CHICANO NOVELS

AND THE

POLITICS OF FORM

CLASS : CULTURE

TITLES IN THE SERIES:

The Syntax of Class: Writing Inequality in Nineteenth-Century America
Amy Schrager Lang

Vanishing Moments: Class and American Culture
Eric Schocket

Let Me Live
Angelo Herndon

Workin' on the Chain Gang: Shaking Off the Dead Hand of History
Walter Mosley

Commerce in Color: Race, Consumer Culture, and American Literature, 1893–1933
James C. Davis

You Work Tomorrow: An Anthology of American Labor Poetry, 1929–41
Edited by John Marsh

Chicano Novels and the Politics of Form: Race, Class, and Reification
Marcial González

CHICANO NOVELS
AND THE
POLITICS OF FORM

Race, Class, and Reification

Marcial González

THE UNIVERSITY OF MICHIGAN PRESS / ANN ARBOR

Published in the United States of America by
The University of Michigan Press
Manufactured in the United States of America
⊗ Printed on acid-free paper

2012 2011 2010 2009 4 3 2 1

A CIP catalog record for this book is available from the British Library.

Library of Congress Cataloging-in-Publication Data

Gonzalez, Marcial, 1953–
Chicano novels and the politics of form : race, class, and
reification / Marcial Gonzalez.
p. cm. — (Class: culture)
Includes bibliographical references and index.
ISBN-13: 978-0-472-07045-9 (alk. paper)
ISBN-10: 0-472-07045-2 (alk. paper)
ISBN-13: 978-0-472-05045-1 (pbk. : alk. paper)
ISBN-10: 0-472-05045-1 (pbk. : alk. paper) 1. American fiction—
Mexican American authors—History and criticism. 2. Politics and
literature—United States. 3. Literature and society—United
States. 4. Fiction—Technique. 5. Mexican Americans in literature.
6. Social classes in literature. 7. Ethnic relations in
literature. 8. Race in literature. I. Title.
PS153.M4G63 2009
813'.540986872—dc22 2008033528

For Valentina

ACKNOWLEDGMENTS

Several of my colleagues in the Department of English at the University of California, Berkeley were enormously and characteristically generous in taking time to read all or parts of my book manuscript and offer suggestions for revision at various stages of the writing process. I want to thank Abdul JanMohamed, José David Saldívar, Kevis Goodman, Steven Goldsmith, and Genaro Padilla. I am especially grateful to Colleen Lye, who read the entire manuscript more than once and challenged me each time to clarify and sharpen my key positions; Ian Duncan, who believed in the importance of the book (and in *me*!) from start to finish; and Mitch Breitwieser, who not only provided feedback on my work but advised me in matters of the profession. Other colleagues who have been particularly supportive include Janet Adelman, Cathy Gallagher, Susan Schweik, Sam Otter, Elizabeth Abel, Richard Hutson, James Grantham Turner, Jennifer Miller, and Hertha Sweet Wong. Thanks also to the 2004 junior faculty reading group: Dorri Beam, Gautam Premnath, Kent Puckett, Michael Rubenstein, and Bryan Wagner.

A number of scholars and writers from outside U.C. Berkeley have also provided support or advice on my writing in one form or another. Thanks to Rosaura Sánchez, Kirsten Silva Gruesz, Donald Pease, Alan Wald, Gregory Meyerson, David Siar, Jonah Raskin, Ronald L. Ruiz, Cecile Pineda, James Smethurst, Krista Walters, Stephen Tatum, the late Jeff Garcilazo, Marijke Rijsberman, Timothy Reiss, and former Berkeley Ethnic Studies professor Patricia Penn Hilden. I am especially indebted to Barbara Foley, Carlos Gallego, Neil Larsen, Anthony Dawahare, and Bill

Mullen for the care they took in critiquing my work, for their long conversations about politics and literature, for their commitment to the working class, and for sharing with me a world view that has provided the philosophical foundation of this book. The earliest stages of this project began during my graduate years in the Modern Thought and Literature Program at Stanford University, where I studied under the direction of Ramón Saldívar and Paula Moya, and with the counseling of David Palumbo-Liu. I am grateful, as well, to Sonia Saldívar-Hull, Norma Cantú, Louis Mendoza, and Ben Olguín for their hospitality during my visit to the University of Texas at San Antonio in the fall of 2004; to Grover Furr, Pat Keeton, Leo Parascandola, Sophia A. McClennen, and Dennis López, members of the Radical Caucus of the Modern Language Association; and to Mary Ann Creadon of Humboldt State University, undeniably the best teacher of literature I have known.

My book prospered from the research assistance of several graduate students, including Marcelle Maese Cohen, Marissa López, Annie McClanahan, María Joaquina Villaseñor, Rebecca Moreno, Gabriela Erandi Rico, Arturo R. Nuñez, and Kristin Fujie. It also benefited from discussions with the students enrolled in my graduate seminars on Marxist literary theory and Chicano literature in the spring of 2001 and the fall of 2004. These students' intellectual curiosity and willingness to engage hard theoretical questions helped me to formulate and refine many of my own arguments in the present work. The comments and advice of colleagues, friends, and students have undoubtedly made my work stronger, but let it be clear that I assume full responsibility for any shortcomings of the book.

Sections of this book have appeared in earlier forms as published essays. A condensed version of Chapter 4 appeared as "Reception and Authenticity: Danny Santiago's *Famous All Over Town*" in *New Directions in American Reception Study*, edited by Philip Goldstein and James L. Machor (New York: Oxford University Press, 2008): 179–94; and the epilogue contains revised paragraphs from "A Marxist Critique of Borderlands Postmodernism: Adorno's *Negative Dialectics* and Chicano Cultural Criticism" in *Left of the Color Line: Race, Radicalism, and Twentieth-Century Literature of the United States*, edited by Bill Mullen and James Smethurst (Chapel Hill: University of North Carolina Press, 2003): 279–97.

This project was supported by funding from various sources: a Career Development Grant from U.C. Berkeley's Faculty Equity Office in the fall of 2002, a Humanities Research Fellowship from the university's College of Letters and Science in the spring of 2003, and a postdoctoral fellowship from the Ford Foundation in 2003–2004. U.C. Berkeley's Committee on Research, the Division of Arts and Humanities, and the Department of English also provided support in various forms and at crucial moments to help bring this project to completion. Additionally, I am grateful to LeAnn Fields and Marcia LaBrenz, my editors at the University of Michigan Press, for their assistance in preparing the book for publication, and to the anonymous reviewers of the original book proposal, whose comments aided me in revising and improving the manuscript. Thanks also to Malaquias Montoya and Lezlie Salkowitz-Montoya for their permission to use Malaquias's artwork on the book's cover.

A valuable part of my education has taken place outside academia. My world outlook has been shaped in a large way by the experiences of growing up in a working-class Mexican American family, working as a farm laborer from childhood to adulthood, coming of age during the Chicano Movement in the late 1960s, attending a Chicano college in the 1970s, and organizing farm workers in the 1980s. In both subtle and overt ways, these experiences have influenced the form and content of this book. I want to acknowledge the following persons for their part in the formation of my ideas and values beyond academia: Epifanio Camacho, Dolores and José Luis Ventura, Lydia and Oscar Martínez, Sofia and Luis Sapien, Salvador Zapien, Consuelo Zavala, and Felix Sánchez, lifelong friends of the Antiracist Farm Workers Union; Tomás González and the late Tony Muñoz, mentors at Colegio de la Tierra Junior College; and the countless novelists who have undertaken the socially significant task of fictionalizing the class-based racialization of Chicanas and Chicanos historically.

I would be remiss if I failed to acknowledge those persons who have contributed to this book by leaving their imprint in the chasms of my unconscious: my parents and first teachers, Inez and Jane González; my six siblings, Lupe Diaz, Johnny González, August García, Rene Quintero, Rachel Anaya, and (a special thought for) Eva Pelayo, who left this world at far too young an age; and my "kids," Marcial Abel, Marina Inez, Octavio, Pavel, Marcial Anthony, Marcellus, Marrion and Marisol, who have shared in my sacrifices through no choice of their own and have humbled me—more than they will ever know—with their courage and perseverance. Finally, I want to express my deepest gratitude to Valentina Holquín-González, my most rigorous critic, for sticking with me all these years, and for not letting me forget where and how we began this long, arduous journey. I dedicate this book to Valentina.

CONTENTS

INTRODUCTION

> He had discovered something. To discover and to rediscover and synthesize. To relate this entity with that entity, and that entity with still another, and finally relating everything with everything else. That was what he had to do. That was all.
>
> —Tomás Rivera, *. . . y no se lo tragó la tierra*

> The peculiar difficulty of dialectical writing lies indeed in its holistic, "totalizing" character: as though you could not say any one thing until you had first said everything; as though with each new idea you were bound to recapitulate the entire system.
>
> —Fredric Jameson, *Marxism and Form*

ONE OF THE CENTRAL AIMS of this book, which draws on the wisdom of the nameless protagonist in Tomás Rivera's novel *. . . y no se lo tragó la tierra*, is to rediscover the specificity of Chicano novels by relating their particularities—in dialectical fashion—with "everything else," that is, with the historical circumstances and social totalities out of which they emerged and to which they are a response. Like Rivera's protagonist, however, I know that the actual task of relating "everything with everything else" is far easier said than done. Notwithstanding the difficulties of such a task, this book shall nevertheless strive toward a theoretical study of the class-based construction of racial identity in several novels written by or about Chicanas and Chicanos. The novels, which include María Amparo Ruiz de Burton's *The Squatter and the Don*, Oscar Zeta Acosta's *The Revolt of the Cockroach People* and *The Autobiography of a Brown Buffalo*, Danny Santiago's *Famous All Over Town*, and Cecile Pineda's *Face* and *Frieze*, narrate the lives of subjects who strive to understand the world beyond their immediate circumstances but ultimately fail to grasp the historicized class character of their experiences. Despite the limited viewpoints of the subjects represented, the novels nonetheless approximate the larger social frameworks that give meaning to the specific experiences they represent by way of their formal operations rather than exclusively through the consciousness of narrators or characters. That is, these novels say as much about history through their formal contradictions as they do in the stories they tell.

Chicano Novels and the Politics of Form does not aim to provide a comprehensive literary history of the Chicano novel, nor does it attempt to delineate a generic anatomy of the component parts of the Chicano novel; my objectives are significantly more modest in scope and subject matter than those projects would entail. In short, I draw on the Marxist theory of reification—a conceptual extension of the theory of commodity fetishism—to examine the relation between history and the ideology of form in a delimited number of Chicano novels. By reification I mean the manner in which the logic of commodity fetishism has pervaded every aspect of social life under late capitalism, including literary forms and consciousness itself—or the manner in which forms of cultural production assume the logic of capital and thus obfuscate their own class content.

From a historical perspective, a theoretical study of Chicano novels at the present is timely. Prior to 1959, only a handful of novels written by Mexican Americans had been published in the United States, most notably, the novels of María Amparo Ruiz de Burton, Daniel Venegas, and Josephina Niggli; their novels were out of print or largely obscure by that year.[1] A few previously unpublished novels from the early twentieth century were put into print after their recovery in the 1990s, including works by Jovita González-Mireles and Américo Paredes.[2] From 1959 to 1969, a period that marked the emergence of the Chicano Movement, fewer than ten Chicano novels were published, among them works by Raymond Barrio, Josephina Niggli, John Rechy, Floyd Salas, and José Antonio Villareal.[3] Outside the few Chicano studies courses being offered on college campuses by the end of the 1960s, these novels were not being taught in American literature courses. From 1970 to 1989—a twenty-year span that witnessed a decline in Chicano nationalism and militancy but an increase in the production of Chicano literature—approximately sixty Chicano novels were put into print. During the 1990s, more than a hundred Chicano novels were published, many of them by mainstream publishers. We are presently witnessing a boom in the production of Chicano novels. Yet few critical studies have been written specifically on the Chicano novel as a literary genre in its own right.[4] Why is this? One of the reasons for the relative paucity of critical studies on the Chicano novel may have to do with the kinds of literary works produced by Chicana and Chicano writers in recent decades. During the 1960s and early 1970s, poetry and teatro (drama) were the dominant literary genres among Chicano writers and social activists. In the 1980s—influenced in part by the rising interests in cultural studies—personal narratives, autobiographies, and mixed-genre texts became popular. (Two works that set a standard for the multigenre personal text in Chicana literature during the 1980s were Cherríe Moraga's *Loving in the War Years: Lo que nunca pasó por sus labios* and Gloria Anzaldúa's *Borderlands/la frontera: the New Mestiza.*[5]) In 1992, Ray González wrote that the short story "is perhaps the strongest genre in Chicano literature today."[6] More than a decade later, now well into the twenty-first century, the novel may or may not be the dominant literary form in Chicano literature, but it has certainly assumed greater importance in Chicano literary production than ever before. The limited number of book-length studies specifically on the Chicano novel—or on a subgenre of it—reflects a need for further research in the field. My particular contribution to meeting this need comes in the form of a book on reification as represented, manifested, and contested in selected exemplary Chicano novels.

Chicano Novels and the Politics of Form includes five chapters and an epilogue. In the first chapter, I outline my theoretical approach to the study of Chicano novels, define my central analytical categories, and situate my project in relation to debates over culture and class within Chicano literary studies. Employing the concept of reification as theorized by Georg Lukács, Theodor Adorno, Fredric Jameson, and Rosemary Hennessy, I suggest a method for Chicano literature that gives importance to both formal and social analysis. Further, I provide a rationale for my use of Lukács as foundational for my argument, challenging the common conception of Lukács's theory of literary realism as unmediated reflection theory. Certain aspects of Adorno's aesthetic theory, I hold, are compatible with the early Lukács of *Theory of the Novel* and—in more problematic ways—*History and Class Consciousness.*[7] Finally, I examine the manner in which Jameson and Hennessy make a case for the continuing relevance of Lukács's theory of reification by revising and extending that theory to make it suitable for the interpretation of contemporary (modernist and postmodernist) literary works, such as Chicano novels.

The next four chapters are structured conceptually in two parts with two chapters in each. In the first part, I analyze the paradigmatic novels of Ruiz de Burton and Acosta, whose works have been widely discussed and written about within Chicano literary studies. Their novels render transparent the class dynamics of two watershed moments of Chicano history: the early 1880s and the late 1960s. The former marked the onset of a long period of Chicano racialization and proletarianization (1890 to the present); the latter represented the most sustained political movement of Chicanos to date against racism and class exploitation (1966–74). In the second part, I analyze the eccentric novels of Santiago and Pineda, whose works have been largely excluded from Chicano literary studies. Their novels call into question the politics of cultural authenticity and identity during the 1980s, a period marked by the culture wars and the waning of the Cold War; they also call into question the criteria traditionally employed in determining the Chicano-ness of Chicano novels. Each of these novels engages in a critique of reified notions of racial identity by drawing the lines of correlation between racialization and its basis in class society. As such, they are valid test cases for my claim that representations of racial and ethnic identity in Chicano novels reveal their class content when placed under the scrutinizing lens of reification theory.[8]

In chapter 2, I study the form and content of Ruiz de Burton's *The Squatter and the Don*, focusing on the conflict between the narrator's reified political outlook (democratic liberalism) and the novel's critique of monopoly capitalism. Critics have read the novel as a "subaltern" text, sometimes disregarding the narrator's derogatory remarks toward mestizos, Native Americans, and African Americans. The novel has also been read as the expression of class privilege, despite its harsh critical stance toward capitalism. Differing with both positions, I argue that the ideological views of the author do not necessarily minimize the social critique in the novel, but rather, the novel surpasses the class interests of the author, whether subaltern or hegemonic. My position resembles the argument Lukács makes about Honoré de Balzac,[9] a nineteenth-century French novelist and a royalist who was better able to represent the objective conditions of his time than were contemporaneous progressive writers because of the influence of his pre-1848 historical moment, and the epistemological possibilities it opened up. Similarly, Ruiz de Burton, a displaced landowner, may have been better able to grasp the essential class contradictions of her time than contemporaneous "subaltern" writers, not because of her skills as a novelist, (though she was evidently a talented writer), but because of the objective circumstances of her moment and her critical class position, which enabled her to write in a manner that lays bare the essential class contradictions of late-nineteenth-century California. *The Squatter* exposes the process that Marx referred to as "primitive accumulation." For the Californios and other propertied Mexicans living in the Southwest after 1848, this process entailed the brutal seizure of their land and the degradation of their social class status; it also transformed the Mexican population into a proletarianized racial group, or what Mario Barrera refers to as a colonial labor force.[10]

My third chapter scrutinizes the politics of cultural nationalism, the mode of reification that both inspires and baffles the narrator in Acosta's *The Revolt of the Cockroach People.* In Acosta's modernist novel, ideological standpoint becomes manifest as stylistic expression. *Revolt* is profoundly paratactic; it relies on the absence of causal connections between temporal moments in the narrative, and on the category of similarity-and-difference, to expose the contradictions of its own themes. Structurally and stylistically, *Revolt* makes use of montage, juxtaposition, repetition, and abrupt transitions similar to cutting techniques in film. In so doing, the novel weighs and balances numerous political strategies that were employed by activists during the most turbulent years of the Chicano Movement, effectively exposing the strengths and weaknesses of these strategies. Cultural nationalism in *Revolt* emerges as a response to imposed racial designations based on skin color and other markers of difference that come to be considered second nature or, to use Acosta's own words, "simply a means of classification" for "determining exactly who one is."[11] But cultural nationalism, understood as the flip side of racialization, or the self-fashioning of a racial identity, proved nearly as problematic—in entirely different ways—as the initial moment of racialization associated with capitalist accumulation. Consistent with its contrastive style, *Revolt* measures the viability of Chicano nationalism against the internationalist politics of the Vietnam War and Third World revolutionary movements of the 1960s. Although the novel is steeped in the nationalist consciousness of a problematic narrator-protagonist, its stylistic maneuvers suggest a standpoint that looks beyond nationalism and the political contradictions of the Chicano Movement. This alternative standpoint is evoked somewhat naively in the narrator's thoughtful reflections on death and the possibilities of a political subject committed to an internationalist struggle against racism, colonialism, and U.S. imperialism.

In chapter 4, I read Santiago's *Famous All Over Town*, the first of three eccentric novels I study, as engaging in the dereification of cultural authenticity. Unlike the novels of Ruiz de Burton and Acosta, which have figured concentrically in Chicano literary studies, Santiago's *Famous All*

Over Town remains a marginal novel in Chicano literature, largely because Santiago himself was not a Chicano. (Danny Santiago was a pseudonym used by Daniel James, a white author.) Upon discovering the author's background a year after the novel's publication, some critics felt deceived; the ones who felt most disturbed by the revelation accused James of being a fraud and claimed that the novel was not an authentic Chicano novel. Despite its marginality, *Famous All Over Town* nonetheless contributes to a comprehension of the manner in which Chicano novels simultaneously embody and contest reification. A compelling novel about a working-class Chicano family living in East Los Angeles in the early 1960s, *Famous* implicitly raises questions about what determines the Chicano-ness of a Chicano novel: Is it possible for a non-Chicano author to write a novel that accurately and convincingly represents Chicano experiences? If so, how does an author acquire epistemic access to these experiences? In responding to these questions, I argue that reification in *Famous* can be conceptualized (among other ways) in the author-reader-text relation, which assumed utmost importance in determining the novel's negative reception among critics of Chicano literature after Santiago's identity had been revealed publicly. *Famous* emblematizes, textually and historically, the problems associated with the categorization of a literary work according to the ethnic or racial background of its author. In my reading of Santiago's *Famous*, I challenge the assumption that the Chicano-ness of a Chicano novel is necessarily dependent upon the ethnicity of the author. By contrast, I argue that a novel's Chicano-ness will be determined primarily by the specific manner in which the novel is able to produce cognition of a particular feature of Chicano experience within a historically situated social totality.

Unlike Santiago, a white author who writes about Chicano experiences, Cecile Pineda, a Chicana, writes novels about non-Chicano characters. Her novels, set in various locations around the globe and in wide-ranging time periods, represent the reification of identity in late capitalism: they emphasize the superficial, fragmented, alienated, constructed character of identity; but they also recognize the manner in which individuals assume identities as a means for coming to know the social world and their place in that world. Pineda's novels highlight the formal similarities between identity formation, commodity fetishism, and novelistic form: categories that have become increasingly ambiguous in a rapidly changing mode of production by the mid-1980s, a decade marked by the buildup of nuclear arsenals among the superpowers of the world, the beginnings of what we now call the "new world order," and the proliferation of postmodernist skepticism and irrationalism among scholars of literature and culture. *Face* and *Frieze* critique the notion of a unified subject, racial or otherwise, but they also distance themselves from the untenable conception of a postmodern nonsubject, emphasizing instead the continuing viability of such concepts as responsibility, intentionality, agency, action, change, and history itself. Because of the importance Pineda's novels give to these concepts and their implications for social praxis, I read *Face* and *Frieze* as examples of what José Limón calls "critical modernism."[12] Pineda's novels may not depict the lives of Chicana or Chicano characters overtly, but the philosophical critique at the center of her novels addresses issues of utmost importance for U.S. ethnic literatures generally, and for Chicano literature in particular. Moreover, the manner in which her novels engage with issues pertinent to a Chicano critique of capitalist accumulation speaks specifically to the reification implicit in narrow notions of the Chicano-ness of Chicano novels.

This study ends with an epilogue that links the book's key theoretical concepts of contradiction, dialectics, commodity fetishism, identity, and novelistic form. A discussion of these concepts leads me to the following conclusion: the novels analyzed in my book imply that racialized subjects must become conscious of themselves as members of a historically situated politicized group but primarily for the purpose of abolishing all divisions based on racial, ethnic, and national difference, including those differences resulting from self-fashioned oppositional identities.

Readers will notice in the pages of my book the positive influence of scholars who study Chicano literature from dialectical or critical-theoretical perspectives—even as I occasionally question or part ways with aspects of the arguments formulated by these scholars. In particular, I draw on Rosaura Sánchez's historical materialist approach in her study of *testimonios*, as well as in her earlier work on Chicano sociolinguistics; Ramón Saldívar's study of Chicano narratives and his theory of the "dialectics of difference"; José David Saldívar's deconstruction of the generic boundaries that separate the various traditions in the literatures of the Americas; José Limón's interpretation of Chicano literature as "critical modernism" in his study of border ballads and Chicano poetry; Ellen McCracken's analysis of "postmodern ethnicity" in the marketing of Latina narratives; Louis Mendoza's argument that Chicano literature represents "the literary making of Chicana and Chicano history"; Paula Moya's theorization of postpositivist realism; and Kirsten Gruesz's call for a philosophical approach to the study of U.S. Latino history. The work of these scholars and others serves as the starting point for my own interpretive approach, beginning with R. Saldívar's description of dialectical criticism.

> Resorting for the sake of exposition to a Hegelian formulation, we might argue that one rationale for studying "ethnic" literatures as part and parcel of the general problematic of American literature as a whole . . . is that the masterworks of the dominant literary culture are the dialogical negations of the marginal texts not sanctioned by the hegemonic culture. As the silenced voices of opposition, these other marginal texts serve to highlight the ideological background of the traditional canon, to bring to the surface that repressed formation that Jameson has called the "political unconscious."[13]

Here I argue that we can resort precisely to this same "Hegelian formulation" not only to examine the dialectical relation of "ethnic literatures" to "the hegemonic culture," but to study also the internal ideological contradictions of Chicano novels themselves. While marginal texts may indeed illuminate a repressed political unconscious in "the masterworks of the dominant literary culture," they also appropriate to some degree the ideology of the masterworks they reject. What's more, the novels in the present study can be considered marginal texts within an already marginal literary tradition, and in this sense they constitute a kind of double negation, twice removed from the center in such a way that, curiously, brings them back to the very issues of centrality negated in the first place. The defining form of the novels I study can be comprehended dialectically as an ideological battleground where antagonistic class discourses come into bitter conflict. But this conflict is not necessarily figured as perpetual. Each novel gestures toward a symbolic resolution of the social contradictions it represents. As such, we can interpret the drive for resolution in Chicano novels as an aspiration toward a standpoint that effectively disrupts reification.

This study represents an effort to contribute to ongoing work on methodology and critical theory in the study of Chicano narratives. Given the theoretical issues examined in my book, I hope it will be useful for the study of narrative form in a number of revisionist literary traditions—not just for Chicano literature, but for U.S. ethnic, working-class, feminist, postcolonial, and minority literatures generally. I endeavor to think through the philosophical as well as the social basis of ethnic literature. Students and scholars interested in theorizing the intersection of reification, race, social identities, and narrative form will find interest in this book, which seeks to pave a path toward their understanding.

I

BEYOND REIFICATION

The Cultural Logic of Chicano Novels

> Commodity production and exchange entail therefore a "phenomenological matrix," a form of consciousness or a cultural logic that alienates many aspects of human life from the network of social relations that makes them possible.
>
> —Rosemary Hennessy, *Profit and Pleasure*

> It became abundantly clear early in my career, that the way I wanted to teach—as well as the way I wanted to critique literature, film, and popular culture—meant needing to understand the mythology around capitalism in the late twentieth century. This has become ever more important as we have moved into the twenty-first century.
>
> —Edén E. Torres, *Chicana without Apology*

IN THE CLOSING LINES of the penultimate chapter of María Amparo Ruiz de Burton's 1885 novel, *The Squatter and the Don*, Doña Josefa Alamar, the matriarch of the displaced Californios in the novel, responds to friendly advice that she should not speak ill of the men who caused the death of her husband because to do so will cause offense. "Oh, very well, let it be so. Let the guilty rejoice and go unpunished, and the innocent suffer ruin and desolation. I slander no one, but shall speak the truth."[1] Thereafter, the novel's nameless narrator, taking a cue from Doña Josefa's promise to "speak the truth," shifts from the conventional storytelling voice of fiction employed throughout the novel to a pseudofactual mode of narration in the final chapter to "speak the truth" about the injustices committed by capitalist monopolies and lawmakers against "the people." Doña Josefa clearly articulates, and the narrator in the last chapter effectively puts into practice, what will become one of the central tenets of Chicano novels for the next 120 years: the attempt to "speak the truth" about experiences that, traditionally, have been largely ignored, excluded, forgotten, or distorted in American literature and history. Chicano novels, to one extent or another, stand as defiant alternatives to the erasure of Chicano experience, but these alternative standpoints also inevitably confront in full force the central problem of representation in our time. How does a novelist go about speaking the truth in a world of pervasive reification, which has become the dominant logic of thought in late capitalism? How can novelists avoid reifying the representation of experience in their efforts to speak the truth? To what degree are novelists able to overcome or disrupt the limitations that reification imposes upon cultural production and consciousness? To what extent can the immediacy of representation in fiction open up access to totality? Can a novel effectively contest reification? If so, what are the narrative strategies best suited for doing so? These questions pertain to novels generally, but they may be even more important for minority literatures, such as Chicano literature, in which speaking the truth has become not only an issue of representational accuracy, but a matter of political agency and empowerment, as well.

Reification has been commonly understood as objectification—making a static object out of a dynamic process—and has been described with such terms as *ossification* and *thing-ification.* But reification can also be understood in other related ways: the shallowness of perception; the naturalizing of social inequalities; the use of immutable or quantifiable laws to explain history; the categorizing of humans according to phenotype and anatomy; the fragmentation and compartmentalization of productive human activity—a development necessitated by the classifying and rationalizing tendencies of a capitalist mode of production; and, most importantly, the manner in which the logic of commodity fetishism has pervaded every aspect of social life under late capitalism, including literary works and consciousness itself.

Rosemary Hennessy instructively characterizes reification as synonymous with the "logic of capital" or, stated differently, as "a logic that binds ways of knowing and forms of identity to changes in the relations of production."[2] This is to say that reification is not a problem of poor intelligence or the lack of education. One does not learn to overcome reified consciousness by getting a college degree or becoming a scientist. Nor is reification a problem of psychology or faulty thought processes. Rather, reification is historically, socially, and materially based; it stems from the experience of living in a social system based on commodity production and exchange. It entails "a form of consciousness or a cultural logic that alienates many aspects of human life from the network of social relations that makes them possible."[3] Drawing on the concepts of commodity fetishism and reification in a critique of anti-Semistism and national socialism, Moishe Postone writes that "the concept of fetishism refers to *forms of thought* that remain bound to the forms of appearance of capitalist social relations, thereby hypostatizing or naturalizing those social relations."[4] Similarly, developmental systems theorist Susan Oyama has the logic of consciousness in mind (though she employs a somewhat different set of analytical terms) in stating that "if we want to fight the good fight, we must know what the enemy is, or we will waste precious time and energy. Note that I say *what* the enemy is, not *who;* I am concerned with ways of thinking, not people."[5] We could interpret Oyama's statement as a call to arms not against armies or other state apparatuses, but against reified consciousness. From these various perspectives, reification can be understood, in one sense, as a way of thinking about (or a form of consciousness that perceives) social relations as natural rather than conditioned by class contradictions.

The theories of reification as formulated particularly and differently by Georg Lukács, Theodor Adorno, Fredric Jameson, and Hennessy[6] provide literary criticism with a conceptual framework for analyzing a novel's various levels of signification implicit in the rift between the immediately given and the socially mediated, between what is apparent and what has been repressed in literary representations, between the anxieties produced by reification itself and the incessant drive to approximate a consciousness beyond reification. In summation of the above, I define reification, echoing Timothy Bewes, as "the failure to think totality,"[7] by which I mean the failure to understand how objects, events, and situations are intricately connected to and constituted by dynamic social processes that have evolved historically at different levels: locally, nationally, and globally.

The novels analyzed in this book represent variations of what Jameson calls "the reified atomization . . . of capitalist social life";[8] they can be read as displaying at different historical moments the anxieties felt by Chicano subjects in their attempts to overcome the effects of reification, which become manifest as racialization and proletarianization. Each novel stands out for the manner in which it simultaneously embodies and resists reification, a novelistic feature that I refer to as contradictory form. I set out to elucidate each novel's contradictory form by analyzing closely a particular mode of reified consciousness: democratic liberalism in María Amparo Ruiz de Burton's *The Squatter and the Don;* cultural nationalism in Oscar Zeta Acosta's *The Revolt of the Cockroach People* and *The Autobiography of a Brown Buffalo;* cultural authenticity in Danny Santiago's *Famous All Over Town;* identity thinking in Cecile Pineda's *Face;* and the ideology of individualism in Pineda's *Frieze.*

These modes or types of reification give shape to the arguments in each of the chapters that follow, as well as to the organizational trajectory of the book. One might conclude that all modern novels to one extent or another represent and pose challenges to the social and epistemological problems associated with reification, a conclusion with which I would agree. I have, however, selected these particular novels for my study because reification is a central and pervasive characteristic thematically and formally in each one. In making this argument, I am not claiming that Chicano novels generally—or the novels I study in particular—are locked into a prison-house of reification with no possibility of escape, no "outside" of reification. The centrality of contradiction in the social realities that inform Chicano subjectivity contributes to the impossibility of complete reification in Chicano novels. Complete reification would mean the absence of contradiction. By contrast, Chicano novels simultaneously and contradictorily embody and contest reification because of the inevitable condition that Edward Said refers to as "crisis,"[9] or the contradictions that cause reification to become transparent and thus open to critique. Consequently, for Chicano novels, reification both precludes and enables their approach to totality; which is to say, the critique of reification in Chicano novels reveals their social class content even in cases where class is not overtly represented. In a study of working-class narratives of labor, Eric Schocket argues similarly that commodity fetishism and reification are "mediations that do not reveal class as an ontology or as an identity but that nevertheless testify indirectly to the way that class processes inescapably permeate the textual field."[10] The point Schocket makes with regard to labor narratives can be made equally in reference to Chicano novels.

The fact that literary figures, both characters and writers, have had to contest the reification attendant upon being racialized constitutes a key component of reified consciousness in Chicano novels. In *Reification, or the Anxiety of Late Capitalism*—one of the few comprehensive studies on the theory of reification since Lukács's classic *History and Class Consciousness*—

Timothy Bewes writes, "In the broader socio-political sphere, reification is what happens in every instance of racism and sexism, where the objects of prejudice are perceived not as human beings but as things or 'types.'"[11] If Bewes is correct (and I believe he is), then it follows logically that to fight against racism is also to contest reification: antiracism in Chicano novels constitutes an attempt to go beyond reification. Reification, however, happens not only in acts of racism and sexism, but somewhat more complexly and problematically in instances of self-constructed racial identities: on the one hand, a self-conceptualized racial identity may serve as an act of resistance against racism; on the other hand, it potentially contributes to the "reified atomization" or alienation perpetually and necessarily produced in a system founded on commodity production and exchange. To contest reification effectively, Chicano subjects thus find themselves not only needing to fight racism but also in the contradictory position of needing to go beyond their own constructed oppositional identities—beyond reification. I shall have more to say on this point later.

My argument is inspired, in part, by Kirsten Gruesz's bold claim that contemporary U.S. Latino studies lacks a "philosophy of history." In making this claim, Gruesz is not arguing that "Latino studies lacks a *history*, in the sense of the reconstitution of a missing archive or repressed past." She acknowledges that a significant amount of critical and biographical work has been undertaken to construct a U.S. Latino literary tradition, and that this work has been recorded in projects such as the Recovering the U.S. Hispanic Literary Heritage book series published by Arte Público Press. Gruesz argues, rather, that Latino studies requires "a way of theorizing a new relationship between past, present, and future that avoids the pitfalls of both an antiquarian historicism and the denial of the past" so as to avoid "museumifying" the object of study.[12] Concurring with Gruesz's proposal, I would add that a similar assertion could be made with regard to the need for a philosophical approach to the interpretation of Chicano/Latino literature—in particular, Chicano novels. With this thought in mind, the present project is guided, in part, by the following declaration: we need to be able to theorize the production of meaning in Chicano novels without "museumifying"—or reifying—the subjects represented in the novels, or the representation itself.

To this end, two observations about current methodological approaches in Chicano literary studies—and my response to these approaches—are in order. First, Chicano criticism has tended toward thematic rather than formal methods of analysis. Understandably, the criticism has focused on analyzing certain themes in the literature to legitimate Chicano culture and history; it has served to counter the nonrepresentation and misrepresentation of Chicanos and U.S. Latinos in American literature historically. The criticism has also demonstrated the manner in which Chicano literary works lay claim to cultural identity as an act of political resistance. Thus the concepts of "culture" and "identity" have become primary analytical categories in the field. But thematic criticism also runs the risk of reifying cultural production if it comes to understand culture as an immediately given reality isolated from larger social processes. By contrast, the analytical categories I am proposing endeavor to disclose the manner in which social contradictions become internalized as the content of cultural production—or, in the present study, as the content of the novel's form, with "form" being understood here as roughly synonymous with the ideological "world" of the novel or its totality, an issue I address more fully subsequently. When a novel's form is taken into account, we discover a literary work that is much more complex—thematically, structurally, and artistically—than previously considered, but the most significant payoff in the critique of form in Chicano novels lies in the broadening of historical consciousness beyond the immediacy of the local realities represented in the literature. The critique of form in this sense seeks to deepen our understanding of the historical processes that inform the literary work and to which the work is a response. To be clear, I am not arguing for a return to the kind of ahistorical formalism practiced by weaker versions of the New Criticism and neo-Aristotelian criticism, though I must admit my affinity for the close textual analyses and the attention to linguistic detail usually associated with these methods, as reflected in my readings of Chicano novels in what follows.[13] In an effort not to limit my approach to "close reading," I seek to uncover the determinate relation between ideology and narrative form in Chicano novels. In this regard, this book serves as an alternative to both formalism, in the narrow sense, and the kind of thematic criticism that places the weight of interpretation on the critic's most immediate level of engagement with a literary work: its surface content.

Second, Chicano criticism has excelled in specifying the uniqueness or difference of Chicano literature, a task I hold as indispensable. It is also necessary, however, to illuminate the aesthetic features, whether of form or theme, that Chicano novels *share* with other literary traditions. Such an endeavor could aid in averting the potential problems associated with making a fetish of cultural uniqueness; it would also potentially enrich other literary and theoretical traditions with its particular contributions to those fields of study. José Limón has these same issues in mind when he writes,

"Lest they become insular and parochial, local ethnic studies must be consistently exposed to the most globalizing interpretive theory. Lest it lose touch with specific practices that test its validity and lest it become elitist and exclusivist, global theory consistently needs to be questioned and revised in terms of the local."[14] One of the goals of this study is to bring Chicano literature into conversation with "globalizing interpretive theory" in such a way that it benefits both the literature and the theory. My approach can be considered pluralist in that I draw on various methods, but I have also clearly made a conscious decision to situate this study specifically and centrally within a Marxist theoretical paradigm. I hope to broaden the scope of Chicano criticism by demonstrating—as Neil Lazarus has argued in a study of postcolonial literature—that "the conceptual reach of Marxism is superior to that of the problematics currently prevailing in the field."[15] A project that makes use of Marxist theory for the interpretation of Chicano novels, I hold, can greatly enhance its critical capacity; conversely, the usefulness of Marxism for the study of U.S. ethnic literature will be extended by a critical project that gives importance to the specificity of race and ethnicity in Chicano literature.

In putting such a project into practice, this book will address the following question: What are the potential benefits of reading Chicano novels as embodiments of class consciousness or as critical commentaries on reification as manifested in novelistic form? In responding to this question, the book shall also raise other related questions as points of inquiry for possible future studies: How can a theoretical study of Chicano novels contribute to a general theory of the novel? How can such a study widen our understanding of literary modernism and realism? What can be gained from reading Chicano novels not only as representations of Chicano experience, but more broadly as critiques of modernity and postmodernity, as interventions in current discussions centered on the meaning of "postcolonial," as commentaries on the future of minority studies, or as engagements with the politics of globalization, transnationalism, and empire? Such an attention to shared concerns in literary theory, I believe, will accentuate rather than efface the difference of Chicano novels and may afford a fuller knowledge of the distinctive quality—the "Chicano-ness"—of Chicano novels.

Race and Class—Content and Form

For analytical purposes critics find it useful and necessary to isolate the categories of race and class in the study of literature, but such separations ultimately prove useful only if we simultaneously keep an eye focused on the fact that in actuality these categories are inseparable. The thorny task of theorizing the relation between racialized identities and social class—along with the equally challenging problem of defining the relation between content and form—in Chicano literature was brought to the forefront by Joseph Sommers in his controversial 1977 essay, "From the Critical Premise to the Product: Critical Modes and Their Applications to a Chicano Literary Text,"[16] in which he called into question "the assumptions" of Chicano literary criticism. Though this essay is dated and no longer regarded as central to contemporary debates on Chicano literary and cultural criticism, it raises issues about the relation between literary form and politics that we may find still relevant for the study of Chicano novels. Thus we will benefit from taking some time to revisit this essay and review its critical insights. Sommers argued that the criticism of Chicano literature in its short existence as an academic discipline[17] had not up to that point made use of recent advances in "European and Anglo-American" literary theory, referring particularly to interests deriving from structuralism, poststructuralism, and Marxism. He also claimed that critics of Chicano literature had for the most part relied almost exclusively on two conceptually restricting methodological approaches: formalism and culturalism. The formalists, according to Sommers, gave more importance to the structural unity of a literary work while avoiding its function as social commentary. A common practice among formalists was to compare the structural or generic aspects of, say, a Chicano novel with novels of other literary traditions. A formalist critic might argue—as did Sommers himself—that Tomás Rivera's 1971 novel, . . . *y no se lo tragó la tierra*, bears generic similarities to the modernist novels of "Faulkner, Joyce, Dos Passos and Rulfo."[18] Implicitly, the formalists attempted to give validity to Chicano literary works by demonstrating their structural similarities to canonical works in the literary traditions of the United States and Mexico.

By contrast, the culturalist approach, Sommers argued, was "based on the notion of Chicano literature as culturally unique." Most critics employing this method sought to locate the value of Chicano literature in "the expression of the distinctive features of Chicano culture." Consequently, they tended "toward the descriptive rather than the interpretive."[19] More problematically, culturalists by and large overlooked the fact that "culture" is constituted by historically specific social class contradictions. For Sommers, the concept of "culture" signified "race" because it had become the reified exteriority of a Chicano racialized identity. "In placing culture (and by implication, race) at the center of Chicano experience, the critic underestimates the all-important factor of class, a factor which shapes and influences the process by which cultural expression is generated."[20] Thus critics displayed an inclination to place more importance in identifying aspects of Chicano literature that reflected "traditional culture" than analyzing the constitutive relation between class and the process of racialization in literary representations. As an alternative, Sommers argued for the importance of "class" as an analytical category, and "class contradiction" as a determining social force, in the interpretation of Chicano literature. One of the assumptions of the culturalist approach was that, "precisely because of its unique qualities," Chicano literature could "be *understood* only by Chicanos."[21] By extension, authentic literary representations of Chicano social experiences could be *written* only by Chicanos.[22]

According to Sommers, both approaches, formalism and culturalism, were based on the assumption that the purpose of analyzing Chicano literature was to promote the validity of the literature, either by revealing the literature's similarities to other traditions or its differences from them. The formalists emphasized the commonalities between Chicano literature and other traditions, especially American and Mexican modernism; the culturalists gave importance to the uniqueness of Chicano literature, isolating the representation of "culture" (i.e., race) as the literature's primary difference. The predetermined political objectives of critics who employed these approaches, supposedly, led them to overlook other aspects of the literature, including the capacity of a literary work to represent history in a manner that surpasses the local representation of racial identity: "formalism tends to ignore the past, focusing on modernism and its virtues," and "culturalism tends to ignore the present, stressing in nostalgic and idealized tones the predominance of the past."[23]

Sommers does not stand alone in arguing against culturalist approaches to the study of Chicano literature and history. In recent years, for example, Gilbert González and Raul Fernández have found that "much Chicano historiography has been built on cultural and culture-conflict models focusing on race and nationality as the bases for social relations and, ultimately, for historical explanation." Alternatively, they make use of "Marxist taxonomies when appropriate" to investigate interpretive models based on economics, modes of production, social relations, and class power.[24] Similarly, Edén E. Torres argues that cultural critics need to become "amateur economists" to understand and explain the causal connection between the global economy and culture—that is, to comprehend and critique the fine lines of determinacy that run from the profit needs of global capitalism to cultural production and formations of identity. Torres does not claim, reductively, that the economy determines culture; she argues rather that contemporary culture is a manifestation of a global political-economic system based on class exploitation, capitalist expansion, and the practices of neoliberalism. She also criticizes cultural critics who ignore the connection between culture and the economy.[25]

The culturalism that Sommers criticized might be understood in terms of what Arif Dirlik has called "cultural fundamentalism," which he defines as "the reification of ethnicity and culture."[26] Sommers, however, argued for an explanatory system that did not dismiss culturalism and formalism out of hand, but brought them together with a third method that he termed "historical-dialectical." This threefold method was based on the assumption that Chicano literature does not merely reflect or represent experience; it "carries in *its form and its structures* an interpretation of this experience."[27] Additionally, Chicano literature is "intimately bound up with the historic pattern of economic and social oppression which has characterized the Mexican American experience since 1848."[28] In particular, the literature is informed by and responds to racism, sexism, state repression, and the proletarianization of Mexican Americans and other Latinos. Sommers described his system as "totalizing" and capable of analyzing the "resistant and political perspective"[29] in a literary work without glossing its ideological contradictions. As such, the interpretation of Chicano texts must incorporate ideology critique as an essential category. (Interestingly, Sommers's three-level approach—theme, form, and history—bears a skeletal resemblance to the three-horizon dialectical method that Fredric Jameson develops much more elaborately and convincingly four years later in *The Political Unconscious*, a method Jameson had already begun to theorize in his earlier works. The methods proposed by Sommers and Jameson are similar not only because of their threefold structures, but because Sommers takes methods he finds reductive—culturalism and formalism—when employed individually and incorporates them into an expanded, dynamic system of interpretation, similar to what Jameson does with his theory of "metacommentary.") I revisit Sommers's essay not to assert the correctness of his assessment, nor to propose that we put his system into practice as some kind of ideal model, but because his essay raised issues about Chicano literature and criticism three decades ago that can potentially serve to theorize a dialectical criticism for the study of Chicano novels today. It will therefore help to review briefly some of the discussion generated by Sommers's proposed method.

Sommers's essay prompted strong critical responses, both negative and positive. One of his harshest critics has been Juan Bruce-Novoa, who chastises Sommers for "using criticism as a weapon against those with whom he did not agree" and for pursuing a "pseudo-Marxist orientation . . . no less dogmatic than the one he attacked in others." He denounces what he considers Sommers's insistence on the "reduction of literature to reality," characterizing Sommers's interpretive approach as "vulgar reductionism," "misrepresentation," "censorship," and the reflection of an "inability to read beyond the surface of a text." More scathingly, he asserts that Sommers fails in his efforts to read Chicano texts correctly because of the latter's status as a "cultural outsider,"[30] given that Sommers was white, not Chicano.

Taking a more substantive but no less critical position, Ramón Saldívar writes what is perhaps the most theoretically challenging response to Sommers. In his 1979 essay, "A Dialectic of Difference: Towards a Theory of the Chicano Novel," Saldívar agrees generally with the need to reassess the methods employed in Chicano literary criticism and acknowledges that the gauntlet thrown down by Sommers cannot be ignored. Saldívar clarifies, however, that Sommers was "not in a position to recognize . . . that this reassessment [was in 1979] already taking place"; he cites essays by José David Saldívar, Juan Rodríguez, Raymund Paredes, and Bruce-Novoa as examples of critical work that make use of poststructuralist, Marxist, and neoformalist methods in new and exciting ways for the interpretation of Chicano literature. More significantly, R. Saldívar writes a "survey of the Chicano novel, based on a 'poststructuralist' methodology" in an effort to outline what he considers a "new, revolutionary critique of narrative structures."[31] In effect, R. Saldívar responds to Sommers not only argumentatively, but demonstratively: he *performs* his answer to Sommers, displaying his own critical capacity to engage poststructuralist theory in a study of Chicano novels. In so doing, he enacts his conviction that imaginative writing itself produces meaning not only as representation but also as a socially symbolic act—that is, not only by what it says, but by how it says it, and by the very fact of its utterance. Bruce-Novoa recognizes this aspect of Saldívar's essay, summarizing the difference between Saldívar and Sommers as follows: "The latter saw [literature] as the product of an exterior reality which the author and work should serve . . . while the former studies [literature] as a reality capable of producing concrete effects in the world. Sommers saw and analyzed the message; Saldívar accepts that symbolic action constitutes a real praxis in itself."[32] In Saldívar's own words, "the Chicano novel's ideology of difference emerges from a . . . complex unity of at least two formal elements: its paradoxical impulse toward revolutionary deconstruction and toward the production of meaning,"[33] which is to say, the form of the Chicano novel is productively contradictory. Drawing on a host of dialectical thinkers, including Lukács, Adorno, Jacques Derrida, and Jameson, among others, R. Saldívar theorizes what he refers to as "the dialectics of difference": the assertion that Chicano narratives engage in the "production of meaning" by deliberately establishing their difference from traditional canonical literary works in order to expose the specific social experiences that constitute Chicano subjectivity—hence, R. Saldívar's much quoted premise that "for Chicano narrative, *history* is the subtext that we must recover because history itself is the subject of its discourse."[34] Despite their differences, Sommers and R. Saldívar both call for a dialectical criticism—a call that has gone largely, though not entirely, unheeded in Chicano literary studies.[35]

For my purpose, José Limón writes perhaps the most useful assessment of Sommers. Limón refers to Sommers's controversial piece as "a landmark essay in Chicano metacriticism," and he acknowledges that his own work has been "inspired" by Sommers's Marxism.[36] He also maintains that Chicano criticism has evolved beyond the reductive methods of culturalism and formalism, incorporating many aspects of the "historical-dialectical" approach that Sommers proposed in 1977. According to Limón, "a new set" of Chicano and Chicana critics (as of his writing in 1992) were developing what he called the "new Chicano criticism." The "new Chicano critics" included Hector Calderón, Angie Chabram, Teresa McKenna, José David Saldívar, Ramón Saldívar, Rosaura Sánchez, and Limón himself.[37] This new approach to Chicano criticism "include[d] Marxism, but it [was] a Marxism articulated in a poststructuralist critical discourse." Some of the "new Chicano critics," in particular Chabram and Sánchez, were "sympathetically suspicious of some dominant versions of poststructuralist thought."[38] Limón linked the historical evolution of the "new Chicano criticism" not only to Sommers, but to Jameson.

> [T]he new Chicano criticism attempts to rupture the idealistic constraints of mainstream American criticism, including its latest deconstructivist phase, and end up in a subsuming critical position—an ultimate horizon of reading, as Fredric Jameson might say—that, indeed, centrally draws on Jameson as well as other Marxist cultural critics sensitive to the historicity and social fluidity of discourse. The new Chicano critics recognize . . . Jameson's work as the prime example of a new kind of American criticism.[39]

Jameson's work indeed represented a "new kind" of criticism for Chicano literature in the 1980s, but it was one that nonetheless drew on a long tradition of Marxist dialectical theory. Like Limón, I hold that Chicano criticism will benefit from drawing on Marxist theory, but I am hesitant to agree entirely with his assessment that Chicano criticism has outgrown the limitations of methods that rely on reified conceptions of culture and form.

In any case, the critical exchanges among the various critics responding to Sommers's proposed method, either favorably or unfavorably, have been productive for Chicano literary criticism. Moreover, some of Sommers's key critical assertions continue to be instructive today: (1) Chicano literature has emerged historically as a response to colonization, racism, class exploitation, and other kinds of social oppression dating back at least to the U.S. annexation of the Southwest in 1848; (2) Chicano literature may indeed be characterized by its uniqueness for the specific themes it represents related to Chicano experience;[40] (3) the specificity of Chicano literature, however, lies not exclusively in its immediate or local representation of Chicano experience, but also in the specific ways that the literature takes shape as a product of (and in response to) class contradictions and the perpetual crises of capitalism, nationally and globally; (4) the social content of Chicano literature is expressed not only in its themes and stories, but also in its various *forms;* and (5) the categories employed, whether thematic or formal, in the interpretation of Chicano literature must themselves be thoroughly historicized.

Despite the positive aspects of Sommers's essay, some of his claims—three in particular—about Chicano literary criticism now seem dated or in some other manner obviously out of synch with recent scholarship in Chicano literature. First, and most notably, Sommers claimed that critics of Chicano literature had not yet done enough genealogical work aimed at reconstructing a Mexican American literary tradition. Such a claim certainly cannot be made today, and his observation was not entirely accurate in 1977 either. Sommers of course wrote his essay well before the recovery and publication of novels by María Amparo Ruiz de Burton, Jovita González, and Américo Paredes, not to mention the large body of critical work that has grown around these novels.[41] Additionally, since 1990 Arte Público Press has published a large collection of literary and critical works as part of its Recovering the U.S. Hispanic Literary Heritage series.[42] These works stand at the center of efforts to reconstruct a Chicano literary tradition, focusing on literature written prior to the publication of José Antonio Villareal's 1959 novel, *Pocho*, often described as the first Chicano novel. Further, as Bruce-Novoa points out, Phillip Ortego, Luis Leal, and Doris Meyer were already writing historical criticism in the late 1960s and early 1970s that laid the groundwork for a reconstruction of a Chicano literary tradition: "contrary to [Sommers's] complaints that [Chicano literary] criticism tended to ignore historical content or context, the dominant method" prior to 1977 "was historical and descriptive."[43]

Second, Sommers could have done more to acknowledge the importance of Chicana feminism as a critical intervention, historically, in Chicano literary studies, even at that early moment. Chicana feminism has not only produced the sharpest critiques of sexism and homophobia as manifested within the Chicano Movement; it has also linked these critiques to analyses of the contradictions of cultural nationalism. The influential literary and critical works of Cherríe Moraga, Gloria Anzaldúa, Ana Castillo, Norma Alarcón, and other Chicana feminists in the 1980s and 1990s must be acknowledged here. Sommers cannot be faulted for not having had the foresight to predict the publication of works by these writers, but Chicana feminism did not emerge in the 1980s; it grew contemporaneously alongside and within the Chicano Movement. From 1968 to 1977, Chicana feminists published a fairly large body of work on history, politics, and culture, mainly in small journals and periodicals. For a sampling of these works, one can begin with *Chicana Feminist Thought*, a collection of writings edited by Alma M. García.[44] Of the eighty-two works included in this collection, sixty were originally published or written before 1977. In addition, *De Colores*, the journal that printed the original version of Sommers's essay in its 4:4 issue, had published a special issue just months earlier devoted to Chicana literature. The 4:3 issue of *De Colores*, entitled *La Cosecha: Literatura y La Mujer Chicana*, featured a number of essays and literary pieces—including the first work of fiction published by novelist Lucha Corpi, a short story entitled "Tres Mujeres"—that made a strong case for the importance of Chicana literature.[45] Two years earlier, *De Colores* had published another special issue (2:3) on "La Chicana." In one article, "World Women's Challenge—a New Society Based on Justice and Peace," Lupe Anguiano reports on the United Nations International Women's Year Conference, both the "official U.N. Conference and the Non-Government Tribune Conference," which were held in Mexico City in the summer of that year. The report is a telling revelation of the internationalist, anti-imperialist political perspectives of some Chicana feminists at that time. Anguiano writes, "The necessary base for Equality of Women and

Men, as well as for Development and Peace must be a new 'International Economic Order—the liberation of developing and underdeveloped countries from foreign controlled military regimes and the Independence of all countries from foreign economic exploitation.'"[46] Anguiano's internationalist politics represent an advanced critique of global capitalism from a Chicana feminist point of view. Sommers's analysis of Chicano criticism would have benefited from acknowledging the work that Chicana feminists were doing in the emerging field of Chicano studies at that time. While I do not focus specifically on issues of gender and sexuality in the present work, the Chicana feminist critiques of sexism and nationalism (not to mention reification) are presupposed in the general political and theoretical positions of my book.

Third—and most important for the purposes of this study—Sommers's proposed "historical-dialectical" method is more synthetic than dialectical. He combines somewhat mechanistically the thematic, formal, and historical approaches in his study of literature, which makes for a more comprehensive approach to reading literature but is not necessarily "dialectical" in a Marxist sense. He emphasizes the importance of social class in the analysis of literature, but he does not make use of other central critical categories of Marxist dialectics, in particular, mediation and reification. These exclusions become most pronounced in his conceptualization of narrative form. In writing about form, Sommers refers mainly to the literary work's structural or component parts: narrator, author, protagonist, point of view, characterization, plot, language, style, and so on. He writes about form as a fixed feature of the text, rather than as the dynamic social aspiration of the text—that is, he thinks of form as a congeries of things rather than a set of relations. By contrast, I hold that the study of Chicano literature—indeed, the study of literature generally—benefits from a dialectical conception of literary form.

To illustrate this point, let us consider the following two instances of dialectical interpretations of form: Adorno's theorization of form as mediation; and Limón's description of form (following Jameson) as the ideological embodiment of the conflict between competing modes of production. In *Aesthetic Theory*, Adorno describes the form of artworks as a kind of mediation, a view reflected in such statements as "form is essential to art [because] it mediates content,"[47] and "[f]orm repudiates the view that artworks are immediately given. If form is that in artworks by which they become artworks, it is equivalent with their mediatedness, their objective reflectedness, into themselves. Form is mediation in that it is the *relation* of parts to each other and to the whole."[48] Conceptualized in this way, the form of a novel can be understood in one sense as the "world" of the novel, or its totality; in another sense, it can be understood as the interconnected logic of the novel's ideological field, which makes each individual part of the novel intelligible on its own, but also gives the sum of the parts a feeling of unity.

Limón defines form in a manner similar to that of Adorno, but his definition is grounded in less abstract terms. In *Dancing with the Devil*, Limón, a cultural anthropologist and literary critic, describes a study he conducted of folkloric narratives of the devil in South Texas: stories of the devil appearing in public places such as bars and celebrations. He collected the narratives from interviews with numerous working-class Mexican Americans living in south Texas: women and men; young and old; urban and rural; English-speaking and Spanish-speaking, and so forth. Of the persons he interviewed for this study, some believed firmly in the appearance of the devil; others were incredulous. Of those who believed in the devil, a good number interpreted the significance of the narrative by focusing on its details, on the themes and events in the narrative itself. Limón observes that only the "elders" tended to comment on the significance of the narrative's form—not in the traditional sense of the component parts of narrative structure (point of view, characterization, setting, etc.), but form as social class conflict. Citing Jameson's "third horizon" of interpretation from *The Political Unconscious*, Limón explains that, at this third level, "form becomes the focus of the interpretive move," but he clarifies that in focusing on form he is mainly "concerned with what Jameson calls the 'ideology of form.'"[49] We will recall that for Jameson the "ideology of form" in his "third horizon" refers to the manner in which a social formation at any given historical moment is constituted not by one mode of production, but by various competing modes of production: traces of modes from the past, a dominant mode from the present, and anticipatory modes not yet having come into existence. The form of literary works resembles the form of social formations in this regard: literary form becomes a battleground of ideologies representative of the various modes of production that gave rise to these ideologies. Interestingly, it is only the "elders" in Limón's study who interpret the devil narrative at this level because

> it is only they who seem to be concerned with form, with the form of society, with their folk sense of the modes of production. The narrative for them signifies something more historically embracing, namely, the per-

> ceived long-term changes in their lives as they have undergone conflict and change in what they perceive from a folk perspective as shifts and overlaps in the modes of production. . . . [F]or in the historical lives of the elders they, in fact, experienced a more virulent and intense race and class domination both in Mexico and in Texas: strict codes of racial segregation, lynchings, hurrying to step off the sidewalk when an Anglo approached, picking cotton at dirt wages from sunup to sundown, unchecked diseases treated only by *curanderos* because no Anglo doctor would accept Mexican patients.[50]

Form as described by Limón in this passage refers to historically specific social relations within which class conflicts, often manifested and felt as racial oppression, and conflicts between competing modes of production, better understood as a battleground of ideologies, leave their imprint on the symbolic content of narratives that, on the surface, may appear to have little or nothing to do with class struggle. The elders recognize the class content of form in the devil narratives because they have the most direct and longest-standing experience in class conflict. Limón seems to be suggesting also that cultural anthropologists and literary critics may be able to learn a lesson from the wisdom of the elders, namely, to interpret culture and literature with an understanding of form as ideology reflective of class conflict and the conflict between modes of production. Limón, like Adorno and Jameson, conceptualizes form in terms of mediation: a social totality that gives meaning to the individual parts of a narrative—to its themes and organization—and provides the conceptual logic for comprehending the relation among the various parts of the narrative as a whole. My purpose for this discussion of form is to emphasize the fact that the dialectical conception of literary form as theorized by Adorno, Jameson, and Limón (not to mention Lukács, Sartre, and Benjamin) is noticeably absent from Sommers's proposed "historical-dialectical" method, even though the critique of form is presumably one of the main argumentative threads in his essay.

In my use of the term *form* I am not referring to the different types of literary expression: novels, short fiction, biography, poetry, or drama; these designations might more aptly be labeled genres or literary conventions. Nor do I want to equate the terms *form* and *structure*, though the concepts referred to by these terms are not entirely unrelated. For my purpose, *structure* refers to the component parts of a narrative and their organization. By contrast, I employ the concept of form to designate the manner in which social relations become ingrained in the various levels of significance in a particular literary work. In this study I follow Limón's emphasis on the importance of understanding the form of narratives as the embodiment of the "form of society"—specifically, the internalization of the conflict between class discourses. By defining form in this way I am also drawing on Jameson's claim that "form is immanently and intrinsically an ideology in its own right."[51] Thus, by extension, the analysis of novelistic form—in the way I am using the term here—is roughly synonymous with ideology critique.

Earlier I stated that contradictory form is a marker of the Chicano-ness of Chicano novels, by which I mean to say the novels simultaneously embody and contest reification. Granted, there are many literary traditions that can also be characterized as inherently and formally contradictory. Fifty years ago, Richard Chase proclaimed that American novels by and large are expressions of acute alienation, and thus they can be characterized by their inherent contradictoriness. He distinguished the American novel from the English novel, describing the latter also as contradictory but as representative of a kind of fiction that consciously strives toward the resolution of its contradictions. The American novel, in his view, resides in its unresolved perpetual contradictoriness, reflective of the conflicted experience of modern American life.[52] In one respect, Chase's argument is similar to that of Marxists, such as Jameson, who also emphasize the contradictoriness of narrative form. Like Chase, Jameson argues that modernist novels do not resolve the contradictions they represent and embody, which is to say, they do not achieve ideological closure. But Jameson also differs from Chase, the former asserting that the modernist novel, at the level of form, nonetheless aspires toward a symbolic resolution. We might explain the seemingly paradoxical content of Jameson's claims by stating that the modernist novel simultaneously manifests reification and attempts to surpass it. Chicano novels can be understood in this way: they are indeed examples of contradictory forms, but they do not necessarily resolve their contradictions thematically, which is to say, in the thoughts and actions of characters or in the narrator's point of view. Nor do they achieve ideological closure. The contradictions faced by the characters remain for the most part unresolved, bathing in their full spectrum of irony and dissonance. The novels nonetheless contest reification formally in striving toward a comprehension of—or at least an allusion to—the relation between the specificity of the novel and social totality.

Even if the forms employed in American novels generally can be considered contradictory, as Chase argues, the particularity of contradiction in specific literary works constitutes their difference. The assertion that novels within a literary tradition are distinguished by their contradictory form could apply to all U.S. ethnic or minority literatures. The contradictoriness of Chicano novels, however, stems from the specific manner of response to the long historical process of racialization as it has been experienced by Mexican Americans for a century and a half. In particular, Chicano novels historically can be read as critiques of dispossession, disenfranchisement, proletarianization, racism, state repression, and various other kinds of social oppression, all of which can be contextualized and traced back historically to the general process of capitalist accumulation beginning in 1848 in the Southwest and continuing up to the present. The themes of dispossession, proletarianization, racism, and so on, are not exhaustive in Chicano novels since issues of gender, sexuality, nationality, language, religion, and family hold important representational places in Chicano literature. My point is that what is particular to Chicano literature beyond the commonalities it shares with other traditions is the critique of being racialized in class terms—a reified, racial subjectivity defined by its proletarianization historically. This is to say, Chicanas and Chicanos have been constructed in the national imaginary as part of a subservient laboring class—a social construction that Chicano novels attempt to dereify.

Debates over form and content in literary interpretation, of course, have not been limited to Chicano literature. In a 1986 survey of theories of narrative, Wallace Martin traces the various form-content debates in American literary studies throughout the twentieth century. He maintains that scholars of various methodological persuasions—from New Criticism and neo-Aristotelian criticism to structuralism and poststructuralism; from subjective and biographical criticism to myth and historical criticism—attempted for decades to resolve or synthesize in one manner or another the form-content antithesis, but no important theoretical approach adequately addressed this problem, in his view, "until later, when the criticism of Lukács was translated into English" in the early 1970s and Jameson subsequently "extended Lukács's dialectical conception of form and content"[53] in *Marxism and Form* and *The Political Unconscious.* If Martin is correct, then Lukács's theory of reification assumes the utmost importance for the critique of narrative form because the concept of reification—along with its counterpart, "totality"—is by far the most significant dialectical category that Jameson inherits from Lukács as a Marxist critic; it is also the central critical category (or code) at work in *The Political Unconscious.* As such, it will prove beneficial to examine in some depth the manner in which Jameson extends Lukács's dialectical conception of reification in order to argue for its continuing relevance, focusing on the relation of that extension to the purpose of the present book—which is to say, the interpretation of Chicano novels.

Reification and the "Standpoint of the Proletariat"

Perhaps the best place to begin an analysis of Jameson's extension and revision of Lukács's theory of reification is not with *The Political Unconscious*, but with his essay "*History and Class Consciousness* as an 'Unfinished Project.'" Published in the inaugural issue of *Rethinking Marxism*, it is structured roughly in two parts: an argument for a reassessment of Lukács's theories of reification and totality; and a comparison of Lukács's "standpoint of the proletariat" with contemporary identity politics. In the first part, Jameson takes issue with what has become the "conventional narrative" of Lukács's personal history and its relation to his life work. As this "conventional narrative" goes, the young, critically astute, Hegelian-Marxist Lukács was attacked and disciplined by the Comintern for his criticisms of "reflection theory" in *History and Class Consciousness*, originally published in 1923. Lukács supposedly caved in to these criticisms and, consequently, all of his works published after 1930 were rectified to conform to the party line and were thus intellectually compromised. This older, Stalinist Lukács presumably relied dogmatically on the same reductive reflection theory that the young Lukács had opposed. Diverging from this "conventional narrative" and simultaneously pointing up the ideological motive behind its emergence and proliferation, Jameson writes that "as long as Lukács is used as a rallying cry (or bogeyman)" against orthodox Marxism and dialectical literary criticism, "there is not much likelihood of any measured assessment of his work as a whole."[54] Obviously not haunted by the specter of such a bogeyman, Jameson argues that critics should refrain from reading Lukács's later works as breaking radically with the earlier ones in every respect. On the contrary, throughout his career and in all of his major works on philosophy, politics, and aesthetics, Lukács remains consistently interested in theorizing the concept of *narrative*.[55] More to the point, Jameson argues, Lukács's conception of narrative can be ascertained through an examination of three critical categories that form the theoretical basis of his lifelong work: reification, totality, and realism.

For Jameson, the Lukácsian theory of reification not only specifies the objectification of the social world, but also explicates the manner in which a capitalist mode of production necessitates the classification, fragmentation, and atomization of social relations—"the Taylorization, not merely of the work process, but also of the mind"[56]—as in the Weberian concept of rationalization. Further, the contradictions of capitalism impose a priori limits on the inner logic of speculative thought, and consequently consciousness comes to assume a form similar to that of the commodity: an abstraction of concrete social relations in which those relations are obfuscated or repressed nearly to the point of oblivion. A reified consciousness is thus able to grasp the world only in its apparent forms—as an infinitely fragmented world of discrete objects, disconnected from their social origins and from each other. Reification is "what suppresses the ability to grasp totalities [and] the capacity to think in terms of process."[57] Moreover, a reified consciousness self-consciously conceptualizes itself as independent from its objects of contemplation. Thus reification refers not exclusively to the thing-ification of social relationships, but also, and perhaps primarily, to the split between subject and object, to the false notion that a subject can somehow become knowledgeable of the objective world from an external standpoint or from the perspective of a purely contemplative consciousness. As Lukács himself states in *History and Class Consciousness*, reification refers to the "contemplative dualism between thought and existence,"[58] to the "unbridgeable abyss between concept and reality."[59] Lukács's critique of reification exposes the essential problematic of bourgeois epistemology, namely, the separation of a knowing subject from a discernable objective reality.

Just as Lukács's theory of "reification has scarcely been appreciated, so also the fundamental message of 'dereification' which *History and Class Consciousness* bears . . . has only intermittently been audible."[60] Inescapably, "dereification" is intricately bound up with Lukács's concept of totality. That is, if the system of commodity production and exchange produces a reified conception of the world by making the fragmented pieces of social reality appear as discrete entities unto themselves, then logically the undoing of reification requires a consciousness that strives to comprehend the historical connections and interconnections of discrete objects within larger social totalities across time and space. Totality with regard to a literary work does not mean that the work has somehow represented every aspect of some immense social reality at a given place and time in history; it would be absurd to think a work of symbolic fiction could reproduce such a reality. In novels, totality refers to (1) the imagined world of the novel, which always implies much more than what is written on the page, and (2) the assumed existence of social totality—always present but never fully graspable or capable of being represented—that gives meaning to the novel and to which the novel repeatedly alludes. As Jameson suggests, the "*aspiration to totality*, famously evoked by Lukács in *History and Class Consciousness*, would then in the narrative realm involve a refusal of these habitual limits and boundaries and even a defamiliarization" of the immediately given.[61] Both Jameson and Lukács conceptualize the possibility of rupturing reification via the critical study of literature—and particularly, in the interpretation of narrative form. For Lukács, the kind of narrative that most successfully aspires toward dereification is the realist novel.

According to the "conventional narrative" mentioned above, Lukács promoted a reductive notion of realism as a transparent reflection of reality in his post-1930 criticism. Even in his later works, however, Lukács did not write about realism as a transparent "reflection" of reality, but as a literary approach that tends toward the dereification of represented realities and consciousness. Realism resists the extreme fragmentation and rationalization caused by the elaborate systems of commodity production and exchange under capitalism by aspiring toward a kind of representation that implies a determinate relation between events and their causes, emphasizing historical continuity rather than discontinuity. Realism for Lukács has "the same function as 'the consciousness of the proletariat' in *History and Class Consciousness*. It is the bearer of the force of dereification."[62] Implicit in Lukács's theory of realism lies the conviction that realist novels possess the potential to produce cognition of the social totality not through unmediated reflection, but through abstractions. It is not that the author of a realist novel *contemplates* social reality and then represents it in some kind of objectively accurate written form; it is rather the other way round: the social relations within a particular mode of production establish the formal limits of narratives internally. Thus, the dialectical critic will recognize the structural similarities between irony in novels and class contradictions in society, between the reified consciousness of characters and the general alienation produced in capitalist society, between the repression of history in novels and the mystery that lies hidden in commodity fetishism.

Further, Lukács's concept of *totality* in the social sphere corresponds roughly to the concept of *narrative* "in the aesthetic realm,"[63] which is to say that the realist novel constitutes a formal totality—the ideological world of the novel—that compensates for and takes the place of the social totality lost to reification.[64] The realist narrative, according to Lukács, resists the fragmenting and objectifying tendencies of reification in a way that the naturalist or modernist text does not. As literary traditions, modernism and naturalism (and the enormous range of aesthetic innovations these terms designate) are very different from one another as far as their stylistic qualities and the specific historical circumstances to which they respond, but they are generally similar, Lukács argues, in that both convey reified conceptions of historical causality: naturalism depicts events as occurring in accord with some natural law or ahistorical process; modernism critiques the effects of alienation and social fragmentation but represents these effects as inescapable consequences of our historical moment or existential condition.

By contrast, realism reveals—or, at the very least, implies—a causal relation between social conditions and class conflicts: between events and the totality that gives them meaning; between the particular and the general. Lukács's critiques of modernism and naturalism in his post-1930s work have been criticized for being dismissive of these important traditions. Anyone who has read Lukács's arguments for realism carefully, however, knows that he is not arguing for some kind of "photographic accuracy" of social reality in literature. His critiques of naturalism and modernism do not necessarily take issue with how empirically faithful characters and events are depicted in these traditions; he challenges rather their formal logic and, in particular, the implied absence of a history-based conception of causality through which events can be more fully comprehended and traced back to real social class contradictions. Further, his political commitments do not necessarily contradict his views of literature. To a large extent, Lukács's Marxism enabled him to develop a critical conception of literary forms from the perspective of totality. Despite his weaknesses and miscalculations—among them, that the world was on the brink of a proletarian revolution in 1923—Lukács criticizes naturalism and modernism because, in his view, they embody the logic of capital, which is to say, a reified consciousness that conceptualizes the social world as fragmented, disconnected, static, and ultimately unexplainable. In this manner his critiques of naturalism and modernism in his later works remain consistent with the theoretical formulations from his earlier period. "What becomes clear when Lukács's positions are grasped in this interrelated and dialectical way is that their philosophical underpinnings remain those of *History and Class Consciousness* and in particular specifically presuppose the theory of reification."[65]

It bears mentioning here that despite Jameson's favorable recognition of the dialectical "underpinnings" of Lukács's critique of literary modernism, and his general feeling that aspects of this critique are indeed salvageable, the former does not fully accept the latter's firm repudiation of modernism.[66] Nor does he assimilate Lukács's theories of realism, modernism, and reification wholesale; he revises them to make them consistent with and thus useful for the interpretation of modernist and postmodernist narratives. Acknowledging that modernism is indeed an "ideological expression" of capitalist reification, Jameson qualifies this claim to assert that "modernism can at one and the same time be read as a Utopian compensation for everything reification brings with it."[67] In a 1995 interview with Xudong Zhang, he offers the following reassessment of Lukács: "[W]hat Lukács meant to me is that ideally, one should somehow get to the content through the forms . . . . [But] Lukács always talked about achieved form, successful form. It seems to me rather that we have to look at failures of form, the impossibility of certain kinds of representation in a certain context, the flaws, limits, obstacles, which become the clue to the social truth or social meaning, and not so much canonical success in that old Lukácsian sense."[68] In effect, Lukács's method of reading realist novels can be adapted for the reading of modernist and postmodernist narratives, in addition to popular forms of art and literature, by analyzing not only the unity of their thematic content, but their formal contradictoriness, as well.

Jameson's revisions of Lukács open up inviting possibilities for the interpretation of literature and culture. For example, postmodernism's attack on the concept of totality can be interpreted as falling headlong into reification because postmodern theory embraces a way of understanding and explaining the world that favors the very fragmented condition that produces its own alienation.[69] Nonetheless, from a dialectical perspective, postmodernist narratives—and here I am thinking of the novels of Dagoberto Gilb and Alejandro Morales as well as those of Thomas Pynchon and Don DeLillo—can be interpreted not only as contemplations on depthlessness and fragmentation, but as implied references to social totality. The noticeable absence of interconnectedness and "depth" in postmodernist narratives calls attention to an implied social reality, imagined in terms of a grand narrative that has produced a sense of disconnection and superficiality. To take the analysis further, one can employ the category of reification to critique the micro-movements of identity politics, multiculturalism, and the "new social movements."[70] Jameson argues that identity politics, like postmodernism, reproduce the fragmenting process of reification in the celebration of "difference" and the rejection of social class analysis, though he steers clear of an oversimplified analysis of the relation between identity politics and postmodernism. In "The Antinomies of Postmodernity," he acknowledges that "the political movements that emerged in the 1960s were [flawed]; most were excessive, ideological[ly] ill-conceived, and poorly executed, with insufficient leadership, dogmatic attitudes, [and] misplaced hopes." They were doomed to failure because of their internal weaknesses, "let alone the overwhelming power of the enemy's productive infrastructure." But he complicates the matter in stating that "the enthusiasm raised by such movements . . . was itself a powerful and objective force whose absolute disappointment could not but have objective consequences in its own right."[71] So it was not the internal politics of the 1960s movements and later the "new social movements" per se that opened the doors to postmodernism and ideological defeatism; rather, these movements emerged alongside postmodernism as symptoms of an intensified reification of a capitalist society in severe economic and political crisis.[72] Thus even though the separatism of cultural nationalism (or identity politics) can be interpreted as reflecting and reproducing the general fragmenting tendency of reification, it can also be understood in terms of its class content insofar as it manifests a response to the general crisis of global capitalism.

Here a similar analytical procedure might be conceptualized for the interpretation of Chicano novels, considering that most twentieth-century Chicano novels cannot be categorized as *realist* in the strict Lukacsian sense since they do not contain the totalizing breadth of class relations characteristic of, say, a Tolstoy novel. Most Chicano novels might reasonably be characterized as modernist or postmodernist, in part, because they have subsumed so deeply the reification and fragmentation that has increasingly become the trademark of capitalist culture in the twentieth century. Nevertheless, they can still be interpreted as aspiring toward a kind of epistemological realism made possible not by a direct correlation between representation and object, but by the logic of their formal contradictoriness—a logic that will be found to be consistent with the structural limits of late capitalism. This formal contradictoriness does not necessarily reflect a weakness in the literature; on the contrary, it offers the possibility of elucidating the specific historical circumstances and social processes within which Chicano novels have been produced and to which they are a response. Nor should the reified consciousness of narrators and characters in Chicano novels lead us to conclude that the novels have failed to aspire toward (or be inspired by) totality; it simply means that totality is implied by its absence rather than its explicit presence. Thus the "social truth or social meaning" of Chicano novels can be derived not only from the representation of experience—and for that matter, not only from their "achieved form"—but from the logic of their imperfect forms, from the absences, inconsistencies, and contradictions of form.

Enter José Limón, who argues that the modernism of Chicano writers should not be interpreted strictly in terms of the limitations of earlier literary modernisms, particularly works characterized by acute alienation and defeatism. Drawing on the critical works of Raymond Williams and Paul Gilroy, Limón reads Chicano literature as "critical modernism," a concept that differs substantively from Lukács's negative judgment of modernism as decadent. For Limón, "critical modernism" challenges the pessimism and notions of discontinuity of earlier modernisms. To support his case, he argues that beginning in the 1960s Chicano writers produced literary works that resulted in "a traditionally reinforced 'native' conversation with modernism from 'below,' a conversation that appropriates and revises modernism as much as it revises the strong folk precursors" of Chicano culture itself.[73] Chicano literature reinvigorates "traditional modernism, now viewed as exhausted in its ability to generate social change."[74] For Limón, if we are going to read Chicano literature as modernist, "we must then speak of a modernism of critical difference."[75] (In one sense, it is not possible to write a novel today—Chicano or non-Chicano—that is not modernist, which is to say, we have not yet outlived the historical epoch of capitalist modernity and the aesthetic sensibilities it produces; the differences among the various kinds of modernisms are distinctions of degree rather than of kind. Postmodernist works, for that matter, need not be considered as qualitatively different from modernist works, but as intensifications of the anxieties generated in the latter.)

After reading the first half of "*History and Class Consciousness* as an 'Unfinished Project,'" one might assume that the second half will lead to a dialectical critique of the limits of identity politics by exposing the manner in which these projects are complicit, even if unwittingly, in reproducing reification. In the second part of his essay, however, Jameson quite surprisingly argues instead—as if undergoing a dialectical reversal—that Lukács's "standpoint of the proletariat" has been misinterpreted by his defenders on the left as well as by his opponents on the right. The only critics who have been able to grasp what Lukács meant by this theoretical formulation, he declares, are certain proponents of identity politics: feminists such as Sandra Harding;[76] writers of "Black theory as it emerged from the 60s and the Black Power movement";[77] and "Jews and so many other ethnic groups."[78] These various groups have staked out theoretical positions similar to what

Jameson, following Harding and other feminists, calls "standpoint theory," or what is more commonly referred to as "standpoint epistemology." He also claims that Lukács's "standpoint of the proletariat" is not based on "*abstract concepts* such as '*class*' or '*production*,' but rather on *group* experience."[79] This move seemingly departs from what Lukács refers to as "orthodox Marxism" and the primacy it grants to the category of class. Jameson contends, however, that the efforts of writers who represent sexism, homophobia, racism, and anti-Semitism can potentially rupture the effects of reification. In so contending, however, he appears, at first sight, to be minimizing the differences between social class and group identities.

Jameson's comparison of standpoint theory and the standpoint of the proletariat is risky, to say the least, for a Marxist critic; the former is premised upon experience, while the latter is premised upon class as structure. For traditional Marxism, the proletariat as a social class possesses the potential to comprehend (in a way that the bourgeoisie does not) the transformation of society beyond capitalism precisely because it has a material interest in doing away with class exploitation, that is, abolishing capitalism. Marx of course argued that knowledge comes from efforts to transform society and that the most critically concrete interpretations of social transformation therefore come from class struggle, not abstract contemplation.[80] Individuals who have an interest in changing society possess the material incentive to seek a more truthful or meaningful analysis of social relations and the causes of social conditions. We cannot make this same claim about the group identities to which Jameson refers. In general, these other group formations promote strategies for unity directed at correcting democratic inequalities—broadening the possibilities for civic inclusion and participation—which are worthy causes in and of themselves, but which are not aimed at comprehending, much less eliminating, the systemic causes of inequality. Thus, in the Lukacsian sense, group identities are more likely to obfuscate or mystify these same relations, especially with regard to social class, than to encourage revolutionary change to take place. This is not to dismiss the exceedingly important work (in academics and political practice) undertaken in the name of identity politics, especially work directed at exposing and challenging racism, sexism, homophobia, and other harmful and potentially deadly forms of oppression. Political practices aimed at challenging oppression are important and absolutely necessary, but without a class standpoint they nonetheless remain contained within an ideology of systemic maintenance and reform, despite the many admirable, courageous, and even sometimes life-threatening actions carried out against the various forms of social abuse and injustice.

More significantly, in writing about the standpoint (or consciousness) of the proletariat, Lukács is not referring to the psychological consciousness of individuals—not even that of individual workers. He makes clear that class consciousness does not refer to "the inherent or natural possession of the proletariat as a class (let alone of proletarian individuals). On the contrary . . . the conscious subject is not defined here as in Kant, where 'subject' is defined as that which can never be an object. The 'subject' here is not a detached spectator of the process. The proletariat is more than just the active and passive part of the process."[81] To be a worker and to be aware of being a worker does not mean that the worker automatically possesses the key to social transformation. Lukács's proletarian consciousness signifies rather a form of consciousness that would be possible only when the material basis of reification (capitalist social relations) has been transformed into nonreifying social relations, which is to say, a classless society. Since no such society has existed in modern times, the "standpoint of the proletariat" refers not to a condition obtainable in the foreseeable future, much less to an actual condition, but to a methodological postulate, much like the concept of totality, against which reified consciousness can be measured and thus comprehended.

Even if we grant, as we must, that group identities cannot be mechanistically separated from social class, we would still have to distinguish between the kinds of knowledge produced from experience and what Lukács means by "proletarian class consciousness," which is not the positive identification of ideas belonging to a particular group of workers, but a methodology based on the negative (dialectical) critique of the pervasive logic of commodity culture, that is, reification. In *History and Class Consciousness*, "[T]he knowledge of reality provided by the dialectical method is . . . inseparable from the class standpoint of the proletariat. . . . [It] can arise only from the point of view of a class, from the point of view of the struggle of the proletariat. To abandon this point of view is to move away from historical materialism."[82] One need not dismiss the importance of group identities and the kinds of knowledge they are capable of producing to find that not all forms of consciousness are necessarily equal, which is to say, not all forms of *oppositional* consciousness can be categorized as dereifying consciousness.

Despite the potential political and theoretical problems encountered by attempting to draw too close a comparison between the standpoint of the proletariat and identity politics, Jameson's project need not be understood as a retreat from Marxism, but could be considered an attempt to expand Marxism's conceptual and interpretive reach. Ultimately Jameson may be correct in implying that theorizing the connections between class and social identity is a risk Marxists must be willing to take, especially those of us involved in the study of minority literatures. In teasing out the similarities between the standpoint of the proletariat and identity politics, Jameson has not given up on the importance of class as a central analytical category; he is arguing that our access to social class in literature—especially in minority literatures—may have to be gleaned from representations of the various social identities rather than from specific representations of class struggle. Elsewhere he writes, "If we want to go on believing in categories like social class, then we are going to have to dig for them in the insubstantial bottomless realm of cultural and collective fantasy."[83] Jameson's analytical move here is similar to that in his revision of Lukács's theory of reification in which he redirects our attention from "achieved form" to "imperfect form" so as to make the theory useful not only for the interpretation of literary realism, but for modernism and postmodernism, as well. With regard to reification, Jameson "rewrites Lukács in the secular tones that befit a postmodern age."[84] We could say he also revises the concept of the standpoint of the proletariat so as to make it a useful category not only for overt representations of class in literary works, but for those of race, ethnicity, gender, sexuality, and nationality, as well—a revision that "befits" our contemporary era of identity thinking.

Jameson's comparison of the standpoint of the proletariat and identity politics serves a much different purpose than Rey Chow's argument in *The Protestant Ethnic and the Spirit of Capitalism* about the centrality of Lukács for contemporary ethnic studies. Most critics would not associate the standpoint of the proletariat with ethnic studies since Lukács clearly posits the primacy of class as a social and analytical category, reflected in such concepts as class consciousness. By contrast, proponents of identity politics in ethnic studies primarily employ the category of experience to formulate theories of subjectivity; to a large extent, ethnic studies also rejects the primacy of class for the study of race and racial inequality, treating class as one among several subcategories of experience. Given these different conceptions of primacy, one would assume that Lukács has little to offer ethnic studies. But Chow interestingly reverses the traditional conception of Lukács, reading him not for the importance he gives to class but for the structure of the narrative he constructs, supposedly about the proletarian subject coming to consciousness much in the manner that ethnic subjects become enlightened once they discover their identity. Chow rejects the consciousness-raising implications in both cases. She nonetheless argues that Lukács's work has served, intentionally or unintentionally, as a foundational framework for theorizing subjectivity in ethnic studies.

> Lukács's work remains, I believe, one of the most influential models for imagining consciousness—or subjectivity-in-exploitation. Be they through feminism, postcolonial theory, alternative sexual preferences and lifestyles, or other types of minority discourses, numerous contemporary versions of identity-based critical thinking have, wittingly or unwittingly, been replicating Lukács's modernist narrative with its telos of self-ownership, and self-affirmation in both individual and collective senses.[85]

Whereas Jameson reads Lukács's "standpoint of the proletariat" as an "unfinished project," which holds the promise of being brought to its fruition via the interpretation of literary works by ethnic and women writers, Chow reads Lukacs's *History and Class Consciousness* as having already outlived its usefulness (if in fact it ever was useful) for the study of literature, and as theoretically sterile for the study of ethnicity. To arrive at this conclusion, Chow reads Lukács's standpoint of the proletariat erroneously as subjectivity—a worker-centered consciousness or working-class identity—rather than as the postulated *other* of reification. Unlike Jameson, who argues that Lukács's "standpoint" can be employed to "dig up" class consciousness and class struggle in narratives about racial and ethnic identities, Chow reads *History and Class Consciousness* as a narrative essentially about identity itself—a narrative of captivity in which a proletarian subject struggles to break free from the confines of bourgeois thinking and comes to consciousness of its own qualities and potentialities. In so doing, Chow has effectively cleansed Lukács's classic text of its critical historicism.[86]

Rosemary Hennessy also recognizes Lukács theoretical shortcomings, such as his overemphasis on "the pervasive invasion of consciousness by commodification," but unlike Chow she acknowledges his "monumental elaborations of commodity culture in *History and Class Consciousness*."[87] Lukács is important for Hennessy because of the way he theorizes and historicizes the relation between the logic of commodity fetishism and the formation of social identities—or more succinctly, between capital and culture. Tracing the formation of sexual identities to social developments in the nineteenth century, Hennessy argues convincingly that much more research is needed to disclose "the historical relationship between the formation of new sexual identities and the reifying cultural logic of an emergent commodity culture." Taking into account the paucity of such theorizations in both the humanities and social sciences, she explains, "Confronting these questions makes me aware of how much historical work on the parallel emergence of commodity culture and heteronormative sexuality still waits to be done."[88] While Hennessy is interested mainly in theorizing sexual identities, her work opens up avenues for thinking about the relationship between the logic of capital and the formation of other kinds of social identities (including those based on race, ethnicity, gender, and nationality). For that matter, we can also think about relation between the logic of capital and cultural production—such as literature and, for the purpose of this book, the novel itself.

Jameson's comparison of standpoint epistemology and the standpoint of the proletariat bears greater similarities, theoretically and politically, to Hennessy's critique of the logic of capital than to Chow's repudiation of Lukács. Both Jameson and Hennessy shed light (though perhaps the latter to a greater degree) on an area of Marxist criticism that remains underdeveloped: the relation between class and the various social identities represented in literature—especially in minority literatures. Whether or not one agrees with the specific revisions Jameson and Hennessy propose to Lukács's theory of reification and the standpoint of the proletariat, what remains unquestionably (even if only implicitly) useful in their revisions for the interpretation of Chicano novels is the attempt to analyze class consciousness and class struggle via the representation of racial identity. In the course of this study, I intend to test Jameson's proposition to read representations of identity and experience as symbolic allusions to a "proletarian standpoint," as well as Hennessy's critique of social identities as based on the logic of capital, via the interpretation of Chicano novels.

Timothy Bewes describes reification as a "once celebrated, lately disparaged metaphor."[89] However, the category of reification—in its different modes—not only continues to be relevant for literary analysis, but allows for going beyond the relative abstraction in propositions about class epistemology, and finding ways to make them concrete. The category of reification as theorized by Jameson and Hennessy provides a bridge—epistemological, rhetorical, and mimetic—between identity as experience and class as structure. It is precisely this theoretical bridge afforded by reification that interests me in the study of Chicano novels. In this regard, this book not only contributes to theories of reading Chicano literature, but extends and explores a range of ways in which reification figures in literary representation generally as both object of representation and stance from which representation is essayed.

2

AN AESTHETIC SOLUTION TO OBJECTIVE PROBLEMS

Liberalism in Ruiz de Burton's *The Squatter and the Don*

> If our legislators could only be induced to adopt Herbert Spencer's view of the duties of law givers, there would be far less misery in the United States. If they could but stop to see how clearly it stands to reason that "legislative deductions must be based on *fundamental morality*."
>
> —María Amparo Ruiz de Burton,
> *The Squatter and the Don*

> Ruiz de Burton's novel deals with several forms of accumulation of capital. . . . But . . . there is also a discussion of a more primitive type of accumulation that is more akin to the conquest, plunder and piracy practiced by European colonizers in the Americas.
>
> —Rosaura Sánchez and Beatrice Pita,
> introduction to *Who Would Have Thought It?*

> Californios moan like husbands of the raped,
> husbands de la tierra,
> tierra de la madre.
>
> —Lorna Dee Cervantes,
> "Poema Para Los Californios Muertos"

MARÍA AMPARO RUIZ DE BURTON'S two novels, *The Squatter and the Don* (1885) and *Who Would Have Thought It?* (1872), are the first known novels written in English by a Mexican American writer, male or female, and published in the United States. As such, they have come to be considered not only concentric works within contemporary Chicano literary studies, but foundational texts that mark a central formational moment in Chicano literary history. The novels were out of print for over a century and virtually unknown until the recovery and reprinting of *The Squatter* in 1992 and *Who Would Have Thought It?* in 1995 by Arte Público Press.[1] Since then a fairly large number of articles, dissertations, and book chapters have been published on these novels, including a collection of critical and pedagogical essays edited by Amelia M. de la Luz Montes and Anne E. Goldman.[2] One of the most provocative works of criticism, however, might be the introduction to the Arte Público edition of the *The Squatter and the Don.*[3] In this assertive and ambitious essay, Rosaura Sánchez and Beatrice Pita provide a biographical sketch of Ruiz de Burton's life, contextualize the novel historically, and analyze its generic/structural features. In so doing, they suggest a genealogical link (in terms of social identity and literary history) between late-nineteenth-century Californios and late-twentieth-century Chicanos based on a common expression of "resistance" to racism, capitalist accumulation, and imperialism. But Sánchez and Pita, like other critics who have written on Ruiz de Burton, are confronted with the task of accounting for the seemingly racist and antiworker declarations made by the narrators and characters in Ruiz de Burton's novels, especially in *The Squatter*. Can a novel in which the narrator unabashedly refers to Native Americans and working-class mestizos in a racially derogatory manner be considered politically resistant?

Critics of Ruiz de Burton's novels, as I discuss in what follows, have grappled with this question to one extent or another: Sánchez and Pita read the novel as the "voice of the subaltern"—as evidence that the subaltern can indeed speak—despite the narrator's occasional offensive remarks toward Native Americans and mestizo workers; by contrast, others have read the novel as the disgruntled expression of class privilege, despite the novel's stinging critique of monopoly capitalism and the proletarianization of Mexicans. Sánchez and Pita account for the narrator's contradictory point of view by arguing that Ruiz de Burton brings together various incommensurable discourses in *The Squatter* to create "a narrative space for the counter-history of the sub-altern" and that in so doing her critique "necessarily require[s] the appropriation of the very political discourses that she set out to denounce."[4] From another angle, Ana Castillo recognizes in the introduction to the Random House edition of the novel that references to Indian and mestizo characters in *The Squatter* are "ascribed with the worst of stereotypes," but adds that from a contemporary perspective she is "also obliged to say that this was not the 'point' of the story."[5] Castillo does not dismiss the racial stereotypes but does not acknowledge the critical importance they deserve either.

Because of their contradictory politics, *The Squatter and the Don* and *Who Would Have Thought It?* implicitly raise important questions for critics of Chicano literature. How can we interpret the politically problematic aspects of Chicano novels, such as those of Ruiz de Burton, without minimizing the problems for the sake of celebrating a Chicano literary tradition, or enlarging them because they do not measure up to some imagined conception of ideal Chicano politics? In an essay on *Who Would Have Thought It?* Anne Goldman maintains that recognizing the novel's contradictory political positions "does not mean we should either discard it because of its sustained classism nor romanticize it as the Moviemiento's orginary text."[6] I agree with Goldman's advice but would add that we should not shy away from analyzing the political contradictions in Ruiz de Burtons' novels. On the contrary, critiquing those contradictions will enable us to develop a deeper appreciation for the social and aesthetic dynamism of Ruiz de Burton's works. One way to do this, as I proposed in chapter 1, is by employing the category of reification, which affords several advantages for the interpretation of Chicano novels. With regard to *The Squatter and the Don,* a critique of the narrator's reified outlook will allow us to assert the following premises: (1) the novel's critical standpoint as a whole cannot be reduced to the narrator's views, or to the thoughts and actions of characters; (2) the social and aesthetic significance of the novel surpasses the class allegiances and ideology of the author; (3) what the narrator and characters learn in the novel is not necessarily equivalent to what the reader potentially stands to learn; and (4) the significance of the novel lies not exclusively in the immediacy of its thematic representations of Californios, but also—and perhaps primarily—in its aspiration toward the representation of a concrete historical moment.

In asserting these premises, I do not mean to imply that Ruiz de Burton's class affiliation is unimportant, but rather, that her class position does not exhaust the production of meaning in the novel. Consequently, we can be critical of the author's ideological commitments and still derive a critical standpoint from the literary work as a whole. In this way, *The Squatter* can be read as simultaneously embodying and contesting reification. Such a reading may lead us to conclude that if there is a genealogical link between Ruiz de Burton's novels and contemporary Chicano literature, it might have to be described not only in terms of a common anticapitalist, antiracist politics of resistance, but as sharing in the expression of hegemonic discourses, as well. Ruiz de Burton's novels indeed might be considered foundational texts for Chicano literature not because they are politically progressive in some kind of pure, absolute sense, but because they are politically and formally contradictory—a characteristic of post-1970 Chicano novels I scrutinize in later chapters. *Who Would Have Thought It?* satirizes the hypocrisy of New England abolitionists and Washington politicians during the American Civil War, and *The Squatter and the Don* criticizes monopoly capitalism and the unjust treatment of Californios by an Anglo-dominated society in the 1870s and early 1880s. Both novels, however, are also complicit with the ideological interests of a growing industrial capitalism, albeit, from the perspective of the liberal wing of capitalist discourse. This ideological contradiction—simultaneously defending and criticizing capitalist ideology—constitutes the *form* of Ruiz de Burton's novels, and it is even more pronounced in *The Squatter* than it is in *Who Would Have Thought It?* It is for this reason that I shall be focusing on Ruiz de Burton's second novel rather than the first. I shall, however, from time to time find it appropriate to comment on *Who Would Have Thought It?* as well.

The contradictions represented in *The Squatter and the Don* cannot be explained fully by relying on biographical or psychological methods exclusively. Rather, our interpretation of the novel will be enhanced with a study of the *relation* between the novel's standpoint and the historical moment within which the novel was produced. In a different context, Roberto Schwarz characterizes such a relation as "an aesthetic solution to objective problems,"[7] a characterization that informs my reading of *The Squatter*. The success or failure of a novel, in one sense, depends on the effectiveness with which the author is able to manage this relation. In *The Squatter*, the narrator's political positions represent the views of a privileged social class; thus the narrator displays an acute capacity to comprehend the internal workings and conflicts among various factions of the ruling elite, but is unable to provide the same depth of comprehension in addressing the needs and interests of subordinated workers and racialized groups in the novel. Nonetheless, the narrator's inability to represent subalterns as anything more than reified cardboard cutouts of race and class speaks volumes in itself. The distance between the narrator's ideological standpoint and the social context of the novel simulates the structure of reified consciousness: the novel performs, if you will, a formal enactment of reification and thus calls attention to its own inherent formal contradictions. That is to say, the novel implicitly thematizes—and thus lays bare for possible critique—the dominant cultural logic of nascent industrial capitalism in the Southwest during the late nineteenth century. It is in this sense that the novel can be understood as an "aesthetic solution to objective problems."

To tease out the nuances of this point, I shall examine several examples of contradictory representations of race, class, and the state in the novel before reviewing several key interpretations, including that of Sánchez and Pita, of these contradictory positions. This review will distinguish the interpretive approach I am proposing from those of other critics, but it will also serve to acknowledge my points of convergence with their methods. In short, I draw on Lukács's method of reading Balzac's novels as a suggestive interpretive model. Like Balzac, a royalist who was—according to Lukács—better able to represent the objective conditions of his time than were his progressive contemporaries, Ruiz de Burton, a displaced landowner from an elite social class background, may have been better able to grasp the essential class contradictions of her time than were contemporaneous subaltern writers. Subsequently, to provide the historical context of the novel, I will be focusing on the manner in which the rapid transitions in modes of production in the late nineteenth century, and the accelerated accumulation of capital during this period, were intricately related to the racialization and proletarianization of Mexican Americans, a social process that continues to this day. I argue that Ruiz de Burton, an organic intellectual who both endorsed and contested this process, inherited an ideological outlook—similar in substance to that referred to by Lukács as "the Romantic critique of capitalism"[8]—from such intellectuals as Herbert Spencer and Thomas Carlyle, quoted liberally by the narrator and characters in *The Squatter*. This Romantic critique did not make Ruiz de Burton a revolutionary by any stretch of the imagination, but conversely her privileged class background does not necessarily diminish the sharp social critique of capitalism and the racialization of Mexicans represented in her novel.

Despite the romanticism of the narrator, the novel can nonetheless be considered realist. By conventional standards, most critics would not categorize *Who Would Have Thought It?* and *The Squatter and the Don* as realist novels because they obviously employ narrative strategies that make use of sentimentalism, satire, and romance. To some degree, they might even be considered antirealist. My assessment of Ruiz de Burton's novels, however, again borrows from the work of Schwarz, who reasons that "if we think of the distinctive spirit of realism as the ambition to capture society in motion,"[9] then the criteria we use to determine a novel's realism changes entirely. Schwarz is not referring here to stylistic realism, but to what I referred to in chapter 1 as "epistemological realism": narratives that succeed in bridging to one extent or another the wide gap between immediacy and totality. This is an issue I shall revisit in each of the chapters that follow on the novels of Acosta, Santiago, and Pineda—an issue I consider central for the study of Chicano novels generally. In the present case, what aided Ruiz de Burton in developing the capacity to write epistemologically realist novels was, to a significant degree, her privileged class background, which provided her with, in Castillo's words, "the kind of elite education seldom offered to women in her day [especially Mexican women] and which allowed her to demonstrate a true gift for the written word."[10] Ruiz de Burton's gift for writing novels that offer "aesthetic solutions to objective problems" established a formal precedent that not surprisingly has been adhered to in Chicano novels written throughout the twentieth century.

As Sánchez and Pita point out, and as Castillo concurs, Ruiz de Burton was not without political contradictions. These contradictions become evident in the narrator's reified conceptions of dark-skin people, the disparaging fear of workers, and the idealist conception of "good government" based on the principles of "fundamental morality." Despite the narrator's reified views, the novel as a whole nonetheless renders naked the objective conditions of Ruiz de Burton's moment, spearheaded by its sharp critique of monopoly capitalism. The conflict between the narrator's limited viewpoint and the novel's aspiration toward totality opens up the possibility of developing critical insight into the novel's key zone of reification—democratic liberalism—which I shall be targeting in this chapter.

Race, Class, and the State

The Squatter and the Don begins in 1872, twenty-four years after the U.S. annexation of Mexico's northern territories and a year before Tiburcio Vásquez was found guilty by an all-Anglo jury and eventually hanged near San Diego, according to Rodolfo Acuña, because the "ricos" believed he was attempting to incite a revolution in Southern California against the "Yankee invaders."[11] The novel ends in 1880 with the Mussel Slough massacre, a violent confrontation in California's San Joaquin Valley that marked the climax of a power struggle between family farmers and railroad barons, ending victoriously for the latter. Framed within this historical setting of racism, class struggle and state-condoned political violence, *The Squatter and the Don* tells the story of the Californios' political demise and exposes the ruthlessness by which they lost their land to Anglo settlers, facilitated by the economic power plays of the Central Pacific Railroad. In the midst of this turmoil, Mercedes, the daughter of Californio Don Mariano Alamar, and Clarence, the son of squatter William Darrel, fall in love. The romance ends in marriage for the lovers after a series of obstacles nearly prevents their eventual union, but the social contradictions experienced by the wealthy Californio landowners are not resolved in their favor. Like most Californios, Ruiz de Burton and her family eventually lost their property and social class standing as Alta California's semifeudal ranching economy was transformed with the industrialization of the state in the latter half of the nineteenth century. Given the historical experience of the Californios, it comes as no surprise that Ruiz de Burton's narrator seeks to negotiate a social space for Californios within the privileged sectors of a fast-developing capitalist society. In so doing, the narrator expresses a series of contradictory ideological positions. We will benefit at this point from a summary of these ideological positions, focusing on the novel's representations of race, social class, and the state.

The Squatter offers conflicting views of Mexican Americans as a racialized group. On one hand, it demystifies stereotypical images of Mexican Americans and legitimizes their contributions to the building of the Southwest; on the other hand, it de-Mexicanizes the propertied class of Mexicans and displays derogatory images of mestizo and Indian workers. Regardless of where Ruiz de Burton's Mexican characters are positioned racially, ultimately they do not escape the reality of class exploitation and racism. Historically, Mexicans have been depicted as dirty, lazy, inherently subservient, and stupid in American literature. John Chávez explains, "[E]xcept in a few works . . . Mexicans in [nineteenth-century] Anglo-American literature were most often treated in a thoroughly negative way, as a racially inferior, ignorant, half-savage people blocking the advance of the US frontier in the same way as the Indians."[12] Writing against the grain of this American literary tradition, Ruiz de Burton inverts the stereotypical images of race in her novel, describing whites instead of Mexicans as "greasy" and characterizing them as thieves, liars, murderers, and drunkards, and as coming from broken families. Unlike many of the white writers of her period, Ruiz de Burton dismantles the traditional debilitating images of Mexican Americans by portraying the aristocratic Californios as clean, dignified, industrious, and intelligent. Her characters and narrator speak articulately on subjects as diverse as economics, business, politics, history, philosophy, literature, and art, and quote or allude to numerous literary figures from Homer and Shakespeare to Charles Fourier and Ralph Waldo Emerson. Don Mariano demonstrates more intelligence than do the white squatters who have settled on his land; he forms a practical plan to allow his family and the squatters to live together peacefully. The Californio elder and the squatters, of course, are in a legal dispute over who owns the land that once belonged entirely to the don.

Ruiz de Burton effectively demystifies stereotypes of Mexicans, but she also de-Mexicanizes them, especially those who own property. The narrator refers to the Californios as "Spanish," "Spano-Americans," or "native Californians." (In *Who Would Have Thought It?* Lola, initially thought to be a "black Indian girl," turns out to have "pure Spanish blood," and her skin actually lightens as the novel progresses.) Nowhere in *The Squatter* are the Californios referred to as "Mexicans." In the novel's introduction, Sánchez and Pita point out that, for nineteenth-century Mexican Americans, identifying themselves as "Spanish" meant "identifying with a different history and being interpellated continentally by discourses in another language" (39). The de-Mexicanization of Mexicans in the novel, however, goes beyond self-naming. Their physical features are European, not Indian. The Alamar family does not look Mexican. Nor do they bear any resemblance to mestizos. Their skin is fair and their eyes blue: "They look like Englishmen," (89) says Clarence Darrel when he first sees them. Another white character says that Don Mariano's youngest son, Victoriano, "is so light he looks more like a German" (89). Mercedes has golden hair, soft white skin, and blue eyes (159). Don Mariano himself has "mild and beautiful blue eyes" (64). Moreover, the three interracial marriages in the novel display the characters' desire to become deracialized—or to become white—as opposed to maintaining a distinct racial or ethnic identity. Further, as Jesse Alemán explains, "[T]he novel's emphasis on Mexican whiteness itself comes at the expense of Native, Irish, and African Americans, who all remain on the racialized margins of white Mexican privilege."[13]

The physical descriptions of Mexicans in *The Squatter and the Don* are based on historical inaccuracies. Social historians and cultural critics alike have pointed out that the earliest "Spanish" settlers who migrated to the region that is now the Southwest were almost exclusively mestizos, not pure-bred Castilian conquistadors. Ramón Saldívar explains that early inhabitants of the Southwest were "racially no different from the people who made up the first major wave of immigrants to the United States after 1890 and were . . . the products of a Mexican, that is to say a *mestizo* cultural identity."[14] While doubtless there were light-skinned, blue-eyed Mexicans who married white U.S. citizens 130 years ago in California, these characteristics are misleading in the novel because the fictional Alamar family stands symbolically for Californios in general, who for the most part were not white but mestizos. The novel further problematizes the question of race through its treatment of Mexican and Indian workers. The narrator, for example, takes offense when Anglo squatters claim that Californios are indolent but then makes an about-face and accuses Mexican workers and Indians of being lazy. Don Mariano calls his workers "stupid Indians" (260), and referring to Chapo, one of Don Mariano's Mexican workers, the narrator declares that he was a "lazy Indian, who first had to stretch himself and yawn several times, then hunt up tobacco and cigarette paper, and smoke his cigarette" (278) before getting up to work. Despite the de-Mexicanization of Californios and the derogatory depiction of mestizo workers in *The Squatter*, none of the Mexican characters escapes racism. The squatters repeatedly call Californios "dirty greasers," and when Gabriel Alamar and his wife Lizzie (who is white) become impoverished in San Francisco, her white friends turn their backs on them because of his racialized status. Lizzie herself comes to know what it feels like to be racialized as a result of having married a Californio, and she realizes that they are victims of class-based racism: "The fact that he was a *native Spaniard*, she saw plainly, militated against them. If he had been rich, his nationality could have been forgiven, but no one will willingly tolerate a *poor native Californian*" (351).

Given the dual depiction of Mexicans—rich landowners as clean and intelligent, workers as dirty, dumb, and lazy—the narrator obviously privileges class above race as a strategy to preserve an elite social status for Californios. With regard to class, however, the narrator is not without contradictions: at one moment criticizing monopoly capitalists; at the next, demonstrating a strong desire to integrate the Californios into an entrepreneurial class. The narrator's ambivalence toward social class in *The Squatter* exemplifies the anxieties felt by Californios during the 1880s. By the time the novel was published in 1885, most Californios had lost great portions, if not all, of their land. Many had become penniless. The narrator expresses the resentment felt by Californios for the way their lands were effectively stolen.

In the novel, urban monopolists destroy the localized power of the landowners by building their political clout in Washington, which involves bribing politicians and other unlawful acts. They monopolize the railroad industry, dictating the cost of transporting agricultural goods, thereby indirectly regulating the exchange value of land. Eventually, they crush whatever vestiges of political and economic power were still held by the landowners on a local level. The deaths of Don Mariano and his good friend Mr. Mechlin, an Anglo settler, signal the ultimate demise of the landowning-ranching class that once held state power in Alta California. But while this older generation of landowners is effectively eradicated, their sons and daughters become entrepreneur capitalists who continue to oppose the power of the industrial monopolists. Clarence Darrel, a squatter's son, becomes a wealthy individual entrepreneur: he inherits a large sum of money from a distant relative, buys a bonanza iron ore mine, makes healthy investments in the stock market that increase his wealth, finances the founding of a bank, and purchases the 47,000-acre Alamar rancho. By the novel's end, his worth surpasses $12 million, an astronomical amount by contemporaneous standards. His marriage to Mercedes Alamar symbolizes the continued (re)generation not only of the class represented by the white squatters-turned-entrepreneurs, but also of the Californios, who by the end of the novel have become bankrupt, financially and politically.

If the narrator's attitude toward the capitalist class can be characterized as one of desire, the attitude toward the working class must be described as one of fear, to say the least. After Don Mariano dies and the Alamar estate is on the brink of bankruptcy, Gabriel, his son, must seek employment as a day laborer. He finds a job as a bricklayer. His wife, Lizzie, objects to the idea of her husband becoming a worker. Aside from the humiliation of working for a wage, Gabriel suffers an accident on the job—a hod of bricks falls on him as he is climbing a ladder—and almost dies. One might say that the "proverbial ton of bricks" came down on the Californios once they were subjected to a working-class way of life. Interestingly, the narrator not only describes the action of this scene, but editorializes as well. The narrator not only shows but tells—a narrative technique that becomes increasingly utilized as the novel progresses, culminating in the final chapter in which the narrator soliloquizes her discontent. In this particular passage, quoted often by critics, the narrator comments on the significance of Gabriel's accident, instructing the reader on how to interpret the scene: "In that hod full of bricks, not only his own sad experience was represented, but *the entire history* of the native Californians *of Spanish descent* was epitomized. Yes, Gabriel carrying his hod full of bricks up a steep ladder, was a symbolic representation of his race" (352). In this passage and others like it, the narrator reveals disdain for the manner in which Mexicans were racialized and proletarianized in the nineteenth century, shedding light on the novel's critical engagement with social issues beyond the narrator's reified conception of the order of things. Gabriel escapes death when Clarence Darrel, now a multimillionaire, arrives in time to place him in a hospital. Clarence begins a banking business, loans money to Gabriel, and then makes him a partner in the bank. The aristocratic Gabriel finds his *natural* abilities more suited to being a banker than a bricklayer. Capital not only becomes the savior of the Californios, but also—we might reasonably conclude—the protagonist of the novel. I shall have more to say on this point below.

What then does Ruiz de Burton's narrator posit as a solution for the dispossessed Californios in *The Squatter and the Don*? Unskilled urban workers, Mexican vaqueros, and Indian servants are depicted contemptuously, implying a fear of proletarianization, even though that would be the outcome for most Californios. The narrator makes no argument for the need to preserve a Mexican identity as a form of self- or group empowerment, or as a means to counter the apocryphal racialization imposed upon the Californios. Rather, the interracial marriage of Clarence and Mercedes signifies the narrator's comprehension that whiteness correlates with an escape from forced proletarianization—a desire to become part of the capitalist class despite the antagonism toward Californios by industrialist bosses and politicians.

In addition to depicting social class in a contradictory manner, the narrator also represents a conflicted view of the state: the narrator unleashes a grand assault on the corrupt nature of the government while clinging to the state for protection from greedy capitalists. The narrator argues that the state serves those who can afford to bribe the lawmakers but also appeals to the state to correct the injustices committed against Californios, arguing that laws should be based on "morality," not the profit motives of monopoly capitalists. Throughout the novel, the narrator repeatedly makes impassioned pleas to lawmakers to pass laws that are based on morality, not profits, seeming to believe that the legal system will actually remedy the injustices committed against the Californios by protecting their property rights. The language in the novel reveals a marked preoccupation with the law through an exaggerated and repetitive use of legal words: "laws," "law-makers," "law-givers," "lawyers," "legality," "legitimate," "legislate," and "litigate." In this respect, the language of *The Squatter and the Don* resembles that of Charles Dickens's *Bleak House*. In fact,

Ruiz de Burton's narrator quotes the following passage from Dickens's novel: "The one great principle of English law . . . is to make business for itself. There is no other principle distinctly, certainly and consistently maintained through all its narrow turnings. Viewed by this light, it becomes a coherent scheme, and not the monstrous maze the laity are apt to think it" (88).[15] The narrator then responds to Dickens, stating, "The one great principle of American law is very much the same; our law-givers keep giving us laws and then enacting others to explain them. The lawyers find plenty of occupation, but what becomes of the laity?" (88) The narrator sagaciously draws a clear correlation between laws and the profit motives of capitalism, pinpointing the anxieties suffered by Californios over losing their land, wealth, and power in large part through "legal" means. Acuña describes how some Mexicans, such as Tiburcio Vásquez and Juan Cortina, rejected the futility of fighting Anglos through the courts and became convinced that the only way to protect their property was through armed struggle.[16] These Mexican folk heroes, of course, became "outlaws" in the eyes of an Anglo-controlled state.

On a wider scale, however, Mexican Americans challenged the appropriation of their properties by going to court. Much like the absurd thirty-year court case in *Bleak House*, brought on by John Jarndyce, with its endless hearings, appeals, and mountains of bureaucratic paperwork, the Californios were subjected to a judicial system that prolonged cases until, unable to continue an expensive legal battle and driven to bankruptcy from court costs, they lost their lands by default. (It should come as no surprise that Ruiz de Burton looks to Dickens as an intellectual precursor worthy of being quoted to support her defense of the Californios. *Bleak House* was published serially from March 1852 to September 1853. Arguably its literary power and socially critical insight derive from its apprehension of totality, afforded by its proximity to the 1848 European moment described in greater detail subsequently. For now, it is enough to state that Dickens's novel, like Balzac's later novels, lends itself to a reading that keenly emphasizes the relationship between transparency and totality.) As several critics have pointed out, including Sánchez and Pita in the novel's introduction, the Land Law of 1851 required Californios to prove ownership of land that had been guaranteed to them under the 1848 Treaty of Guadalupe Hidalgo. To satisfy legal requirements, the Spanish-speaking Californios encountered hearings conducted in English only, lawyers who never intended to represent their interests but instead demanded outrageous fees often payable only in the very land for which they were fighting, and squatters who occupied the land without paying rent until "legal" ownership was decided by the courts.[17] Needless to say, the Land Law of 1851 led to a tremendous loss of Californio property. Martha Menchaca emphasizes the relationship between the formation of racial identities and class power in arguing that the "process of racialization" in the Southwest during the nineteenth century was consolidated in large part by "the legal system," which was used "to confer privilege upon Whites and to discriminate against people of color."[18] Or, in the historically insightful words of Ruiz de Burton's narrator, "All would be done 'according to law' and in this easy way more land was taken from its legitimate owner" (76). In the final pages of the novel, the narrator vehemently urges the people of California to "*take the law into their own hands*" (366) to seize control of both the state and the property of the monopolists. Such drastic action is necessary, according to the narrator, because the lawmakers serve the interests of monopoly capitalism and will therefore always act in favor of the corporations. With such thought-provoking—albeit, contradictory—declarations by the narrator, readers might be left wondering on what side of the *law* Ruiz de Burton really stands.

Despite such a biting critique of the capitalist state in *The Squatter and the Don*, the narrator makes a 180-degree turn and appeals for justice from the very force, cynical and institutionalized, that has served as a weapon of domination against the Californios—the capitalist state itself. The narrator calls on "law-makers" to reform their methods of "law-making," proposes to replace corrupt legislators with morally responsible ones, and argues that the motive for passing laws should be based on "morality," not profits. She asserts, "If the principles of fundamental morality were better understood and more conscientiously respected, railroad manipulators would find it impossible to organize a lobby" to get their laws passed (217). Similarly, in a conversation concerning the legitimacy of Spanish land grants issued to Alta Californios in the early nineteenth century, Don Mariano exclaims, "I hold that the legislators of a nation are the guardians of public morality, the teachers of what is right and just. They should never enact laws that are not founded upon rectitude" (173).[19] But the narrator's conception of the state, as expressed in the preceding passages, remains idealistically founded on the assumption that the state is a neutral arbiter between classes, rather than an integral aspect of the capitalist political machinery. Although critical of the state, the narrator ignores the function of "laws" in sustaining capitalism and expresses the idealist belief that ideas determine the material world and therefore posits in Spencerian fashion that a few good legislators, driven by moral convictions rather than economic interests, can change society. Thus the narrator's reified consciousness can be understood as entering the novel at the level of ideology via liberalist discourse.

"All to Voice the Bitter Resentment of the Subaltern"

As mentioned above, the contradictory politics of *The Squatter* have both fascinated and bothered critics. In their introduction to the novel, Sánchez and Pita argue that it can be considered both accommodation and contestation in that it simultaneously criticizes and promotes the reproduction of the hegemonic order through its ambivalent discussion of power and subservience. Paying close attention to the issue of genre, they conclude that the novel "calls for a double reading, constructed as it is both as romance and [as] history."[20] Their double reading of the text extends beyond the dichotomized generic structure of the novel and scrutinizes the manner in which the narrator criticizes monopoly capitalism while upholding the values of bourgeois ideology, and similarly, to its "acerbic critique" of Anglo racism toward the propertied Californios while simultaneously representing working-class Mexicans and nonlandowning Indians negatively. In their effort to explain this contradictoriness, Sánchez and Pita argue that the novel takes an oppositional stance toward the hegemony in the subtext, in spite of its hegemonic characteristics at the narrative's surface—an argument in many ways consistent with my own reading, and upon which I have drawn. To make this argument, they employ the structuralist method of A. J. Greimas, à la Fredric Jameson, and make use of his "semiotic rectangle" to identify the numerous class-based ideological antinomies at work in the novel.

Based on these oppositions, Sánchez and Pita contextualize the novel historically to explain the narrator's conflicted attitude toward such issues as class power, racism, gender, and the law. They state, for example, that *The Squatter*, "in keeping with a reformist stance that has no basic quarrel with capitalism in and of itself,—nor with patriarchy for that matter—argues for the full enforcement of existing laws guaranteeing the righting of wrongs and a more principled capitalism."[21] But they also account for the novel's procapitalist positions by arguing that "Ruiz de Burton *dialogues* with a number of contemporary discourses . . . both dominant and minority, *all to voice the bitter resentment of the subaltern.*"[22] Here Sánchez and Pita come close to crediting Ruiz de Burton with the deliberate decision to manipulate the contradictory discourses of dominance and subservience: an assessment of the novel that might be compared to Henry Louis Gates's analysis of African American literature as a form of "signifying," but which might also be misunderstood as inadvertently sliding in the direction of an intentional fallacy—of assuming the novel means exactly what the author wanted it to mean. As Sánchez and Pita correctly intimate, however, we need not jettison the concept of authorial intentionality or the usefulness of biographical criticism to argue that the significance of a text often surpasses the immediate motives of an author. Or as Schwarz explains, "[R]ather than looking for the author's intention, [the reader] needs to decipher the meaning of the whole form, of which intentions are but an element."[23] The idea that Mexican American authors have deliberately written politically contradictory texts, clandestinely resorting to the very ideological discourses they criticize, creates difficulties for both literary theory and political practice. It remains difficult to conceptualize a human subject capable of stepping outside of ideology to construct a narrative that manages various conflicting discourses from a nonattached standpoint. In a different context, R. Saldívar discusses the issue of ideology in a manner that sheds light on this point, declaring that "the utoptian vision of a moment when the individual subject would be completely aware of his or her determination by class ideology and would be able to step outside of this determination by sheer lucidity and clarity of thought is a myth."[24] Drawing on the implications of Saldívar's comments, we can agree with Sánchez and Pita's analysis of the novel as a critique of capitalism and, at the same time, draw a conclusion that builds upon their assessment of the author's motives: the political positions represented by the narrator in *The Squatter* can be interpreted as the ideological contradictions of the author herself, now foregrounded as reified because of the conflict between what the novel can represent of the social totality and the liberal obscurantism of the narrator.

What I am suggesting is a reading that may in some ways differ tactically—though not strategically—from that of Sánchez and Pita: to characterize the novel's ideological contradictions as the embodiment of the repressed, *but also nakedly transparent*, objective conditions of late- nineteenth-century capitalism in the Southwest. In the introduction to the collected letters of Ruiz de Burton, Sánchez and Pita situate the author historically: "Engaged in her writing in oppositional enterprises and in her personal affairs in opportunistic acquiescence to whatever promised capitalist accumulation, the least that can be said about [Ruiz de Burton] is that her life and writing provide an intriguing crucible from which to precipitate out the key and shaping issues of a period that set in motion a whole set of relations still visiting us today."[25] Elsewhere, writing alone, Sánchez argues for a strikingly similar point in her analysis of the Californio *testimonios*, declaring that they engage with history in a manner that often surpasses the immediate intentions of the Californios in telling their stories; this is possible because "'reality' is always already discursively embedded in any text, in its enabling and constraining effects,"[26] despite the ideological contradictions of the Californios themselves and the various mediated levels of influence involved in the recording, translating, and archiving of the narratives. Of most concern to the Californios is the fact that they were being forced to make choices about their future at a time when almost all of their options had already been closed off. Ruiz de Burton's narrator similarly bemoans—perhaps even more precipitously than the other Californios—the fact that a grave injustice has been committed against the "native Californians," and her complaints are laced with class and personal prejudices that taint the forcefulness of her critique. Nonetheless, the novel lays bare the history "embedded" in its pages that undergirds the anxieties, the uncertainty, and the fear of forced proletarianization faced by the Californios and by Ruiz de Burton herself.

Sánchez and Pita's nuanced readings of Ruiz de Burton's novels—sometimes perceived overly sympathetic—have not gone uncontested. Jesse Alemán, for example, describes the two introductions by Sánchez and Pita as "strong readings" because they attempt to "resolve the issue of Mexican American whiteness"[27] in a positive light. Similarly, John M. González claims that "Sánchez and Pita needlessly complicate" the interpretation of the novel by highlighting the "often obscurantist tensions between Chicano nationalism and other interpretive methodologies in examining *The Squatter and the Don*."[28] Unlike Sánchez and Pita, González does not conclude that Ruiz de Burton voices the "bitter resentment of the subaltern." He argues instead that Ruiz de Burton simultaneously criticizes and expresses a desire to become part of the American nationalist project. "Ruiz de Burton," González argues, "contests not the process of incorporation of California's economy and culture into the national core as such, but rather the social position accorded to the Californios within that capitalist order. The Californios show themselves more than willing to participate in emergent capitalist economies."[29] González subtly warns of the potential problems with cultural nationalist readings of *The Squatter* that celebrate the novel solely on the basis of the author's national origin.[30] Manuel M.

Martín Rodríguez also disagrees with Sánchez and Pita, arguing that *The Squatter* cannot be compared equitably to the "protest" novels that emerged during the Chicano Movement of the 1960s and 1970s. Rodríguez admits that, in his view, Ruiz de Burton indeed "wrote a protest novel,"[31] but not to denounce the exploitation of working-class Mexican Americans. Rather, Ruiz de Burton directs her critique at the declining "privileged status" of the Californios that resulted with the emergence of industrial capitalism. Rodríguez argues further that "Ruiz de Burton's protest emanates from a very definitely class-oriented position that many Chicanos/as would not share today, and her social class gives shape to a perceived ethnic identity that many others could not share either."[32] I find myself at once in accord and at odds with Rodríguez's claims. I agree that *The Squatter and the Don* cannot be called a "protest" or working-class novel in the way that one might so describe, say, Oscar Zeta Acosta's *Revolt of the Cockroach People* or Tomás Rivera's *. . . y no se lo tragó la tierra.* But I disagree with Rodriguez's conclusion that Chicanos today "would not share" Ruiz de Burton's ideological aspirations. A close scrutiny of later Chicano works would reveal a web of semblances—though perhaps not an exact parallel—between Ruiz de Burton's narrator, whose views are steeped in the discourses of democratic liberalism, and the desires expressed by narrators and characters in contemporary Chicano novels, the latter often openly expressing a longing for recognition, citizenship, equal representation, and full participation in the democratic process. From this view, one might conclude, as I do, that if a Californio-Chicano literary genealogy exists, it does not emerge exclusively from a common "resistance" to racism and class exploitation, but equally, and in some cases perhaps even more so, from a common desire to be included within the democratic institutions of American capitalism—a desire that, granted, would not necessarily be considered a disabling contradiction by all readers of contemporary Chicano literature.

José Aranda also takes exception with some of the implications in Sánchez and Pita's introduction in his argument against the tendency of Chicano studies to categorize all literary texts written by Mexican Americans as resistant to racism and hegemony generally.[33] He expresses a suspicion of recovery projects that have not sufficiently addressed the antiproletarian and racist aspects of the texts they recover, *The Squatter and the Don* being just one example. Framed within this larger critique of Chicano studies, he challenges Sánchez and Pita's characterization of Ruiz de Burton as a subaltern: "In the growing critical industry built around the reemergence of Ruiz de Burton, many have followed the lead of her recoverers, Rosaura Sánchez and Beatrice Pita, in locating a 'resistance' narrative in her life and writings and historicizing her biography as a 'subaltern.' While some elements of her published writings support these identities, *her life reveals* an individual willing to wage a rhetorical war on her conquerors but also anxious to reassume the privileges of a colonialist."[34]

In providing a detailed biographical account of Ruiz de Burton's life, Aranda demonstrates her social class allegiances and political affiliations. His research leads him to a letter written by Abraham Lincoln in 1861 in which the president reveals that Ruiz de Burton visited him and lobbied to get him to appoint her husband to a higher rank in the military, a request that he attempted to honor.[35] Aranda uses this evidence to conclude that Ruiz de Burton was far from a subaltern, and he questions José David Saldívar's characterization of Ruiz de Burton as a "subaltern supplementary subject" and a "subaltern mediator," stating that J. Saldívar's language "works only if one ignores [Ruiz de Burton's] colonialist history as a monarchist."[36] J. Saldívar indeed refers to Ruiz de Burton also as an "insurgent critic" and a "radical critic."[37] He argues that her characters function as "subaltern ironists,"[38] and he reasons that "Ruiz de Burton functions as a subaltern mediator who is simultaneously an insurgent critic of monopoly capitalism and a radical critic of Anglocentric historiography."[39] In making these claims, J. Saldívar compares Ruiz de Burton to the "anti-imperialist José Martí" and refers to her novels as "anti-imperialist chronicles of the borderlands of Nuestra America."[40] J. Saldívar's assessment of Ruiz de Burton's fiction highlights—correctly, in my opinion—the anti-capitalist aspects of *The Squatter and the Don*, but, granted, he displays less interest in the ideological or hegemonic tendencies in her novels.

By contrast, Aranda acknowledges that Ruiz de Burton's novels criticize the political structures of her day, but argues that she makes this critique essentially as an idealist reformer demanding a kinder and gentler capitalism in the form of a liberal democracy, while characterizing herself as a "Daughter of the Enlightenment."[41] The novels are not the typical colonized versus colonizer texts; they might better be understood, Aranda argues, as representing one side of a struggle between two colonizers. Aranda makes a strong case in exposing the problems with recovery projects and Chicano studies for their reluctance to theorize the social contradictions in texts written by Mexican Americans. The difficulty with Aranda's position, however, is that it places almost all the weight of interpretation on the author's personal background in the customary manner of biographical criticism, evident in such phrases as "her life reveals." Aranda reasons that because Ruiz de Burton came from a privileged class background the ideas expressed in the novel cannot be those of a subaltern group but must represent those of her class position; thus he is "not persuaded" by Sánchez and Pita's reading of *The Squatter* as the symbolic representation of a "concrete historic situation."[42] As stated previously, however, the social and aesthetic significance of novels often surpasses the intentions and class interests of the author because authors are not exempt from the complex and often contradictory influences of the social moments in which they live. Again, as Sánchez persuasively asserts, "'[R]eality' is always already discursively embedded in any text."[43] I have spent time summarizing these various critical positions on Ruiz de Burton's novels because they shed light on the approach I am proposing for the interpretation of *The Squatter*—an approach that is aligned more closely with the historical-dialectical method employed by Sánchez and Pita than with the biographical criticism practiced by Aranda. Such an approach, I believe, will facilitate a comprehension of the conflict between the narrator's reified consciousness and the novel's aspiration toward a critical approximation of the author's "concrete historic situation."

The Squatter and the Don as a Realist Novel

Because my approach is essentially comparative, it may help to review briefly the manner in which critics have compared Ruiz de Burton's novels to the works of other nineteenth-century writers, effectively situating them within various literary genres: historical romance, satire, sentimental fiction, the novel of domesticity, and the novel of manners. Sánchez and Pita, for example, point out the striking parallel between *The Squatter* and Frank Norris's naturalist novel *The Octopus* (1901), highlighting the fact that Ruiz de Burton's novel ends with a commentary on the Mussel Slough massacre, which took place near Tulare, California, in 1882 and which forms the subtext of Norris's novel. Anne Goldman highlights the similarities between *Who Would Have Thought It?* and Henry James's *The Bostonians* (1886),[44] characterizing both as critiques of New England manners. She also compares *The Squatter* to Helen Hunt Jackson's *Ramona* (1884) and the nineteenth-century California romances of Gertrude Atherton, delineating these works as critiques of Manifest Destiny and as representations of attempts to resolve legal disputes over land ownership.[45] Similarly, Julie Ruiz reads *Who Would Have Thought It?* as alluding to Nathaniel

Hawthorne's *The Scarlet Letter*, principally in Ruiz de Burton's critique of the Puritan origins of early New Englanders. Ruiz demonstrates vividly the manner in which *Who Would Have Thought It?* "couples the political and the sexual through the adulterous union of the Protestant minister Hackwell and Mrs. Norval. This mismatch," she argues, "represents the continued adulteration of seventeenth-century U.S. origins in the nineteenth century."[46] Ruiz aligns the adulterated values of the novel's characters with the adulterated politics pervading the doctrine of Manifest Destiny. From another perspective, Carrie Tirado Bramen compares *The Squatter* to Hamlin Garland's short story "Up the Coulee" (1891) and W. E. B. DuBois's "The Negro in the Black Belt; Some Social Sketches" (1899).[47] Tirado Bramen argues that the texts of Garland, DuBois, and Ruiz de Burton deconstruct the notion that regional literatures have little relevance as social commentaries outside their local geographies, demonstrating the manner in which these texts run counter to a "fetish of the periphery" by addressing national and international issues related to the uneven development of cultural groups and social classes. Whereas Tirado Bramen reads Ruiz de Burton's novels as radiating in social significance beyond the immediacy of represented space and time, Leticia M. Garza-Falcón compares *The Squatter* to Jovita González's *Caballero: A Historical Novel* (written circa the 1930s) to argue that both novelists essentially narrate their own personal life stories as elite women who fought against the patriarchy of their specific locations and temporalities. Ruiz de Burton in particular struggled to "maintain a dignity suitable to her landowning background despite her declining financial conditions." Whether *The Squatter* is read in autobiographical terms or as the story of the Californios, the central motifs of failure and defeat remain the same since both the individual and the class-cultural group meet gloomy outcomes. Garza-Falcón emphasizes the fact that Don Mariano is represented as "defeated" and his way of life "destroyed": "Ruiz de Burton's patriarch . . . fail[s] tragically in [his attempt] to deal with the new social and economic order." Though perhaps unintentionally, Garza-Falcón sheds light on the failures of the Californios and their genealogical connection to similar political failures confronted by contemporary Chicanos, explaining that Ruiz de Burton's novels "reveal important historical realities that provide some insight into how the present-day socioeconomic conditions of many Mexican Americans came to be."[48]

The comparisons referenced above are incisive and trenchant. To add to the critical milieu of comparative works surrounding the novels of Ruiz de Burton, I shall, however, propose a comparison of a different kind, drawing a parallel not between the themes and representations in Ruiz de Burton's novels and those of other literary works, but between the critical approach I employ in my interpretation of *The Squatter* and that employed by Lukács in his interpretation of Balzac's novels. That is to say, I shall draw a comparison between the objective conditions of pre-1848 France and those of pre-1890 California. But what are the similarities between these two periods and on what are they based? Lukács argues that before the 1848 Paris insurrection the French bourgeoisie had some residually progressive characteristics, reflected in their idealist commitments to the concepts of freedom and equality, in their relatively peaceful coexistence with the laboring classes, and in the ability of writers of all political stripes to represent social relations objectively. The merciless crushing of workers' movements by the bourgeoisie in 1848 in Europe exposed with naked transparency the class interests of capitalists and the extent to which they would go to protect those interests. The bourgeois backlash resulted in—among other things—the emergence of a kind of literature more steeped in reification than previous literary forms. Summarizing Lukács's argument, Roberto Schwarz writes that after 1848 in France "the fireworks of Romantic-liberal rhetoric, which aimed to unite workers and owners, had given way to General Cavaignac's incendiary bombs. . . . Bourgeois normality, and with it the whole of contemporary language, began to live in a state of siege: words became soaked with incompatible meanings, produced by social antagonism [and] class warfare: on one side, the official acceptations, on the other, those that the words held for the defeated, which were often semi-clandestine."[49] The reality of class oppression came to reveal rather abruptly the shallowness and falseness of bourgeois doublespeak in such concepts as liberty, equality, and universal rights; the disputed meaning of words came to reflect the disputes between classes (or what V. N. Volosinov would characterize some years later as the class struggle in language).[50] Thus, the gap between reality and political discourse in Europe after 1848 became internalized in the reified standpoints of literary narratives.

But 1848 means something different in California than it does in Europe: in the latter, it forecloses (or makes more difficult) the apprehension of totality, whereas in the former it opens up the possibility of this apprehension, at least for some decades. In Europe, this pivotal moment signals the consolidation of class rule by the bourgeoisie; in California, 1848 marks the onset of capitalist relations of production and the beginning of a long process of primitive accumulation, which would result in a transformation of the Southwest from a semifeudal society, or what Rosaura Sánchez characterizes as a despotic, hacienda-based economy,[51] to an industrialized monopoly capitalism by the end of the century. What enabled this transformation, and what was needed for its occurrence, was the expropriation of land, which was acquired when the United States annexed Mexico's northern territories after the war. The features of the political economy—in particular, the emergence of a powerful liberal bourgeoisie in a position of class dominance—that facilitated a Balazacian type of literary realism in pre-1848 France did not develop in California until the 1870s and were made possible, along with other political and economic developments, by the victory of the North in the Civil War and the completion of the first transcontinental railroad in 1869. These two developments allowed for a rapid expansion of industrial capitalism to the West, bringing with it not only "the fireworks of Romantic-liberal rhetoric," but the sharpening of class contradictions and the dehumanization of various nonwhite groups to justify countless acts of virulent racism, exploitation, and violence.

The parallels between Balzac and Ruiz de Burton are not exact. Balzac wrote more than a hundred novels; Ruiz de Burton wrote two. The former was a member of an elite class, a royalist, all his life; the latter lived on the verge of relative poverty much of her life. Moreover, there is no precise equivalent of France's 1848 moment in California. One might even argue that there was never a revolutionary moment of the bourgeoisie in the United States. The closest that U.S. capitalism came to one may have been at the end of the Civil War with the triumph over slavery and the semifeudal slave relations of the South. But no sooner had the Northern industrialists freed the slaves and Southern poor whites from the shackles of unpaid labor than they ceased to be "revolutionary" in any substantive sense and set about the business of exploiting the now expanded pool of so-called free labor. Thus, unlike Balzac who lived through a relatively long bourgeois revolutionary moment, Ruiz de Burton witnessed a similar moment in the United States only as a fleeting possibility. Nonetheless, the political developments and the sharpening of class conflicts in Ruiz de Burton's time are laid bare, first in *Who Would Have Thought It?* and then later in *The Squatter*, just as the class relations of nascent capitalist society in France are rendered naked in Balzac's novels. Hence the reified consciousness that I attribute to Ruiz de Burton's narrator corresponds, in a way, with the royalist views of the Balzacian narrator. In both cases, the class position of the narrator contrasts with the apprehension of totality made available by the text as a whole. The dereifying aspects of Ruiz de Burton's novels are made possible, in part, by the fact that the author is writing from a critical perspective at a historical juncture marked by the large-scale transformation of the economy and political structures in the Southwest from one mode of production to another over a relatively short period of time. The historicity of this transformative moment—which witnessed a rapid shift from primitive accumulation to capitalist accumulation proper—now becomes embodied in *The Squatter* as a constitutive aspect of the novel's contradictory form.

Capitalist Accumulation and the Proletarianization of Mexicans

The decades immediately preceding and following the publication of *The Squatter and the Don* were marked by erratic fluctuations in the U.S. economy, from rampant prosperity to severe depression. The instability of the economy was caused in part by the inability of U.S. industrialists to market the large supply of commodities they were producing, and thus a perpetual crisis of overproduction ensued. To stay ahead of the competition, industrialists were driven to seek more efficient methods of production—new technologies and new systems of organization—in an effort to dominate the world markets. But investing in new technologies of production was costly, cutting into an already falling rate of profit from the sale of commodities and forcing capitalists into a ruthless competition for the control of markets to survive. Consequently, the dominant mode of production in the United States underwent a rapid transition from entrepreneurial to full-blown monopoly capitalism by the end of the century. The competition among late-nineteenth-century capitalists, which inevitably forced most of them out of business, resulted in an increase in the organic composition (or concentration) of capital. As Marx himself states, the expropriation of capital "is accomplished through the action of the immanent laws of capitalist production itself, through the centralization of capitals. One capitalist always strikes down many others. Hand in hand with this centralization, or this expropriation of many capitalists by a few, other developments take place on an ever-increasing scale, such as the growth of the co-operative form of the labour process,"[52] which is to say, socialized labor.

In California and throughout the Southwest, the monopolization of the economy and the socialization of labor necessitated, among other things, the proletarianization of Mexican Americans to meet the large demand for cheap labor.[53] (The proletarianization of Mexican Americans and Latinos generally in the United States continued throughout the twentieth century.) In the Southwest, most of the new workers came from nonelite classes: hired hands, small farmers, craftsmen, and servants. As detailed in *The Squatter*, however, the emergent proletariat was also extracted from elite classes: entrepreneurs and large landowners, such as the Californios, squeezed out of business by the competition with stronger capitalists. Eventually, a rapidly growing capitalism would require the importation of workers from China, Japan, the Philippines, and Mexico to satisfy the insatiable need for cheap labor. But before the massive immigration of laborers from other countries could take place, capitalists first needed to reduce the number of owners of production competing for scarce resources. John Borrego, in an intriguing study of Chicano history as a continuous engagement with capitalist accumulation, describes this process as it developed in New Mexico.

> As increasing amounts of land passed from [New Mexican] family and common land grants to the Anglo . . . a process of proletarianization began with the large numbers of New Mexicans driven from their land . . . [T]hey had to sell their labor to the mines, the railroads and as migrant agricultural workers. The old ruling elite attempted to survive by allying themselves with the conquerors, but the new regime had transformed the old basis of power so radically, that few were able to retain their wealth and power through the late 1880s.[54]

The systematic dispossession and proletarianization of New Mexicans described by Borrego also took place in California and is dramatized in *The Squatter*. This is the process that Marx refers to as "primitive accumulation"—the reorganization of the forces of production, necessary for the transition from an agricultural-based society to industrial capitalism. Primitive accumulation is commonly understood as the starting point[55] of capitalist accumulation, made possible by the blatant seizure of productive resources, especially land, often by brute force and other means of state-endorsed coercion. But the process also implies the forced consolidation of a working class—the proletarianization of a large sector of the population to supply the abundant amount of labor needed by an emergent industrial capitalism.[56] The separation of the former owners of land and the producers of goods from the means of production clears the path for the consolidation of "free" labor: workers are now "free" to sell their labor as a commodity, opening up the potential for capitalists to create surplus value via the exploitation of that labor.[57] The transition from a semifeudal ranching economy to capitalism also required the formation of a state apparatus that served explicitly to maintain a class-based racial hierarchy by systematically consolidating and then subordinating the social group that Mario Barrera refers to as a Mexican "colonial labor force."

In *Race and Class in the Southwest: A Theory of Racial Inequality*, Barrera offers a detailed account of primitive accumulation (though he does not actually use this term) as it relates to Mexicans living in the post-1848 Southwest.[58] He draws mainly on two theoretical paradigms: Marxism and the "internal colonial model" of analysis popular among Chicano historians and sociologists in the 1970s.[59] One of his objectives is to trace the formation of Chicanos as a racial group in the United States. He argues that the racialization of Chicanos was necessitated by the needs of an expanding capitalist system, and that it resulted in the large-scale proletarianization of Mexicans in the Southwest. Significantly, he argues that the process of consolidating Mexican American workers as a "colonial labor force," or as a class-based racial group, began in the nineteenth century and continued throughout the twentieth century and up to the present. Barrera is a sociologist, but like many Chicano historians he marks the U.S. defeat of Mexico in 1848 and the annexation of the Southwest as the starting point of Chicano racialization. He writes that Mexicans living in the annexed territories in 1848 were "the original Chicanos,"[60] an assertion some historians have regarded as problematic. Barrera nonetheless offers a materialist analysis of the racialization of Chicanos, identifying four historical developments that were required to begin the process of consolidating Mexicans as a class-based racial group: (1) the defeat of Mexico in the Mexican-American War; (2) the expropriation of land and the consequential "legal" removal of Mexicans from their land; (3) "the emergence of a labor system in which Chicanos and other minorities constituted a clearly subordinated segment," which he refers to as a "colonial labor force"; and (4) the consolidation of a capitalist state, which became instrumental in "creating [and] maintaining . . . the structure of inequality that characterizes the situation of Chicanos in American society." He elaborates further on the formation of a colonial labor force, referred to in point 3 above, identifying five constitutive aspects of this process: *(a)* "labor repression," or extreme forms of labor exploitation that were similar to "unfree labor," such as debt peonage and bondage; *(b)* a dual-wage system, or the practice of "paying one wage to minority workers and another to non-minority workers who perform the same task"; *(c)* occupational stratification, or "the practice of classifying certain kinds of jobs as suited for minorities and others as suited for non-minorities," which meant employing Mexicans primarily in the dirtiest, lowest paying, and most physically demanding jobs; *(d)* a "reserve labor force," or the practice of maintaining a large supply of unemployed Mexican workers to be readily available in case the demand for labor increased—and also to be used as political leverage against employed workers demanding higher wages or better working conditions; and *(e)* a "buffer role," which essentially meant that Chicano workers were "the last hired and the first fired," depending on the needs of employers to control the supply of labor at any given time.[61] For our purpose, we can draw at least two conclusions from Barrera's theory of racial inequality: one, the racialization of Chicanos, as a historically determined social formation, develops in conjunction with the transformation that take place as a result of the conflict between competing modes of production, which is to say, the transition from pre-1848 semifeudal relations in the Southwest to full-blown monopoly capitalism by the end of the century; and two, my proposal, as outlined in chapter 1, to interpret class consciousness and "class struggle" as epistemic realism in representations of racial identities is rendered not only feasible with Barrera's theoretical model, but compelling—which is to say, representations of Chicano racialization are full of class content.

My purpose for drawing on Barrera's theory of the racialization of Chicanos—in addition to agreeing with his general argument about the class-driven basis of Chicano racialization and his implied analysis of capitalist accumulation—is to assert that Chicano literature has responded to this historical development to varying degrees and in myriad imaginative ways. *The Chicano-ness of Chicano literature has to do with its response, directly and indirectly, to the specific ways that the racialization of Chicanos has been constituted, to a large degree, by capitalist accumulation.* In this regard, Ruiz de Burton's novels can be considered foundational works of a Chicano literary tradition not only because they are the first novels written in the United States by a Mexican American author, but also because they initiate a tradition of novels that respond specifically to the racialization of Mexican Americans in the United States. Moreover, Ruiz de Burton writes during the historical period this process is being put into motion—that is, her novels capture the initial historical moment of Chicano racialization and proletarianization, similar to the manner in which Acosta's *Revolt of the Cockroach People* captures the moment of Chicano contestation against the effects of capitalist accumulation in the late 1960s, as we shall examine in the next chapter. Despite the contradictory ideological positions of the novel's narrator, and despite the contradictory class position of the author herself, *The Squatter* nonetheless adamantly contests the proletarianization and racialization of Mexicans; in so doing, it also effectively opposes the general tendencies of capitalist accumulation, including capitalism's inevitable drive toward imperialism.

While the spread of imperialism was the most obvious reaction to the increase in the organic composition of capital during the waning years of the nineteenth century, equally significant was capital's need to exploit the working classes to a greater degree in order to finance its expansion nationally and abroad. This structural transformation to monopoly capitalism made necessary not only greater extraction of surplus value from labor, but the continued (re)articulation of racial categories as a rationale for class domination. But these developments did not occur automatically or without resistance. Organic intellectuals of the hegemonic classes in the final decades of the century outlined the political, economic, and ideological projects necessary for these developments to occur.[62] For example, the issues of land acquisition and the uneven social mobility among racial groups and social classes in America were central concerns of Frederick Jackson Turner in the 1890s. His well-known thesis was straightforward: the expansion of the frontier and the settlement of "free land" made America great. The logic in Turner's thinking, however, rested in the recognition that expansion within the country's national borders would soon reach its limits because free land would eventually run out, a fact that necessitated expansion beyond U.S. borders through the formation of an imperialist project. In Turner's own words: "With the settlement of the Pacific coast and the occupation of the free lands, this movement has come to a check. That these energies of expansion will no longer operate would be a rash prediction; and the demands for a vigorous foreign policy . . . for a revival of our power upon the seas, and for the extension of American influence to . . . adjoining countries [indicate] that the movement will continue."[63] Turner wrote sympathetically and unapologetically about one of the basic tenets of capitalist accumulation: expansion beyond North America. Other intellectuals did the same with another necessary aspect of this process, namely, the racialization of Mexicans.

The decades immediately preceding 1900 witnessed an increase in the publication of literature that depicted Mexicans in a derogatory manner, paralleled by an increase in the demand for Mexican labor throughout the Southwest. After the passing of the Chinese Exclusion Act of 1882, three years before the publication of *The Squatter and the Don*, Mexicans became the primary source of labor for the railroads. By 1890, Mexicans dominated the labor force in Arizona and New Mexico mines, especially in copper. With Roosevelt's Gentlemen's Agreement of 1907, barring Japanese laborers from U.S. entry, the demand for Mexican labor in agriculture increased. By the 1920s, Mexicans formed a significant percentage of the labor force in the auto and steel plants of the Midwest. Clearly capitalism had a material interest in maintaining an image of Mexican workers as docile, subservient, and loyal; that interest was the large-scale proletarianization of Mexicans to fill the demand for labor, especially in those industries that required workers willing to accept bare subsistence wages. The process of proletarianizing Mexicans and other Latino immigrants in the United States continues to this day, primarily to ensure the steady influx of cheap labor for industries such as agriculture and service, but also as a mechanism that drives wages down for nonimmigrant workers in other industries.

To justify the proletarianization of Mexicans in the late nineteenth century, organic intellectuals of the time needed to develop an image of Mexicans as lacking in intellect and industrious integrity, and thus suited for nothing better than manual labor in the lowest-paying (and usually the dirtiest) jobs. The accusation that Mexicans were indolent and dilatory by nature gave writers license to fashion images of Mexicans as naturally endowed with such negative traits as the *mañana* syndrome to explain their supposed procrastination, lack of industriousness, and downright laziness. The *mañana* syndrome, a bourgeois critique of the backwardness of the hacienda-based Mexican social order, coupled with the ideology of Manifest Destiny, formed an essential element of the colonizing discourse that rationalized the 1846 U.S. invasion of Mexico and resulted in the seizure of one-third of Mexico's territory—what is now the U.S. Southwest. Gilbert González contends that "the economic relation between" Mexico and the United States "that had evolved after 1870 and matured by 1890 contained all the ingredients for defining Mexico as an economic colony of the U.S."[64] González reveals the manner in which the economic and political conquest of Mexico was aided by American writers who constructed derogatory images of Mexicans. The derisive depictions of Mexicans, in turn, facilitated and justified the proletarianization of Mexicans and their relegation to the lowest economic and political rungs of society.[65]

The development of a highly technological mode of production before the turn of the century generated anxieties not only over how to *produce* more efficiently, but how to *reproduce* a hierarchical social order based on racial domination and class exploitation. In a study of literary naturalism, Mark Seltzer writes that "an insistent anxiety about production and generation" marks the late-nineteenth-century naturalist novel. Citing Michel Foucault's concept of "evolutive historicity," Seltzer suggests that this anxiety—or rather a "cluster of anxieties . . . at once sexual, economic, and aesthetic"[66]—made possible "the articulation of a practice of domination" that required "bodies at once regulated and productive . . . within a general tactic of subjection."[67] Seltzer analyzes an aspect of class domination that Frederick Winslow Taylor did not explain in his theory of scientific management, namely, how to convince workers that it is within their own interests to submit to subjection—or, in the context of the present study, how to convince the former landowning Californios (and Mexicans generally) to submit to their inevitable proletarianization. Granted, the "cluster of anxieties" over the need to reproduce the social relations of production was not generated spontaneously in the minds of late-nineteenth-century writers of the Southwest. Rather the objective needs of a rapidly developing monopolist mode of production, especially the need to reproduce new generations of docile workers, found an identical expression in the writing of organic intellectuals during that period.

The changes that occurred in the Southwest during the nineteenth century—the historical transitions from a feudal hacienda-based ranching economy to a competitive-entrepreneurial capitalism to a full-blown industrial boom and monopoly capitalism, followed by the onset of imperialism, all within a span of fifty years—led to transformations in the modes of cultural production as well. Organic intellectuals produced works aimed at shaping the ideas, values, and practices of human subjects in such a way as to reproduce constantly the relations of production. Intellectuals not only served as apologists for capitalist accumulation; some also expressed in contradictory ways opposition to the effects of this process. Ruiz de Burton was an organic intellectual of her time, standing (problematically but critically) both against and in favor of the ideological interests of a rapidly changing capitalist society.

The Romantic Critique of Capitalism

Ruiz de Burton's views on society and history become apparent, in part, in the novel's references to intellectuals who influenced her writing and politics. The narrator and three of the novel's main characters quote Herbert

Spencer, Thomas Carlyle, Charles Dickens, Ralph Waldo Emerson, Joseph Addison, Charles Fourier, and William Ellery Channing, as if they were household names. Don Mariano, Holman, and Mechlin—all patriarchs of their landowning families and all sympathetic to the plight of the Californios—speak with authority on the works of these writers, especially Spencer and Carlyle, almost as if they were speaking through a single consciousness. At these moments in the novel, Ruiz de Burton displays less concern with writing stylistically realistic prose—in which the purpose of dialogue and narration aims to bring out what is distinct or unique about a particular character—than with making sure key passages from these writers are printed verbatim in the awkwardly constructed long speeches of characters or in the words of the narrator. Nevertheless, as a writer and political thinker, Ruiz de Burton was obviously trying to position herself alongside such figures as Spencer and Carlyle, perhaps out of necessity since in her time there were few Mexican American authors—and certainly no Mexican American women novelists that we know of—from whom she could draw inspiration and seek mentorship. But she also seems to have had a genuine interest in the politically problematic views upheld by these men—an interest that in turn reveals much about her attitudes toward history and social relations.

In associating herself with these figures, Ruiz de Burton joined the ranks of post-1848 intellectuals—Carlyle among them—whom Lukács describes as "the heirs of the Romantic critique of capitalism," referring to intellectuals whose ideas represented the residual interests of privileged classes left behind or even repressed by industrial capitalism, such as the petite bourgeois and landed gentry. The romantic critics of capitalism had been supporters of marginalized interests within the capitalist class itself. Some of them, however, moved increasingly in the direction of reactionary politics after 1848. The reason for this had nothing to do with their inability to think critically, but with the objective possibilities afforded by the historical moment, according to Lukács. It was their objective position of being displaced socially, coupled with their subjective sense of injustice, that made them capable of formulating sharp critiques of capitalism in the way they did, albeit from a less than progressive standpoint. After 1850, Lukács writes, "Criticism of the capitalist division of labour, of capitalism's lack of culture etc. enters increasingly into the service of the most reactionary classes."[68] Carlyle, for example, "developed more and more in the direction of clear hostility to democracy and combated the democratic elements still present in capitalism and even in imperialism,"[69] despite his "rebellious protest" against social inequalities and his sympathy for the working class in his early years. In a telling passage, the narrator in *The Squatter* quotes Carlyle, informing the reader that "Great men are the Fire Pillars in this dark pilgrimage of mankind; they stand as heavenly signs, ever living witnesses of what has been, prophetic tokens of what may still be—the revealed embodied Possibilities of human nature" (304).[70] Carlyle, much like Ruiz de Burton herself, champions the individual "hero," rather than the masses, as the makers of history.

Considering the historical references and literary allusions in *The Squatter*, one can have little doubt that Ruiz de Burton was profoundly influenced not only by the pre-1848 romanticism of the young Carlyle, but perhaps more problematically by the post-1848 scientistic mysticism of Spencer, in addition to other intellectuals of her time. One of the intellectual developments of this period, according to Lukács, was a generalized tendency to interpret history and society with methods based on the laws of natural science: the use of quantifiable, immutable laws applicable to the physical world to explain (and in the process, reify) history. Spencer exemplifies, perhaps more than any of the other intellectuals Ruiz de Burton mentions in her novel, the mechanistic and reifying attitude toward history and society informed by the naturalizing laws of science that Lukács criticizes. Spencer believed that political structures and the legal system should be based on morality,[71] an argument that Ruiz de Burton's narrator and certain characters, especially Don Mariano, repeat throughout *The Squatter*. But Spencer also envisioned history as progressing through time according to fixed laws of development and growth similar to the way a biological organism might develop or a natural system might evolve.

> The ever-increasing complexity which characterizes advancing societies is a complexity that results from the multiplication of different parts performing different duties. The doctrine of the division of labour is now-a-days understood by most to some extent; and most know that by this division of labour each operative, each manufacturer, each town, each district, is constantly more and more restricted to one kind of work. Those who study the organization of living bodies find the uniform process of development to be, that each organ gradually acquires a definite and limited function; there arises, step by step, a more perfect "physiological division of labour."[72]

In this passage Spencer prefigures Max Weber's theory of rationalization and Frederic Taylor's concept of scientific management by almost half a century. His view of society as a physiological structure, each part isolated functionally from the others, not only instantiates an early example of advanced reification, but substantiates Lukács claim about the intellectuals in the post-1848 period giving importance to an understanding of history and society through the laws of the natural sciences. Moreover, Spencer's view of society in these terms accomplishes two things that are important for the present argument: he removes any notion of class power as a social determinant from his analysis of social structures; and in so doing he reifies and dehistoricizes social relations. We could safely assume that Ruiz de Burton was familiar with the passage from Spencer just quoted, considering that one of her characters repeats a line verbatim from the same article. When James Mechlin, a friend of the Californios, fails in his attempt to reason with Leland Stanford, a railroad baron and former governor of California, Mechlin exclaims, "'Misery is the highway to death, while happiness is added life, and the giver of life.' Think of this, Governor" (318).[73] *The Squatter*'s narrator does not convey conceptions of historical development and social relations in physiological or scientistic terms, as does Spencer, but does argue for a sociolegal system operating according to what Spencer called the "fundamental law of morality." Such passages seem to confirm the profound influence that Spencer had on Ruiz de Burton's literary and political views.

Nevertheless, even though Ruiz de Burton was influenced by Spencer and Carlyle, she needed to have already developed a certain level of historical consciousness to be attracted to their ideas in the first place—in which case, her literary and political views should be considered characteristic of a common experience made possible by the large-scale political, economic, and intellectual developments during the period of her formation and maturity as a novelist. Further, as Lukács points out, "[I]t is not this philologically demonstrable influence which is important, but rather the *common character of the reactions to reality* which in history and literature produce *analogous* subjects and forms of historical consciousness. . . . If individual historians or philosophers achieved a notable influence in these questions, this influence is not a primary cause, but itself a consequence of the new ideological tendencies among both writers and readers, produced by the social-historical development."[74] Lukács is not alone in theorizing the relation between literature and society as "analogous." Barbara Foley coins the term *analogous configuration* to describe "a process of mediation, through which the universal aspects of the referent are replicated in the individual features of the mimetic text,"[75] emphasizing that the relation between the historical moment of the author and the author's literary representations can best be described as *analogous* rather than *homologous*—that is to say, the relation between literature and society is that of an abstraction rather than a reflection. Some authors possess the potential to capture their historical moment more than others because they are able to reconfigure the social totality figuratively or abstractly. In *The Squatter*, the narrator's liberalism reconfigures the social contradictions of the author's moment analogously in terms of race, class, and the law; it is what provides access to the social totality in the novel. To reiterate: recognizing the direct influence of such thinkers as Spencer on Ruiz de Burton's outlook is less important than understanding her development as a writer, caught up in the social contradictions of her moment and affected by the "common character of the reactions to society," no less than was Spencer himself. Had she not been part of this "common character" of history, Spencer's ideas would have meant nothing to her.

We can draw two inferences from the fact that Ruiz de Burton was an "heir[ess] to the Romantic critique of capitalism": one, an author's critique of capitalism does not necessarily make the author a subaltern or a revolutionary; and two, such a critique nonetheless remains valuable for anyone—even subalterns—interested in gaining a sense of class antagonisms and history as represented in literature. That is, the author's class background does not necessarily diminish the validity of her critique. We can give emphasis to the second point by referencing a scene from the novel in which Don Mariano converses with Leland Stanford. To discredit the liberalism of the Californios, Stanford ridicules the French Jacobins, Georges-Jacques Danton and Jean-Paul Marat, for advocating "the rights of man" and for singing their liberal rhetoric "to the music of the guillotine." In a less than friendly tone, Don Mariano agrees with Stanford but adds, "[Y]ou see Governor, the devil might sing psalms, and it won't hurt the psalms" (318), as if to say that liberal discourse has a life of its own quite apart from the individual who gives it voice. Similarly, the privileged class background and reified consciousness of the narrator, while important, do not necessarily impede the novel's sharp social critique of monopoly capitalism. It is in this sense that I refer to *The Squatter* as an epistemologically realist novel, as a novel that expresses "the ambition to capture society in motion,"[76] despite its antirealist style and quite apart from the reifying views of its narrator. The narrator represents a view of the social world that operates according to the rigid "natural law" of morality consistent with Spencer's scientistic theories of history, but the novel's contradictory form—in particular, the internal contradictoriness of the narrative viewpoint that both supports and takes a principled stance against its own class interests—throws light on the central subject of the novel, which is the ideology of democratic liberalism itself.

The Ideology of Liberalism

One might reasonably ask if *The Squatter and the Don* offers any solutions to the contradictions faced by the Californios. In answering this question, we would be forced to respond affirmatively. Its suggested resolutions are to be found in the very ideological discourse that represents the repression of history: democratic liberalism. If, on the one hand, liberalism in the novel represents an ideological strategy of containment that opts for assimilation and confidence in the capitalist state, on the other, it also imagines (we must admit) a social order in which racial and ethnic identities would no longer be necessary because racial prejudice would no longer exist (at least not for the aristocratic Californios), capitalists would be kind-hearted enough to save the lives of workers rather than exploit them—the way Clarence Darrel saves Gabriel by making him a banker rather than a bricklayer—and the state would function to serve the interests of morality, not profits. Liberalism in *The Squatter and the Don* may fall short of other more radical or revolutionary solutions, but the novel via the discourse of liberalism nonetheless imagines a collective, futuristic society within which the inequalities and injustices of monopoly capitalism have been eradicated. The positive side of liberalism represented in *The Squatter* can be interpreted as an aesthetic symbolization of a egalitarian form of social organization, or a classless society, as symbolized in the novel's conceptualizations of social groups—the Californios, in particular—as the fantasized substitute for an imagined way of life based on equality and justice. Despite its contradictions, *The Squatter and the Don* draws on democratic liberalism to formulate its utopian appeal.

I have characterized *The Squatter*, in one sense, as being forward-looking. I recognize, however, that because the novel is structured generically as a romance, critics might understandably be tempted to interpret the novel as nostalgic, its conflicts understood as the expressed antagonism of the "residual" toward the "dominant," to use the terms popularized by Raymond Williams.[77] This would really be another way of saying that the novel criticizes the replacement of one mode of production (an agrarian hacienda-based society) by another (industrial capitalism). While this interpretation would certainly be compatible with traditional views of the romance as a literary genre that expresses the anxieties and lamentations of subjects nostalgically yearning for a displaced social order, I want to propose an alternative interpretation that would center the novel's ideological allegiances not exclusively within a residual mode of production (a semifeudal ranching economy) displaced forty years earlier, but with the one firmly established and fully hegemonic (monopoly capitalism) at the time that the novel was written and published. I am not arguing that *The Squatter* consciously or unproblematically articulates the most obvious political interests of monopoly capitalism: surplus value, class domination, and interimperialist rivalry. On the contrary, the novel's outward appearance takes the form of a critique of those interests. My point is rather that the novel articulates *one aspect of a contradiction* ideologically internal to the contemporaneous capitalist moment: namely, economic liberalism with a human face. This ideological project was exemplified by the great reform movements of the late nineteenth and early twentieth centuries aimed not at destroying the capitalist system but at making it more bearable for the masses of laborers and other poor people, such as the proletarianized Mexican American population. To state the point from a slightly different perspective (and to borrow a concept from Foley's insightful study of the documentary novel and African American fiction) one might argue that the "supreme social subject"[78] of *The Squatter and the Don* may not be a subaltern Mexican American subject or, for that matter, a dispossessed and defeated aristocratic Californio subject. Rather, it may be capital itself, manifested as a hegemonic social class wrestling with questions concerning the most effective methods to maintain authority and domination—driven on one hand by its need to repress the working class for the purpose of extracting the greatest amount of surplus value possible from their labor; forced on the other to grant both ideological and material concessions to workers to win their "consent" to be governed. As a strategy for effective social control, it is precisely the act of consent as opposed to coercion that marks the most basic ingredient of democratic liberalism.[79]

In this regard, I differ with Vincent Pérez and José Aranda, who read *The Squatter* as harking back nostalgically for an old way of life. Pérez argues that Ruiz de Burton defends her "native region by redeeming its premodern social order," and that she "depict[s] the hacienda as an organic 'true community' set against the post-1848 landscape of capitalist modernity."[80] Similarly, Aranda writes that *The Squatter* represents a "desire to return California to a previous golden age of ranchos, fruit orchards, and vineyards, all of which grew out of the repressive and coercive mission system that colonized native lands and native people into feudal labor."[81] Aranda argues further that "the novel is defending an economic order that originated among nineteenth-century Californios of Spanish/Mexican descent" and supports "new ways of accumulating capital that required little or no change in the social and gender hierarchy of pre-1848 Alta California" (22). But evidence from the novel can be called upon to counter Aranda's claim that *The Squatter* desires a return to a *siglo de oro.* The references to Spencer and Carlyle, descriptions of a government based on "natural law," the depiction of Clarence Darrell as a capitalist savior, and the liberalist discourse of the narrator all point to a novel that is defending not the golden age of the hacienda, but a more humane transition to a modern capitalist society based on liberal ideology. The references to fruit growing that Aranda criticizes as backward-looking in their allusions to the mission system can actually be considered prophetic or visionary in that California's wheat farms and cattle ranches were eventually replaced with truck farming, orchards, and vineyards, which continue to be the mainstay of California agriculture to this day.

By contrast, I have been arguing that *The Squatter,* in its contradictory representations of race, class, and the law, articulates this most basic ingredient of liberalism for the sake of a Californio population that has fallen from grace. Liberalism, because of its contradictions, cannot offer a viable strategy for working-class resistance or antiracist struggle, much less for political revolution. But as a utopian appeal, it nonetheless *figures* as the aspiration for an egalitarian community—an appeal that expresses more than the disgruntled complaints of Californios against the monopolists and their call for a kinder and gentler capitalism, but one that in many respects is futuristic, anticipating a society unencumbered by the proletarianization and racialization of Mexicans. In the end, the solution that the narrator proposes does not offer Californios much more than a reformist fantasy, but it is nonetheless a solution—albeit aesthetic rather than political.

Before bringing this chapter to a close, it will help to reflect briefly on some possible connections between Ruiz de Burton's novels and contemporary Chicana and Chicano literature. I have read *The Squatter and the Don* as a realist novel because it exposes the conflicts between late-nineteenth-century monopolists and other classes: banking capitalists, entrepreneurs, merchants, small farmers, workers, and above all the Californios—the displaced landowners and ranchers. It also reveals essential aspects of the process in which Mexican Americans have been racialized and proletarianized. *The Squatter*, however, can also be considered a proto-modernist novel in that it anticipates the anxieties over social contradictions that already at that time were beginning to preoccupy writers of the early modernist period: in particular, the irresolvable tension between the desire for national belonging and what Terry Eagleton calls "the rootless conditions of an international monopoly capitalism."[82] The Californios in *The Squatter* display a fervent yearning to be part of the same national body and political system that has effectively excluded them. The kinds of full-blown modernist projects that will take shape in the works of later Chicana and Chicano writers will differ in scope and intensity from the pre- or protomodernism of *The Squatter*, but the contradictoriness of their ideological outlooks will remain strikingly similar: the need to feel included in a political system that engenders perpetual social estrangement; and, simultaneously, the need to establish racial or ethnic difference in a socioeconomic system that became increasingly homogenous ideologically by the end of the twentieth century. In this respect, *The Squatter* can be read as establishing a formal template for contemporary Chicana and Chicano novels, not because of its language, style, themes, and generic features, and not because of the author's ethnic background or Spanish surname, but because of its contradictory form. *The Squatter and the Don* serves as a formal precursor for a literary tradition that can be characterized in part as comprising literary works that are at once stylistically modernist and epistemologically realist. Such is the case, as we shall now see, in Acosta's *The Revolt of the Cockroach People*.

3

CULTURAL NATIONALISM AND THE FORMAL LOGIC OF A STYLE

Acosta's *Revolt of the Cockroach People*

During the summer . . . brown buffalos ran practically naked in the sweltering heat of the San Joaquin Valley. The name [brown buffalos] was not meant as an insult. It was simply a means of classification. Everyone in the Valley considers skin color to be of ultimate importance. The tone of one's pigmentation is the fastest and surest way of determining exactly who one is.

—Oscar Zeta Acosta,
The Autobiography of a Brown Buffalo

Thus, in Lukács's theory of reification, art is caught between two forms of idealism that it cannot hope to resolve, a situation that leads directly to the Frankfurt School attempt to develop a relation to art and aesthetics that is neither reductively materialist nor complacently idealist—and eventually to Adorno's aesthetic theory, organized around paradox and parataxis.

—Timothy Bewes,
"What Is a Literary Landscape?"

IN *THE DECLINE OF THE CALIFORNIOS*, published in 1966, Leonard Pitt describes a series of conflicts between Mexicans and whites in the middle years of the nineteenth century as a "race war in Los Angeles." Correlating this "race war" to the experiences of Chicanos a hundred years later, he writes, "Plainly, by 1854 the Spanish-speaking of Los Angeles felt oppressed by a double standard of justice such as some of them had previously experienced in the gold mines. One sees here in embryo resentments about 'Anglo justice' similar to those that have incited Mexican Americans in more recent times."[1] In these comments, Pitt not only links the social conditions confronted by nineteenth-century Mexican Americans to those faced by twentieth-century Chicanos historically; he also references the early stages of what would later be called the Chicano Movement. For several years following the publication of Pitt's book, coincidentally, a wave of demonstrations, many of which resulted in violent confrontations with the police, took place in Los Angeles. The movement reached its apex on August 29, 1970, the day the National Chicano Moratorium Committee held a march in East Los Angeles to protest the Vietnam War and to draw attention to the disproportionate number of Chicano casualties in that war. Most of the demonstrators, however, came to protest more than just the war; they came to denounce racism, police brutality, inequality in schools, and class exploitation. In a sense, they came to stand in solidarity against what I described in the last chapter as the long-term effects of capitalist accumulation. These effects can be summarized as the state-enforced, class-based racialization and general oppression of Chicanas and Chicanos, a process that began in the nineteenth century and by some accounts has continued to this day. Some twenty to thirty thousand persons participated in the march and the rally that took place afterward in Laguna Park. Claiming they were responding to threats of violence and looting, Los Angeles county sheriffs and the Los Angeles Police Department attacked the demonstrators with batons and tear gas. Most of the demonstrators dispersed, but some fought back, throwing rocks and bottles and burning police vehicles. The police responded with arrests, beatings, and bullets. When the fighting was over hours later, three Chicanos were dead, including news reporter Rubén Salazar, who had been shot in the head with a ten-inch tear gas projectile.[2]

Oscar Zeta Acosta, an attorney and novelist, fictionalizes the events surrounding the Chicano Moratorium demonstration in his 1973 novel, *The Revolt of the Cockroach People.*[3] Buffalo Zeta Brown, the fictional militant Chicano lawyer molded into a near replica of the author himself, narrates *Revolt.* Like Pitt, Zeta Brown draws a genealogical link between the nineteenth-century Californios and twentieth-century Chicanos in stating that "the *vato loco* has been fighting with the pig since the Anglos stole his land in the last century" (91). Zeta Brown's comment may smack of historical romanticism or revisionism, not to mention gender bias. The sentence also reflects a reified conception of history from a cultural nationalist perspective, fortified with the metaphor of "land." His assertion nonetheless speaks to objective historical conditions if we are willing to seek its significance beyond the limited and precise meanings the sentence was meant to convey. Like the sentence, *Revolt* itself explores the appropriateness of cultural nationalism as a response to the effects of capitalist accumulation, but it simultaneously contains a deep critical and historical intelligibility that surpasses its own surface content.

As a concentric novel within Chicano literary studies, *Revolt* has been the topic of much criticism centered on both its thematic and its structural aspects, as well as on the author's colorful but tragic life. Hopefully it will become apparent to the reader as she or he progresses through these pages the extent to which I have drawn on the work of other critics in formulating my own arguments. My critique of *Revolt*, however, differs from other readings of the novel in that I interpret Acosta's "style" specifically as performing a dereifying function that seeks to transgress the reified consciousness of the novel's narrator. *Revolt* is written in—to borrow from Jameson's characterization of Jean-Paul Sartre's fictional prose—"a modern style [that] is somehow in itself intelligible, above and beyond the limited meaning of the book written in it." The critical content of style in *Revolt*, however, parts ways not only with "those precise meanings which the individual sentences that make it up are designed to convey,"[4] but with the narrator's reified conception of cultural nationalism, which is the primary mode of reification at work in *Revolt*, and thus the central object of critique in this chapter. When the critical intelligibility of the novel's style is taken into account, we discover a narrative that is not only more complex—thematically, structurally, and artistically—than previously considered; the novel's formal complexities also give us cause to challenge previous critical assessments of *Revolt* as they relate to cultural nationalism and other political strategies promoted by activists and supporters of the Chicano Movement from 1968 to 1971, the period represented in the novel.

In this chapter, I hope to accomplish four objectives. (1) I shall analyze various sets of conceptual antinomies to disclose the dialectical logic of the novel's style. Initially, my analysis centers on one of these antimonies: the opposition between parataxis and hypotaxis in Acosta's narrative sequences and sentence structures. Parataxis refers to a style of writing that places phrases, words, or concepts one after another without subordinating connectives, thus implying rather than positing their relation; hypotaxis refers to a kind of writing that makes use of conjunctions to state overtly the interconnectedness among ranged phrases, words, or concepts. I shall discuss the meaning of these terms at greater length subsequently. For now, suffice it to say that examining the parataxis-hypotaxis opposition in *Revolt* will help us make sense of the relation between social contradictions and literary form in Acosta's novels. (2) As an example of paratactic logic, I shall examine the novel's thematic representation of the Chicano Movement, scrutinizing in particular the narrator's constant juxtaposing of political strategies that were employed by activists during the most turbulent years of the movement. The narrator's naive weighing and balancing of political strategies, I hold, sheds light on cultural nationalism as a reified worldview. (3) In the third part of the chapter, I shall attempt to elucidate the dialectical logic of the novel's generic features. Here I shall focus primarily on *Revolt* but will find occasion to draw some comparisons to Acosta's 1972 novel, *The Autobiography of a Brown Buffalo.*[5] The latter bears stylistic similarities to *Revolt*, but the author's dereifying style matures in his second novel, which is my reason for concentrating on *Revolt* rather than *Autobiography. Revolt* and *Autobiography* are written as autobiographical narratives, but Acosta, noticeably, has taken many liberties in changing actual names, events, and places. Via the intentional distortion of factual information, Acosta's novels effectively formulate a subtle critique of the truth claims inherent in autobiographical narratives. By implication, *Revolt* also strongly suggests that it be read as fiction rather than memoir. (4) I shall argue that *Revolt* strives toward a symbolic resolution of the tension between the poles of the various oppositions it constructs stylistically in its repeated references to death as a metaphor for transformation, and in the narrator's thoughtful but problematic reflections on the possibilities of a political subject committed to a long-term, internationalist struggle against racism and U.S. imperialism.

Like Ruiz de Burton's novels, Acosta's *Revolt* and *Autobiography* express a bitter antagonism toward the effects of capitalist accumulation. But unlike Ruiz de Burton's narrator, who rejects a working-class racial identity, Zeta Brown attempts to fashion a racial identity that embraces his working-class, Chicano heritage. Thus, whereas Lola Medina's skin color changes from nearly black to white in *Who Would Have Thought It?*, Oscar becomes "Brown" in the transition from *The Autobiography of a Brown Buffalo* to *The Revolt of the Cockroach People*. Ultimately, cultural nationalism in *Revolt* turns out to be nearly as problematic as the racialization made necessary by the economic needs and ideological interests of capitalist accumulation from the late nineteenth century to the present. The novel is thus driven by this contradictory predicament—forced racialization versus a self-fashioned racial identity—in which the narrator finds himself. Within this framework, I read Acosta's *Revolt* as aspiring toward the representation of society as a whole, even if this aspiration in the end remains unrealized.

The Logic of Style in *Revolt*

Acosta's style has been described as outrageous, sensational, idiosyncratic, digressive, wildly erotic, perverse, stream of consciousness, naughty, funny, funky, chaotic, and schizophrenic. Raymund Paredes adeptly characterizes Acosta's style as the "literary equivalent of a Molotov cocktail."[6] On a more serious note, Paredes echoes other critics who have observed that *Revolt* and *Autobiography* are "rendered in Acosta's version of Hunter Thompson's 'Gonzo Journalism,' a literary technique that requires the author's participation in the very events he is in the process of recording,"[7] even though the author's participation is often highly fictionalized. The Gonzo stylist endeavors to write a narrative that appears to be unedited. Such a text will produce a sense of spontaneity and immediacy by seeming to remain faithful to the recorder's initial observations and impressions.[8] In actuality, Acosta, like Thompson, spent much time editing and revising his work, as becomes evident when one compares the drafts of *Autobiography* and *Revolt* to their final versions.[9] Most critics who read Acosta's novels as examples of Gonzo journalism focus on the outlandish, egotistical, intentionally offensive, and calling-attention-to-itself qualities of the writing and to the fact that the author becomes the antihero of his own narrative. I am interested, however, not only in the way Acosta's writing style reflects the narrator's (or the author's) personality but also in the manner in which his writing style produces meaning that surpasses the consciousness of the narrator—and perhaps even of the author himself. One of the key aspects of Acosta's writing style in *Revolt* that enables the production of extraliterary signification is the author's use of juxtaposition.

During the trial of the "Tooner Flats Seven," Zeta Brown, the defense attorney, watches the events of August 29 secondhand, in a film shown in the courtroom. Initially, he describes the film with linguistic fragments rather than complete sentences as if visualizing a series of discrete photographs instead of narrating a sequence of causally connected events (198). The descriptive terms—nouns and adjectives without verbs—reflect the stylistic texture of the film itself, as Zeta Brown describes it. Shot on location by someone present at the demonstration, the film remains unedited with no sound track or narration as such. Less concerned with aesthetic quality than immediacy, the filmmakers produced a film that might be characterized as a "compilation documentary."[10] Zeta Brown thinks the film provides an accurate account of the events in question, referring to it as "a real document, not from the movies, not TV, you know it really happened" (200). In this regard, the film lends itself to an audience already familiar with the subject matter, an audience that will be easily persuaded: "you have seen the burnt streets, you have walked them, you recognize some of the faces, some of the stores, you know exactly where the corners of Indiana and Whittier are" (200).[11] But Zeta Brown also feels that not all aspects of the film will be readily apparent to viewers, so he finds himself needing to call attention to details that might otherwise go unnoticed. In one such moment, the police form a skirmish line in front of a liquor store, riot guns in hand. The sun's glare distorts the picture, prompting Zeta Brown to instruct readers, as if they were film viewers, that despite the distortion, if they "look close" they will notice people inside the store peering out through the steel bars covering the windows—if they "look close" they will notice the people are frantic with the realization that the police are about to attack (199). The film, according to Zeta Brown, requires close reading for a proper interpretation. The same might be said of *Revolt* itself.

In commenting on the film, the narrator describes the abrupt cutting of camera shots from one scene to another. Zeta Brown's description of the film sheds light, however inadvertently, on the dialectical logic of the novel's style. The power of Acosta's writing in *Revolt* has to do with its filmic cutting techniques: a style that forces readers to take notice of sharply contrasting images, events, and ideas; one that also encourages the reader to juxtapose the stylistic features of the narrative against the novel as a whole—and by extension, the reified consciousness of a fragmented worldview against the social totality. "SLASH!" the narrator states, to capture the sudden unexplained transition from a scene that looks like a safe and happy family picnic in the park on a sunny Saturday afternoon to one where the police are swinging clubs at young people, bleeding bodies, cars burning, the broken head of a mannequin lying in the middle of the street. "[T]he film shows us a distortion of what we just saw a few minutes ago," Zeta Brown explains. "Then there was order and laughter. Now there is chaos: legs, arms, hair in the wind, running kids, people in scrambling motions, running away from the camera, away from the cops advancing in platoon formation, a phalanx of pigs, guns, smoke, bottles in air. . . . SLASH! Whittier Boulevard is burning" (201). As described by the narrator, the film encourages the audience to view its content critically, the stylistic

"SLASH!" marking the sudden cutting from one scene to another so as to emphasize the contrast between the two. The SLASH! defamiliarizes what was previously felt to be known, forcing the audience to think in terms of conflict and tension rather than unity and coherence. A few critics have noticed the slashing quality of Acosta's writing. According to Smith, "One of the interesting features of Acosta's descriptions—of his style—is the manner in which he sets the tone and mood of an episode by striving for a cinematic quality,"[12] and Juan Bruce-Novoa writes that Acosta's novels, especially *Revolt*, are filled with "Thompson-like leaps from one subject to another and the constant juxtaposition of temporal planes and levels of reality."[13] Smith and Bruce-Novoa ably describe Acosta's cutting technique. I argue, however, that Acosta's contradistinctive writing style in *Revolt*—a style that ceaselessly draws on the dialectical category of similarity and difference to produce meaning—constitutes not only a literary technique but the very logic of the novel's form, symptomatically reflecting and dereifying the author's urgent desire to comprehend the social contradictions of his historical moment.

The Parataxis-Hypotaxis Antinomy

Literary theorists have described the kind of writing we find in *Revolt* as parataxis. According to Erich Auerbach, a paratactic narrative produces meaning through the juxtaposition of narrative moments rather than through linear coherence; a paratactic style is more akin to a montage of images or a compilation of discrete statements than to a story told as a series of events connected temporally and causally. The individual units or narrative moments of the paratactic text produce meaning in their stark contrast to other moments of the narrative totality without the use of conjunctions or explanatory connectives, but they also function as self-contained expressions of the social totalities out of which they emerge: parts that express the whole. Auerbach identifies three operating features of paratactic narratives that I find particularly useful for the interpretation of Acosta's *Revolt:* one, paratactic narratives contain words, phrases, ideas, or actions that are repeated in varied ways to produce a sense of newness, of constant renewal, or of repeatedly returning to a point of origin; two, an individual moment of a paratactic narrative produces meaning emphatically by standing in sharp contradistinction to other moments; and three, the *event* in a paratactic text "contains one decisive gesture with only a loose temporal or causal connection with those [events] that follow or precede."[14] The paratactic strategy in *Revolt* is particularly effective because of the hybrid[15] or eclectic structure of the novel. *Revolt* cannot be read exclusively as a paratactic text; it is rather hypotactic in its outward appearance, with a paratactic form operating covertly as a kind of "inside narrative."[16] Hypotaxis—the syntactic subordination of one clause to another connected by explanatory conjunctions—becomes the appearance (or the immediacy of narrative cognition) that obfuscates the more fundamental parataxis at work in *Revolt.* For Richard Lanham, hypotactic narratives "desire to rank, order, [and] build carefully from evidence to conclusion," while the paratactic text "works by putting things next to each other and letting the reader make the most of the juxtaposition."[17] Whereas the formal logic of hypotaxis is diachronic and metaphoric, the logic of parataxis is synchronic and metonymic. Hypotaxis resides in the unity of a narrative's thematic content or story; parataxis operates at the level of structural conflict.

Significantly, the paratactic structure of *Revolt* takes shape as the expression of a long history of racial and class antagonisms as experienced by Chicanos. The form of the novel assumes an internal identity with the contradictoriness of Chicano social experience: violent confrontations with a class-based criminal justice system, intentional distortions of factual information as in trials and other legal proceedings, and severe social inequalities in education, employment, and basic civil liberties. As Smith has stated, "The impressions of Acosta's montages, particularly in *The Revolt of the Cockroach People*, give far more insight into the frustrations of the oppressed than could a straightforward narrative."[18] Indeed, the experiences of being criminalized because of physical appearance, arrested without cause, abused and brutalized physically, forced to serve extraordinarily long periods of incarceration, and killed while in the custody of the police are acted out rhetorically by ruptures in narrative time sequence, the juxtaposition of sharply contrasting events, and the shocking disjointedness of the narrative voice itself. Consequently, the novel assumes the posture of a self-reflexive commentary that suggests similarities between political realities and novelistic form, an aesthetic feature developed to a higher level in Pineda's *Frieze*—examined in the last chapter of this book—in which the modernist novel takes on a formal semblance to commodity fetishism. In *Revolt*, however, the conflicting categories of parataxis and hypotaxis function to defamiliarize the immediately given or, more directly, to contest reification.

We may be tempted to read Acosta's novel exclusively as a hypotactic narrative—as an episodic construction of events connected chronologically and ordered spatially with conjunctions or associating terms that not only conjoin but explicate and justify the reasons for bringing two or more narrative moments together. The temptation to read the novel hypotactically should come as no surprise: at first glance, *Revolt* appears to be a straightforward narrative. Upon a closer inspection, however, we will recognize not only that *Revolt* employs both hypotactic and paratactic narrative strategies but that they produce a socially significant tension when brought together in the novel. As a hypotactic text, *Revolt* traces the formation and development of the narrator's consciousness through a series of narrated events and reflections; as a paratactic narrative, the novel produces a level of signification not necessarily attributable to the narrator's consciousness. As such, the paratactic impulse of the novel disrupts (or dereifies) the anticipated trajectory of hypotactic thinking—or what Lanham refers to as the "hypotactic habits of the mind."[19]

Consider the following minor example. When first arriving in Los Angeles in 1968, Zeta Brown visits his cousin Manuel, who had been a high jumper at USC in the early 1950s. Manuel had been good enough to try out for the Olympics, but his coach was racist against Chicanos and had deliberately refused to train him properly. Thus Manuel failed to qualify for the Olympics. Now in his late thirties, he remains bitter about his coach's racism. Ironically, when Zeta Brown asks him what he thinks about the Chicano Militants who are fighting against racism, Manuel accuses them of being lazy and of blaming others for their problems. He calls them "a bunch of young punk communists who don't know their ass from a hole in the ground" (27). Zeta Brown feels perplexed: he sympathizes with Manuel but is also fascinated by the energy and boldness of the Chicano Militants. He thinks about Manuel's opinions on his way home. Arriving at his hotel room, he concludes, "In a way, I agree with Manuel: the best way to accomplish what you want is simply to work for it, on an individual basis." In the very next sentence, he announces, "I open my room and an army of cockroaches disperses into the cracks and darkness" (28). The contrast between these two sentences can be read as a paratactic moment; the absence of an explanatory connective between them can be interpreted as performing the same function as the SLASH! The first and second sentences end and begin a paragraph, respectively; the slight pause when reading the transition from one paragraph to the next emphasizes the contradistinction between the two declarations. More significantly, the tension between the sentences reflects two levels of knowing: read literally, Zeta Brown and his cousin are too individualistic to recognize their own interest in joining an organized fight against racism; read structurally, the logic of the narrative order—the placing of these two particular sentences side by side—draws attention to the possibility that Chicano Militants have joined the movement because working-class Mexican Americans historically have been kept in "darkness" and forced to live in "cracks in the wall." The second sentence reveals the ever-present specter of social unrest (an "army of cockroaches"), sharply contrasting with the cynicism expressed by Zeta Brown and Manuel. What's more, nowhere is it apparent that the narrator is aware of the significance to be drawn from the tension between these two sentences. On the contrary, he seems oblivious to the implied social conflict embedded in the order of his statements: he is simply telling a story. Logically, Zeta Brown is not the ultimate authoritative agent giving meaning to the novel's organization and "inside narrative."

Though I am mainly concerned with the paratactic logic of the novel's narrative structure, the same logic can be identified in Acosta's sentences. Robert Hullot-Kentor explains that in paratactic texts readers will notice the "recurrence to abrupt, staccato, sometimes delphically abbreviated expression." He adds that because parataxis "rejects certitude as a standard of truth in favor of exactness of insight, it necessarily tends toward the apodictic."[20] If we look closely at the language of *Revolt*, we will notice the staccato style and paratactic logic of Acosta's sentences: "Silence comes hard and heavy" (23); "I am a stone peacenik, albeit with violent tendencies" (28); "I am divided against myself, torn in two" (42); "I am where I am, always" (65); "I feel like I'd like to feel like I think he must be feeling" (174); "It is a night for interrogation and I catch them wondering in the corners of their eyes" (211); "Cockroach is a big word" (230); "Our smiles and good humor are the professional touch of deadly enemies" (245); and "What would happen if I ever got serious? I am serious" (257). Auerbach teaches us that a paratactic sentence will present the relation between two moments in its structure more emphatically than will its hypotactic counterpart, accomplishing this reordered emphasis by substituting the neutral conjunction *and* for such subordinating connectives as *but* or *however*. The paratactic sentence at once equalizes and more sharply distinguishes two moments or thoughts. The paratactic construction, "He opened his eyes and was struck," is stated more dramatically, Auerbach explains, than the hypotactic sentence, "Upon opening his eyes, he was struck."[21] Acosta's sentences tend toward parataxis with their emphatically declared, internally conflicted constructions, and they demonstrate how profoundly the logic of parataxis informs *Revolt* at every level. Some critics, obviously moved by Acosta's writing style, have attempted to capture the *feel* of contradiction and parataxis in their own sentences. Jeanne Thwaites argues that *Autobiography* "cannot be accused of being simplistic. . . . The book is tragic. It is also hilarious."[22] Similarly, Arthur Ramírez describes *Autobiography* and *Revolt* as "tragically funny, hilariously sad," and he claims that Acosta "cannot help but tell the truth—and it hurts, but it also humanizes and raises consciousness."[23] Ramirez refers to Acosta as a "truthful liar."[24]

It is understandable that some critics will associate paratactic writing with postmodernism, even though there is no necessary correlation between them. In an illuminating essay N. Katherine Hayles compares the writing style in Don DeLillo's *White Noise* to the linguistic-like codes used to explain the way genetic information is encoded and translated in DNA. She also argues that "postmodern literature, with its suspicion of traditional liberal values, is more likely to manifest" a paratactic orientation. By contrast, the connective logic or teleological thrust of hypotaxis remains consistent with the "liberal humanism" of modernist literature.[25] For Hayles, hypotaxis gives structure to narratives that represent historical continuity, while parataxis "marks a discontinuity both in language and cultural formation."[26] The concept of "postmodern parataxis" as defined by Hayles presents potential theoretical obstacles for the dialectical critic because, for Hayles, paratactic narratives do not lend themselves to the representation of historical continuity, an assertion with which I take issue in the last section of this chapter. Despite the brilliance of her comparisons between the languages of literature and genetics, little in her analysis of parataxis has to do with negation: the concept of postmodern parataxis implies the necessity—perhaps even the desirability—of perpetual oscillation between the poles of antinomies or between contrasting images and stands opposed to dialectical sublation, which is essential for any historical analysis of social transformations.

Further, not all scholars define parataxis strictly in terms of periodization: hypotaxis as modernist; parataxis as postmodernist. Auerbach, for one, studies the paratactic structures in Homeric poetry to theorize the evolution of mimesis in narrative forms from the epic to the novel. But the social significance produced in the paratactic structures of antiquarian narrative forms differs markedly from that produced in contemporary narratives. Whereas the significance of the epic, according to Auerbach, lies in its mimetic immediacy, the formal problematic of the modernist novel, quite to the contrary, stems from the difficulty in delineating a direct correspondence between an event and its cause. As Alan Munton writes, a "paratactic [narrative] structure means . . . that a breakdown in the signifying chain has occurred, as in Lacan's account of schizophrenia."[27] This breakdown, however, need not lead to the conclusion that modernist or postmodernist novels are marked in some absolute sense by the absence of historical continuity; on the contrary, it can also facilitate a comprehension of the modernist novel as obfuscating or complicating rather than eradicating the relation between events and their causes—or, for that matter, between language and reference. In a related context, Theodor Adorno declares, "[F]rom my theorem that there are no philosophical first principles, it follows that one cannot construct a continuous argument with the usual stages, but one must assemble the whole from a series of partial complexes . . . whose constellation not [logical] sequence produces the idea."[28] Adorno does not reject the notion that the whole can be reassembled conceptually; he argues rather that the assembler must make use of appropriate critical tools when the connections between the parts of the whole are not readily apparent.

Thus the paratactic novel requires the critic to employ various analytical and social categories as mediations to give a sense of totality to a narrative that is apparently fragmented and discontinuous. (In the present work I am employing the categories of reification, totality, and epistemic realism to dereify representations of racialized identities.) Following the logic of Adorno's argument, paratactic narratives represent historical continuity in a manner that differs pronouncedly from that encountered in hypotactic texts: by negation and absence rather than positive assertion. Lanham articulates this argument in simpler terms: "Both paratactic and hypotactic styles can work in complex ways but the principle remains the same. Is the ranking done for us (hypotaxis) or left up to us (parataxis)?"[29] We could ask the same question in this way: Are the connections between events and their causes stated overtly (hypotaxis) or are they implied covertly (parataxis)? In my interpretation of *Revolt*, I argue that, despite the paratactic logic of its style, the novel does not reflect historical stasis or signify a perpetual oscillation between the poles of unresolved binaries, but aspires toward—or at least alludes to the possibility of—social transformation. To ground these theoretical claims, we will do well at this point to relate the concept of parataxis back to the issues of cultural nationalism as an expression of standpoint politics and to the larger questions of reification and totality. We can accomplish this task, in part, by examining the manner in which the novel repeatedly juxtaposes the various political strategies employed and rejected by activists during the heyday of the Chicano Movement.

Juxtaposing Political Strategies

Shortly after *Autobiography* and *Revolt* were reissued by Vintage Books in 1989 (both novels having been out of print for several years), Alan Hunsaker wrote a sympathetic review, highlighting the author's seductive prose style as well as the significance of the historical events represented in the two novels. Hunsaker also reviewed *Destructive Generation: Second Thoughts about the '60s* by Peter Collier and David Horowitz—a book about the radical social movements of the 1960s and the New Left politics that informed them. Curiously, Hunsaker notes, "not a word is written [in *Destructive Generation*] about the Chicano Movement . . . which grew out of the radical politics of the 1960s." Collier and Horowitz do not reflect kindly on the New Left movements in which they themselves participated. "Instead, the . . . 'Second Thought' people . . . have decided that they'd rather finish life's journey in existential peace than continue the struggle for what they now claim is merely a 'romanticized Idea,' namely, the idea of a communist utopia."[30] Hunsaker concludes that politically active Latinos who read *Destructive Generation* today "may react as Buffalo Zeta Brown did years ago when a Communist Party official approached him during a Chicano demonstration at the central jail in Los Angeles."[31] Aware that some political activists avoid any contact with Communists for fear of being redbaited, Dorothy Healey[32] says to Zeta Brown, "If you think it'll be embarrassing to your group, we'll leave." Zeta Brown puts his arm around her and replies, "Listen, Dorothy, you can march with me anytime . . . and besides, the Chicanos are ten times to the left of the Communists now" (58). Hunsaker highlights this moment in *Revolt* to accentuate his critical assessment of *Destructive Generation* by contrasting the politics of the "Second Thought people" to those of the "Cockroach People." For my purpose, the brief encounter between Zeta Brown and Healey is instructive because it juxtaposes the militant cultural nationalism of the Chicano Movement and the revolutionary reformism of the Communist Party. Zeta Brown's comment about which group is farther "left" implies a subtle critique of the opportunism of leftists (in this case, Communists) who tail rather than lead the masses. Yet throughout the novel, Zeta Brown expresses considerable respect for Communist Party members, namely, Healey, Rose Chernin, and Angela Davis, despite his subtle critique of Davis's promotion of electoral politics at an antiwar rally (177–79). Zeta Brown's attitude toward these characters might be read as analogous to an expression of sympathy for class-based internationalism, which stands opposed to the reified standpoint of cultural nationalism.

The critical comparison of political strategies in *Revolt*, however, is not limited to cultural nationalism and Communism. From beginning to end, *Revolt* raises a myriad of rhetorical questions that effectively examine the pros and cons of numerous tactical questions and political strategies.[33] For example: Should the Chicano Movement concentrate its organizing efforts on urban youth, given the exuberance of the high school walkouts in East Los Angeles in the late 1960s? Or should the movement place more emphasis on supporting the struggles of agricultural workers, given the immense popularity of the United Farm Workers Union during that same period? Zeta Brown, who grew up in a rural Central California town "picking peaches,"[34] manifests the tension between the poles of this opposition when, after his own authenticity as a Chicano has been questioned, he asks a newfound urban friend, "How many peaches have you picked, priest?" (34). In addition to dramatizing the urban-rural dilemma, the novel raises questions about a whole series of similar tactical oppositions: students versus workers; intellectuals versus *vatos locos*;[35] the working class versus the liberal counterculture; electoral politics versus direct action; acts of terror by small groups versus political actions of a mass movement; clandestine versus public methods of organizing; separatism versus multiracial unity; militancy versus pacifism; nationalism versus internationalism; legality versus illegality; and reform versus revolution.[36] (Political movements associated with feminism and gay rights are noticeably and problematically absent from this catalog of strategies contemplated in the novel.)[37]

To illustrate the dialectical logic of the novel's critique of political strategies, consider the representation of the law in *Revolt*. Critics have analyzed Acosta's representation of the law from a variety of perspectives. Ramón Saldívar suggests that "no single feature of [Acosta's] satire is likely to offend the common reader more than his assessment of the American legal system."[38] By contrast, Michael Olivas reads *Revolt* as a case study in his examination of the problems faced by actual lawyers defending clients who have broken the law intentionally in pursuit of political objectives.[39] From another angle, Michael Hames-Garcia argues that Zeta Brown increasingly comes to believe in the destruction of the legal system and its replacement with "a more fundamental conception of justice" based on "Marxist natural law,"[40] the process of eliminating the political oppression of social classes and groups via legal means. In *Racism on Trial: The Chicano Fight for Justice*, Ian Haney López reconstructs the legal arguments formulated by Acosta in two cases—the East L.A. Thirteen and the Biltmore Six—to formulate a theory of racism based on "common sense."[41] These analyses are provocative and instructive. In my interpretation of *Revolt*, however, I shall not attempt to extract a particular theory of law practice from the novel. The point I want to emphasize here is the manner in which the narrator's actions and thoughts as an attorney illuminate Acosta's critique of political strategies—in this instance, legality versus illegality—as read through the novel's paratactic style and its logic of similarity and difference. In short, *Revolt* juxtaposes legal and illegal organizing strategies to accentuate the futility of working within the law to effect change.

The law is perhaps the most important motif in *Revolt*, in part because it exposes the narrator's internal conflict. Zeta Brown practices law but he hates the law at the same time.[42] He is an "outlaw lawyer,"[43] who complains endlessly that he does not want to be a lawyer. He hates the law so profoundly that he proclaims unabashedly, "I'd rather spit in a judge's eye than stick a pig in the heart" (214). He also confesses that he got his law degree only "to prove that a fat brown Chicano like [him] could do it" (24). In *Autobiography*, the narrator quits his job with a legal aid clinic and goes on a six-month drug binge before joining up with the Chicano Movement in *Revolt*. He renews his law practice for the sole purpose of serving the movement, then bills himself as "the only revolutionary lawyer this side of the Florida Gulf" (214). As might be expected in a novel narrated by a lawyer with an inflated ego, many scenes take place in a courtroom, in jail, or in confrontations with the police. The novel reveals a dilemma confronted by Zeta Brown in his law practice: Should he work within the law to undermine the system? Or should he reject legal practices entirely in favor of illegal, revolutionary activities?

Despite his constant complaints about wanting to quit the law, Zeta Brown provides legal counsel—albeit, in a somewhat unorthodox manner—to dozens of defendants arrested for their political activities. In his most important cases, he serves as chief counsel in the defense of the East L.A. Thirteen, the St. Basil's Twenty-One, and the Tooner Flats Seven. He also begins another large case, the Biltmore Six, which is not concluded by the end of the novel. His main legal strategy in the courtroom is rigorously political: rather than trying to prove the innocence or guilt of his clients by standards set forth in the normal rules of law, he endeavors to expose the inherent class bias of the courts and the LAPD.[44] Zeta Brown does not win all of his legal battles, but he is relatively successful with most of them. He seems to win because his fantastic, chaotic approach to lawyering bears a striking resemblance to Acosta's paratactic writing style: exposing falsehoods by juxtaposing the statements of prosecutors to their own rules of law; antagonizing judges and witnesses with offensive language; intentionally disobeying the protocols of litigation with lines of questioning that show no apparent connective logic; converting the normally tranquil space of a courtroom into a place of chaos so that it takes on a semblance of the social world outside the Hall of Justice; and appealing to the emotions of jurors with his humor, wit, and uncontrolled sentimentality in the courtroom so as to win their sympathy and positive judgment. The narrator's courtroom antics mimic the possibilities and limits of the novel's eclectic prose. Throughout the novel, Zeta Brown plays the part of a Hamlet, torn between a perceived obligation to avenge an injustice that has been committed against him and a felt inability to make the commitment necessary to take action. At certain moments, however, especially in the courtroom, Zeta Brown acts more like the gravedigger clown who outwits Hamlet with his quirky responses to questions. When Judge Alacran exhorts, "I don't want to hear any more of your sass. . . . Do you understand?" Zeta Brown responds, "I went to school." When the judge tells him to wear a tie and dress properly before the court, he replies offhandedly,

> "It's my neck, sir. My neck is too fat."
> "Just see to it that you wear something appropriate."
> "It must be this shirt, Judge. It's from Acapulco."
> "Mr. Brown, you're sassing me again."
> "I'm sorry, Judge. I've had trouble with fat necks."

Zeta Brown's wit takes a sharp jab at the hypocrisy of judicial formalities. To further emphasize this hypocrisy, he subpoenas more than a hundred judges to take the stand and then questions them about their attitudes toward Chicanos and their reasons for not appointing Chicanos to the grand jury. After weeks of hearing testimonies of mere "[w]ords, words, words" (224), he concludes that the judges are either lying or do not recognize the inherent racism in their actions. As such, his staccato responses to Alacran and his disruption of court proceedings do not aim to expose the truth in some absolute sense; they seek rather to approximate the truth via a dialectical logic that is totally alien to the positivistic thinking of the law. That is to say, the narrator's actions dereify the objectifying, class-based assumptions of the law rather than merely posit an analytical corrective to them. Thus, Zeta Brown does not argue his cases; he deconstructs the implied logic of the prosecutor's cases.

Vexed by the legality-illegality dilemma, Zeta Brown insists that "professional revolutionaries"—the designation he gives as his occupation during one of his arrests for contempt of court—can only operate within the legal system if their goal is ultimately to destroy it. He exemplifies this strategy most clearly and emphatically when he runs for sheriff of Los Angeles County, promising to dismantle the department if he wins.[45] In an interview with Roland Zanzibar, a character based on journalist Rubén Salazar, Zeta Brown admits he has no real possibility of winning an election for sheriff. Nonetheless, adopting a platform that differs considerably from the political commitments of Ruiz de Burton's narrator, Zeta Brown declares, "If I were elected Sheriff, I would make every attempt to dissolve the office. The community has no need for professional killers. . . . The police are the violent arm of the rich and I would get rid of them" (136). Zeta Brown discloses his socialist tendencies by promising to replace the Sheriff's Office with a "People's Protection Department," having members of the community establish the policies and methods for state-free, self-regulated protection. The narrator works within the legal system to establish political legitimacy for Chicanos, but with each court case he grows increasingly skeptical of legal strategies. He comes to realize that he can indeed win some tactical battles in court, but in the long run the system cannot be defeated from within its own legal structures—just as it cannot be transformed with elections.

Despite the novel's scathing critique of a racist criminal justice system, not all critics have shared a favorable opinion of Acosta's novels. Bruce-Novoa, who writes sympathetically about *Revolt*, explains that Acosta was a "troublesome novelist"[46] for critics of Chicano literature right from the start. Like John Rechy and Josephina Niggli, whose novels were excluded from Chicano literary studies for years, Acosta was shunned in the 1970s by critics, such as those who directed the Premio Quinto Sol, a national literary award for Chicano literature. He was not seriously considered for the award, according to Bruce-Novoa, because his depiction of the Chicano Movement "was not the picture of ethnic unity Chicanos wanted to see,"[47] even though it was the only substantial fictional representation of the movement extant. That his novels were sometimes considered critiques of the movement's contradictions was not enough to satisfy the skeptics. As Louis Mendoza (another sympathetic critic) explains, for some scholars of Chicano literature it was "a perceived threat . . . to reveal in-group dynamics, weaknesses, or contradictions,"[48] as Acosta's novels do. Following Mendoza, I would argue that *Revolt*'s critical force lies precisely in its critique of cultural nationalism and its revelation of in-group ideological con-traditions. A reading of *Revolt* as a satiric engagement with the pros and cons of various political strategies reveals a narrative that calls into question the cultural nationalist politics of the Chicano Movement and the politically contradictory attitudes and practices it engendered.

Revolt as a Critique of Identity

The paratactic logic of the author's style and the novel's scrutiny of various political strategies make possible an interpretation of *Revolt* as an epistemologically realist novel that, when read in this manner, may need to be reconsidered in light of its particular posture toward various categories of identity, including gender and sexuality along with race and ethnicity. Because *Revolt* foregrounds the Chicano Movement and is narrated from the perspective of a participant-observer in the movement, the novel has been commonly interpreted as a representation of Chicano identity.[49] The overwhelming agreement in reading *Autobiography* and *Revolt* as the author's search for identity points up a particular interpretation of Acosta's novels that cannot be disputed, especially when they are read thematically. By paying closer attention to their formal elements, however, we may open up a space that allows for a reading of *Revolt* as a critique of rather than as a search for identity. Acosta's novels contribute to the formulation of a critical assessment from the inside, if you will: they are essentially case studies in immanent critique. In *Revolt*, the narrator is inextricably immersed in a quagmire of nationalist politics, simultaneously celebrating nationalism and displaying the desire to transcend the limits of a reified nationalist consciousness. Ultimately he fails to overcome those limits. To be clear, Acosta's novel does not critique nationalist identity on moralistic or philosophical grounds;[50] *Revolt* displays a profound wariness toward nationalism based on epistemological and political grounds.

We can support our argument at this point by analyzing the narrative sequences in chapter 6 of the novel. In this chapter, Zeta Brown and four friends—Black Eagle, Mangas, Lady Feathers, and Gilbert—are experiencing an LSD rush while swimming at a lake. The lake is located on private property a hundred miles outside of Los Angeles, not far from Edwards Air Force Base: "home of the strategic Air Command, which keeps B-52s afloat for doomsday" (65–66). The group has come to the lake for a meeting to plan the activities surrounding an upcoming trial. After entering the water, Black Eagle asks Lady Feathers whether she is going to "gang-bang" them. She rejects his advance and tries to steer the conversation toward their political agenda, but Mangas and Gilbert jump in with further allusions to group sex. Mangas, who has taken up "acting" at UCLA, retorts, "I call this orgy to order." Gilbert chimes in lasciviously, "Can we all vote?" (67). Lady Feathers rebukes their remarks as if scolding children, and nothing actually comes of their sexual intimations. The scene nonetheless must be read as offensive to women and men alike. The males, particularly Black Eagle and Mangas, treat Lady Feathers as a sexual object. Perhaps worse, they fail to take her seriously as their group leader, despite the fact that in this scene she is the most committed to the political objectives of the group, which they refer to as the Brown Buffalo Party. On a purely thematic level, these characters, Zeta Brown included, lack political commitment and class consciousness.

But more is going on here than meets the eye. The innuendos of group sex and the relationships among the members of the group reveal a greater tension that unfolds in the narrative's paratactic structure. What happens, for example, if we juxtapose this particular moment—as a discrete unit of the narrative whole—with the ones that immediately follow? Subsequently, the conversation shifts from sexual innuendos to social transformation. Zeta Brown and his friends imagine an egalitarian society, albeit in a slapstick manner: they are tripping on LSD, thus placing in doubt the seriousness of their comments. Nevertheless, Zeta Brown and his friends go through the symbolic motion of stating their desire for social equality and state power: Black Eagle announces, "I think we can run our own country"; Gilbert says he would be happy to receive a parcel of land at the top of a mountain; and Lady Feathers, the most practical among them, states, "Just get me a color TV" (68). Their moment of egalitarian fantasy, however, does not last long. Three white men on a motorboat come along to run them off the property, shooting shotguns into the water to intimidate them, and the members of the Brown Buffalo Party run for their lives half naked and tripping on acid. Some distance from the lake, Zeta Brown stops to catch his breath as he hears the deafening "ROAR" of a B-52 as it passes overhead en route either to or away from Edwards Air Force Base. Even in his intoxicated stupor, Zeta Brown recognizes the symbolic significance of the bomber, "ominous and evil. . . . [I]ts wings wave in the wind from the weight of the bombs it carries in its belly," which will be used to "kill brown babies and fine women and brothers that only want to pick up a chunk of earth and sift it through their fingers." In a rage, he throws rocks at the B-52 in a fruitless effort to bring it down "before it can drop those bombs on downtown LA and East LA and downtown Mongolia or Saigon or

Haiphong or Quang Tri or Tooner Flats and Lincoln Heights or wherever Cockroaches live" (70). The bomber flies away unobstructed as Zeta Brown collapses on the ground, enacting a kind of symbolic death, sand in his mouth, becoming one again with the earth, dust to dust. His merging with the earth evokes nationalist discourse insofar as recovering "lost land" and the feelings of being rooted to a particular geographical location have been central metaphors in nationalist movements. Moreover, Zeta Brown realizes what his commitment to the Party of Brown Buffalos will almost certainly mean "*bang, bang, bang, you're dead!*" (71).

The paratactic logic of this scene sequence requires scrutiny. It lacks apparent connectives that would explain the various moments of the narrative sequence as I have described them, but it nonetheless reflects a movement from → drugs, sexism, escapism → imagining equality and social change → violent repression of egalitarians by private property owners and the state → a renewed commitment to a political strategy that may require armed struggle against the seemingly insurmountable weaponry of an imperialist superpower → intensified repression from the state → the formation of nationalist ideology as a political strategy → the realization that the committed rebel must accept death as a possible outcome of struggle. Now compare the sequential logic of this slapstick scene with the more seriously written sequence that immediately precedes and follows, which has to do with the trial of the East L.A. Thirteen—the trial that the Brown Buffalo Party members were supposed to have discussed during their meeting at the lake.

Historically, the case of the East L.A. Thirteen began when ten thousand Chicano students walked out of five high schools in East Los Angeles in March 1968,[51] two months after Zeta Brown (and Acosta himself) arrived in the city. The students' demands were straightforward and sensible: "[T]hey demanded an end to the racist system in the schools" and "compliance with the [1848] Treaty of Guadalupe Hidalgo, which provided for a bilingual society" (60). The students wanted to be able to study Chicano history and culture in their classes, and they insisted on the hiring of more Chicano teachers. Students and parents were angry at the dismal conditions of schools in Chicano neighborhoods: dilapidated buildings, shortage of books and materials, inadequate funding from the state, overcrowded classrooms, the lack of Spanish-speaking teachers, exceedingly high dropout rates, low test scores, the presence of police on campuses, and the overt racism of the school toward students and their parents. The walkouts—or "Blow Outs" as they were called—lasted only a week before most of the students returned to class. While the immediate crisis was temporarily alleviated as far as the state was concerned, the problems continued to brew in East Los Angeles and elsewhere. The political consciousness and confidence of the Chicano community mushroomed as a result of the Blow Outs, and the protests spread to other cities and states across the Southwest. In an effort to destroy the movement, the state retaliated harshly against the demonstrators. Two months after the East L.A. Blow Outs, the Los Angeles County Grand Jury handed down indictments to thirteen teachers, college students, and community activists, charging them with fifteen counts each of conspiracy to riot.

According to Haney López, the actual "defendants were charged with a variety of misdemeanors, ranging from disturbing the peace to trespassing on school grounds—offenses that would usually result in fines or, at worst, a few days of incarceration."[52] With conspiracy charges, however, the defendants faced extremely stiff sentences: up to forty-five years in prison! Interestingly, the state's plan to intimidate protesters backfired. Rather than subdue Chicano activism, the repressive measures against the defendants further inflamed the Chicano community, and the movement grew. Just as Acosta headed the defense team for the actual defendants in this case, Zeta Brown is the chief counsel of the East L.A. Thirteen in the novel. The point I want to emphasize here is that the narrative logic of the East L.A. Thirteen scene sequence in *Revolt* assumes a pattern that resembles the logic of the slapstick scene sequence: Chicanos, with all their ideological contradictions, imagine social change → they take action in an attempt to effect change → they suffer the full force of state repression → they begin to explore, sometimes desperately, alternative strategies of resistance → they are forced to commit themselves to a higher level of political struggle → they come to understand that death is a possible consequence of their commitment. To some extent, the narrative structure of *Revolt* as a whole can be read as following this same sequential pattern.

Granted, when read thematically, the egalitarian moment of the slapstick scene seems to poke fun at the idea that working-class Chicanos are capable of self-governance, even though this moment could also be read as a strike against machismo. When Black Eagle expresses his desire to "run our own country," Lady Feathers responds, "You can't even fix the sink, *ese*." Structurally, however, the novel somberly traces a pattern of struggle countered by repression that has been repeated over and again whenever "Cockroaches" have attempted to overcome the limitations of their socioeconomic conditions or when they have dared to imagine the possibility of social equality. These characters may indeed express sexist attitudes, the glorification of drug culture, and political cynicism—albeit, in a slapstick mode—but there is nothing frivolous in the novel's critique of social relations and state power. The significance of Acosta's political exposé is to be found in the formal elements of his narrative, while the story's content reveals the author's lighthearted intuitiveness, problematic as his intuition may be. Surely this is what Bruce-Novoa must have had in mind when he stated in Nietzschian terms that *Revolt* "mixes Dionysian content with carefully structured Apollonian form."[53]

As such, Acosta's novel embodies what might be termed an aesthetic of contradiction. The narrator in *Revolt* manifests what some literary theorists call *aporia*—a walking paradox. Zeta Brown can be described as simultaneously obnoxious and charismatic, repugnant and appealing, repellant and seductive, flippant and serious, comic and tragic, misleading and truthful, self-confident and insecure, Dionysian and Apollonian. In this light, would it be farfetched to read the novel as *both* a reflection and a critique of the ideological contradictions of the Chicano Movement?

Juxtaposing Fact and Fiction—or, Lies as Form

As an aesthetic of contradiction, *Revolt* positions facts and fiction against one another formally so as to call into question the authenticity of a narrator who claims to represent the experiences and events of the author. By centering my interpretation of *Revolt* on the logic of the novel's form, I am attempting to avoid some of the problems that have confronted other critics of Acosta's work. Some of these problems, which overlap, can be described as follows: the tendency to read *Autobiography* and *Revolt* at face value rather than figuratively; the urge to take Acosta seriously in a superficial sense rather than reading his novels as satire or as intentional distortions of serious subject matter; the confusion over how to read novels that claim to be autobiographies but in which the author has obviously taken liberties in changing some names, places, dates, and events; (thus) the decision to read *Autobiography* and *Revolt* strictly as autobiographies rather than as novels; the inclination to locate the meaning of the novel exclusively or largely in the personal history, political views, and ideological positions of the author; (thus) the conflation of the author and the narrator, that is, reading Zeta Brown as if he were Acosta; and the proclivity toward thematic interpretations of Acosta's novels at the expense of formal analysis. To clarify further, I am not arguing that critics should refrain from reading *Autobiography* and *Revolt* as autobiographies. They certainly represent many aspects of the author's personal life and ideological commitments, but I hold they are much richer in symbolic content and social significance when read as novels.

Despite the novel's autobiographical veneer, Acosta takes many liberties in changing the names of key figures (including his own), the dates and locations of actual events, and other factual pieces of information: *LA Times*/KMEX reporter Rubén Salazar becomes Roland Zanzibar, LA County sheriff Peter Pitchess is called Sheriff Peaches, Judge Arthur Alarcón is now named Judge Alacran,[54] the Brown Berets are the Chicano Militants, and so forth.[55] Acosta's playful attitude toward the cogency of self-representation should not be taken as naive skepticism. Nor should it be considered an indictment against the genre of autobiography generally. The intentional distortion of facts in *Revolt* and *Autobiography* draws attention to the pseudoautobiographical form the novels assume almost as if to insist that readers rethink the categories of fact and fiction through the lens of intentional deceptions. In *Autobiography*, for example, the narrator lies several times to other characters.[56] On one occasion he claims to be a Samoan; on another he identifies himself as a Black Foot Indian chief from Oklahoma who raises buffaloes. He lies to his family, friends, and lovers. He lies to his students—mainly "San Blas Indians . . . black Jamaicans . . . and brown Panamanians"—in his Bible study class at Chilebre, Panama in 1956, continuing to teach Christianity to them three months after quitting the Baptist church and after coming to the conclusion that religion "was all a crock of shit." He states, "I despised myself for being a hypocrite, but it seemed the right thing to do" (133). He changes his name several times in the two novels, calling himself Oscar Acosta, Brown Buffalo, Henry Hawk, Buffalo Zeta Brown, and Big Bear. In the end, he prefers to be called just plain Zeta. Guajardo complains that the narrator's lies "are means to avoiding his Mexican identity, his culture, and his painful past,"[57] but such a complaint severely misreads the symbolic significance of the narrator's recalibrations of the truth. Rather than criticizing the author for creating a narrator who has a penchant for fabricating stories, critics should welcome the rich complexities of such a scenario. The narrator's lies can be read as formal moments of the narrative that offer self-reflexive commentaries on the difficulties of both representation and the interpretive act. Zeta Brown deliberately lies to other characters (in the same way that Acosta misrepresents facts to his readers as a fiction writer) because he gains more from lying than from attempting to represent facts and events transparently. The interpretation of Acosta's novels must begin with the seemingly obvious but often neglected premise that fiction relies on the manipulation if not the outright distortion of events as recorded and experiences as remembered. More significantly, fiction distorts the truth not only because it is the product of a creative imagination attempting to convey a sense of real experiences in symbolic terms, but also and mainly because fiction writers and the narrators they create tend to reify the social world in their efforts to deliver a sense of immediacy or to produce the effects of realism.

Hunsaker suggests a possible way to interpret Acosta's distortion of facts. He admits a lack of clarity in trying to figure out why Acosta changes some names but not others: "Was he trying to make his book more of a roman à clef and less of a historical document, or was he merely trying to avoid a lawsuit?"[58] Given Acosta's insights as an attorney and his propensity for writing narratives in which the narrators tell blatant lies to others as well as to themselves, the easy answer to Hunsaker's question might be *both*. It is also possible that such changes allowed Acosta the emotional distance to reconstruct a difficult story. In my interpretation of *Revolt*, however, I find it preferable to shift the focus of Hunsaker's question to emphasize less the author's conscious motives for changing factual information and more the effects of such changes on the way we read the novel. That is, I am interested in understanding the significance of *Revolt* as a totality—as well as the novel's engagement *with* totality. This approach requires that I treat the author's personal reasons for writing the novel in the manner he did as just one aspect to consider in determining the novel's social significance and aesthetic quality. In this way, *Autobiography* and *Revolt* taken together can indeed be read as a *roman à clef*. The "clef" or "key," however, that unlocks the symbolic order of the novels will not be found in some secret list of real names and dates that simply need to be inserted in place of their false counterparts. It will instead be discovered in the complex interplay of form and content, in the tension between structure and story, and in the riotous battles that take place between what is normally taken for fact and what is customarily understood as fiction—battles that ultimately take shape as the formal expression of the complex social contradictions of the historical moment that came to bear on Acosta's writing.

Autobiography and *Revolt* complicate and dismantle their external appearance as autobiographies because Acosta repeatedly estranges himself as author from the fictive narrators of his books. Kimberly Kowalczyk takes this premise to heart: she reads *Autobiography* and *Revolt* as novels, but she also seeks to identify the moment in the novels wherein the facts of the narrative cease to be consonant with the actuality of history and Acosta's experiences—wherein autobiography ends and fiction begins. The schism between fact and fiction results in a "distancing between Acosta, the autobiographer, and the 'I' of the autobiography."[59] The narrator of *Autobiography* and *Revolt* shares many similarities with the author. "Nevertheless, he is not Acosta."[60] Logically, then, the separation of author and narrator in *Autobiography* and *Revolt* marks their formal distinction as novels rather than autobiographies, despite the pseudoautobiographical exteriority behind which the novels parade. As such, the eradication of a direct correlation between author and narrator transforms the immediacy of literary self-representation into a far-reaching politico-aesthetic symbolization. I find Kowalczyk's separation of the author and the narrator-protagonist—a separation also emphasized by Frederick Aldama[61]—provocative and useful for my own reading of Acosta's novels, even as I recognize that *Autobiography* and *Revolt* indeed reflect an autobiographical content not because they assume a pseudoautobiographical stance outwardly, but because Acosta's experiences and his ideological views inform both the form and content of his novels.[62]

Richard Weisberg, a scholar in the field of literature and law, has written extensively about lawyer-narrated novels in a manner that may afford an interpretive approach for *Revolt.* Weisberg points out that "lawyers in Flaubert, Dostoevsky, Melville, Kafka, Faulkner, and Camus, or for that matter in Barth, Malamud, and Doctorow . . . influence us to be skeptical of the word, precisely of the word as most effectively employed, by clever, articulate beings in positions of institutional and cultural power."[63] Skepticism of "the word" in *Revolt* can be approached from two perspectives. On the one hand, the narrator takes offense at the way language is manipulated by lawyers, judges, witnesses, and the police. In a much cited passage, Zeta Brown insists that "*every single witness, both prosecution and defense . . . is lying.* Or not telling the truth. The bastards know exactly what we have done and what we have not done. . . . But they have all told their own version of things as they would like them to be" (251). He comes to sense that "truth" is not determined by an absolute relation between language and reality. As Saldívar points out, truth in *Revolt* is determined by the "struggle between embattled groups"[64] and ultimately by the group that possesses the most power. Zeta Brown dramatizes his realization of this fact in the courtroom through his skepticism of legal language and procedures. On the other hand, Acosta is himself a master at manipulating language. Readers should be appalled by the way Acosta appropriates language for deceptive purposes. *Revolt* is not only "one big ironic statement,"[65] as Thwaites adeptly characterizes Acosta's writing. It is also one big lie: one big satirical, farcical, intentional distortion of facts that nonetheless approximates truth. Only it does not do so directly; it sneaks up on truth by way of the back door, so to speak. Zeta Brown is indeed a "truthful liar," as Ramirez notes. In an autobiographical sketch, Acosta himself warns readers not to take him too seriously, but rather to attempt to understand the seriousness of his writing beneath the heap of flippant rhetoric. He writes, "Of course I joke a lot. I'm not always entirely serious. If ever. It is the game I have played all my adult life. I play it even with myself. When all is done it may be that I was nothing but a big fraud. Time will find me out."[66]

Though we may feel inclined to attribute the ideological contradictions of the characters to those of the author himself, we could still recognize the author's ideological contradictions without necessarily diminishing the social critique of the novel as a whole. I arrive at a similar assessment of *The Squatter and the Don* in chapter 2, arguing that Ruiz de Burton's privileged class background does not lessen the sharp social critique of capitalism and the proletarianization of Californios represented in her novel. This same basic argument holds true for *Revolt.* The author's personal beliefs and background certainly leave a significant mark on the novel—it could not be otherwise—but they do not determine the *totality* of the novel's social and aesthetic significance.

Generic Features of the Autobiographical Novel

Of the many liberties Acosta took with factual information in writing *Revolt,* I shall comment briefly on one that may be the most significant: Acosta's decision to place Zeta Brown in Acapulco vacationing in chapter 14 on the day the National Chicano Moratorium held a demonstration in East Los Angeles against the Vietnam War. Acosta himself was in East L.A. for the demonstration and the subsequent police riot.[67] Zeta Brown, however, returns to Los Angeles the day after the demonstration to begin his legal defense. Acosta's decision to remove Zeta Brown from Los Angeles during one of the most significant moments in the history of the Chicano Movement is interesting. But why is this discrepancy between fact and fiction significant? Aside from the obvious legal question of avoiding prosecution or a lawsuit, the discrepancy may simply serve the practical purpose of storytelling—arranging events to produce dramatic effects, or so that they remain consistent with the narrator's personality. In this case,

Zeta Brown has been in Los Angeles involved in the daily struggles of the movement for the past thirty months. He complains about being tired and needing a rest. Thus he decides to travel to Acapulco for relaxation, but the trip also allows him to establish a critical distance from the Chicano Movement to better evaluate the merits of his political work. He becomes a passive detached observer rather than an active participant-observer of the movement. Bruce-Novoa refers to Zeta Brown's sojourn in Acapulco as an escape from the front lines of struggle and as the narrator's "attempt to distance himself from the chaos of his reality."[68] Bruce-Novoa is right, of course, but I shall attempt to complicate chapter 14 even more by pointing out two other significant aspects of Zeta Brown's retreat to Acapulco.

First, the chapter is consistent with the paratactic logic of the novel as a whole. It stands in sharp contrast to the novel's other eighteen chapters; it is the only one in which Zeta Brown is removed from the epicenter of political struggle. The chapter also resonates with themes from other narrative moments in the novel. The story of Lopitos as recounted by Jesús parallels the paratactic structure of the East L.A. Thirteen sequence discussed earlier: "Cockroaches" imagine equality → they take action to achieve their goals → in the process they win some battles → inevitably their victories are followed by violent state repression. The chapter ends as abruptly as it begins. After a summer of drugs, alcohol, and kinky sex with prostitutes and underage girls—a summer of moral corruption—the prose cuts back to political reality with a SLASH! The headlines of the *LA Times* report that Roland Zanzibar has been killed and Corky Gonzales is in jail (195). Zeta Brown immediately calls the Chicano Militants and talks with Black Eagle, but he tells an outrageous *lie:* he reports that he has been in Mexico "working" to establish a sanctuary for political activists escaping persecution. Yet one must wonder: has the entire chapter been constructed as a lie? Zeta Brown pleads with Black Eagle to believe him: "tell the dudes that I've been working. . . . All right?" (197). Can one sense a bit of authorial transparency here—a plea to his audience to grasp the truth behind the lie?

The second point I want to make about Zeta Brown's retreat to Acapulco has to do with the way chapter 14 highlights formal similarities and differences in Acosta's two novels. Because I have been focusing on *Revolt*, it may be helpful to provide a brief description of *Autobiography*'s formal structure before proceeding. *Autobiography* is structured essentially as a dialogue between Oscar, the narrator, and Dr. Serbin, the narrator's "Jewish shrink." With the exception of one brief moment, Serbin never appears as a character in his own right. His presence in the novel surfaces almost exclusively in Oscar's imagination, thoughts, memories, fantasies, and delusions. Oscar is haunted by ten years of psychiatric therapy with the doctor. A. Robert Lee refers to Serbin as Oscar's "accuser . . . whose voice echoes like some mock Freudian throughout"[69] the novel. To build on Lee's insight, we could say that Serbin represents one side of Oscar's contradictory consciousness: the side that recognizes the validity of analyzing his present condition in terms of his past experiences—especially the trauma of being interpellated as a racial, gendered class subject. The other side of Oscar's consciousness—the acid-dropping, paranoid, suicidal side—narrates the entire novel seemingly in search of identity but actually on the run from Serbin. Guajardo states that the psychoanalytical is the least developed aspect of *Autobiography*, an assertion with which I disagree, but he nonetheless makes the following insightful comment: "Serbin becomes Acosta's own worst self, something of an alter-ego, someone that knows him intimately, but also someone who uses that knowledge to exploit his insecurities."[70] The separation between Oscar as the conscious narrative voice and Serbin as a haunting unconscious might be described as a tension between the ego and the superego. But if so, this is an ego in bad faith: an ego that represses the past but is fully aware of that which it has repressed. More simply, Oscar remembers exactly what he wants most to forget. One cannot help but recall Mary Helen Ponce's illuminating declaration: "The memory is a mysterious—and powerful—thing. It forgets what we want most to remember, and retains what we often wish to forget."[71] Oscar fits Ponce's characterization of self-imposed historical amnesia perfectly: he is terrified by a traumatic past, but he is horrified even more by the realization that the past has given substance to an equally terrifying present. Serbin symbolizes Oscar's desire to overcome his fears. Yet Oscar constantly argues with Serbin, criticizes, ridicules, denigrates, curses, and tries to ignore him, but ultimately he cannot escape him—because he cannot escape his historically determined subjectivity. On the surface, Oscar appears to elude Serbin, leaving the doctor behind as he takes flight from San Francisco and goes on a self-intoxicating spree half way across the country. Structurally, however, the Serbin side of the narrator's contradictory consciousness wins out—not because Oscar comes to an enlightened understanding of his identity crisis (he does not, though he thinks he does) but because Serbin constitutes an essential aspect of the novel's form, which can be described as the conflict between a paranoid Chicano subject and his "Jewish shrink" with his "ancient history hangups" (42). To state it differently, Acosta transforms the internal Serbin into a historically conscious psychoanalysis. Serbin's hounding presence places an exclamation point on Oscar's unresolved predicament: the inability of a self-perceiving subject to break free from the confines of a reified consciousness. Thus, *Autobiography* begins and ends in the same way: a naked man standing before a mirror feeling nauseated and revulsed with what he sees.

If *Autobiography* begins and closes with the narrator standing before a mirror, disgusted and confused within his solipsistic prison of self-inspection, *Revolt* begins with a protest demonstration at St. Basil's Cathedral that evolves into a riot against the police, and it ends with the bombing of a courthouse that accidentally kills an innocent Latino man. If Acosta's first novel essentially looks inward, his second novel looks outward. Critics have correctly characterized the movement from *Autobiography* to *Revolt* as a thematic "progression" from a search for individual identity to the realization of cultural/collective identity, but the novels can also be read as a progression of form. *Autobiography* assumes the form of mirrorlike psychic introspection: the self-reflexive account of an alienated subject attempting to understand who he is and why he exists. *Revolt* takes the form of subject formation via social critique: the standpoint of an individual subject looking at himself through the lens of historical events and political struggle. Perhaps more than any other chapter in the two novels, chapter 14 in *Revolt* brings these two formal approaches together. Zeta Brown retreats to Acapulco to reflect on his political activities, but he also immerses himself in a space of psychological self-indulgence (as if standing before a mirror) nearly to the point of self-pity where he calls into question not only the significance of his political activism but the very basis of his existence. In *Autobiography*, the narrator's alter ego is represented by Serbin. In *Revolt*, the Serbin figure is now replaced by Zeta Brown's identical twin brother, Jesús.[72] Looking at his twin, Zeta Brown exclaims, "It is like looking in a mirror . . . he looks just like me" (186). Genaro Padilla reads Jesús as a doppelgänger, Zeta Brown's "other, anti-romantic self,"[73] a shadow self that no one else can see. Formally, Serbin and Jesús perform the same narrative function: they allow the narrator to create an alternative self, a kind of mask or talking prop, through which the narrator can inspect himself from the perspective of the Other. The doppelgänger in both novels is a fictive construct, a lie to one's self that aims to uncover a truth about the self—and in the case of *Revolt*, a truth about political struggle and history—unavailable through direct contemplation. In this respect the two novels are both similar and different. When considered together they constitute a movement from interiority to exteriority, from psychology to history.

The tension between the paratactic antinomies constructed in the novel—competing political strategies, autobiography versus the novel, truth and lies, psychology and history—comes to a head in the narrator's repeated references to death, which serves as a metaphor not only of negation, but of transformation. Death is dramatized most emphatically in chapter 14, which also marks the novel's sharpest critique of the Chicano Movement via the story of Lopitos. Jesús relates this story to Zeta Brown not to point out the *similarities* between Lopitos's struggle and the Chicano Movement, but to emphasize their *differences*. Jesús does not believe that Zeta Brown and the Chicano Militants possess the commitment necessary to achieve victory in their struggle against U.S. racism and capitalism. What Zeta Brown and his cohorts do not understand—and what Lopitos understood perfectly, according to Jesús—is that the political rebel must be committed to death. As Jesús explains, when Lopitos and his people "took over the mountain there was no turning back. . . . It was life or death on the mountaintop. . . . They chose death and they beat it. You've got to accept it, look for it, stick your nose into it and fight your way out of it. You've got to find your death before you can find your life" (188–89). Zeta Brown responds defensively that he received thousands of votes in his run for sheriff and that he is helping to lead the Chicano Movement, but Jesús counters, "It amounts to nothing. It's just an exercise in ego-tripping" (189). Jesús's advice causes Zeta Brown to experience an existential crisis, coming to question the validity of his political commitments. Consistent with the contrastive logic of the novel, *Revolt* pits Chicano cultural nationalism against a kind of political consciousness characterized by the political rebel's acceptance of death as a possible outcome of struggle. The narrator's many references to death, more than any other single motif in the novel, signal the possibility of social transformation. In the final section of this chapter, I shall bring my interpretation of *Revolt* to a close with comments on this last point.

Death as Transformation

The Autobiography of a Brown Buffalo begins in July 1967 and ends in January 1968. *The Revolt of the Cockroach People* picks up where *Autobiography* leaves off, tracing events in Los Angeles from January 1968 to April 1971.[74] Aside from everything else that was going on historically during these politically turbulent years, including the emergence of the Chicano Movement, the period covered by Acosta's two novels witnessed the most intense fighting of the Vietnam War and was marked by a great loss of life for both

U.S. soldiers and the Vietnamese population. During the seven-month period narrated in *Autobiography*, 6,775 U.S. soldiers and 70,000 Vietnamese were killed. During the forty months that transpire in *Revolt*, 35,404 U.S. soldiers and almost 700,000 Vietnamese soldiers and civilians lost their lives in the war.[75] *Autobiography* ends and *Revolt* begins in January 1968, the same month the North Vietnamese Army and the National Liberation Front launched the Tet offensive against the United States and its allies. Over the next two months, 4,000 U.S. soldiers and more than 50,000 Vietnamese were killed in a campaign that not only produced the highest number of daily causalities in the conflict, but eventually proved to be the turning point of the war.

These statistics do not appear in any specificity in *Revolt*. The novel does not represent the Vietnam War; nor does it narrate the lives of soldiers who were directly involved in it.[76] The war nonetheless provides historical substance and background to Zeta Brown's narrative. This is so partly because of the war's pervasive impact on all aspects of social life in the United States during that time, but also because *Revolt* situates the Chicano Movement within an international context. The significance of the Vietnam War becomes most apparent in *Revolt* with the series of events that unfold during and after the Chicano Moratorium Anti-War March, which is one of the central narrative threads in the novel. Zeta Brown describes the purpose of the march as "a protest against the burning of peasants in Vietnam" (209). The centrality of the war as historical backdrop, however, becomes evident in at least two other important ways, one more noticeable than the other. First, Acosta's narrative repeatedly compares and juxtaposes the political struggles of Chicanos with those of Vietnamese rebels. Zeta Brown makes many references, sometimes only in passing, that link the battles of Chicanos against racist police brutality in Los Angeles to those of the anti-imperialist rebels fighting the occupation of Vietnam. For example, he refers to James Francis McIntyre—the Catholic cardinal who orchestrates the planned police attack on Chicano protestors at St. Basil's Cathedral in the novel's opening scene—as a "man who encouraged presidents to drop fire on poor Cockroaches in far-off villages of Vietnam" (13). Zeta Brown also refers to Chicanos as "the Viet Cong of America" and "Tooner Flats [a]s Mylai" (200). Responding to a film showing Whittier Boulevard filled with smoke and flames, police cars burning, cops attacking protesters, and debris scattered in the streets, Zeta Brown states, "An ordinary day in Saigon, Haiphong, Quang Tri and Tooner Flats" (201). In *Revolt*, racism against Chicanos is not merely a local issue; it is not even strictly a national issue. It is a systemic problem that transgresses U.S. borders, a symptom of the political and economic contradictions of global capitalism, intensified by U.S. military aggression in Vietnam. Acosta endeavored to show that the relatively small struggles in East Los Angeles against police brutality and a racist educational system were part of an international class struggle against capitalism. In this regard, I think Alurista is partly correct when he states that the "object" of critique in *Revolt* is "the Yankee militarist empire and its 'democratic' gymnastics."[77]

Less noticeably, *Revolt* focuses not only on the object but on the subject of this critique: it displays a profound curiosity about the kind of subject committed enough to risk death fighting against U.S. imperialism. The Vietnam revolutionary becomes the ideal political subject against which Zeta Brown compares the commitment of the Chicano militant. Acosta was certainly not the only thinker of his day to inquire into such issues. In an essay entitled "The Revolted," published in 1967, Carl Oglesby, a former president of the Students for a Democratic Society, analyzes both the rebel's reasons for fighting and the misconceptions of many Americans about why people rebel. He tells of a U.S. Special Forces major who was extremely impressed with the "high motivation" and "high dedication" of NLF guerrilla fighters after a particularly hard-fought battle at Plei Me in 1965. The major described the rebels as "the finest soldiers I have ever seen in the world except Americans. I wish we could recruit them. . . . I wish I knew what they were drugging them with to make them fight like that."[78] The major, of course, wanted to understand the "guerrilla fighters" to know how to defeat them. Nonetheless, his comments, according to Oglesby, get to the heart of the question: What makes the rebel fight in spite of the likelihood of death? Seemingly influenced by the existentialist underpinnings of writers like Oglesby and others in the antiwar movement of the 1960s, Acosta displays an interest in understanding the rebel as a political figure. This interest is played out in *Revolt* through the narrator's repeated references to death.

Death recurs in *Autobiography* also, but in a much different way. In several scenes Oscar imagines himself dead. At these moments death performs essentially the same narrative function as does Serbin: death becomes an Other in which the narrator observes himself from a detached perspective. On one occasion, Oscar takes pleasure in observing his imagined funeral, paying particular attention to the grief of a girlfriend and a teacher who happen to have the same initials as his mother (95). Serbin finds Oscar's death fantasy fascinating from his therapeutic point of view. Oscar's many imagined deaths in *Autobiography*, however, serve no purpose other than to allow the narrator to assume a psychoanalytical posture: Oscar's death wish in *Autobiography* has been metamorphosed; it is a psychosocial death rather than an actual death.[79] The narrator's imagined death contains no social content beyond the construction of subjectivity via self-analysis. By contrast, the deaths in *Revolt* are all fundamentally and specifically political: Roland Zanzibar and two other Chicanos are shot by sheriffs deputies at the police riot following the August 29 antiwar demonstration; Lopitos is assassinated either by the Mexican police or the CIA; a nameless Latino man is killed in a courthouse bombing intended to kill a judge; and Robert Fernandez is killed by police who then conspire to cover up his murder. Cumulatively, the deaths in *Revolt*, like the references to the war in Vietnam, gesture toward a totality that surpasses the immediacy of Chicano experience in East Los Angeles.

Zeta Brown pays considerably more attention to Robert's death than to the others. Robert, a young Chicano, dies while in police custody shortly after being taken in for questioning. The police claim Robert committed suicide; his relatives accuse the police of murder, and they retain Zeta Brown to represent them. As attorney for the family, Zeta Brown requests that an autopsy be performed to search for evidence of death at the hands of another. He also agrees to direct the autopsy; essentially, he tells the medical staff where to cut the body and how much to cut. When Zeta Brown arrives at the morgue, he is overwhelmed by the sight of dead bodies but forces himself to look at them: "Don't turn away from it, goddamnit! Don't be afraid of bare-ass naked death" (99). But the horror of looking at corpses pales in comparison to watching the mutilation of Robert's body during the autopsy. Zeta Brown not only feels personally responsible for having Robert's body exhumed only to be butchered, he internalizes the young man's "second death" and makes it his own. "For the rest of my born days," he cries, "I will suffer the knowledge of your death and your second death and your ashes to *my* ashes, your dust to *my* dust" (104; emphasis added). As Paredes explains, watching a team of pathologists "cut out chunks of the boy's face, neck, and chest . . . reminds [Zeta Brown], in the strongest possible terms, that in Los Angeles, Mexican Americans, dead or alive, count for nothing."[80] The killing of Robert by the police and the failure of the coroner's inquest to determine homicidal intent signify first and foremost a sharp condemnation of a racist criminal justice system in the United States. The subject of death, however, also reflects Zeta Brown's conceptions of art to which he alludes in declaring, "I first encountered death as a world of art" (89), after witnessing Robert's autopsy. In describing the mutilation of Robert's body, Zeta Brown's language slips into an almost exaggerated paratactic style.

> Slit. One slice. Slit. Up goes the chin. Lift it right up over the face . . . the face? The face goes up over the head. The head? The head is the face. Huh? *There is no face!* . . . The face is hanging down the back of the head. The face is a mask. The mouth is where the brain . . . The nose is at the back of the neck. The hair is the ears. The brown nose is hanging where the neck. . . . Get your goddamn hand out of there. (103)

In *Revolt,* death becomes a metaphor for Zeta Brown's conception of art—with literature as the pertinent art form—because death signifies negation and transformation. Accordingly, literature does not merely reproduce an object; it negates the object, transforms it into something else, a new object, qualitatively different from the original. Robert's mutilated body is no longer Robert; it has been transformed into something else. Zeta Brown affirms, "This ain't Robert no more. It's just a . . . . no, not a body . . . body is a whole . . . this is a joke" (102). The racist fragmentation (or reification) of Robert's body requires an alternative conception of totality as cause, but Zeta Brown has no recourse to such an alternative with his limited worldview. Death establishes the conceptual model for the making of a new political subject in Zeta Brown's world because it signifies the symbolic annihilation of one kind of identity and its transformation into a new and qualitatively different condition of existence.

In the final pages of *Revolt,* Zeta Brown participates in a bombing at the Los Angeles County Hall of Justice. He and his friends plant a bomb in a restroom on the floor directly below the office of Judge Alacran, hoping to destroy the judge's chambers and kill the judge. But the bombers succeed only in killing a Latino bystander by mistake. The fact that Acosta ends *Revolt* with the death of a Latino killed by Chicano militants in a political action aimed at a representative of the state in a novel about the Chicano Movement is fraught with political symbolism—especially in light of the fact that the dead man is not given a voice, a name, a history, or the consideration afforded the deaths of Robert Fernandez and Roland Zanzibar. Given these observations, I propose to read the novel's final scene not as a political blunder on the part of inept militants or as Zeta Brown's defeatist demoralization, but as a symbolic negation of failed Chicano nationalism—a negation that necessarily implies transformation to a broader level of political commitment in the manner prescribed by Jesús. When Jesús insists that the Chicano activist must be committed to death, he argues essentially that the political subject must be committed to a kind of negation that leads to social transformation. Zeta Brown comments on the presuppositions of such a transformation late in the novel:

> Lots more will die before this fight is over. The truce we've signed for the moment doesn't mean anything. Just because the Viet Cong or the Chicanos temporarily lay down their arms doesn't prove shit. . . . Somebody still has to answer for Robert Fernandez and Roland Zanzibar. Somebody still has to answer for all the smothered lives of all the fighters who have been forced to carry on, chained to a war for Freedom just like a slave is chained to his master. (257–58)

Zeta Brown's prognostication of future battles falls short of an advanced theory of social revolution despite his steadfast resolve as expressed in this passage. *Revolt* after all is fiction, not political theory, and the narrator is an imperfect rebellious Chicano writer and a disgruntled lawyer, not a social theorist. Nonetheless, by the end of the novel Zeta Brown conveys a desire (one that he does not actually achieve in the novel) to transcend the narrow limits of Chicano identity politics—not his Chicano-ness, but the lack of commitment he encounters in himself and others involved in the Chicano Movement and the antiwar movement. He cannot change the fact of his ethnic background, the place of his birth, the names of his parents, or the color of his skin; these aspects of his existence are merely accidents of history and circumstance. He seeks rather to shed the limited perspective of the social identities he has criticized throughout the novel in favor of a broader, more critical world outlook—internationalist in scope. Interestingly, he evokes the Hegelian master-slave dialectic to describe the predicament of the kind of political figure he imagines as the ideal rebel type. Chicanos and the Viet Nam Cong San now merge into a singular designation—that of the slave locked in a duel to the death against a common enemy. If one senses a resigned unhappiness in this passage it is because Zeta Brown feels that Freedom as an ideal abstraction is not achievable under the present conditions, perhaps not even in his lifetime. The slave merely exchanges one kind of servitude for another—giving up submission to U.S. imperialism for absolute commitment to social revolution. Some readers may find the slave's alternatives depressing: a choice between two masters. In "The Revolted," Oglesby asks, "[W]here is the freedom of this ex-slave who, instead of cutting cane, is now sharpening knives? That [s]he has removed himself [or herself] from one discipline to another does not hide the fact that [s]he remains under discipline."[81] But the two disciplines are not equivalent, and the difference lies in this: whereas to be a slave to the master is a dehumanizing condition, to choose to be chained to the fight for Freedom is a humanizing affair. Nonetheless, by the novel's end Zeta Brown finds himself confronting—what we might call, appropriately—an arrested dialectic: he remains firm in his commitment to fight in a "war" he believes cannot be won—at least not "for the moment."

Cockroaches on the Page

As we have seen in chapters 2 and 3, the novels of Ruiz de Burton and Acosta have been concentrically situated within Chicano literary studies, in part, because they represent Mexican American experience vividly, but also because they render with realistic transparency the class politics of two watershed moments in Chicano history. *The Squatter and the Don* critiques the onset of Mexican American racialization and proletarianization in the late nineteenth century, a process that would continue throughout the twentieth century. *Revolt*, to recall Roberto Schwarz's definition of literary realism,[82] "captures society in motion," providing an aesthetic solution to a key historical moment of sustained protest and revolt during the late 1960s against the various forms of subordination associated with capitalist accumulation and its effects on Chicanos. There are differences, however, between these two novels. Whereas the key zone of reification in *The Squatter* is democratic liberalism, as articulated by Ruiz de Burton's narrator, the central mode of reification in *Revolt* is cultural nationalism. Both novels, however, partake in dereifying these ideological discourses, the former in the contradictory standpoint of the narrator, the second in the paratactic narrative logic and writing style of the author. For this reason, both novels can be considered instances of epistemological realism, as defined in chapter 1, despite the fact that *The Squatter* is considered a historical romance and *Revolt* assumes modernist techniques in its flamboyant and chaotic narrative style.

In the next two chapters, I will be analyzing the eccentric novels of Danny Santiago and Cecile Pineda in an effort to reassess the criteria critics employ in determining the Chicano-ness of Chicano novels. This reassessment will involve questioning the boundaries traditionally established around conceptions of the Chicano novel and suggesting a need for their deconstruction. I hope to elucidate the strong similarities between paradigmatic and eccentric novels in Chicano literature within the context of the categories that have been guiding this book: reification, totality, realism, and standpoint, in addition to liberalism, nationalism, cultural authenticity, and class consciousness. If Acosta's paradigmatic novels were considered threatening to Chicano nationalists because, as Mendoza explains, they were perceived as revealing "in-group dynamics, weaknesses, or contradictions,"[83] then the eccentric novels of Santiago and Pineda, traditionally excluded from Chicano literature, have been perceived—if not in word then in deed—as posing an even greater threat, considering they have been almost unilaterally neglected by critics of Chicano literature. It should come as no surprise, then, that the mode of reification that I shall be targeting in the next chapter on Danny Santiago's *Famous All Over Town* is cultural authenticity.

Before tending to that issue, though, a few final comments on Acosta are in order. Cultural nationalism in *Revolt* is represented as a response to Chicano racialization, but the self-fashioning of racial identities creates a whole new set of contradictions—different in political substance, but just as problematic in effect. The paratactic style of *Revolt*, however, suggests a standpoint that critiques nationalism and the political contradictions of the Chicano Movement, establishing a formal pattern or trajectory from a reified consciousness to a standpoint beyond reification: class subjects feel the effects of racialization → they become politicized → imagine social change → take action to effect change → suffer the effects of state repression → explore alternative strategies of resistance → commit themselves to a higher level of political struggle → and come to understand that death is a possible outcome of their commitment. Ironically—and tragically—Acosta himself went missing a year after the publication of *Revolt*. Eventually, amid rumors that he had been killed in a drug deal gone bad or assassinated by the CIA, he was declared legally deceased. Despite Acosta's untimely disappearance and death, the voice and personality of his narrator remain with the reader long after finishing the novel and setting it down. Like a ghostly unconscious, or like the visual line drawings of cockroaches creeping across the pages of the novel, the urgency and immediacy of Acosta's narrative style are haunting reminders of the ever-present potential of revolt by the cockroach people.

4

THE DEREIFICATION OF CULTURAL AUTHENTICITY

Santiago's *Famous All Over Town*

> James is not a Latino and his work should not be valued as a Hispanic work or as a work that sheds any particular "insider's" knowledge about Hispanic East Los Angeles. It should be valued as a work about Latinos by a non-Hispanic. Let it stand muster on its own merit—not on a fable of identity.
>
> —Felipe de Ortego y Gasca, "Danny Santiago and the Ethics of Deception"

> The book, the book. That's the important thing.
>
> —Danny Santiago (Daniel James), quoted in Burt A. Folkart, "Daniel James Who Masqueraded as a Latino"

UNLIKE THE NOVELS OF Ruiz de Burton and Acosta, which have figured paradigmatically in Chicano literary studies, Danny Santiago's *Famous All Over Town*[1] remains eccentrically situated in Chicano literature, largely because Santiago himself was not a Chicano. In this chapter I shall argue that, despite its marginality within Chicano literary studies, *Famous All Over Town* contributes to a comprehension of the possibilities and limits of Chicano novels insofar as it simultaneously represents Chicano experience and contests cultural authenticity, by which I mean the reification of ethnic identification categories. A compelling novel about a working-class Chicano family living in East Los Angeles in the early 1960s, *Famous* implicitly raises questions concerning cultural authenticity: What determines the

Chicano-ness of a Chicano novel? Some writers and scholars have proposed that the ethnicity of the author is the primary determinant of a literary work's authenticity. Poet Ricardo Sánchez, for example, writes that "Chicano literature can only be written by Chicanos, for only Chicanos understand the nuance of the Chicano way of life from a living/feeling/existential/experiential perspective—others can write about how they observe us, but they cannot possibly know why and how we valuate life, for that is a cultural/linguistic process."[2] But *Famous*, given its thematic content along with the circumstances surrounding its production and reception, broaches the question: Is it possible for a non-Chicano author to write a novel that represents Chicano experiences convincingly—a novel that effectively enters the "cultural/linguistic process" that Sánchez refers to? If so, how does an author acquire—to use Felipe de Ortego y Gasca's words from the epigraph—an "insider's knowledge" of Chicano experience?

In many of the novel's theme-packed scenes, Santiago explores the problematic of what it means to possess an "insider's knowledge" of ethnic experience. In one such scene, the novel's fourteen-year-old narrator, Chato, pays a visit to Max Pilger, a sympathetic but somewhat idealistic school counselor. Pilger recognizes Chato's potential, despite the boy's poor grades. But the counselor remains puzzled by a dramatic drop in Chato's IQ test scores from 135 to 95 in just one year. He decides to examine Chato himself with a series of Rorschach inkblot tests and other images. Chato reads all the images pessimistically, while Pilger counters with more optimistic interpretations. The boy says of one image, "A giant man-eating butterfly [with] blood dripping from its mouth." The counselor explains that most people see "happy dancing girls." Pilger asks Chato why he sees sadness in all the pictures; the boy replies that all the pictures are sad. "The sadness is in you, son," Pilger says. "I don't see sadness at all." Then Chato blurts out, "You're not a Mexican." Without understanding the profundity of his brusque comment, rooted in the practical experience of growing up Chicano in East Los Angeles during the 1950s and early 1960s, Chato insinuates that Pilger cannot comprehend what it means to be a Chicano because he comes from a different, more privileged background. Pilger pauses before responding with his own equally incisive words: "No, Rudy. I'm not a Mexican. I'm a Jew." He describes his experience growing up poor in New York City tenements, having to fight the anti-Semitism of teachers who would make fun of his "Jew-boy haircut" and "oiyoi accent." Even as Pilger recognizes his lack of firsthand knowledge of what it means to live as a Chicano, he suggests that his background as a Jew enables him to form knowledgeable opinions about Chato's personal history. Pilger raises an extremely important issue: if we fail to recognize a common ground or mediatory space within which the experiences of others can be represented, interpreted, and comprehended, we will remain forever locked in a quagmire of cultural relativism, where epistemic access remains primarily, if not entirely, the property of those who possess firsthand experience.[3]

We can safely assume that Santiago reflected on his own situation when he wrote this scene, years before John Gregory Dunne scandalously disclosed Santiago's "real" identity to the literary world. Dunne published an article in the *New York Review of Books* sixteen months after the novel's release, revealing that Santiago's birth name was Daniel Lewis James and that he was not a young Chicano fiction writer from East Los Angeles, as most readers had assumed, but a "septuagenarian ex-Stalinist aristocrat [originally] from Kansas City,"[4] a "prize-winning playwright," and a "graduate of Andover and Yale."[5] Moreover, he was an "Anglo" and a former member of the Communist Party.[6] Consequently, scores of critics and educators effectively censored *Famous*, excluding it from Chicano literature courses and research projects. Dunne's article ignited strong responses from both critics and supporters of the novel; the respondents focused mainly on issues of ethnic authenticity and authorship. As Jonah Raskin puts it, Dunne "opened the floodgates to cultural controversy."[7]

Many of those who criticized James were angered because they felt he had exploited the use of a Latino pseudonym for the purpose of getting his novel published while Chicano and Chicana writers generally continued to be ignored by mainstream publishers. They directed this anger primarily at the author, not at the novel itself, but their attitude toward the author resulted in the novel being shunned or deemed inauthentic. In criticizing James for his use of a Latino pseudonym, critics implicitly posited that fiction writers can represent specific experiences authentically only if they have lived those experiences firsthand. This assertion also implies a determinate relation between an author's personal background and the aesthetic value of the literary work. I discuss the criticisms of James's use of a Latino pseudonym at greater length subsequently. For now it is enough to clarify that James worked as a volunteer social worker in East Los Angeles for more than two decades, so he was not entirely isolated from the kinds of experiences he writes about in *Famous*. But we must also admit that he wrote about a reality he had not experienced personally: he did not know what it *felt* like to be born into a Mexican working-class family or to live in

East Los Angeles for the first fourteen years of his life, as does Chato. How then could he write such a compelling representation of a Chicano family?

The content of James's personal experiences differs from that of the characters he develops in *Famous*, but the author and his protagonist nonetheless share a common ground: both experience the collapse of a belief system—different in content but similar in form. A parallel can be drawn between the novel and the author's life, between the destruction of Chato's world and the collapse of James's confidence in the Communist Party, which he quit in 1948. Nowhere is the parallel between the author's Marxist past and Chato's story more evident than in the following passage from James's 1984 interview with Raskin:

> I realized that the Chato character was me. . . . Of course, he has none of the advantages that I had. He didn't go to college, and didn't study Marxism. He comes from a poor Mexican family and has little formal education and no ideology. But Chato and I are also very much alike. We're both writers. Like him I wanted to put my mark on the wall. His ruined street became all the constructs of my past, including the Communist Party, which had collapsed for me.[8]

As implied in the preceding quotation, James did not set out to write a novel deliberately about the collapse of a Chicano family in the 1960s as a way of representing his loss of faith in the Party, even though this loss apparently weighed heavily on his mind as he was writing the novel and afterwards. I do not propose to argue, however, that *Famous* correlates allegorically to the author's political views. Rather, to remain consistent with my readings of *The Squatter and the Don* and *The Revolt of the Cockroach People* in the previous two chapters, I hold that the social and literary significance of *Famous* goes beyond both the reified consciousness of its narrator and the author's immediate purposes in writing the novel; it lies rather in the novel's aspiration toward a representation of the link between Chicano identity and society as a whole. That is to say, the novel is driven by its attempt to dereify notions of cultural authenticity that restrict our understanding of the complex interconnections between Chicano identity and history writ large.

The author's engagement in class struggle and antiracist practices at many levels from the 1930s to the 1980s nurtured his ability to gain an "insider's" perspective on the specific Chicano experiences he writes about in *Famous*. Epistemic access was made possible by James's personal history on two fronts: his Marxist praxis during his early years, prior to testifying before the House Committee on Un-American Activities (HUAC) in 1951; and his involvement with the Chicano community in his post-HUAC years. To develop my argument, I devote considerable space to examining Santiago's life: his accomplishments as a writer, his membership in the Communist Party in the 1930s, his participation in Party debates over the doctrine of "art as a weapon" in the 1940s, his blacklisting by the Hollywood movie industry in the 1950s, his social activism in a Chicano neighborhood from the 1950s to the 1970s, and ultimately his writing of a novel (which he wrote in the 1970s and 1980s) about a working-class Chicano family living in East Los Angeles in the early 1960s before the emergence of the Chicano Movement. These experiences gave Santiago/James the grounding—or epistemic access—to be able to write *Famous All Over Town* from a Chicano standpoint. Notwithstanding its Chicano-ness, *Famous* has not been well received since its publication in 1983. It has been largely rejected or ignored by scholars and teachers of Chicano literature in the main because the author was not a Chicano, but also because problematic notions of cultural authenticity continue to influence ethnic literary studies generally.

In an effort to continue developing the arguments I have been making up to now, I shall broaden my critique of reification as it relates to *Famous All Over Town.* In chapters 2 and 3 I analyzed reification in relation to the author's class position, the narrator's ideological standpoint, and the stylistic-structural components of the narrative. To some extent, I shall read *Famous* from these categorical perspectives as well. But I also argue more centrally that reification in *Famous* can be conceptualized in the author-reader-text relation, made evident, in part, by the novel's negative reception among critics of Chicano literature after Santiago's non-Chicano identity had been revealed publicly.

The rest of this chapter will be organized in three sections. In the first section, I discuss briefly a methodological approach that treats biographical criticism as a *mediation* (or common ground) to explore the points of connection between an author's values, beliefs, and practices, and the social totality out of which they emanate. In the second section, I examine James's personal history, focusing on his accomplishments as a writer, his membership in the Communist Party, his blacklisting by the Hollywood movie industry, and his social activism in East Los Angeles. I also review the novel's reception, highlighting the manner in which *Famous* was largely, though not entirely, rejected or ignored by critics because of the author's background. I read Santiago's personal history not as a set of contextual factors that provide unhindered access to the novel's content, but as a mediation that elucidates the novel's standpoint with regard to the categories of race and class as they relate to Chicano experience. In the final section, I turn my attention to the novel itself, which relies on formal mechanisms to formulate a self-reflexive critical commentary aimed at the dereification of cultural authenticity in literary representation and interpretation, an aspect of the novel that, ironically, was overlooked by critics who condemned *Famous* because it was not, in their view, an authentic Chicano novel.

Biographical Criticism as Mediation

In the pages that follow, I discuss Daniel James's personal history in some detail, employing a critical approach that makes use of biographical criticism as a mediation to bridge the gap between the novel and its object. In its most fundamental sense, the concept of mediation stands opposed to that of immediacy. Mediations can be thought of as totalities (imagined or real) against which the particularities of a given existence are measured; their analysis allows for a critical approach that transcends and gives depth to the empirically given. Mediation is not strictly a Marxist concept, but it is a central critical category for any dialectical theory of literature; it enables the critic to analyze the correlation between the particularities of a literary work and the larger social framework that gives meaning to those particularities. We might think of mediation, in one sense, as the "common ground" that enables Pilger to comprehend Chato's social experiences, despite the fact that he's "not a Mexican." The critique of mediations also allows for an interpretive method aimed at deciphering the various dialectical categories that constitute a novel's form: subject/object, consciousness/being, representation/referent, and so on. Fredric Jameson defines mediation in the classical Marxist-Hegelian sense as "the dialectical term for the establishment of relationships between, say, the formal analysis of a work of art and its social ground." It will prove useful to quote several passages by Jameson on mediation to fully explain my use of this concept. In literary terms, mediation can be understood as "a process of *transcoding*, as the invention of a set of terms . . . such that the same terminology can be used to analyze and articulate two quite distinct types of objects or 'texts,' or two very different structural levels of reality."[9] Jameson explains further that "by being able to use the same language about . . . quite distinct objects or levels of an object, we can restore, at least methodologically, the lost unity of social life, and demonstrate that widely distant elements of the social totality are ultimately part of the same global historical process." The analysis of mediations can lead us to suggest that "the same essence" is at work in the literature of racialized groups and the relations of production within which the literature was produced. With regard to Santiago's novel, we might wonder if "the same essence" is at work in *Famous* and, say, Tomás Rivera's . . . *y no se lo tragó la tierra*—that is to say, the racialization, proletarianization, and criminalization of Chicanos in the middle decades of the twentieth century.

Marxism employs a fairly large number of mediations or "mediatory codes, the most obvious ones being social class, mode of production, the alienation of labor, commodification, the various ideologies of Otherness (sex or race), and political domination."[10] In *The Political Unconscious*, Jameson draws on reification as a primary "mediatory code," particularly in his study of Joseph Conrad, but he also calls upon other codes. In the chapter entitled "Realism and Desire," he uses biographical criticism as a mediatory code to analyze "the problem of the subject" in Balzac's *La Vieille Fille (An Old Maid)* and *La Rabouilleuse (The Black Sheep)*. He distinguishes his approach, however, from two other types of biographical criticism, common to literary studies. The first can be identified as the type "against which the older New Criticism very properly reacted"[11] and which sought to determine the meaning of a literary work by drawing a direct correlation between the text and the author's social, intellectual, or personal background. Jameson refers to the second type of biographical criticism as "psychobiography," which reads the author's psychological profile as a key that parallels the content of the literary work in question. These two types of biographical criticism are based on the assumption that the significance of a literary work can be located primarily in the personal experiences or the psychical conflicts of the author, positing the author's life as the source, origin, or ultimate determining factor of the literary work's significance. Both types of criticism err by not treating the author's personal history as only one of many factors to consider in determining the various levels of socially symbolic significance in a narrative. Both arrive at faulty conclusions because they are informed by the logic of a genetic fallacy: what is true about the author must be true about the literary work.

As an alterative to these two author-centered approaches, Jameson argues for a kind of biographical criticism "neither as a set of empirical facts, nor as a textual system of characteristic behavior, but rather as the traces of the symptoms of a fundamental *family situation* which is at one and the same time a fantasy master narrative."[12] Three aspects of this passage deserve attention. First, the relation between an author's personal life and the literary text should be read not as a causal relationship wherein the author's life determines the meaning of the text, but as a symptomatic relation in which the narrative manifests, thematically and formally, "traces of the symptoms" of the historically specific social contradictions that shaped the life and psyche of the author. In the case of James/Santiago, these contradictions were linked to the sharpening of class struggle in the United States during the depression years, the emergence and decline of the proletarian literature movement of the 1930s, World War II and the global fight against fascism in the 1940s, the anti-Communist McCarthyism of the 1950s, and the formation of a Chicano literary movement in the 1960s. Second, biographical criticism as mediation allows for a reading of the literary work not as a reproduction of the author's psyche, but as the construction of a "fantasy master narrative"—not as psychology, but as ideology. The representation of ideology in the novel lays bare the "symptoms" of a social totality that resists representation. The novel's ideology does not merely mystify the social world; it also reveals much about the social world's structures and relations. This method implies an inverted logic: the critic does not begin with the "base" to arrive at conclusions about the "superstructure"; on the contrary, the critic starts with a critique of ideological "symptoms" (superstructure) in the narrative and works backward to draw inferences about the social system (base) that gave rise to those symptoms. Third, in reading the novels of Balzac, Jameson emphasizes the conflicts within the author's immediate family, in particular, Balzac's relationship with his mother and father. Drawing on Jean-Paul Sartre's theory of mediation as articulated in *Search for a Method*, Jameson argues for the "institution of the family [as] the basic mediation between the experience of the child (object of psychoanalysis) and the class structure of society at large (object of Marxist analysis)."[13] In the present work, I am arguing that James's political commitments can serve as the "basic mediation" between ethnic identity as experience and class as structure.

Sartre employs his theory of mediations in *The Family Idiot*, which includes a meticulous study of Gustave Flaubert's family. He argues for the need to analyze Flaubert's family relations as a topic worthy of critical inquiry in its own right before arriving at conclusions about the social class contradictions and psychoanalytical repressions represented in Flaubert's novels. He effectively demonstrates his conviction that the dialectical critic must travel the long and arduous road of mediations before attempting to disclose a sense of immediacy. That is to say, one must not totalize too quickly. Despite the preference he gives to the family as the "basic mediation," Sartre also identifies an array of other possible mediations: groupings based on ethnicity, race, sexuality, and political affiliations. The "mediatory code" or "invented set of terms" that assumes the role of a transcoding device in my interpretation of *Famous* lies not in the author's immediate family, but in two sets of family-like relations: James's affiliation and disaffiliation with the Communist Party, which assumed for him the role of a kind of second family; and his relationship with families in a Chicano neighborhood, where he was essentially adopted into the families of others, becoming a *compadre* and a *padrino* to numerous individuals in East Los Angeles. Not coincidently, the novel itself tells the story of a symbolic family, which collapses under the weight of its internal contradictions. The centrality of the category of family in *Famous* can be considered the point of entry for an analysis of mediations. With that stated, I shall now take an extended excursus into James's personal history to discuss specific aspects of his family-like relationships—the Communist Party and the Chicano community—that will then serve as a transcoding device for a close reading of the novel itself.

Politics and Literature: A Personal History

Daniel Lewis James was born in Kansas City, Missouri, in 1911, the only child of wealthy parents. His paternal grandfather was the first cousin of the notorious Frank and Jesse James. Unlike his famous outlaw cousins, however, James's grandfather was part of the Missouri gentry: he attended Brown University, married a woman who graduated from Vassar, and started a business in Kansas City, selling imported china and fine glassware to the social elite throughout the Midwest. James's father graduated from Yale and became the manager of the family business. Daniel James graduated from Andover Academy in 1928. Five years later, he received a bachelor's degree in Greek classics from Yale. During his senior year in college, at the height of the Great Depression, James joined the John Reed Club, a branch of the Communist Party that encouraged young writers to promote working-class culture and politics in their work. A few years later, James joined the Young Communist League, another Party structure. During this time, he was also actively involved in the activities of the Unemployed Council, whose main objective was to win unemployment insurance for workers.[14]

From the beginning of his career, James's literary interests were clearly informed by his politics. In 1936 he collaborated with his father in writing a play entitled *Pier 17* about the San Francisco longshoreman's strike of 1934, but the play was never produced. One year later, he played a small part in *Marching Song*, a play written by John Howard Lawson. A Communist, Lawson recruited James to the Party in 1938. From 1938 to 1940, James worked with Charlie Chaplin as an assistant screenwriter for the classic film *The Great Dictator*. His name appears on the credits as "assistant director." When the Nazis invaded the Soviet Union in 1941, he contributed to the antifascist effort by writing a play entitled *Winter Soldiers*, in which guerrilla groups from occupied territories on the eastern front force a six-hour delay of a Nazi train en route to Moscow, thwarting the Nazis' plans to invade and occupy that city.[15] Burns Mantle included *Winter Soldiers* in *The Best Plays of 1942–1943*, stating, "It embodies the will to win of freedom-loving peoples all over the world and is, I think, one of the truly significant dramas inspired by the global war."[16] Years later, James felt less positive about the play than did his critics. In his 1984 interview with Raskin, he describes *Winter Soldiers* as a "bad play that got good reviews. . . . It was art as a social weapon, but there was a lot more weapon than there was art."[17] Not surprisingly, Dunne characterized the play as "pure propaganda" and "a true Stalinist play."[18] In 1944, James collaborated with his wife, Lilith James, in writing the play *Bloomer Girl*. Lilith developed the original idea at a Party workshop on women's rights. The drama takes place in the antebellum South, where a group of progressive women become politically active, exchanging their hoop skirts for bloomers and helping in the operation of an underground railroad. The play opened on October 4, 1944, in New York and ran on Broadway for 654 performances over eighteen months.[19] In the late 1940s, James worked with Paul Robeson in writing a dramatic adaptation of Howard Fast's novel *Freedom Road*, a fictional account of the Reconstruction era, and in 1948 James wrote a novel entitled *The Hockadays*,[20] which was never published.

In 1951, three years after James had severed ties with the Party, Richard Collins, his friend and a former member of the Party, "purged himself" before HUAC, naming 152 persons in the movie industry as Communist members or sympathizers. "In private session, Collins not only named Dan James as a Party member but also suggested that he might be a cooperative witness."[21] Subpoenaed in the summer of that year, the Jameses appeared before HUAC on September 19, 1951.[22] About the hearings, Lilith James said, "They thought we would snitch,"[23] but the

Jameses refused to cooperate, and thirty-three years elapsed before they spoke again to Collins—and then, only by telephone. After the HUAC hearing, James was blacklisted and could no longer find work in Hollywood. During this time, he first began to use the pseudonym Danny Santiago and write stories about Mexican American life in East Los Angeles, though none of these stories was ever published. During the next years, James used the pen name Daniel Hyatt, while writing the screenplays for two low-budget monster movies: *The Giant Behemoth* (1959) and *Gorgo* (1961). In 1970 three of his short stories appeared under the Santiago pen name: "The Somebody" came out in *Redbook;* "A Message from Home" and "Goldilocks and the Three Beers" were printed in *Playboy.* "The Somebody" was subsequently reprinted in several anthologies, including Martha Foley's *Best American Short Stories, 1971.* The short stories eventually evolved into *Famous All Over Town,* which James began to submit to publishers in 1976. After sixteen rejections, it was accepted by Simon and Schuster in 1982 and published in March 1983. A year later, at the age of seventy-three, Santiago won the prestigious Richard and Hilda Rosenthal Foundation Award, sponsored by the American Academy and Institute of Arts and Letters, but his failure to show at the ceremony on May 16, 1984, to receive the award and a five-thousand-dollar prize fueled suspicion about his identity.[24] Two months later Dunne published his article revealing Santiago's personal history.

For more than two decades, beginning in the late 1940s, Dan and Lilith James worked as volunteer social workers with the Los Angeles Church Federation. Their work was concentrated in the Lincoln Heights community of East Los Angeles. During those years, they started several youth clubs, which involved young people in social and cultural activities and promoted education as an alternative to gang violence.[25] More importantly, they established close friendships and kinship ties with a large circle of families in the neighborhood.[26] Raskin states that Dan and Lilith James underwent "an initiation into another culture."[27] The Jameses became part of the social fabric in Lincoln Heights, building a base of support and trust in the neighborhood because they were profoundly committed to their beliefs in social responsibility and in leading an egalitarian lifestyle. To integrate themselves into one of the poorest and roughest Latino neighborhoods in East Los Angeles during those years also suggests their strong antiracist sympathies. James himself discloses the change he underwent living in East Los Angeles among working-class Chicanos: "I gradually stopped thinking about abstract ideas. I got rid of the 1930s Marxist insistence on art as a social weapon. I began to use my eyes and ears, to watch and to listen, and out of that process began to emerge the writing that finally was published as *Famous All Over Town*."[28] Because of his involvement in helping three generations of Chicanos overcome the hardships of barrio life, James was posthumously honored by the City of Los Angeles on October 8, 1988, at the Sixth Annual Scholarship Reunion of the Clover Street Club.[29] Eight hundred persons attended the event to eulogize him.[30]

"Where art is a weapon, it is only so when it is art"

James was a member of the Communist Party for ten years during the 1930s and 1940s. Before that, he spent half a dozen years in the Party's umbrella organizations. Ultimately he lost confidence in the Party and quit in 1948. His critics have tended to conclude that when he left the Party, he gave up on Marxist politics and theories of literature once and for all. But James's decision to leave the Party was not entirely a Marxist apostasy, at least not as far as his writing was concerned. It was, rather, a decision that reflected his desire to develop a writing style that was at once free of melodrama and formulaic resolutions to social problems, yet consistent with the Party's doctrine of "art as a social weapon." I arrive at this conclusion not from James's own comments in interviews, but from the historical record and, more importantly, from a close reading of *Famous* itself.

Dunne argues that *Famous* stands as proof that James was finally able to rid himself of his Marxist influence: "There is no trace of the didacticism of *Winter Soldiers*, no hint of the author's history, either his communism or his apostasy. This is not social realism, not a proletarian novel; James's Southern Pacific is not Frank Norris' octopus."[31] For a writer who knew James personally, Dunne does not seem to have read the novel closely. James may have been critical of literature that was "more weapon than art," but he was certainly in favor of literature that was both "art" and "weapon." He succeeded in writing *Famous* from that point of view. Actually, Dunne was partly right in his evaluation of *Famous* but for the wrong reason. He correctly declares that *Famous* is not mechanistic didacticism, but he fails to recognize the novel's genealogical link to the tradition of proletarian literature. Raskin suggests that, in writing *Famous*, "James was following the US Proletarian tradition" of the 1930s and 1940s, "but also breaking with it."[32] *Famous* certainly differs in form and style from the proletarian novels of that period but also bears similarities, particularly in its critique of social injustice. The last chapter of the novel was originally published as a short story entitled "The Somebody." The story's title alludes to Nelson Algren's *Somebody in Boots* (1935),[33] a proletarian novel in which the Southern Pacific Railroad also plays an important role in distinguishing class interests. Dunne misses the mark in reading the novel as art with no trace of weapon.

Other critics have highlighted James's criticisms of Marxism without diminishing the novel's social critique. Raskin writes that James quit the Party precisely because "he was increasingly uncomfortable with Marxist prescriptions for the arts."[34] He explains that *Famous* does not romanticize working-class characters, and he adds, "There is a strong sense of defiance and protest, but it is individual, almost anarchist, rather than collective and Marxist."[35] Alberto Huerta also describes James as becoming disillusioned with "Marxist ideology."[36] As an alternative to the rigid strictures of Marxism, in Huerta's view, James found solace in the nonconfining relations of the Chicano community: "Everything that the rational, effete discussions with Communist comrades had lacked, the Mexican American *compadres* and *comadres* quickly supplied to the Jameses, with warmth and spontaneity."[37] Huerta does not seem wrong so much as incomplete in his assessment; one could argue, as I do, that James's newfound relations within the Chicano community complemented rather than negated his Marxist sympathies.

Undeniably, James rejected aspects of Marxism and the Party, but he also made clear that he still believed in "much of Marxist economic thinking."[38] His falling out with the Party came as a result of specific events that signaled a crisis in the Party's leadership role among the working class. In his 1984 interview with Raskin, James revealed that he began to lose confidence in the Party "from the time of the Hitler-Stalin Non-Aggression Pact [1939–41], but increasingly after 1945."[39] He explains how Party members became isolated as a result of the failures of the "wartime coalition," a policy that followed the Tehran Conference of 1943 and essentially resulted in the Party's support of imperialist powers, namely the United States and Great Britain, in the fight against fascism. He also points out how the Party lost credibility with workers because of its "wartime no-strike stand," which amounted to a strategic suspension of class struggle. Not least of all, "the debacle of the [Henry] Wallace campaign in '48 sealed the coffin."[40] As a writer, James also rejected certain aesthetic theories promoted by the Party. He explains—echoing Albert Maltz[41]—that "in the '30s, Marxist aesthetics came to be terribly debased, both here and in the Soviet Union. We were all supposed to be writing socialist realist novels about the class struggle and the triumph of the working class."[42]

To be clear, *Famous* does not represent the failures of the Communist Party; it allegorizes the collapse of James's loss of commitment to the politics and policies of the Party as he understood them. James's decision to leave the Party does not mean that his criticisms of post–World War II Marxist politics and aesthetics were necessarily correct; his criticisms may have had more to do with his own weaknesses than those of the Party. It also bears mentioning here that the political weaknesses of the CPUSA in the 1940s stemmed from its embrace of an American nationalism that foreclosed analysis of the antagonistic relationship between labor and capital—that is, between classes—which is the core concept in the Marxist theory of totality. Left intellectuals today doubtless gain much from analyzing the political weaknesses of the Communist Party in the 1940s, but they must also recognize the important historical role of the Party (warts and all) in the fight for working-class interests. James's decision to leave the Party had to do, in part, with his perception of its political weaknesses. It is not clear, however, that James criticized the Party from a more principled left position. Nor is it clear, in this context, that he linked the political weaknesses of the Party's leadership in the 1940s to the debates over art and literature among Marxist intellectuals during that time.[43]

Despite his loss of confidence in the Party, James continued, ambivalently, to express interest in Marxism, and he remained committed, even if only tentatively, to certain aspects of his Marxist past. According to James, he had two "surrogate fathers": the first was Charlie Chaplin; the second was the Communist Party. Of the first, James explains, "I'm sure that Chaplin felt the Nazis could capture me and pull out my fingernails . . . and I would never turn against him."[44] Obviously, James believed that Chaplin trusted him immensely, and he felt in turn a profound sense of loyalty to Chaplin's professional and political mentorship. If James felt this way about his first surrogate father, could the same be said about the second? Like others who became the targets of McCarthyism, Daniel and Lilith James refused to name names at the HUAC hearings, even though it meant the end of their careers in Hollywood—even though it meant a metaphorical "pulling out of their fingernails." His commitment to his surrogate fathers does not support Dunne's claim that James joined the Party as "a romantic adventure."[45] As Raskin acknowledges, "[R]eaders may or may not see the hand of a writer shaped by the 1930s, by Marxism, the contact with Charlie Chaplin, and experiences on Broadway and in Hollywood. . . . There are some obvious legacies there."[46] He also writes that James left the Party "without rancor or bitterness."[47] James himself describes how difficult it was for him to leave the Party: "When I left, don't get the idea that it was a purely intellectual decision. There was plenty of fear in there, really chilling fear and . . . shame because of that fear."[48] He kept a close guard on the memories and feelings associated with the turmoil and conflict involved in deciding to leave the Party. His pain, shame, and fear—together with his class consciousness and political commitments—leave their impression in complex and sometimes problematical ways as "traces of symptoms" of social contradictions on the pages of *Famous All Over Town.*

In the 1980s, James continued to recall the importance of debates that took place in the Party in the 1940s over the doctrine of art as a social weapon. Most Party members who participated in those debates argued that the aesthetic value of a literary text cannot be separated from the political views and practices of its author. But a few writers, Albert Maltz among them, argued that the doctrine of art as a weapon tended to stunt the creative efforts of politically committed writers, and they maintained that great literature does not necessarily reflect the author's social status or background.[49] Significantly, another intellectual exchange took place over issues of authorship after the publication of *Famous* and Dunne's revelatory essay—not among Marxists concerned with the relation between an author's political commitments and the aesthetic value of a literary work, but among scholars and teachers of ethnic literature concerned with the relation between an author's racial background and the authenticity of the literary work. I shall now turn to that critical exchange, fast-forwarding some forty years, to review the reception of *Famous All Over Town* among critics in 1983 and afterward who focused on Santiago's racial background to measure the authenticity of his novel.

The Authenticity of a Latino Pseudonym and the Ire of Critics

Despite Santiago's social integration into a Chicano community before he published *Famous,* the novel was not well received by critics and teachers of Chicano literature after they learned that he was not a Chicano. When Dunne published "The Secret of Danny Santiago" in the *New York Review of Books* he ignited the ire of many writers and educators across the country, prompting some of them to state their opinions or write commentaries on the appropriateness of the Santiago pseudonym.[50] On the one hand, this exchange of opinions was useful because it questioned the assumptions of publishers and literary critics in evaluating the work of U.S. ethnic fiction writers. On the other hand, the literary merit of the novel itself was nearly lost in the crossfire between critics and defenders of Santiago's use of a Latino pen name. Representatives of the novel's publisher, Simon and Schuster, insisted that their decision to publish the novel was based on the merits of the writing, not the identity of the author. Julia Knickerbocker, a publicity director for Simon and Schuster, confirmed that the editors thought so highly of the novel they "wanted to submit it for the Pulitzer Prize," but the Pulitzer rules required submitting a photograph and biography of the author along with the book. "We didn't have any to submit," Knickerbocker confessed.[51] In an interview, Santiago conceded he deliberately decided against submitting a biography even though the publishers had requested one because doing so would have meant fabricating his background or disclosing his identity, neither of which seemed advantageous to him at the time. Even though he did not win the Pulitzer, Santiago did in fact win the prestigious Rosenthal Award.

Contrary to the praise lavished upon *Famous* by its publisher, however, some critics have argued that winning the Rosenthal award and being considered for the Pulitzer do not necessarily provide an accurate assessment of the quality of the novel because of discriminatory attitudes toward the work of minority writers historically. R. W. B. Lewis, chair of the committee that picked *Famous* for the Rosenthal prize, reports, "I don't think when I was reading it I was too much concerned with whether the author was a Chicano or not, but now that I know I think I admire the novel all the more."[52] Nonetheless, Gerald Haslam asserts that the way many U.S. intellectuals evaluate the work of ethnic writers "smacks of elitism."[53] He implies that publishers and critics *expect* a lower quality of work from minority writers. Consequently, they judge such work by a lower standard than that used for Anglo writers. By assuming a Latino pen name, Haslam suggests, James gave himself a better chance for publishing his novel and, as it turned out, for winning the Rosenthal award. From Haslam's point of view, James's novel was not as good as was claimed by "overcompensatory critics."[54] He argues that literati will conveniently "confuse political and social values for aesthetic ones" when judging the literature of ethnic writers. "As a result, a good story like [Santiago's] 'The Somebody' is called great by critics and scholars who are reading the author's Hispanic surname with greater intensity than the tale."[55] Publishers find interest in a Hispanic surname, Haslam claims, because they are motivated by the "profit potential" in marketing a novel written by a Latino writer.

José M. Ferrer, cofounder of the Latino magazine *Nuestro*, which published one of Santiago's stories before Dunne's article appeared, voices a similar concern. Ferrer wonders if James's motive in deciding to use the pen name "had to do with cachet, with trying to get onto the bandwagon of minorities who might be more publishable these days."[56] James responded to Ferrer's insinuation, pointedly asking, "What bandwagon?"[57] He was referring no doubt to the fact that Latino writers during the decades he was writing the novel were largely shunned by mainstream publishers. To some extent, rather than opportunistically jumping on a bandwagon, he may have been running the risk of making his novel susceptible to the publishing industry's kiss of death by adopting a Latino pen name and writing about a working-class Chicano family living in East Lost Angeles.

Notwithstanding the recognition of the Rosenthal award, a flood of negative comments and reviews appeared in newspapers and journals in the months following the revelation of Santiago's "secret." Some of the more agitated critics refer to Santiago with such terms as "masquerade," "fraud," "fake," "hoax," and "deception." Ortego y Gasca accused James of needing "to deceive."[58] José Antonio Burciaga exclaimed that "1951 is a long way from 1970," rejecting the argument that Santiago was forced to begin using a Latino pseudonym following his testimony before HUAC and his subsequent blacklisting. For Burciaga, having been blacklisted in the 1950s for his membership in the Communist Party during the 1930s and 1940s was no excuse for James to assume a Latino pen name in the 1970s and 1980s. Ron Arias, after finding out about Santiago's real identity, described Santiago's fiction as "cute but without substance," and Arturo Islas boldly asserted that *Famous* "has no literary merit."[59] Not to be outdone, Ilan Stavans reported that many cases of "imposters" who "take a Hispanic name and pretend to write a realistic account of growing up Hispanic" can be cited, but the case of Santiago was "the most outrageous" case of all.[60]

(In an essay on the way Chicano literary studies has excluded certain works from the "Chicano canon," Juan Bruce-Novoa suggests, admittedly with tongue in cheek, that if works by "Anglos" about Chicanos are to be included in the Chicano canon, then "we would be faced with a situation, intolerable to many Chicanos, in which our best novelist could well be John Nichols," author of *The Milagro Beanfield War* and other novels.[61] He proposes, playfully, that rather than include the works of white writers in the Chicano canon, "what we need is yet another category of 'casi-casis,' or 'almost-almosts' in English."[62] Bruce-Novoa subtly mocks the criticisms of

"James' impersonation of a Chicano novelist." To emphasize the slipperiness of such criticisms, he compares James to Chester Seltzer, a white writer who was married to a Chicana named Amada Muro. Seltzer used the pseudonym Amado Muro, a male derivative of his wife's name. With the Seltzer example in mind, Bruce-Novoa writes satirically, "James almost passes—perhaps he still has time to divorce his Anglo wife and remarry a Chicana.")[63]

In 1985, a year after Dunne's article, Haslam summarized the general reception of Santiago's novel: "Presently, an 'I-disliked-it-before-you-did' upsmanship seems to be in effect, especially among Chicano scholars."[64] Despite recognizing the questionable motives behind the attacks on Santiago, Haslam too finds fault in Santiago's constructed identity. He writes that "the deception implicit" in James's use of a Latino pseudonym must be held in contempt, despite the author's "genuine commitment to America's downtrodden, especially poor Chicanos."[65] What seemed to hide behind the ire was not the fact that Santiago had used a Latino pseudonym, but that readers had actually been fooled by the "authenticity" of the writing. Santiago's editors were quick to point out, "James never claimed that Danny Santiago was Mexican-American. He never said that Danny Santiago grew up in the Latino neighborhoods of East Los Angeles. Those were assumptions readers made—largely, many now admit, because the writing was so vivid, so accurate. Who else but a Mexican-American could have written so perceptively about life in a Mexican barrio?"[66] The attacks against Santiago reached their apex six months after his exposure. On January 26, 1985, the Before Columbus Foundation sponsored a symposium entitled "Danny Santiago: Art or Fraud" at the Modern Times Bookstore in San Francisco. Although James was invited to attend, he declined. The panelists included Rudolfo Anaya, Myrtha Chabrán, Juan Felipe Herrera, Gary Soto, and Tomás Ybarra-Frausto. One hundred twenty persons attended the symposium, including Stanford English professor Arturo Islas and Berkeley novelist Ishmael Reed. "With the exception of Soto," who defended the novel's integrity, "every one else at the symposium censured James and called him a fraud."[67]

Despite the personal attacks on Santiago and the near total censorship of *Famous* in Chicano literature courses and research projects, several writers and educators held a positive view of Santiago and *Famous*.[68] Richard Rodriguez, who stood at the center of yet another scandal surrounding issues of ethnicity and authenticity, reports that in a "perverse way" he welcomed the Santiago revelation. "We've been working under an assumption for the past 25 years," Rodriguez argues, "that only Hispanic writers can write about Hispanic experiences, that only black writers can write about black experiences, that only women can write about women. I think those are really dangerous assumptions."[69] Novelist Rolando Hinojosa-Smith comments, "I can understand James taking a pen name after what he'd been through in the 1950s. . . . I don't think that an injustice was done to the Chicano or the Mexican community. It's a funny novel and it's authentic."[70] Roberto Cantú affirms that "the novel was not accepted by many Chicano critics because [Santiago] was not a Chicano. . . . In fact a colleague of mine and I almost ended our friendship over it." Cantú expresses hope that Santiago's novel will "destroy the myth that only Chicanos can write about Chicanos."[71]

Huerta also writes sympathetically of Santiago, staunchly opposing those who have censored the novel. "James fell into controversy twice," he proclaims, "first, black-listed by the Communist-hunting House Un-American Activities Committee in 1951 and then, several decades later, 'brown-listed' by certain established Hispanic writers when it was revealed" that Santiago was not Latino but white.[72] Arguing that James was "brown-listed" for having the audacity to speak up "for a *barrio* kid named Chato," Huerta states that he knows "of no other activist-writer in California history who suffered such double-jeopardy."[73] Alexander Cockburn makes a similar claim. But rather than voice disagreement with scholars who "brown-listed" James, Cockburn directs his displeasure toward Dunne for the implicit anti-Communism of the article he wrote to "expose" Santiago/James. Cockburn maintains that

> the way *The* [*New York*] *Times* ran the story from *The New York Review* [*of Books*], it seemed a reenactment, a mime, of the ritual of naming names. McCarthyized in 1951 and forced into pseudonymity, James has been McCarthyized all over again in 1984. Dunne's narrative, self-regarding, contrived and conservative . . . had the whiff of the witch hunter while purporting to be something else.[74]

Huerta and Cockburn certainly had good reason to take issue with Dunne and others for their treatment of Santiago/James. Nevertheless, at the center of the debate about James's use of a Latino pen name was also the thorny issue of authenticity. Haslam, expressing a commonly held belief with respect to literary representations of ethnicity, writes, "All other things being equal, it is safe to assume that a gifted Chicano will write better novels of Chicano life than will a gifted Anglo."[75] Henry Louis Gates Jr. disagrees with these kinds of claims. To make his point, Gates tells of the "great black jazz trumpeter Roy Eldridge [who] once made a wager with the critic Leonard Feather that he could distinguish white musicians from black ones—blindfolded." Eldridge claimed that an essential difference existed in the music of blacks that distinguished it from that of whites. Feather took him up on the bet and played several albums by musicians unknown to Eldridge. "More than half the time, Eldridge guessed wrong."[76] The story emphasizes the manner in which the reification of ethnic identification categories will result in reified interpretations of literature and art. "Our literary judgments," Gates asserts, "remain hostage to the ideology of authenticity."[77] He sees a huge problem with the contemporary assumption that works categorized according to their authors' race, ethnicity, or gender represent the authentic experiences of their social groups in a way that literary works by persons outside the group cannot. For this reason Gates believes "that exposing the true author of *Famous All Over Town*," which had been previously "hailed by Latino critics for its vibrancy and authenticity . . . was a form of violence against the book itself."[78] When Santiago's personal history was disclosed, an awful truth was also revealed to many Latino writers and critics: if "blindfolded" to the ethnicity of the author, they could not necessarily tell the difference between a work written by a Chicano author and one written by a non-Chicano about Chicanos.

The critics who attacked James for his use of a Latino pseudonym based their arguments almost exclusively on the author's racial background. In so doing, they effectively reified both the author's personal history and the novel he wrote, overlooking the manner in which an author's praxis can potentially grant access to a comprehension of the experience of others. What is tragic but also ironic about the negative reception heaved upon *Famous* is that the novel centrally critiques and attempts to dereify the very same concept that surfaced as ideology in its rejection and neglect: cultural authenticity. I have now come to the end of this excursus on James's personal history and the reception of his novel. In the next section of this chapter, I shall turn my attention to the novel proper with the aim of uncovering the "traces of symptoms" of the master narrative that shaped the life of James himself and that left its mark on the form and content of *Famous All Over Town.*

Collapse of Ideology: "Shamrock Street looked like the end of the world"

Famous All Over Town complements but also differs from the novels analyzed in previous chapters. Whereas *The Squatter and the Don* and *The Re-*

volt of the Cockroach People contest the reification associated with democratic liberalism and cultural nationalism, respectively, *Famous* disrupts the reification implicit in notions of "cultural authenticity." It does this in two ways. Thematically, it critiques the network of ideological discourses that holds the family together but also causes its dissolution; and structurally, it produces a tension between the reified consciousness of a naive narrator and the standpoint of the reader. These two aspects of *Famous* turn on a number of interrelated issues: the relation between the contradictions faced by Chato's family and those faced by the author in his family-like relationships (the Communist Party and a Chicano neighborhood in East Los Angeles) as detailed above; the analysis of mediations, which helps to understand the link between author and novel as analogous rather than causal; and the irony in the relation between the novel's critique of cultural authenticity and its negative reception among critics who dismissed the novel as inauthentic because of the author's non-Chicano background.

Famous All Over Town addresses issues that, historically, can be situated both before and after Acosta's *Revolt.* Santiago's training and participation in the political movements of the 1930s and 1940s left their mark on the novel, which reflects the influence of issues debated by writers within and close to the Communist Party during that period—issues such as the role of art and literature in class struggle, and the relation between the political consciousness of an author and the value of the literary work. The novel also addresses pre-Movimiento issues, taking place in a Chicano barrio in East Los Angeles just a few years before the periods represented in Acosta's *Revolt*, which takes place from 1968 to 1971. *Famous* is set in the early 1960s, and there are only vague references to political organizing and the militant struggles that will erupt later in the decade. Chato, Santiago's fourteen-year-old narrator, would have been a senior in high school during the 1968 walkouts in five East Los Angeles high schools (a struggle that is dramatized in *Revolt*), but *Famous* ends before Chato can experience that historical moment. More significantly, Santiago's novel also addresses post-Movimiento issues: in particular, notions of cultural authenticity associated with identity politics of the 1980s, when the novel was published with its less-than-favorable reception from the Chicano literary community. The Chicano Movement, along with other separatist movements of the 1960s, contributed to the emergence of the new social movements, multiculturalism, and second-wave identity politics of the 1980s. The novel's reception reflects the contradictions of these political formations.

Before examining the novel in more detail, I shall describe briefly the novel's four main characters, who are all members of the same family. Chato, the novel's narrator and protagonist, is an eighth-grade student, a poor achiever in school but a brilliant storyteller. Despite his intelligence, he is oblivious to what makes his world tick, quickly adopting his father's ideological worldview, especially with regard to race, nationality, and gender. Dunne refers to *Famous* as a "Chicano bildungsroman,"[79] but the novel does not fulfill the terms of a typical bildungsroman because Chato does not become wiser or more mature from the lessons of life. In fact, he begins his narrative not at the age of fourteen, but at twenty-eight, reflecting on the neighborhood where he had lived "half [his] life" (8) and which was destroyed six months after his fourteenth birthday. At twenty-eight Chato has not matured but continues to speak in the voice of a fourteen-year-old boy. Chato's father, Rudy Medina Sr., represents the values of nationalism, racism, individualism, and sexism; he imposes his views on the other members of his family, either through persuasion or with his fists. Chato's seventeen-year-old sister, Lena, has a hot temper but is also sensitive. More significantly, she challenges the authority of her father at the risk of physical abuse. At times, however, her loyalty to the patriarchal order of her household outweighs her rebelliousness. At one point, to console her distraught father, she humbly tells him, "You could hit me, Papa . . . if it would make you feel better" (117). Eleanora, Chato's mother, at first appears to be the stereotypical Mexican housewife, taking her licks and her husband's infidelity passively. But her strength lies in her ability to operate clandestinely within the confines of her patriarchal environment. She has control over her life only to the extent that she knows what to reveal and what to keep to herself—much like the control James wields over his own life through his use of a pseudonym. Whatever judgment we may pass on these characters, and despite their obvious ideological defects, they are complexly developed.

The novel begins with the narrator-protagonist contemplating the failures of the past. Chato, approximately twenty-eight years old, returns to Shamrock Street, where he had lived "half [his] life" (8) before the Southern Pacific Railroad razed the neighborhood to build a parking lot. He admits his reason for returning to this place is "to dig up various long-buried corpses" (7), but he also feels the need to reconstruct the past in an effort to better understand the present and to gain a sense of direction for the future. "One hour I stood there listening to the dead and gone. It was a bad time in my life. I couldn't see my next step, should it be Left or Right . . . ? Maybe if I relived my yesterdays I could be surer of my tomorrows" (8).

Despite Chato's romanticism, the novel does not look to the past nostalgically to lament the failures of history or to locate some lost origin; it accepts the collapse of the past but hopes to derive something useful from the depths of its ruins. This point is emphasized in the novel's epigraph, written circa 1521 by Bernal Díaz del Castillo, who looks upon the ruins of Tenochtitlán, the Aztec city destroyed by the Spanish during the conquest. Díaz del Castillo recalls how the city looked just a few short years before the Spanish invasion: the magnificent stonework and cedar woodwork, the majestic architectural designs, the Edenic gardens grown over the lake. "But of the wonders I then beheld," he writes, "today all is overthrown and lost and nothing is left standing" (5). This passage accurately resembles the outward projection of the novel's formal posture: a narrator reflecting on a historical moment of collapse and failure in a manner that mirrors a similar set of circumstances experienced by the author during a totally different historical juncture.

James's world collapsed in 1948, beginning with his retreat from the Party, followed by his blacklisting in the movie industry and his subsequent inability to write for a number of years. He wrote the novel decades after his blacklisting when well into his sixties, looking back to a moment when he was half that age and his life had collapsed around him. Similarly, *Famous* is a novel about collapse and failure. Chato and his family live on Shamrock Street in a working-class Chicano neighborhood of dilapidated houses, extreme poverty, gang violence, and police repression. The neighborhood has the feel of a police state, and the school operates more like a prison than an educational institution. The Southern Pacific Railroad, with the help of the state, forces the residents of Shamrock Street to sell their homes as the company plans to raze the neighborhood and build a parking lot for its transport cars. Not least of all, Chato's family falls apart due to its own internal contradictions, namely, nationalism, racism, sexism, and individualism on the part of Chato's father. As Huerta states, "Chato's intentions and actions are thwarted from the very beginning; everything seems to go wrong."[80] The collapse of Chato's world, both the physical destruction of his neighborhood and the disintegration of his family, fuels Chato's unsuccessful efforts to achieve unity and coherence, to replace the fragmentation and alienation he experiences.

By comparing James and Chato, I do not wish to argue that *Famous* is an autobiographical novel. I am suggesting that the novel assumes a relation to its characters that bears a resemblance to the relation between the author and the historical events that shaped his life. In *Famous*, the author's collapsed ideals are reconstructed and transformed into a narrative about the collapse of a Chicano family and the destruction of their neighborhood. Several critics have commented on the obvious motif of destruction and collapse in the novel. David Quammen maintains that *Famous* "is full of poverty, violence, emotional injury and other forms of major disaster."[81] Flores reports that "[a]n air of impending catastrophe pervades the book."[82] Raskin reads the novel as the death of a community: "The old neighborhood is destroyed, the Medina family falls apart. . . . Chato watches as bulldozers batter his home and the homes of his neighbors."[83] Huerta takes his observation a step further, pointing up the link between the collapse of James's aspirations as a Marxist writer and Chato's story, which "comes from a whimsical if not fatalistic disposition toward failure."[84] Like the political movement that collapsed, in James's view, as the result of external forces (McCarthyism) and internal weaknesses (the suspension of class struggle), Chato's family also succumbs to outside and inside pressures. Flores maintains that "these two plots are intricately interwoven in the novel: the family drama which devastates the Medinas and the actions triggered by the external forces which end up destroying the entire neighborhood."[85] Chato expresses his frustration when the bulldozers come to "murder" Shamrock Street. To him, "Shamrock Street looked like the end of the world" (276). But what collapses, what fails, is not only the physical neighborhood and the family structure, but the ideological structure that holds the family together.

To better grasp this point, we can turn to Rodolfo Acuña's *Anything but Mexican*, which traces the long "troubled" history of Chicanos in Los Angeles. Acuña makes no effort to disguise his political views in discussing the Los Angeles Police Department and Sheriff's Department: he bluntly accuses the police of committing murder and getting away with it. But even if one disagrees with Acuña's political adamancy, it would be difficult to deny the wealth of statistics and documented evidence he offers in support of his argument. The police in Los Angeles, as in most major urban centers, do not possess a clean record in their treatment of racial minorities, especially in working-class neighborhoods. Acuña, however, does not see the police as the cause of the problems, but as a symptom. He argues that historically the tensions between Latinos and the police in Los Angeles, which can be traced back to the annexation of the Southwest in the nineteenth century, stem from *systemic inequalities*—both economic and political. I want to point out two important aspects of his argument that relate to the specific social critique represented in *Famous*.

On the one hand, Acuña argues that young people of all ethnic or racial groups—but especially minorities—join gangs because of racism and the lack of economic opportunities. Crime could be nearly eradicated, he insists, if everyone had a decent job and a safe place to live. Instead of looking for ways to provide better living and working conditions for the communities that need it the most, the state often relies on a repressive police force that is not always held accountable for its abuses and flagrant violations of civil liberties. Additionally, because of racism, poor people and ethnic groups are often blamed for the very conditions in which they are forced to live. Acuña cites two articles from the *Los Angeles Times* that report the results of polls taken shortly after the Rodney King uprising in 1992. According to the polls, "44.6 percent of non-Latinos rated Latinos as less intelligent," while "52.2 percent of non-Latinos . . . believed that Latinos were more likely to *prefer* living on welfare."[86] Historically, according to Acuña, Latino neighborhoods in Los Angeles have been attacked and even destroyed by these *external* forces: the lack of jobs, state repression, and racism.

On the other hand, Acuña asserts that Latino neighborhoods have also suffered because of *internal* problems: namely, young people join gangs because they lack role models or what he calls "moral authority." Schools, churches, community organizations, political groups, and families have not been able to provide the moral leadership, or the sense of right and wrong, that young people need to understand their social situation, or, more significantly, to do something about it in a constructive way. Unlike some politicians who are quick to isolate parents, showering them with blame for raising bad children and neglecting to recognize the state's role in sanctioning a system (political, economic, and legal) that perpetuates crime and child abuse, Acuña acknowledges both the *internal* and *external* factors that contribute to criminal behavior. He does not state explicitly that the internal is primary, but one might reach this conclusion from the implicit inferences of his essay. These two points in Acuña's chapter—the social repression of a community by external factors and the destruction of that community by its own internal contradictions—characterize an important narrative strain in *Famous*. Acuña's analysis generates an interesting question: Are the internal weaknesses in Chato's family the primary cause for the family's disintegration? By extension, we might ask: Were the internal ideological contradictions of cultural nationalism the primary cause for the failures of the Chicano Movement? Are the discourses of cultural authenticity the primary internal contradictions of contemporary identity politics and multiculturalism?

Externally, the family's neighborhood is destroyed by political interests and depressed economic conditions. The Southern Pacific Railroad with the help of the Los Angeles City Planning Commission demolishes the homes on Shamrock Street for the sake of profits. The conditions at Chato's school are also dismal: he explains, "All we lacked was machine-gun towers" (64). Even Pilger feels bitter about how the school operates, and he asks Chato, "Doesn't it bother you that your class is reading at fourth-grade level? Doesn't it bother you that every youngster with a Mexican name gets shunted into Metal Shop or Carpentry?" (66). After taking the Rorschach tests with Pilger, Chato requests a pass, which he needs to return to class. "Pilger clap[s] his hand on his forehead. 'Passes! Fences! Policemen in the restroom!' he explode[s]. 'What are we running here, a penitentiary?'" (68). Chato, not catching the pun, replies, "More or less, maybe."[87] If the schools are run like prisons, the streets are controlled like a police state. Chato's best friend, sixteen-year-old Pelón, is killed by the police, shot in the back of his head. An investigation happens, but the officer who shot Pelón receives only minor disciplinary action. Pilger asks, "You mean to tell me . . . two weeks' suspension is all that killer gets?" The novel can be read as an explosion of pain and frustration directed mainly at the police but also at the many decades of social injustice resulting from the effects of capitalist accumulation, as I described in chapter 2.

In this sense, the residents of Shamrock Street in *Famous*—like the Californios in *The Squatter* and the Chicano militants in *Revolt*—respond with anger and class hatred toward the historical fact of their racialization and proletarianization, even though they do not fully comprehend all the ramifications of the social processes that led to their subjection as members of a racialized colonial labor force. Like the novels of Ruiz de Burton and Acosta, *Famous* renders the objective conditions of its moment at a level that surpasses the comprehension of its characters. Contrary to Dunne's assertions that "there is no trace of didacticism" in *Famous* and "[t]his is not social realism," the novel speaks volumes in sharply criticizing the racism and repression of a capitalist state, while simultaneously indicting the ideological discourses of cultural authenticity for being complicit in complicated ways with that repression. It is in this sense that I refer to *Famous* as aspiring toward the dereification of cultural authenticity.

The collapse of Chato's world in the novel is not limited to the physical destruction of the neighborhood. The novel is not only about the destructive intrusion of external forces; it is also a story about the deterioration of the social space inside the Medina home caused by Rudy's racism, nationalism, and sexism, which lead directly to the collapse of the family's internal cohesion and belief system, despite the fact that these discourses also function as the ideological glue that holds the family together—contradictory as this may seem. Rudy Sr. stands at the hub of machismo in the Medina home. In an age of political sensitivity for difference, most readers will find Rudy's comments about women repugnant and sometimes too outlandish to take seriously. The father tells the son that "you'll find it out some day, they have a certain ugly little smell, women do, and never lose it, not even after showers, not even sprayed with perfume" (142). "Never criticize an Indian or a mule or a woman," he says, "it's a waste of time" (257). Rudy's sexism is overdetermined by his rabid nationalism, his racism, and his feelings of class superiority over immigrant workers. The father becomes angry when he finds out that Lena has been having a romantic relationship with an undocumented Mexican worker. He refers to the boyfriend as "one of those bracero devils, those no-good son of a bitch rapers" (104), and he calls the immigration office to deport the young man. When Eleanora does not deny that she knows about their daughter's lover, Rudy hits her. Chato intervenes to stop the beating because he feels "sympathy" for his mother. But he quickly clarifies that "in another way, [he] was on [his] father's side" because his mother "knew more than she admitted" (104). Chato is the heir apparent of his father's sexism, uncritically accepting his father's ideological views as a kind of second nature. Thus, he too makes misogynist comments: "I should have slugged her. Knuckles are the only language a woman understands" (101).

Despite the overwhelming and devastating power of the ideological discourses—especially nationalism and sexism—that grip the family, the novel nonetheless offers moments in which some characters resist the effects of reification. One such character is Fujita, Chato's sympathetic Asian American probation officer. When Fujita first visits the Medina family, he makes clear, "Please don't think of me as a policeman. . . . Regard me as a counselor, or family doctor" (194). Fujita's actions expose the fractured unity of Chato's family and the ideological time bomb in their household, on the verge of exploding. Fujita not only counsels Chato, he also scolds Rudy for the physical and psychological abuse he inflicts on the other family members. He criticizes the father for not having "man-to-man discussions" with his son and for not being a good role model. Not only does Fujita expose the denial of the family and Rudy Sr.'s hypocrisy, he also deconstructs the stereotype of the unsympathetic, monolithic Asian American character and the nationalist myths that accompany it. Here I agree with Laura Browder, who reads *Famous* as "a critique of ethnic essentialism." As Browder argues, it is the non-Chicano characters in the novel who "hold the key to understanding . . . a new perspective on the idea of ethnicity."[88] In particular she calls attention to the "Anglo" Dr. Penrose, the African American juvenile hall officer Bozeman, and the Jewish school counselor Pilger for the manner in which they challenge notions of ethnic authenticity. But Fujita stands out because he is the only character to confront the family with the truth of their situation. Unfortunately, they do not want to hear the truth, and Lena voices the defensive thoughts of a family in denial, defending her father as a hard worker, a good provider, and an upstanding citizen.

At the most basic level, Lena's defense of her father signals a need for the family to stick together to protect itself from the state, which has no right to intrude on family matters. In a more significant way, however, her fabricated version of the family's unity reveals the real threat Fujita presents in his criticism of the father. To criticize the father is to attack the very core of the ideological structure that holds the family together; it is a structure that each of them has accepted for truth, if not for a sense of stability or for convenience. The father's ideology, as the Subject with a capital *S*, has, to a large degree, interpellated the family members (including the father), who are subjects with a small *s*. As subjects, they possess little aside from their belief in the validity of their subjectivities, despite the fact that these subjectivities are fraught with contradictions. In criticizing the father for his defects as a parent and, more troubling, his ideological weaknesses, Fujita threatens to expose to the rest of the family the defectiveness of their own existence. Thus Lena defends her father because in doing so she is also defending the fragile subjectivities of her brother, her mother, and herself.

The final descent from what was always a shaky stability in the family to its total collapse comes the day after Eleanora, Lena, and Chato defy the father's authority because he has spent the night with a prostitute. Chato's family is visiting his grandmother's home in Titatlán, Mexico, at the time. Chato describes his father's role in maintaining the family's unity and the consequences of challenging his authority.

> When you're a kid your father is like the sun in the sky. Your whole family circles him like a bunch of planets. He gives you your winters and your summers, your good days and your bad, and it's black night when his back is

> turned to you. But we had disobeyed him. We had shamed him in public and now our Gravity was all gone. The only thing that held us together was the Buick. (254–55)

The Buick—a status symbol of middle-class American mobility and freedom in the commodity culture of the early 1960s—remains nothing more than an empty shell, a false formal structure that contains no significant social content other than the deep contradictions that are now threatening to obliterate the family's superficial unity. The conflicts that divide the family during their long drive home from Mexico in the Buick can be read evidently as an expression of the underlying ideological contradiction of the novel as a whole. In the world of the novel, Rudy's reified views function in the manner of a narrative that the various family members come to accept and live by despite its destructive effects.

To some degree, the family's contradictory commitment to the father's worldview resembles Althusser's oft quoted characterization of ideology as "a 'representation' of the Imaginary relationship of individuals to their real conditions of existence."[89] Althusser argues that subjects construct ideologically informed narratives to explain their own fictive *relation* to the real social world. Similarly, the fictive world represented in *Famous* is a projection of a symbolic form onto external reality in an effort to make the authorial subject's *relation* to that reality intelligible or meaningful, but what remains immediately visible to the naked eye is the form (or the *relation*) itself, not the reality. The world of the novel functions like ideology; it gives order and meaning to the narrator's imagined relation to real conditions of existence based partly on the author's experience and ideological commitments, but also on the objective conditions of his historical moment.[90] In *Famous*, the family's beliefs in the father's world outlook are consolidated, reinforced, and regenerated via the specific relation of each family member with the father.

Chato's father is simultaneously the center of the family's universe and the force responsible for its destruction. The son rejects his father's betrayals, but he desires the unity and stability—tentative as that stability may be—that his father brings to the family structure. Chato cannot escape the love-hate relation with his father; it presents a problem for him. He finds a partial solution—albeit a symbolic one—in writing his name on the walls of commercial buildings near his destroyed neighborhood. Not coincidently, as Chato searches the rubble of his demolished home he finds a "red Crayola," which he decides to use to sign his name on buildings "all over town." Yet he feels ambivalent about separating himself entirely from his ideological origins, expressing a desire for his audience to realize that he is in fact a legacy of his ideological past. "Why not sign myself there and prove somebody's left alive at least? Or else why did I pick up that *red* Crayola?" (278; emphasis added). Santiago/James almost seems to be alluding to his *red* past to "prove" that it remains "alive"—that he has retained some of what he learned during his formative years as a Marxist writer. Like Chato's writing on the wall, James's novel is written in a sense to "prove" the novel's connection to a social history that surpasses the immediate lives of the characters represented as well as that of the author himself.

Given that all the characters in the novel suffer such pathetic outcomes, we might wonder if the novel suggests solutions to their ideological contradictions. Chato ends up homeless, cynical and alone. Rudy betrays his family and his friends: his compadre, Chuchu, calls him a *vendido* for selling his home to railroad behind everyone's back. Throughout the novel, Lena takes inspirational stances against the abuses of her father, standing up to him even as he beats her. She represents a source of strength and courage in the home, and one might expect that she will end up in a positive light. But she willingly enters a relationship potentially as abusive as that of her parents, marrying a man who is "kind of the jealous type" (272). For most of the novel, Eleanora is the least developed of the four main characters, and she seems the least likely of the characters to persevere. Unlike Lena, she is reserved. We do not learn that her name is Eleanora until two-thirds through the novel (200). Nor does Chato know that her friends call her Nellie: an indication of her invisibility within her own home. But clues emerge to contradict Eleanora's character as passive and submissive. Chato notices that she always seems to be withholding something from him. Eleanora's strength lies in her ability to withhold knowledge and to use that knowledge to her advantage. More importantly, Eleanora's stance against the sexism of her husband can be interpreted as the novel's symbolic attempt to dereify gender-based stereotypes.

More than any other character, Eleanora represents the desire to overcome the limits of ideology in *Famous;* her actions open up the one small thematic space in the novel wherein we glimpse the possibility of an imagined resolution to the family's predicament. Despite her reticence, Eleanora knows more than the other characters in the novel, including how to garner a sense of agency and control in a situation of near total domination. She stands as the glue that keeps the family together, even as she aborts her final pregnancy, essentially imposing a death sentence on the family as a patriarchal institution of dominance to wield power and take revenge against her husband. More significantly, she is the only character to change and to display a sense of agency by deliberately acting to take control of her life. She rejects the patriarchal world of Shamrock Street and returns to Mexico to live with her mother. Eleanora is the most complex character in the novel, despite the fact that her outcome remains unclear at the novel's end. Thematically, her actions stand opposed to the destructive ideologies of working-class Chicanos who have internalized the discourses of their own oppression. Eleanora's actions also invoke an implicit critique of sexism within the Chicano Movement, given that the novel was written largely from the late 1960s to the mid-1970s. Ultimately, however, Eleanora does not resolve the contradictions of the family. Short of some conception of the total transformation of society, the characters in *Famous*, Eleanora included, cannot overcome their ideological contradictions, any more than James was able to resolve the ideological conflicts he faced as a class-conscious writer during the early years of his career. The novel nonetheless offers a valuable theme-based object-lesson for the critique of ideology via Eleanora's story.

Content Masquerading as Form

In addition to representing the family's ideological contradictions, Chato's story functions as a kind of disguised form, that is, content masquerading as form: a narrative that thematizes self-reflexively the very assumptions of cultural authenticity implied in its reception. The pseudonymity of the author becomes the model or the starting point for the pseudoformal stance of the novel itself: the pseudonym serves to escape the censor of McCarthyism; the pseudoform serves to elude the ideological implications of naive realism, which reports on events as if it were indeed possible to represent them in the immediacy of their empirical forms. Thematically the novel assumes a pseudorealistic posture in an effort, clandestinely, to expose some social significance that cannot be revealed overtly.

My view of *Famous* as thematizing form draws on Theodor Adorno's assertion that the position of the narrator in contemporary novels is a paradox: "it is no longer possible to tell a story, but the form of the novel requires narration."[91] Because society has reached the point of near pervasive reification, the "true subject matter" of the novel qua novel is "the conflict between living human beings and rigidified conditions."[92] The novel's capacity to reproduce the social world mimetically is "prevented by the administered world," which has become standardized and total. As Adorno reminds us, "The more strictly the novel adheres to realism in external things, to the gesture that says 'this is how it was,' the more every word becomes a mere 'as if,' and the greater becomes the contradiction between this claim and the fact that it was not so."[93] The universal contradiction of the novel lies in the fact that it endeavors to represent that which cannot be represented. Almost as if heeding Adorno's admonition, James/Santiago does not write a novel that claims to present events as if to say, "This is how things were," despite the realistic effects he employs in representing Chato's life. On the contrary, *Famous* thematizes its own form as reification via the thoughts and actions of its characters, especially the narrator.[94]

Raskin points out that "*Famous All Over Town* is a novelist's novel, a story about the making of a writer."[95] We could add to his perceptive assessment that *Famous* is also a narrator's novel, in which case the interpretation of the novel would then hinge on coming to terms with a fictive world constructed entirely through the problematic consciousness of a naive narrator. The fact that Chato usually knows less about his world than do other characters produces a formal tension between the text and the reader who has no choice but to rely on an unreliable narrator. Chato offers no guarantee that his descriptions of the actions and thoughts of other characters are accurate, and he constantly reveals the fact that he knows even less about the events he describes than does the reader. The various characters in the novel themselves demonstrate different levels of knowledge about the causes and the effects of events, but no character possesses a comprehensive understanding of the novel's totality. Chato's narrative does not always correspond to the reality it claims to represent; the truths that readers come to discover in the novel are not necessarily revealed (or at least not fully) by the narrator's description of events. Chato desires to be more knowledgeable about his world and even undergoes a minor change of consciousness during the course of his narration, but that change is limited to a mere suspicion that his strong feelings of despair and social disconnectedness have something to do with the loss of his family and the destruction of his neighborhood.

Chato's naive point of view in *Famous* is similar to that of Huck Finn, who expresses a blend of caginess and naïveté that the reader is invited, indeed required, to see through and around to get at the novel's aspiration toward totality. There is nothing distinctly "Chicano" about Santiago's use of a naive narrator, or even about the problems that it presents, but it is worth noting here that both Daniel James and Mark Twain are white male authors who have written narratives addressing the sensitive issues of racism and the reification of racial categories. The naïveté of the narrator in both *Famous* and *The Adventures of Huckleberry Finn* functions as a strategic mechanism that not only makes for a likable protagonist but also produces a formal tension between the narrator and the reader. This narrator's point of view consistently challenges the reader's assumptions about representation and interpretation. Chato's youthful innocence and his natural ability to tell a story—not to mention his capacity to amuse readers with wit, humor, and charm—function as narrative maneuvers to make the harsh social critique of the novel more bearable. These maneuvers are so effective that readers may be seduced into overlooking the obvious critique of racism and class bias altogether, but Chato's seductive voice does not diminish the novel's critique in the least.

Famous produces meaning, however, not only by direct correlation between the consciousness of the storyteller and the object of representation, but also—and perhaps primarily—in the tension that develops between the different levels of knowing among the various characters, including the narrator, and in the conflicts that erupt when a character realizes that he or she has been kept in the dark about some event or some crucial bit of information. When Rudy finds out that his daughter has a Mexican boyfriend, he becomes angry more from his realization that the truth has been kept from him than from the fact of the relationship itself. The tension between knowing and not knowing, however, gets played out at many levels in the novel not only when characters withhold knowledge from one another, but also in the relation between the reader and the narrative itself. The tension in this relation is reinforced by the irony in the fact that readers initially were kept in the dark about the author's background. Strangely enough, Chato suffers from the same predicament as the reader, desiring to know more than what is revealed on the narrative surface. The way Chato's mother always spoke with guarded words bothered him: "Could there be mysteries in my home I didn't know about?" (97). Chato senses the sharpening of problems in his home but agonizes over being kept in the dark: "Whenever my mother mentioned my father, her voice got edgy, I wondered why. . . . There were too many secrets in this house" (103). When Chato finds out that his father is having an affair with a woman who lives on Forney Street and that the woman is pregnant, he becomes demoralized and his world begins to fall apart. His anger stems from the fact that everyone knew about his father and the other woman except him: "She knew, they knew, the whole town knew, except only dumb stupid me" (146).

The conflict between knowing and not knowing simulates the formal distance between the reader and the text. That simulation does not imply that Santiago/James prognosticated the reception of his novel or consciously wrote a built-in response to that reception in advance. Rather, the novel addresses and critiques the general problem of interpretive approaches informed by limited notions of authenticity—the same problem that produced shortsighted criticisms of Santiago and his novel based on the author's racial origin. That Santiago did not anticipate the novel's reception does not abrogate the fact that Chato's naïveté as a storyteller resembles the naïveté of readers who attempt to read a novel transparently but objectify and reify it instead. Despite that resemblance *Famous* does not overcome the problem of naïveté; it embodies and embraces it, staging the problem and thus exposing it to inspection by perceptive readers and critics.

Lauro Flores addresses the problem of the narrator's naive point of view, maintaining that the novel can be read as a critique of racism and social injustice, but the critique is formulated from the perspective of a narrator who "apparently lacks any coherent social or political consciousness. This technique is not only consistent with the psychology of the fourteen-year-old narrator-protagonist, but with the reality existing in many barrios where spontaneous outrage sometimes outweighs organized action."[96] I agree with Flores's assessment, except I would add that the gap between the narrator's naive consciousness and the complexity of his social world can be attributed to more than the immaturity of an adolescent narrator or the spontaneous reactions of the victims of racial discrimination; it also reflects the problem of reified consciousness, a condition associated with the logic of commodity fetishism, which can be characterized, in one sense, as a symptom of the general crisis of epistemology in modernity, or as a split between subject and object, consciousness and being, representation and referent, and—in the present case—knowing and not knowing. Reified consciousness comes to be considered as a discrete concrete entity with an independent life of its own, rather than an abstraction and a manifestation of the social totality. (The relation of commodity fetishism and literary form will figure more centrally in the next chapter on Cecile Pineda's *Face* and *Frieze* than it does here in my study of *Famous*.)

In a different context, Adorno refers to this split as "the anti-realism of the modern novel," as the moment the novel calls forth "a society in which human beings have been torn from one another and from themselves."[97] Unable to represent the external world as unmediated reflection, the modern novel turns inward to reflect self-consciously on the act of novel writing itself, narrating in effect its own drive to achieve self-knowledge. The self-reflexive structure of the modern novel is not simply a stylistic feature of the narrative; rather, as in Acosta's *Revolt*, it replicates the process of self-recognition that constitutes subjectivity itself. Adorno finds that "the novel's true impulse, the attempt to decipher the riddle of external life," ultimately cannot be solved. Thus the novel qua novel self-consciously reflects on its own essence, its own inner form—the reification of consciousness—which "itself has become an aesthetic device for the novel."[98] This is another way of saying that the novel thematizes its own formal contradictoriness.[99]

One way the novel thematizes form is in its self-reflexive commentaries on narrative interpretation. I discussed one such moment at the beginning of this chapter: Chato's visit with Max Pilger, a scene in which the two characters differ in their interpretations of various images. Their differences suggest that narratives produce meaning not only internally through symbolic representation, but externally in the subjective viewpoint of the reader as well. The novel's tendency toward self-reflection is repeated in a number of scenes. The many self-reflexive commentaries on narrative interpretation in *Famous* point up the novel's concern with attempting to overcome the problem of reification, instructing readers that a sound critical interpretation of *Famous* will require that the novel itself be rigorously historicized rather than subjected to a predetermined assessment.

Consider a scene that dramatizes the role of the reader's ideological standpoint in the interpretive act—an issue that has been almost entirely overlooked by the novel's critics. When Chato comes home from the hospital after having his appendix removed because of peritonitis, his mother puts him to bed in Lena's bedroom, which Lena has recently decorated. "The floor was dazzling white, the walls were black, the ceiling was white again" (40), the curtains black and the window trim white. A white vase with black lilies sits on the black dresser. He suspects the bizarre color scheme of Lena's room has something to do with a boyfriend. To find out, he attempts to interpret the symbolism of her room in the way readers or literary critics might analyze the symbols in a narrative. But since Chato lacks the critical skills to arrive at a satisfactory interpretation of the room's colors, he decides to gain knowledge from a primary source: Lena's diary. He reads a few entries in it but finds nothing too revealing until September 25: "It was pure stars and hearts and moons and flowers. The only human word was potato salad. Why? What happened? Was that the day some son of a bitch nailed her?" (42).

Chato attempts to analyze the symbolism of his sister's bedroom, but the static, one-sided outlook of his sexism prevents him from penetrating the significance of the room's two-sided color scheme. Thus he remains epistemologically impotent. For Lena, the black-white design of her bedroom represents, somewhat romantically, her desire for a healthy female-male relationship. In the symbolic world of the novel, however, the color-coded room emphasizes the great divide between the family's patriarchal order and the female characters who must continuously seek new ways to challenge or escape gender-based oppression. Ultimately, Chato cannot decipher the symbolic colors of Lena's room. Nor can he interpret to his satisfaction the figurative doodles in her diary. For him, the colors suggest "the Los Angeles Police department" (43). As Chato later explains, a "black-and-white on Shamrock is like a cloud passing across the sun, it chills you. Loud guys get quiet, quiet guys get loud . . . and everybody feels Wanted For Murder" (90). Tellingly, the scene ends with Lena, who has joined her brother on the bed, cutting Chato's hair. She tickles him and playfully threatens to castrate him with scissors. "Hold real still," she orders. "I'm gonna make a little girl out of you" (45). The entire scene suggests that before Chato can decode the symbolism of Lena's room he must first exorcise his machismo by coming to view the world from a woman's point of view. But because of his sexism, Chato fails to identify a common ground (or mediation) that will enable him to comprehend that symbolism.

It would not be farfetched to draw a parallel between Chato's reified consciousness and the views of critics who failed to appreciate the significance of Santiago's novel. To comprehend the socially symbolic significance of *Famous*, those critics would need to examine their own ideological presuppositions with a critical microscope. Santiago may not have anticipated the negative responses of critics upon discovering that he was not a Chicano writer, but the novel nonetheless speaks to those responses. In so doing, it strives to overcome the relativism associated with naive notions of cultural authenticity.

James Meets Santiago

When Santiago's identity was revealed in 1984, Chicano critics had reason to be angry, given the many decades of institutionalized racism and neglect toward U.S. Latino writers on the part of the mainstream publishing industry. But the antagonism expressed toward Santiago was for the most part misdirected; it needed to have been aimed at the systemic causes of racism, rather than at the author or the novel itself. As Rodolfo Acuña observes, the problem is not "with who [Santiago] is or is not. . . . It is more a commentary on our system than anything else."[100] The problem with the concept of cultural authenticity does not lie primarily in the accusations against writers for not possessing the proper credentials or experiences to be able to write about such topics as ethnicity—wrongheaded as these accusations may be. It lies instead in the fetishism of literary objects, or in the reification of their formal properties and social categories. Through such reification the critic comes to assume a role similar to that of Chato, whose reified consciousness remains at a considerable distance from the object of contemplation.

We could argue that Chicano literature would be enhanced rather than hindered if more non-Chicano writers followed the example of James/Santiago, who became so deeply immersed in the cultural realities of a Chicano neighborhood that he was able to write about those realities persuasively. Gates offers this same basic assessment more succinctly: "No human culture is inaccessible to someone who makes the effort to understand, to learn, to inhabit another world."[101] What enabled James/Santiago to write a compelling novel about Chicano experiences was not his ethnic origin; it was his social practice, his political convictions, and the fact that he made a conscious choice to live and work in a Chicano community for decades. His writing was also the product of his years in the Communist Party, where he acquired antisexist, antiracist, working-class sympathies. For James, antiracism and class struggle served as the "common ground" that enabled him to comprehend and write about "a *barrio* kid named Chato." Despite its status as an eccentric novel within Chicano literary studies, *Famous* contributes to the broadening of our understanding of the specificity of Chicano novels.

By way of a conclusion, it may help to recall the ways in which the novel's engagement with reification can be compared to the other novels I have been studying. In *The Squatter and the Don*, Ruiz de Burton lays bare the objective conditions of her historical moment in the late nineteenth century, taking a staunch stance against emergent monopoly capitalism and capturing symbolically the onset of a long process of socialization in which Chicanos over the next century will be continuously racialized and proletarianized in accord with the needs of capitalist accumulation. In *The Revolt of the Cockroach People*, published almost a century after *The Squatter*, Acosta fictionalizes a moment of rebellion against the continued effects of capitalist accumulation in the late twentieth century, and the historical consequences of the formation of Chicanos as a class-based racial group, but *Re-*

volt also critiques cultural nationalism: the central oppositional discourse among activists in the Chicano Movement. Santiago's *Famous All Over Town* critiques the reification inherent in notions of "cultural authenticity," which ironically was reflected in the negative reviews of readers who refused to accept *Famous* as an "authentic" Chicano novel. Moreover, it critiques the long-term effects of capital accumulation on Chicanos, especially with regard to racism, nationalism, state repression, class exploitation, and sexism.

Chato's narrative does not emphasize the actual life of the author so much as it draws the implicit linkages between the history that constituted the author's life and the history that informs the writing of the novel. One such linkage can be found in the similarities (though there are differences, too) between the proletarian literary movement of the 1930s and 1940s, and the emergence of a Chicano literary movement in the 1960s.[102] The connection between these two large cultural systems remains an unfulfilled gap in both Chicano cultural studies and Marxist literary history. This is an area of research that has not been given sufficient attention and deserves a comprehensive study in its own right. Such a study would enrich Chicano studies by exposing it, as José Limón suggests, "to the most globalizing interpretive theory," but the critical horizons of Marxism would be broadened, as well. A comprehensive comparison of this kind, however, remains beyond the scope of this book.

In the next chapter, I shall analyze two more eccentric novels, Cecile Pineda's *Face* and *Frieze*, focusing on the manner in which they deconstruct the reification inherent in notions of postmodern nonidentity, and draw a comparison between novelistic form and commodity fetishism, respectively. I shall argue that, like *Famous*, Pineda's novels should be studied in Chicano literature courses and research projects because they challenge traditional conceptions of the Chicano novel and encourage readers to rethink the concepts of authenticity and authorship as they relate to the categorization of novels as "Chicana" or "Chicano."

Before proceeding to the next chapter, however, I shall end my discussion of *Famous* with an anecdote. In August 1984, the same month Dunne made public Santiago's "true identity," the *Los Angeles Times* asked Santiago/James to write an article for the newspaper, allowing him to respond to critics who were calling his novel a hoax and giving him the opportunity to explain his reasons for publishing *Famous All Over Town* with a Latino pseudonym. James wrote the article, but he did not explain or defend, much less apologize for, his decision to write as Santiago. Instead, he wrote a personal account in the voice of Danny Santiago who pays a visit to Daniel James to demand an explanation for the masquerade. Upon arriving at James's home, Santiago notices a "1937 Hermes typewriter" on James's desk, "cold to the touch."[103] Obviously the old man had not been writing much the past three or four decades. The young Santiago—cocky, exigent, and a bit obnoxious—demands a response to the charges of fraud and deception; the old James—complacent, indifferent, and fatigued—sees no reason to respond to such accusations. A pseudonym is after all a false name, an invented persona. It was true: Santiago was a construct, not real. (I suppose James could have explained to his counterpart that Santiago was not so much unreal as he was the projection of a contradictory aesthetic form to make sense of experience. He could have explained that the Santiago pseudonym was an extension of the pseudoform of the novel itself, and that the invention of Santiago was necessary to develop a dereifying, defamiliarizing aesthetic—that he needed to create *greater distance* between the novelist and the novel in order to shorten the distance between the novel and history. But he offered no such explanation.) After a brief conversation during which James fails to satisfy the young writer's desire to learn why the old man had created him, Santiago departs, but not before tucking the "ancient Hermes under [his] elbow" and leaving the aging James "to the enjoyment of his ill-gotten fame." The young Santiago had planned to use the Hermes typewriter, a relic from the golden age of the 1930s, to write two or three more novels about Chato and the other characters from Shamrock Street, including one where James and Santiago meet. Unfortunately, he was unable to complete that goal because Daniel James died of a heart attack in the spring of 1988, taking the vibrant Danny Santiago with him to the grave.

5

REIFIED IDENTITIES AND THE FETISHISM OF NARRATIVE FORM

Pineda's *Face* and *Frieze*

When Marx speaks of reification, he does not mean to show that we are transformed into things but that we are [humans] condemned to live humanly the condition of material things.

—Jean-Paul Sartre,
Search for a Method

Art is the negative knowledge of the actual world.

—Theodor Adorno,
"Reconciliation under Duress"

Art must occupy itself in breaking barriers, upsetting comfortable mythologies, whether of content or form.

—Cecile Pineda quoted in Jeff Biggers,
"Pineda Unbound"

UNLIKE THE OTHER NOVELS I have been analyzing, Cecile Pineda's novels do not represent Chicano experiences explicitly. For this reason, her works have been largely excluded from Chicano literary studies. Yet Pineda's works, especially her first two novels, *Face* and *Frieze*,[1] are exemplary cases for Chicano literature because they force us to reconsider, among other things, the distinctive quality—or "Chicano-ness"—of Chicano novels. Despite their differences, *Face* and *Frieze* bear similarities to the novels of Ruiz de Burton, Acosta, and Santiago, insofar as they take a staunch critical stance toward the long-term effects of capitalist accumulation, namely, the racialization and proletarianization of U.S. Latinos. They also highlight the formal similarities in identity formation, the commodity form, and novelistic form. In *Face* and *Frieze*, the mystification of social relations implicit in commodity fetishism bears an analogous relation to the repression of class consciousness in social identities, as well as to the erasure of class content in novels narrated from the perspective of a reified consciousness.

Because *Face* and *Frieze* are so intently invested in imagining the possibility of change in the midst of social stagnation, I read them as instances of what José Limón calls "critical modernism." The novels represent a preoccupation, almost to the point of obsession, in trying to understand how individuals effect change in a social environment marked by apparent changelessness. This preoccupation is expressed in terms of the novels' thematic and formal conflicts, four of which I shall analyze in this chapter: the reification of identity; the realistic content of modernism; the rupturing of historical stasis; and the opposition between narrative and narration. Before analyzing the significance of these conflicts, I shall first review the neglect of Pineda's novels to contextualize their intervention in Chicano literature. Pineda's novels may not depict the lives of Chicanas or Chicanos overtly, but they nonetheless stand as sharp critiques of the reification implicit in narrow notions of literary Chicano-ness.

The Politics of Reception and Neglect

Whereas Danny Santiago's *Famous All Over Town* has been ignored and deemed inauthentic by critics of Chicano literature because Santiago was not a Chicano, Cecile Pineda's novels have been similarly neglected but for the opposite reason: Pineda is a Chicana who does not write specifically about Chicano characters. The neglect of Pineda's novels, however, has not been for a lack of literary production on her part. Since 1985, she has published six novels: *Face; Frieze; The Love Queen of the Amazon; Bardo99; Redoubt;* and *Fishlight: A Dream of Childhood.*[2] Prior to her career as a novelist, Pineda founded the ensemble company Theatre of Man, which she directed in San Francisco from 1969 to 1981, staging a dozen dramatic productions, including original adaptations of T. S. Eliot's *Murder in the Cathedral* in 1969 and Franz Kakfa's *The Trial* in 1975. Despite Pineda's prolific creative career, only a small number of critical essays have been written about her work in journals, books, and dissertations. As is the case with many fine works by Chicana and Chicano writers, Pineda's novels have not come on the radar screen of contemporary American literary criticism generally. More surprisingly, as Juan Bruce-Novoa points out, "[E]ven now, after the extraordinary success of *Face* . . . Pineda remains, for the most part, ignored by Chicano criticism."[3] Her theater work has also gone "unnoticed by Chicano or Latino critics, even by those most active in drama."[4] In recent years, critics have begun to recognize the importance of Pineda's fiction,[5] but the number of critical works on her novels remains relatively small compared to the quantity and quality of her creative accomplishments. Barbara Rodriguez explains that "Pineda's work is routinely overlooked by scholars of Latino and 'minority' literature"[6] and adds, "Although Cecile Pineda identifies herself as a Chicana and thus as a woman writer of color, [*Face*] has not received the attention of the Chicano literary establishment."[7] What makes the shunning of Pineda's fiction more startling is the fact that her first three novels were published contemporaneously with the works of other Chicana writers in the 1980s and early 1990s—writers who received much acclaim for their work within the Chicano literary community and beyond. As Francisco Lomelí points out: "Whether by chance or design, writing by Chicanas came to dominate the general Chicano literary scene in the 1980s, thanks in great part to the experiential resonance of the works of such writers as Ana Castillo, Cherríe Moraga, Pat Mora, Denise Chávez, Gloria Anzaldúa, Margarita Cota-Cárdenas, Sandra Cisneros, Lucha Corpi, Helena María Viramontes, and Naomi Quiñones."[8] The praise these writers have received no doubt remains well deserved, but this still does not explain why Pineda's work has lacked similar recognition and acceptance within Chicano literary studies.

One might suspect that Pineda's novels have been neglected because she does not write specifically about Chicana experience. Pineda does not write the kind of novels Chicanas are expected to write: she does not represent Chicano identity as a cultural formation that originates in Aztlán, in the barrio, or on the U.S.-Mexico border. She does not celebrate nor does she criticize the Chicano Movement. Moreover, she does not represent history in a temporally limited or geographically local manner. On the contrary, her novels transgress continents and expand across centuries in narrating stories from a world-historical perspective. Because of the settings, historical periods, and particular kinds of conflicts represented in *Face* and *Frieze*, Lomelí concludes that Pineda's novels "function more aptly at the metaphorical instead of the purely sociological level."[9] Similarly, Bruce-Novoa argues that Pineda "exemplifies a trend toward a less regional and ethnically specific, more international and universal approach," and he adds that her "novels are allegories for our time and place."[10] One could also argue, as does Rafael Pérez-Torres with regard to John Rechy's novels, that "the absence of 'ethnic content'" in Pineda's work could "in its silence evoke a most interesting relationship between"[11] ethnicity and other categories of experience.

Even if we accept a description of Pineda's novels as metaphorical, allegorical, and universal, as we surely must, *Face* and *Frieze* also engage with issues that have been of immediate and oftentimes urgent concern to Chicana and Chicano writers at least since the 1960s: representing the contradictions of social identities that are both externally determined and socially necessary; imagining a subject capable of effecting historical change; criticizing sexism and racism; exposing the devastation caused by forced migration; destabilizing traditional conceptions of national boundaries and nationalities; depicting social class contradictions and the exploitation of labor; arguing for a conception of art and literature as political; and experimenting with narrative styles that elucidate the complexities of the novel as an art form. Considering that Pineda's novels address themes and social issues traditionally important to Chicano literature, the question remains: Why have her works been neglected?

In a different context, Michael Bérubé writes about the politics of neglect in a study of African American poet Melvin Tolson. Author of *Harlem Gallery* and several other works, Tolson was credited with seeking to incorporate African American poetry into university curriculums immediately following World War II. But he "has become our era's most neglected and undervalued modernist poet of consequence."[12] He has been neglected not only by critics of American literature generally, but by those of African American literature as well. In Bérubé's view, "[N]eglect constitutes a kind of reception, and . . . certain kinds of reception attempt to provide justification for neglect."[13] Neglect by scholars in one's field reflects more than professional silence; it implies a critical assessment just as powerful as an essay published in a flagship journal. In the case of Tolson, "[N]eglect by Houston Baker or Henry Louis Gates, say, is not the same thing as neglect by Hugh Kenner or Frank Kermode."[14] Similarly, the neglect of Pineda's works by critics of Chicano literature carries more weight than that of critics who write on other areas of American literature. Neglect can determine the place of a writer within a literary field or the academy itself. "The partiality of neglect yields the kind of misrepresentation that authorizes nonrepresentation: it tells students, literary professionals, and the general literate public that they don't have to read Tolson."[15] The neglect of Pineda's novels can be understood in a similar manner: it constitutes a critical assessment within Chicano literary studies.

It would not be farfetched to suggest that Pineda's works have been disregarded by Chicano criticism at least in part because they implicitly call into question assumptions in determining the Chicano-ness of Chicano novels, taking issue with notions of cultural authenticity and reified identity in two ways. First, Pineda challenges the view that the works of Chicana writers should be deemed authentic only if the writing focuses on the experiences of being a Chicana. In taking up this challenge, she rejects the implication that Chicanas are unable to write about anything other than the specificity of an immediate cultural experience. In a 1997 essay, she responds to those who hold such views:

> Subjecting the vast scope of the human imagination to the fetters of time, place, culture, or ethnicity is a prescription for artistic sterility, and for the kind of stilted polemic that precludes the splendid accidents that occasionally illuminate human life. We of Mexican origin—Chicanas—are entirely capable of reading (yes, we read books); we are entirely capable of thinking for ourselves, even imagining the unimaginable (yes, Sor Juana Inés de la Cruz); and we reflect the deracination of our lives in the culture of our exile.[16]

It is not that Pineda believes the immediacy of experience is unimportant. On the contrary, it is precisely the experience of being uprooted and displaced—physically, politically, and intellectually—that grants to individuals, as members of a group, a certain epistemic access to a broader body of social knowledge. As Sophia A. McClennen argues, "[E]xile writing challenges certain conclusions central to contemporary cultural theories. . . . The urgency of [exile] writing lies in the way that literature serves as a memory of the past and an imaginative version of alternative realities."[17] In this regard, the philosophical implications of Pineda's comments are compatible with my comparison (detailed in chapter 1) of standpoint theory and the standpoint of the proletariat. That is to say, the experience of being constituted socially as a racialized or gendered subject creates the conditions of possibility for conscientious women and men to develop not only an acute familiarity with their most immediate form of inequality or oppression, but a critical and oftentimes futuristic outlook on the social world from a class or global perspective. This outlook, in turn, becomes embedded, thematically and formally, in representations of experience.

It is from this perspective, second, that Pineda challenges U.S. Latina and Latino writers to expand the thematic and formal boundaries that have become a commonplace in Chicano and U.S. Latino literature. Specifically, she calls on writers to transcend the reifying limits of localism. In an interview, she was asked if she shared the sentiments of Chicano novelist Alfredo Vea, who states pointedly that U.S. Latino writers have "allowed ourselves to applaud the provincial in literature." Vea adds, "That time is over. The artistic bar of literary fiction has been set for our time by Nabokov, Bellow, Faulkner, et al. We should study that bar—aim at it with every intention of leaping over."[18] In response to the question, Pineda proposes to raise the bar even higher than Vea would have it:

> I would set the bar past the province of Nabokov, Bellow and Faulkner (another male axis) to encompass the great ocean of letters, Gaia split into many continents: Frame of New Zealand; Abe of Asia; Coetzee, Breitenbach and Achebe of Africa; Beckett and Joyce of Ireland (a literary continent unto itself); Schulz and Bachmann of Europe; Lispector of South America; Hedayat of the Middle East; and that greatest prestidigitator of all, Juan Rulfo of Mexico, who discovered the possibility of creating a novel devoid of any of the traditional locators, depending only on the signature phrases of each character's voice, as if to say: "Look, Ma, no hands!" because hands may not be required at all, except by outdated literary conventions. . . . [A]rt must occupy itself in breaking barriers, upsetting comfortable mythologies, whether of content or form.[19]

Challenging the boundaries of tradition, however, comes with a cost. For Pineda, the price has been a kind of literary ostracism, despite the fact that she has honed her writing skills nearly to the point of being able to narrate, like Rulfo, "with no hands," and despite the fact that she succeeds as much as—and in many cases, more than—any Chicana or Chicano novelist today in breaking with the rigid provincialism that Vea criticizes. She accomplishes this task not entirely in the themes she represents or in the actions and thoughts of her characters, but in the formal features of her narratives as well. This holds true for Pineda's *Face* and *Frieze*, which are rife with thematic and formal contradictions, but it is precisely their contradictoriness that allows readers a slight opening into the social history that lies beyond the surface content of the stories they tell.

At first glance, readers will find *Face* and *Frieze* to be quite different from one another. The former is set in Brazil, the latter in Java and India.

The first takes place in the mid–twentieth century, the second in the ninth century. One tells the story of an individual's lost identity and his efforts to construct a new identity; the other is about the exploitation of an artisan's labor and the repression of class content in art forms. *Face* is narrated in the third person, making liberal use of free indirect discourse; *Frieze* is told in the first person, drawing freely on dreams and memories. Even the writing process differed with the two novels. As Pineda explains, *Face* took several years to write and was finished only after a long, arduous process of composition and revision. By contrast, *Frieze* took only a year to write, coming quickly on the heels of *Face*, as if Pineda felt compelled to write a second novel to complete the unfinished business of the first.[20] Despite their differences, *Face* and *Frieze*, each in its own way, engage imaginatively with the same problematic: the effort to transcend the reification of identity in narrative form.[21] No doubt, each novel stands on its own and can be read independently, but because of their common themes and similar formal qualities we will benefit from reading them together as two complementary novels, or as two parts of a singular novelistic project.

The Reification of Identity

Reading *Face* thematically, we will inevitably conclude that the novel is centrally about identity. Pineda herself confirms that "with *Face*, certainly the question has to do with identity: identity lost, identity found, identity lost again, and found again, and again and again and again (as in life)."[22] But *Face* should not be read simplistically as representing a search for identity, much less a celebration of identity; Pineda's novel is rather an imaginative, philosophical investigation into the limits and possibilities of social identities in late capitalism, a historical period marked by pervasive reification that both constitutes and destroys social identities at the same time. *Face* is set in the Whale Back, a "slum district" in Rio de Janeiro, Brazil, and tells the story of Helio Cara, a barber who suffers an atrocious accident. He falls down a flight of stairs, and the accident disfigures his face beyond recognition. Significantly, Helio's last name means "face" in Spanish and Portuguese; it can also mean "expensive." Too poor to afford reconstructive surgery, and rejected by his lover, coworkers, and neighbors, Helio leaves the "Capital" and returns to his home village in the "Hinterland." The novel is structured in two parts, entitled "Capital" and "Hinterland," respectively. The abrupt change in the setting of the narrative half way through the novel marks not only a significant shift in the thematic trajectory of the story, but a sharp disjuncture in the novel's structure, as well, formally replicating the sudden crisis of identity experienced by Helio as a result of his accident. In the Hinterland, Helio teaches himself basic surgical techniques to undertake the arduous task of reconstructing his face. In the process, he uncovers the repressed memory of his father's murder. *Face* emphasizes the superficial, fragmented, crisis-ridden, socially constituted character of identity in late capitalism; but it also recognizes the inescapable need for individuals to assume social identities as a means for coming to know the social world and their place in that world. *Face* represents the reified identity of a character who unwittingly confronts the dangerous frailty of his existence in the world.

By "reified identity" I am referring to individuals who think of their identities and those of others as natural, eternal, constituted by inherent qualities, self-generated, or otherwise autonomous from the determining effects of society and history. Because the concept of reification is often associated with objectification, reified identity might be understood as producing discrete, objectified individuals. But as Sartre reminds us: "When Marx speaks of reification, he does not mean to show that we are transformed into things but that we are [human subjects] condemned to live humanly the condition of material things."[23] Drawing on Sartre's clarification, we can read *Face* as representing reified identity in three ways: Helio and other characters take their identities for granted, uncritically accepting them as natural; Helio's identity becomes a commodity, measurable on a quantitative scale as an exchange value; and Helio comes to lead a dehistoricized life, lacking in class consciousness and incognizant of the history that gives substance to the formation of his identity.

Helio undergoes an acute crisis of identity. The rigid exteriority of his normalizing selfhood is ruptured with the physical demolition of his face. He also reconstructs his physical face and thus effectively establishes a new identity, but his newly constructed identity is not much different from the one he had before. Like the old self, his new identity is reified, despite the fact that he *chooses* his new identity. Choosing an identity does not necessarily diminish its condition of reification. Helio fashions for himself an "unremarkable face" that "evokes neither origins nor class" (191–92). The importance of this development, however, does not lie in the fact that he consciously desires and deliberately manufactures a socially sterile face, void of class or racial markers. Rather, in making what ultimately amounts to a utilitarian decision to create a face that will allow him to resist the material effects of being a racialized and proletarianized subject—which is to say, a face that will allow him to survive unnoticed in a world of social bigotry and exploitation—he constructs an identity that invariably comes into conflict with his class interests as a working-class mestizo.[24]

To be sure, political identities, such as those based on race, ethnicity, gender, sexuality, and religion, are internally contradictory. On the one hand, they provide subjects with epistemological focal points—social locations from which they are able to become knowledgeable of their roles within society, possibly even for the purpose of changing the social conditions in which they live.[25] On the other hand, identities can also limit an individual's capacity to comprehend social relations and history if the politics of identity become the disguise for a reified consciousness. In either case, one thing is certain: despite the contradictoriness of social identities, we cannot live without them. Helio Cara ponders this issue in recalling the question others skeptically pose to him: "You need a face to live?" (84). He realizes that he does indeed need a face—an identity—to function in society, difficult as this becomes for him once he experiences the loss of his face.

Prior to his accident, Helio had taken his social circumstances for granted, naively and uncritically accepting his identity as a given fact, or as natural. He was a worker who had no working-class consciousness, no sense of history and no conception of his place in the social world. Helio does not assume a reified identity *after* his accident; he had been living as an alienated subject all along. The accident that caused him to lose his face—a perverse kind of poetic justice—initiates a chain of events that produces the unwelcome opportunity to develop a critical awareness of the instability of his identity, but that opportunity is no guarantee that he will come to comprehend fully the significance of his identity crisis. The injury to his face exposes to some degree the facade of his alienation. After his accident, he imagines "taking his life—the old one, before—taking it off like a coat and leaving it, on this step perhaps, high, overlooking the bay, and quite calmly walking away, leaving it there, still warm" (10–11). Helio's preaccident identity is the part of him "condemned to live humanly the condition of material things." With his fall, he suffers not only the physical and emotional pain of losing his face, but an existential crisis as well. He must now learn to live without the particular reified identity with which he had been uncritically accustomed, but living without a face presents as many problems as having one. No longer can he walk the streets comfortably or safely in broad daylight. He loses the friendship of his employer and coworkers, the companionship and loyalty of his girlfriend, and his home because he cannot pay the rent, not to mention that his neighbors set it afire. The response of those who reject him and feel repugnance at the sight of his disfigurement reflects the ignorance of bigots—persons who cannot see beyond the facade of their own reified identities. For his part, Helio does not seek to attain a critical consciousness of his situation; he would be satisfied with affection from his lover, compassion from his friends, acceptance from his neighbors and coworkers, and medical assistance from the state for reconstructive surgery. If he could, Helio would jump at the chance to reassume his former self, to regarb himself with his coatlike identity that he leaves lying on the steps, still warm. But such a return is impossible, so instead he does the next best thing: he constructs a new identity similar to "the old one, before," in which case we must ask: how much has he really changed?

The violent obliteration of his face and the response of loved ones to his loss can also be explained from the perspective of a critical framework that analyzes the function of identity as an exchange value. After leaving the hospital, Helio returns to work at the barbershop where he has been employed for sixteen years. The Padrão (or boss) is not happy about his return; he fears losing customers who will not want their hair cut by a man with a disfigured face. At the end of Helio's first day back at work, the Padrão counts his earnings. "'Look at the take.' The boss thrusts the figures at [Helio]. 'There's no way. No way I can make it.' [Helio] gives the figures a perfunctory glance before handing back the sheet" (61). Soon thereafter, the Padrão fires Helio, contradicting David E. Johnson's argument that the value of a face cannot be recorded on an "economic register."[26] The value of Helio's face appears quite clearly on the Padrão's balance sheet, even though his identity no longer serves profitably as a commodity.

The reification of identity refers not only to the naturalizing of identities or to notions of self that assume commodity-like characteristics, but also (and perhaps more significantly) to individuals who have no sense of history and no understanding of how their identities are determined by social relations that extend far beyond immediate experiences. It refers to the lack of class consciousness and the absence of any meaningful comprehension of the manner in which history has been repressed in consciousness as well as in the daily practices of social life. Without a job, broke, destitute, abandoned by his lover, and with threats increasingly made against his life, Helio flees the Capital and returns to his home village in the Hinterland. His journey home, however, does not represent a nostalgic lament for the passing of an old social order; it does not steer the novel in the direction of a romance. On the contrary, given Helio's troubled return home, *Face* could be read as a rejection of attempts to locate an authentic identity in cultural origins. Upon returning to his home village, Helio finds that his parents are both dead, and the residents of his village reject him. The villagers feel as threatened by his disfigured face as did his neighbors in the city.

The opportunity arises to recover a repressed or forgotten history when he stumbles upon a personal story that had been kept from him—a story that remains largely undocumented and unrecoverable. Helio possesses only one photograph (and a poor one at that) of his face as it was before the accident; he cannot receive mail directly in Rio das Pedras because the houses there have no addresses and the streets have no names; there is no record of his father's death; and his father's name is never mentioned in the novel. Readers have access to Helio's history only in the same way that Helio himself finds it—in the unexplained fragments of memories and dreams, from narrative allusions, in the narrator's poetic voice and playful gestures, and in references to objects that serve to spark remembrances, now transformed into narrative reconfigurations, as in a dream, where ambiguous images stand in for a personal history that has been displaced. *Face* utilizes a narrative strategy that alludes to rather than represents Helio's personal history.

While it is true that, as readers, we are left only with fragments of Helio's history, we nonetheless gather enough background information to draw some conclusions about his class origins and the class conflicts he experiences. We know enough to conclude, for example, that his identity is overdetermined by class relations. In Rio das Pedras, the economy is in a state of severe depression, there are few jobs, and Helio has great difficulty finding work. When he does find a job as a farmworker, he earns barely enough to survive. The depressed economic situation in Rio das Pedras has developed in part because of the expansion of industrial capitalism in Latin America. Farmworkers and peasants have been forced to migrate to the cities, to look for work. These rural workers become a modern industrial proletariat. Those who do not possess employable skills become lumpens or beggars, roaming the streets of the city at night; those who rebel against the alienating and repressive conditions of their displacement must also suffer the consequences of fascistic terror:

> In the city at sleep, in the deserted alleys, or in the Whale Back, he had come to know them, the creatures that roamed the night, parasites, like

> himself... But of the other creatures, those of his own kind, he is less knowing: Indians from the Interior living on the outskirts, roaming like the night creatures, restless, always on the move, never even pausing to build a shelter. The mill hands locked out since the strikes, and the fugitives from the police squads,[27] some of them, too, must roam the same streets. (90–91)

The destruction of living conditions in the countryside, the displacement of agricultural workers, the making of an urban *lumpenproletariat*, and the erasure of personal histories are dramatized in the scandalous secret surrounding the murder of Helio's father, a farmworker, by Julião Cara, a businessman. When Helio is a child, Cara murders the father, then marries the boy's mother and gives Helio his last name. Years later the mother dies in poverty on the very day, incidentally, of Helio's accident. The secret withheld from Helio correlates roughly and symbolically to the obfuscation of social relations that takes place in reification itself. As Roberto Schwarz writes in a study of the Brazilian novel: "Once reality has migrated into abstract economic functions, it can no longer be read in human faces. Observation of life in a former colony," such as Brazil, "where social divisions remain stark, might then seem more rewarding. But such concreteness too is suspect, since the abstractions of the world market are never far away, and belie the fullness of spontaneous perception at every moment."[28] In *Face*, Helio's reality has migrated into the abstract economic function of the commodity. The concreteness of social life in the novel is no longer recognizable in Helio's face, which has been replaced with a monstrous nothingness.

The expropriation of land and the proletarianization of the peasantry in *Face* recall a historical period that parallels the primitive accumulation represented in *The Squatter and the Don* but from the perspective of the late twentieth century, emphasizing the continuity of a social process represented in two novels published exactly one hundred years apart. We might also compare *Face* to Ana Castillo's *Sapogonia*, a novel about the colonial history of the Americas, in which the effects of colonialism and imperialism on the proletarianized mestizo population drive the perception of reality into abstract dream states. Similarly, Pineda's *Face* speaks to the manner in which capitalist speculators as agents of primitive accumulation historically have wreaked havoc in Latin America, wiping out entire cultures in their quest for progress and profits, erasing histories, breaking up families, and destroying communities. This kind of development marks the historical transition from agrarian backwardness with its leftover remnants of the

but makes those limitations pleasurable. Thus he exposes the fragmented aspects of Pineda's novel but does not fully appreciate its unity and historicity.

Taking a position that differs markedly from that of Christie, José Limón reads the modernism of Chicano literature, as critical rather than mystifying. Limón argues that the modernism of Chicano writers should not be interpreted strictly in terms of alienation, fragmentation, and defeatism, but that, alternatively, Chicano literature partakes of what he calls a "critical modernism" that challenges the pessimism and discontinuity unfairly attributed to literary modernism. Thus he reads Chicano literature as a "modernism with a critical difference."[35] For an interpretation of post-1980 U.S. ethnic novels, generally, and *Face*, in particular, I find Limón's conception of critical modernism much more useful than Christie's assessment of Latino modernism as inescapably restricted to its concerns with fragmentation, discontinuity, and necessary failure. Building on Limón's argument, I shall consider some of the generic mechanisms at work in *Face* that necessitate its categorization as a "critical" rather than a playfully chaotic literary modernism. On its surface, Pineda's modernist narrative may indeed fail to display the interconnectedness of its fragmented parts—in particular, the relation between Helio's accident and the social basis of his accident—but the very fact of the novel's fragmentation implies an external reality that generates a sense of disconnectedness in literature, as well as in everyday consciousness. *Face* calls attention not only to a "heap of broken images" in the novel, but to the implied interconnectedness of social structures that lurks in the background of a multifarious world like a haunting unconscious. It does this in four ways.

First, the fact that *Face* has been interpreted as adhering to various generic traditions reveals the complexity of its narrative structure. The collapsing of multiple generic systems is one of the distinguishing features of modernist novels. The modernist novel not only brings together aspects of various genres—or, more accurately, systems of signification—drawing from each what it needs to provide a sense of completeness in the fictional world it constructs; it also produces a competition among its various generic approaches, as if a formal struggle for dominance is being waged in the background while the story is being told. Schwarz offers an insightful critique of the eclectic form of the Brazilian modernist novel from which we can derive a characterization of modernist novels, generally, and of Pineda's novel, in particular. Commenting on novels that make use of various literary styles at once, he points out that "the result of this combination is strident, like a family secret dragged out into the middle of the street, like treachery to one's own class. It is literally an absurdity—this is the first impression it gives—however, the misfit reveals to the onlooker a real historical abyss, a junction of different stages of capitalist development."[36] Drawing on Schwarz's eloquently stated insight, which emphasizes both the appearance and essence of the conflict taking place at the level of form, we could say that the junction among the various generic approaches in *Face* is roughly analogous in form to the conflicts among coexisting stages of capitalist development—and their corresponding ideologies—competing against one another within a singular social formation.

To be clear, I am not arguing that the various styles in the novel correspond directly to specific modes of production in conflict, as in some one-to-one allegorical relation; I am saying that the general state of stylistic conflict in the novel's aesthetic is analogous on the whole to the general state of social conflict under late capitalism. The point raised by Schwarz about the strident combination of signifying systems in modernist narratives can be compared to Volosinov's argument about a similar tendency in language itself, namely, his concept of the "multiaccentuality of the ideological sign," or more simply, language "as an arena of class struggle."[37] From this point of view, *Face* does not merely represent the chaos of a "multifarious world" for the sheer "delight in the absurdity of the attempt," as Christie claims, but rather, it embodies formally a kind of "multiaccentuality" of ideologies struggling for dominance via the medium of its various generic features. *Face* embodies a modernist sensibility not because the author has employed a fragmented writing style, but because the novel joins a literary tradition that reproduces, aesthetically, the anxieties of living in a contradiction-ridden society. As Eugene Lunn writes, modernism represents the "implicit avowal of the inability of a social system to solve its growing crises."[38] *Face* points us in the direction of such an "implicit avowal."

Second, the "critical modernism" of *Face* signifies more than simply the multiplicity of genres and the tension among competing class interests or modes of production. It also points up—albeit, in a superficial sense—the cancellation of realism: superficial because that which has been canceled continues to maintain a presence in the text, even if only by way of its absence (in a manner reminiscent perhaps of Godot's absent-presence in Beckett's play, an issue I discuss later). This is to say, the modernist novel continues to bear the residues of the "realistic content" it has negated. Jameson takes issue with Lukács's position that modernism is an "ideological distraction, a way of systematically displacing the reader's attention from history and society to pure form."[39] Unlike Lukács, Jameson maintains that realistic content is not totally erased in the modernist project. He argues that to negate realism, the modernist text must be conscious of the very realistic content it wants to cancel.[40] Adorno arrives at a similar conclusion about the realistic content of modernist literature, arguing that the "shabby, damaged world of images" in Beckett's work "is the negative imprint of the administered world," which is to say, the work is the manifestation of a totalizing reification that closes the access to realistic representation of the social world without necessarily sealing off the knowledge produced from experiencing the effects of a reified world. Adorno's interest lies less in stylistic realism than it does in epistemological realism. "To this extent Beckett is realistic [because] even in what passes *vaguement* under the name of abstract art, something survives of the tradition it effaced."[41] It is from this perspective that Adorno justifies his assertion that "Beckett is more realistic than the socialist realists who counterfeit reality by their very principle. If they took reality seriously enough they would eventually realize what Lukács condemned when during the days of his imprisonment in Romania he is reported to have said that he had finally realized that Kafka was a realist writer."[42] Even if one takes issue with Adorno's generalization of socialist realist writers by pointing out the many fine works that have been produced under this rubric—which would surely have to include the works of Bertolt Brecht, among others—Adorno's argument nonetheless holds sway: the negation of realism in the modernist text is inextricable from modernism's self-reflexive concern with its own realistic content. It is in this way that I refer to *Face* as a modernist novel with realistic content.

Third, the contradictory form of Pineda's novel implies not only fragmentation, but totality. In an insightful essay, Bruce-Novoa makes two seemingly opposing claims about *Face* and *Frieze* that shed light on this point. On the one hand, he argues that Pineda's novels are "a lesson in aesthetic asceticism."[43] On the other, he asserts that her narratives "attack" logocentrism and that in so doing they denounce "the word as signifier of meaning and as conveyor of a message known to . . . the speaker."[44] The former conveys the concept of absolute knowledge; the latter categorically refutes the possibility of knowledge. As lessons in "aesthetic asceticism," Pineda's novels seek the *true meaning* of existence through a spiritual transcendence of the Self; as prototypes of texts that deconstruct themselves, they stand for the unequivocal *negation of meaning*. How is it that these novels can do both? What remains absent from Bruce-Novoa's interesting observations is a recognition of the dialectical relation between contradictory form and social reference—or, more precisely, between reification and totality. "Despite all claims," he writes,

> no human reduction can adequately convey, much less take the place of . . . the multiple discourses that intersect the text in its phenomenological field of full intertextuality. At the same time, since the polivalent [*sic*] discourse is unable to have itself experienced in its entire being by readers of humanly limited capacities, its totality is fated to be a continually differed difference, always eminent, but only known as a possibility suggested, glimpsed, or perhaps recalled like the fragmentary traces of a lost lover.[45]

It would be difficult to dispute the fact that ultimately our "limited capacities" as human subjects prevent us from grasping the full significance of a novel's aesthetic and discursive complexities, especially in modernist novels such as *Face* and *Frieze*. Nonetheless, my hesitation with Bruce-Novoa's argument has to do with his view of "totality" as a "continually differed difference," which leaves readers stranded in the wide, unbridgeable gap of indeterminacy between the text's multiple discourses and the novel's social referent. Such views run the risk of establishing static binaries that privilege one side of their dichotomous structures over the other: difference instead of sameness; fragmentation above unity; particularity rather than universality.

We might, however, gain a better understanding of the "multiple discourses that intersect the text" if these discourses are analyzed from within the context of larger social structures and historical processes. In rejecting the positivist claim of an unproblematic correlation between concepts and the objects to which they refer, we need not replace one static paradigm with another by seeking refuge in a conception of narratives as lacking any cognitive correlation to social objects. Or, as Keya Ganguly pointedly maintains in an essay on postcolonial studies, "[I]f the rock-kicking realism of positivistic thought is untenable, the consequence does not have to be a pendulum swing to the opposite extreme of epistemological uncertainty and theoretical relativism."[46] What I am arguing here is that the allusions, suggestions, gestures, vague references, and absences in *Face*—indeed, the very aspects of Pineda's writing that might be considered indeterminate, fragmented, and discontinuous—do not necessarily negate the possibility of conceptualizing totality; on the contrary, they provide what might be our best access as critical readers to some approximation of history. In referring to novels that approximate totality, I do not mean to argue that a novel is capable of representing every aspect of some immense social reality in its immediacy. I am referring rather to the assumed existence of a social totality that informs the writing of the novel, and to which the novel is a response, but which is never fully graspable or capable of being represented. The concept of totality is a critical category—a mediation, or rather, a set of mediations—projected onto the social world (or the world of the novel) for the purpose of approximating the relation between local experience and empirical structures; it is a methodological postulate against which reification can be conceptualized and critiqued.

Finally, the fact that *Face* has been categorized into various generic traditions stems not only from a detailed accounting of the specific features of the novel itself, but from our own ideological suppositions as readers with regard to the relation between literature and history. *Face* displays the anxieties of alienated labor in late capitalism, but alienation, the exploitation of labor, the slipperiness of identity, and history itself are torturous topics to swallow. It is much easier to read *Face* as a nonrealistic allegory (Lomelí), an "aesthetic asceticism" (Bruce-Novoa), a "fiction of assimilation" (Johnson), a "heap of broken images" (Christie), or a rejection of "obvious political themes" (Magill). To read *Face* in one of these ways heightens the conflict between the ideology of the text and the ideology of the reader, a point I made in my reading of Santiago's *Famous All Over Town* in the last chapter. This conflict can be described in traditional literary language as dramatic irony in that it takes shape as a tension between Helio's reified identity and the reader who stands to learn more from the object lesson of the novel than does the protagonist himself. Helio's actions can be applauded or denounced, depending on the reader's standpoint. In either case, *Face* adopts a critical stance toward the reification of identity. Like *Revolt of the Cockroach People*, Pineda's novel exposes the contradictions of identity rather than merely celebrating its formation, and such exposés have not necessarily displayed "the picture of ethnic unity Chicanos [have] wanted to see."[47] Unlike Acosta's novel, however, *Face* accomplishes its critique of Chicano identity by way of deflection and suggestion rather than in the consciousness of its protagonist.

"Godoy Would Wait"

Via allusions to a number of modernist and existentialist writers, Pineda emphasizes the interpenetrating relation between historical stasis and change. In *Face*, there are obvious allusions to Sartre, Kafka, and Camus, but the most interesting allusions may be to Samuel Beckett, beginning with—but not limited to—the similarity in the names of two key characters: Beckett's Godot and Pineda's Godoy. The novel begins with a prologue: an excerpt from a speech delivered by the fictional Teofilho Godoy, a plastic surgeon, at the Twenty-fifth Annual Meeting of Plastic and Reconstruction Surgery in Rio de Janeiro, Brazil, in June 1975. The doctor reports the case of a man who suffered a terrible fall and disfigured his face. The man was too poor to afford reconstructive surgery and therefore left Rio de Janeiro for Rio das Pedras and was not seen again after that. The doctor wonders, "You may ask what this man was doing all this time he was in hiding" (4). Thus the novel is framed as a response to the doctor's query, setting in motion a story that follows several years in the life of Helio Cara during which he reconstructs his own face with self-taught surgical techniques and with the most elementary instruments imaginable: a needle, gossamer thread, and painkiller.[48]

Pineda's Godoy is not an exact replica of Beckett's Godot. The former is an actual character in *Face*, albeit a minor character. The latter never actually appears in *Waiting for Godot*, and the audience does not know with certainty if Godot is a character in absentia or a symbolic reference to an absent cause. Both characters, however, play immensely significant roles in the fictional worlds of their respective works. Like Beckett's illusive noncharacter, Pineda's doctor evokes the concept of God with the first letters of his appelative, reinforced by the fact that his first name is Teofilho, the Portuguese translation of *Theophilos* (or a "friend of God").[49] Both Godot and Godoy hold in their godlike hands the power to shape the future of their protagonists, either by acting or not acting. Godoy promises to reconstruct surgically Helio's damaged face before circumstances prevent him from doing so. As a doctor working for a government-sponsored institution, Godoy represents the omnipotent role of science and the modern capitalist state in determining *en masse* the lives of human subjects; in this sense, he is the symbolic figure of modernity itself. More significantly, both *Godot* and *Face* are ultimately balanced on similar questions: Will the future for these characters (and perhaps for humanity generally) be determined by an external force, or will it be shaped by the deliberate actions of socially conscious individuals? Will the subjects of these works have to wait for a deus ex machina to save them from their predicaments, or must they take matters into their own hands?

To elaborate further on the significance of these questions, and simultaneously to shed light on the approach I am proposing in my reading of

Pineda's novels, I shall digress briefly to recall Adorno's interpretation of Beckett's plays, especially *Waiting for Godot.* As Adorno points out, Beckett's plays and novels have been commonly interpreted as pessimistic and absurd, or as allegories of the general existential predicament of human existence, rather than as realistic representations of specific human experiences. Adorno himself refers to Beckett's plays as "crepuscularly grey as after sunset and the end of the world."[50] In reading Beckett, however, Adorno is faced with a theoretical conundrum. On the one hand, he accepts the characterization of Beckett's works as representations of meaninglessness. On the other hand, he finds that the absurdity of the modernist text is historically "merited," which is to say, meaninglessness is a product of history. Hence, how does the critic arrive at a historicized interpretation of meaninglessness in a modern literary work without succumbing to the absurdity of such an endeavor in itself—or without slipping back inadvertently into a reifying interpretation of the work? In an effort to solve this puzzle, Adorno argues, ultimately, that Beckett's works are most illuminating not for their sad commentaries on the gravity of the human condition, but for their contradictory aesthetic forms, which take shape as the "imprint" of the real social contradictions that gave rise to a seemingly meaningless social world. As he does over and again throughout his work, Adorno dialecticizes the problem rather than relying on an either-or solution. To illustrate this point, consider the following passage in which he argues that Beckett was essentially correct in believing that

> the need for progress is inextricable from its impossibility. The gesture of walking in place at the end of *Godot,* which is the fundamental motif of the whole of his work, reacts precisely to this situation. . . . His work is the extrapolation of a negative καιρός . . . . His narratives . . . no more offer objective descriptions of social reality than—as the widespread misunderstanding supposes—they present the reduction of life to basic human relationships. . . . The novels do, however, touch on fundamental layers of experience *hic et nunc,* which are brought together into a paradoxical dynamic at a standstill.[51]

Adorno refuses to read Beckett's *Godot* exclusively as the expression of some universalizing principle, void of reference to real experiences. At the same time, he rejects the idea that the play can be read as a literature of sociological transparency. Instead, he reads *Godot* as a dialectic of immediacy and mediation, evident in his reference to a "negative καιρός." The Greek word καιρός *(kairos)* means "time" in English. In philosophy and theology, the term is understood more in the sense of "propitious time" than "chronological time," which is to say, the appropriateness of a situation rather than a diachronic construct. Adorno's use of the term connotes a kind of eternal here and now, *hic et nunc*, the collapsing of space, time, and materiality into a simultaneous "moment," or "the present" in its most essential manifestation. Thus a "negative καιρός" is everything that the καιρός is not; it is the totality outside the frozen moment; the real social experiences that are external to yet integrally part of a given situation, which on its surface appears motionless and emptied of historicity. Whereas the καιρός is conceptualized as temporally and spatially static, the negative καιρός is historically dynamic. Accordingly, in Adorno's view, Beckett's works construct a social world at a standstill, but in so doing they also call attention to the very historical reasons for such social stagnancy.

It is precisely this idea of a "paradoxical *dynamic* at a standstill," a concept he inherits from Walter Benjamin's *Arcades Project*,[52] that makes Adorno's reading of Beckett fascinating and useful for our own interpretation of Pineda's novels. Adorno reads *Godot* as the expression of (what we might call) movement within a frozen moment, transcendence within an arrested history, or totality within particularity. He refers to the association of dynamism and stasis as "paradoxical" because the nondialectical thinker will not normally speak these opposing concepts in the same breath. From Adorno's dialectical perspective, however, the concepts constitute the contradictory aesthetic at work in Beckett's play. Rather than read *Godot* one-sidedly as pessimistic *or* hopeful, meaningless *or* realistic, static *or* transcendent, Adorno reads it as a symbolic representation of contradictory existence. Beckett's works are absurd not because they reflect a general skepticism toward meaning, but "because they put meaning on trial; they unfold history";[53] they offer a symbolic reflection on the fact that meaninglessness is paradoxically full of social and historical significance. Struck with the realization that they live in a world wherein one has no alternative but to try to resolve an irresolvable contradiction, Beckett's characters display an urgent desire to find a way out of the confines of an enclosed contemporaneity. It is precisely the urgency of the need to strive for change in the face of its impossibility that drives Beckett's plays and novels.

Beckett's works are important to Adorno because the literature of the former exemplifies the theory of the latter. As the editors of *Aesthetic Theory* write, Adorno's aesthetic "demands the solution of a problem of whose ultimate insolubility, in the medium of theory, Adorno had no doubt. At the same time, however, the bindingness of theory is bound to the obligation that labor and the effort of thought not renounce the effort to solve the insoluble."[54] It is the "labor" and "effort" to resolve the contradiction that is important in Beckett and Pineda—the drive, the desire, the *intention* toward resolution—not the actual resolution itself. Vladimir and Estragon do not resolve their predicament of being confined eternally to the present, waiting for Godot (or God, or some other external force) to save the day. Had *Godot* ended with a resolution to this problem, it would have dissolved into melodrama and ceased to be tragicomedy. Nonetheless, the expressed desires of the play's characters to resolve their stagnant situation, repeated down to the very last lines of the play, endow *Godot* with a social significance that surpasses mere absurdity. God may be dead—but if so, the reason for his death is rooted in history.

Face and *Frieze* are driven by a formal contradictoriness similar to that in Beckett's works, and the argument I am making about Pineda's novels resembles some of the basic conclusions Adorno reaches in his reading of *Godot*. Specifically, *Face* and *Frieze* should not be read unilaterally as promoting universality *or* particularity, allegory *or* realism, change *or* stasis (or, for that matter, they should not be read primarily to determine whether they are Chicano novels *or* non-Chicano novels). They should be critiqued rather for the manner in which they establish these various conceptual oppositions formally as symbolic allusions to the inescapable social conflicts of our times: contradiction, as the defining quality of all consciousness in late capitalism, constitutes the form of Pineda's novels. We stand to gain more from reading Pineda's novels—like Beckett's works—in a manner that specifically inflects the negativity of Adorno's dialectic: as "the extrapolation of a negative καιρός," or as implying the presence of an absent totality.

But *Face* and *Frieze* also differ from *Godot* in one essential aspect. To describe that difference, I would propose inverting Adorno's declaration: rather than stating that "the need for progress is inextricable from its impossibility" (which places emphasis on the final word, "impossibility," as the end product of the assertion), we can characterize Pineda's fiction more productively in declaring that "the impossibility of change produces the need for change," (emphasizing "change" as the end product of the assertion rather than its "impossibility"). The impossibility creates the need for imagining an outlook and praxis aimed at overcoming that impossibility. Unlike Vladimir and Estragon, who are still waiting to be saved from an eternal contemporaneity at the end of *Godot*, Helio seems at first glance to take a decisive step toward shaping his own future via the reconstruction of his face and the making of a new identity.

We must, however, be careful here not to grant too much agency to

Pineda's protagonist, especially since, as I have already suggested, the changes he makes ultimately result in the formation of a self similar to the old reified self. The significance of Helio as a character does not lie mainly in his thoughts or in his deliberate efforts to build a new face; it lies rather in the socially significant symbolism of his actions. Helio's consciousness remains critically truncated. He constructs a new identity, but he does not change the fact that he must continue to rely on the recognition of others in order to survive in his social world. Like the "NO EXIT" sign (recalling the title of Sartre's play) that captures Helio's attention in the waiting room of an indifferent social services department (49), *Face* can be read as a critique of the absence of options available to human subjects attempting to change themselves and the world in which they live. Ultimately, Helio does not escape the condition famously referred to by Sartre's character, Garcin, who discovers that "Hell is other people," a statement meant to convey the idea that by accepting an image of himself as determined by others, Garcin had relinquished the possibility of determining his own future.[55] On the contrary, Helio continues to seek the recognition of others in order to feel a sense of security, perhaps even authenticity, as is evident even in the final lines of the novel. Granted, in the process of remaking his life, Helio discovers aspects of a personal history that had been repressed, as stated above, and he may be more sensitive to his social class origins as a result of his personal investigations. But at the novel's end he has not developed a class consciousness in the Lukácsian sense of a "proletarian standpoint." Far from it: Helio desires nothing more than to possess an "unremarkable face" without class markers, a face that will allow him to live an "unremarkable" life (191–92).

Helio's efforts to change himself, to whatever degree they are successful, are indicative of concerns that surpass his immediate consciousness: What would it take to bring about change on a broad scale—that is, social change? In describing her purpose in writing *Face*, Pineda asks, "How do people change? . . . How can the writer emblemize the slow, minute increments that accompany cellular change? Is there a correlative measured in terms of daily existence? . . . Where and how does a transformative moment come about?"[56] Pineda's interest in the categories of identity, otherness, nothingness, absence, consciousness, accident, contingency, and change discloses her willingness to revisit old questions raised decades ago by existentialism, many of which still seem relevant today, to shed light on the particular dilemmas of her own historical moment. Just as *Godot* and *No Exit* were written at a time when artists, writers, and philosophers world-wide were struggling to comprehend the senselessness of war, fascism, and genocide—and to make sense of such notions as responsibility, choice, and passivity in the face of such large-scale death and devastation—so too, *Face* and *Frieze* were written during the very dangerous final decade of the Cold War, which witnessed a massive proliferation of nuclear weapons and an increased realization that a nuclear spring was not only a conceivable threat but a real possibility. (Pineda could very well have included, among the many epigraphs in her books, Adorno's much quoted passage: "No universal history leads from savagery to humanitarianism, but there is one leading from the slingshot to the megaton bomb. It ends in the total menace which organized mankind poses to organized men, in the epitome of discontinuity.")[57] *Face* and *Frieze* were also written in a period marked by a growing intellectual skepticism toward the knowability, not to mention the transformability, of the social world. In the midst of this situation, Pineda's novels implicitly raise the question that too often remains unasked, and even more often unanswered: What can we do to change the world? How can our actions as individuals transform a world that seems so insurmountably unchangeable and so "crepuscularly grey"?

Pineda's novels offer a partial, albeit artistic, response to these questions, though they do not pretend to provide easy answers. The relationship between Godoy and Helio, for example, can be interpreted as representing a conflict between opposing epistemologies. On the one hand, Godoy, sympathetic as he may be, represents religion, science, the state, and bourgeois culture—several of Althusser's Ideological State Apparatuses all rolled into one. In modern capitalism, these apparatuses have come to assume a godlike character, leading us to believe that change can only be initiated from above: the most we can do is to wait for some higher authority—a specialist, expert, leader, hero, superhero, politician, doctrine, cultural icon, or army—to change our bleak situations. On the other hand, Helio's symbolic actions represent a kind of working-class or subaltern knowledge, derived from the commonsense belief that actions speak louder than words, not the other way round: in philosophical terms, that social practice precedes theory and knowledge. Helio approaches his problem by acting to resolve it, rather than waiting for the problem to be solved for him, implying that if change is to happen it will have to be initiated not from the top down, but from the bottom up. Toward the end of *Face*, after Helio has nearly completed the reconstruction of his face while still living in the Hinterland, he receives a note from the Capital. Godoy has sent for him; there are now sufficient funds and means to perform surgery on Helio's face. Godoy urges him to come immediately. Helio ponders the invitation before concluding that he no longer needs to rely on the good doctor's knowledge. The narrator, reading Helio's mind freely and indirectly, informs us that "Godoy would wait."[58] The inversion of the Beckettian motif points us in the direction of the need to take action rather than waiting for action to be taken for us by some higher power.

The Object of *Frieze:* "Tell it in stone"

Whereas the tension between change and stasis constitutes one of the central formal concerns in *Face*, one of the primary conflicts in *Frieze*, Pineda's second novel, might be described as the opposition between *narrative* and *narration*—between the story being told and its telling, or between the narrative as a finished product and the social circumstances that govern the act of narration. *Frieze* is informed by a history that surpasses the specific experiences of the narrator-protagonist, Gopal, and other characters, but the narrative does not necessarily reflect that history first hand. On the contrary, the novel deflects or, at most, alludes to its own social content. Consequently, the narrative takes on the characteristics of a reified object even though the conditions under which the narrator narrates remain fluid and "paradoxically dynamic." The tension between rigidity and fluidity in the novel is thematized in the story of Gopal, a sculptor of friezes, and the narrative he carves on the walls of the Borobudur temple. That is, the conflicts in Gopal's story can be compared to the conflicts in the form of *Frieze* itself.

To gain a better understanding of the conflict between narrative and narration, we might describe it in nonliterary terms as bearing an analogous relation to the oppositions between structure and history, determination and agency, or necessity and freedom. But for literature, and specifically for the novel, the problem takes shape as a contradiction between narratives that present themselves as if "written in stone," such as the 120-frieze narrative that Gopal carves on the inside walls of the Borobudur temple, and the attempt of storytellers to reach beyond the reified limits of their own stories by evoking the history out of which their stories were born. We can think of the tension between narrative and narration as one of the defining formal aspects of the modern novel. J. M. Bernstein takes up this very issue in his study of Lukács's *Theory of the Novel*, arguing that what we learn from Lukács is that "the novel is a dialectic of form-giving and mimesis, a dialectic of interpretation and representation. . . . [T]he dialectic of the novel is the attempt to write the world *as it is* in terms of how it *ought to be.*"[59] Bernstein's analytic ably describes the form of Pineda's novel: *Frieze* reproduces its social world mimetically not by representing that world transparently, but by constructing a symbolic-fictional world that *gives form* to real social experiences, thus making them intelligible. *Frieze* "writes the world *as it is*" in terms of the symbolic contradictions confronted by the novel's protagonist. In short, Pineda attempts to rupture the representational limits of her own narrative by appealing to the real social experiences that gave cause to the writing of the story in the first place: forced migration, class exploitation, ideological deception, and the repression of history—motifs that have been central to Chicano literature generally.

From this view, *Frieze* lends itself to an interpretation on three levels: the novel's thematic content, or what we normally refer to as "story"; its narrative structure, or the particular manner in which events and other important details are ordered spatially and temporally; and the novel's aspiration toward its own historicity, which is to say, totality. More significantly, the novel itself calls for such an approach by thematizing the three levels of its own construction. When Gopal arrives in Java to begin carving stone in the Borobudur temple, he meets Gunadharma, the head overseer at the worksite. The overseer shows the stone carver the master plans of the monumental construction project, but he also speaks to Gopal about the belief system upon which the temple's design is based. "Our world is of three, so is our temple three: shrine, stupa, cosmos" (105). Gunadharma explains that the temple is to be built on three levels, escalating from lower to higher. The first level, in the temple's "basement," represents the "sphere of desire," comprised of stone carvings that depict "good and evil." The second level constitutes the "sphere of form—but form free of desire"; it includes four galleries, one of which is the gallery that Gopal was recruited to carve. The third level, "surmounting all," encapsulates the sphere of formlessness, "the world where being and nothingness collide, beyond form, beyond appearance, beyond all desiring" (105), or, to evoke one of this book's themes, beyond reification. Gunadharma's description of the three spheres reveals the logic and the philosophical basis of the temple's design, but we can also infer from his interpretation that the three levels serve as a metaphorical model for the triadic form of the novel itself—not in the spiritual sense of Gunadharma's Buddhism, but in a manner that retains the organization of the architectural design without its ecclesiastical content. The three spheres of the temple correlate roughly to three levels of significance in *Frieze:* theme, structure, and the historicity of art forms.

Thematically, *Frieze* tells the life story of Gopal, who lives in India in the ninth century. As a sculptor of friezes, he is an artisan, a highly skilled laborer, better off than the slaves but still exploited by the ruling classes. His employer in India contracts his labor to a Javanese ruling sect. Thus he migrates unwillingly to Java, leaving his family behind, to carve 120 friezes in the temple of Borobudur. The friezes narrate the life of Siddhartha Gautama, the Buddha, or, "The Enlightened One." The rulers of this distant land promise to pay Gopal "ten pieces of gold at the successful completion" (76) of the project, which takes twenty years to finish. Instead, because Gopal has seen the beauty and truth of Gautama's narrative, a privilege granted only to the deity, the rulers send their henchmen to blind him by putting hot iron to his eyes. Gopal reflects critically on various aspects of his life: his three marriages; his special feelings for his first wife, Maya, who is also his muse; his pride in his work; his artistic pursuits; and his exile to Java. Despite the fact that the story centers on the life of an individual, spanning some fifty years, the novel does not take the form of a quest. It is rather the recollection of a failed quest that has already happened by the start of the novel. Gopal recalls his pursuit to produce an artistic masterpiece and in the process earn ten pieces of gold, all the while paying little heed to the class conflicts that surround him and determine the limits of his artistic endeavors. In his remembrances, he recognizes not only the fact that he had failed, but the reasons for his failure. This recognition enables him in his old age to develop a critical awareness of the historicity of his art but only after the fact of his blindness, and only from the perspective of a distanced recollection. Nonetheless, Gopal, as opposed to Helio, acquires a critical insight of, ironically, the blinding effects of ideology on his life and on that of so many others like himself.

> How easily we accept the yoke! Twenty monsoons. Curious how we become so sunk in the pursuit of craft, so harmless, while they!—playing with kingdoms, whole peoples, with never a thought. Issuing orders, keeping records, counting out measures of grain, of sheep, with the same efficiency they use to pluck a life—or a way of living—thinking of nothing but making profit whether by war, or husbandry, it matters little which. (70)

One of the questions that readers will predictably extract from Gopal's reflections is this: How can a relatively small ruling class force the much larger exploited classes to submit to rules and laws that benefit the interests of the former? Pineda displays an interest in class conflict and social control in *Frieze;* indeed, she first conceptualized the novel after visiting the actual Borobudur temple in 1984. During that visit, she was overcome by the thought of the labor that was required to build this monument. She "discovered that Boroburdur was raised with forced labor," mainly peasant farmers who had been taken from the rice fields. The temple "required some one million carved stones, mostly of volcanic rock, to build, [and] it measures one hundred thirteen meters corner to corner, and thirty-one meters high. For a temple of its size and period . . . Sanskrit sources relating to other monuments suggest that it may have required nearly ten thousand workmen to be on the site at any given time during the more than eighty years it took to build."[60] Obviously, coercive methods needed to be implemented to maintain control over so many forced laborers for so many years, but one must assume that noncoercive methods also needed to be employed, winning at least a sector of the laboring population to accept their condition of servitude with promises of material benefits, improved social status, or salvation in the afterlife. To a large degree, the critique of ideology in *Frieze* may be more appropriate analytically for the period in which the novel was written than for the time of its historical setting, given the advanced technologies of social control that have been developed in modern capitalist democracies. My reading of *Frieze*, however, mainly focuses not on the politics of the novel's ideology critique, but on the formal similarities it draws between ideology as dehistoricized consciousness and reified narratives that obfuscate their own historical content.

Because of the attention it pays to ideology as class domination, *Frieze* can be described as a working-class novel, though not necessarily a social realist novel in a strict sense.[61] The writing style in *Frieze* is allusive rather than representational. The novel produces meaning in the formal embodiment of its content. That is to say, the style reflects the manner in which knowledge is denied to workers as part of systemic class control and subordination. Thinking back about how, as a young man in India, he was easily manipulated by his "merchant-assassin" employer who essentially sold him to other "merchant-assassins" in Java, Gopal comments, "So much, so much is never known to us, not with any certainty, is not given to us to know" (77). The "us" Gopal refers to is obviously the exploited classes, comprising individuals who are fully capable of becoming knowledgeable of the world, and of representing the world in their art, but who are systematically and tragically deprived of knowledge. Pineda's writing style in

Frieze hints at this dualism, not allowing readers to know the whole truth of the story with certainty, leaving many loose ends and unanswered questions, but at the same time tantalizing readers with gestures toward a more transparent revelation of her subject, encouraging readers to want to know more, to see through the haze that is the world of her fiction.

In *Frieze*, Gopal finds himself in a situation similar to that of the modern novelist, torn between the act of narration, which for him means the actual work of carving 120 friezes in stone and the narrative itself, which tells the sacred life story of the Buddha from before his birth until just before the teaching of his first sermon. In carving the Borobudur friezes, Gopal develops close ties with his personal assistant, Karto, a slave who was forcibly taken from the rice fields along with thousands of others to build the magnificent temple. Gopal (from India) and Karto (from Java) learn to speak one another's language and become friends. Before Gopal can begin to carve the friezes, he has to sketch all 120 of them with charcoal. One of Karto's tasks is to apply a coat of clear paint over the sketches to protect them until Gopal can start the carving, which could take years. On one particular day, Gopal is sketching a frieze that shows Queen Maya, the Buddha's mother, as she journeys through the countryside. Struck with the thought that the countryside in the frieze must resemble Karto's home, Gopal blurts out, "[T]ell me about your village" (132). After a moment of reflection with eyes closed, Karto exclaims, "[T]here, almost as far as the eye can see, the rice fields lie in rows—for we live in the valley" (132). Gopal listens and sketches. Karto studies the sketch, then calls over a stonecutter and they discuss the drawing together, as if they were art critics. Another worker joins them. They decide collectively to include in the sketch an oxcart because "[a] road is no road without an oxcart." Upon demand, Gopal also sketches "a pair of buffalo, their sharp horns lowered, struggling to pull their burden," and then he draws ducks in the sky, Karto's mother singing in the field, standing in water up to her knees and wearing a large hat that looks like an umbrella to protect her from the sun, and whole families working side by side in the "paddy fields." The indentured workers easily conjure up images that are meaningful to their own experiences as exploited laborers. Gopal is extremely pleased with the sketch, almost as much as Karto and the stonecutters.

It takes Gopal three years to complete the 120 sketches. But before he can begin carving the friezes, three overseers, including Gunadharma, inspect the sketches to make sure they accurately reflect the Buddha's narrative. All of the sketches pass the inspection with the exception of the panel showing Queen Maya on her journey through the countryside. Gunadharma asks Gopal to explain his reason for including the rice fields and workers in this particular panel. Gopal answers, "No reason. It is the countryside. What more reason can there be?" But Gunadharma replies, "To everything there is meaning. Nothing is accident. The fields, the planting have no place in the procession" (135). He orders Gopal to remove the rice fields and the farmers from the panel. The next day, Gopal and Karto work together to erase the rice fields; they use pumice stone to remove the coated sketches, but the charcoal does not come off easily. Then Gopal notices that Karto has begun to weep. "Tears set rivers in the stone dust on his face" (136). Gopal whispers that this was not his doing, and he tries to comfort the stricken man. Karto replies:

> "Year after year we struggle for them here. This temple. This temple is none of our affair. We are farmers. It is we who plant the rice. We make the ground yield for them, season after season. Without rice, nothing happens: no life, no food, nothing that is beautiful. Only emptiness, emptiness as empty as that sky there, or that earth."
>
> "Look," he whispers to [Gopal] in altogether a different tone. "Look if anywhere here, in any of the hundred panels, you see rice anywhere but in the golden bowls of princes!" (137)

For Gunadharma, the narrative of the Buddha must be carved in stone so that its truth will last thousands of years. There can be no deviations in the storyline for there is only *one meaning:* the coming of a prophet. There is no room for class content. Thus the overseer orders Gopal to remove the rice fields from the frieze. But for Gopal, the act of narration contradicts everything the narrative stands for; unlike the narrative itself, the narration is full of class content not only because the temple is built with the forced labor of slaves, but because these now-enslaved peasant farmers themselves sustain the economy upon which the political structure is built. In this scene, Pineda has constructed a perfect thematic representation of the formal conflict between narrative and narration: a narrative literally carved in stone that excludes the history and social experiences of the ones actually constructing the narrative.

The author's response to the narrative-narration conflict can be found partly in the many structural devices she employs in *Frieze*, beginning with the parallel between the 120 friezes carved by Gopal in the Borodudur temple and the 120 chapters of Pineda's novel, some of them no longer than vignettes. We can infer from this structural correlation that Pineda wants to highlight the resemblance between the formal limits of her own narrative and those of the narrative that Gopal carves in stone, starting, perhaps, with the displacement of her own historical conditions of production eleven hundred years into the past. In effect, her structural comparison draws our attention to the fact that she includes in her novel the very "rice fields" that were forcibly removed from the Borobudur friezes. The parallel between Gopal's narrative and Pineda's novel will be noticed not only in the number of friezes and panels, but also in the shape of their structures. Gopal's narrative in the Borobudur temple has a rectangular structure. The friezes are carved on the four inside walls of a gallery, thirty on each wall, beginning at one corner of the gallery where two walls meet and continuing around the room until the friezes meet once again at the point of origin. The novel is structured like the friezes in Borobudur, beginning exactly at the point where it ends. The fact that the novel ends with a colon signifies that it has not achieved closure. The colon—like the final frieze of Gopal's narrative—brings us back to the beginning, and encourages a rereading of the novel: a repetition. To understand the first pages of *Frieze* fully, one must first read the novel in its entirety.

Pineda's technique produces the effect of drawing the reader back to the beginning of the novel to start again, to revisit the same vague language, the same allusions and poetic gestures, but now with fresh eyes and armed with a familiarity that the reader did not possess on reading the narrative the first time through. The structure, however, should not be understood as a never-ending cycle in which one finds no exit, as if caught up in a Möbius strip, but as a technique designed to satisfy the urge to return repeatedly to a defining moment in one's life, revisited each time from a new perspective and each time building on the meaning of the experience. What might be more important, however, than either the original defining moment or the return to that moment is the space between the two—a space that J. Hillis Miller (drawing on Benjamin) refers to as "the image": "The image is the meaning generated by the echoing of two dissimilar things . . . in repetition. It is neither in the first nor in the second nor in some ground which preceded both, but in between, in the empty space which the opaque similarity crosses." Miller describes this "empty space" as similar in form to what Freud identified as "trauma."[62] The structure of *Frieze* reinforces the concepts of repetition and return, even though thematically the novel itself does not perpetuate the view that a return to the past is ever really possible; and the importance of the repetition lies not exclusively in the original moment nor in its revisiting—not in the novel's opening lines nor in its final colon. It lies rather in the emptiness symbolized by Gopal's blindness. After his loss of sight, Gopal begins to trace the events of his life with greater scrutiny than he had when he was actually experiencing those events. In his endeavor to recall the defining moments of his past, he tries to understand the very mechanisms that had prevented him from remembering in the first place: "Perhaps it began there, this journey into night . . . the point where return was no longer possible, return, if return could be, to something remembered or something perhaps that never really was" (37). Gopal's "journey into night" speaks to the loss of his physiological sense of sight, but it also refers to another kind blindness that has more to do with ideology than with physiology. He cannot restore the function of his eyes any more than he can recover what was lost to ideology in the many years before he was blinded.

Dereification as Remembering

As should by now be evident, commodity exchange and the exploitation of labor are central themes in *Frieze.* Rice is a basic staple in the novel, but it also functions in Gopal's world as a medium of exchange, or what Marx calls *the universal equivalent.* The rulers impose taxes on farmers, which the farmers pay in rice; over time, the rulers accumulate huge storage rooms full of surplus rice. With this surplus in hand, the rulers can afford to round up farmers (both men and women—anyone old enough to work) and force them to labor in the building of the temple. The rulers sustain the laborers with the very rice that the workers themselves produce. When the surplus runs low, the rulers cut back the amount of rice allotted to the workers to near-starvation levels but force them to continue working on the temple since they have deadlines to meet and are already behind schedule. Eventually the worker-slaves rebel, but the rebellion is crushed, and the cycle of economic crisis and political turbulence repeats itself. Class struggle is the *real content* of the act of narrating the life of the Buddha: the symbolic rice fields were forcibly removed from the narrative, just as the labor of the peasants is disassociated from the rice itself once it assumes the form of a commodity. The erasure of the rice fields represents the *repression of class content* in the narrative, and, in a broad allegorical sweep, calls attention to the particular development in the evolution of class societies that Marx refers to as the division of intellectual and manual labor or, more simply, the separation of head and hand.

While *Frieze* is certainly an allegory of class exploitation, it is more than that. It is also a meditation on the fetish character of art forms, exposing the formal similarities between the novel's form and commodity fetishism.[63] This particular comparison is not articulated explicitly by the narrator or any other character in the novel; it is implied in Gopal's contemplations on topics as seemingly mundane as the meaning of stones. After his blindness, which makes him more dependent on his other faculties, Gopal begins to study the substance of stones with his sense of touch. He not only familiarizes himself with the texture of their exteriority, but he deliberates on their fetish character. He ponders the history of their formation and transformation—a history that lies embedded yet obfuscated within their very concreteness. Holding some stones in his hands, he describes them in the following manner: "I ran my thumbs over their contours. If it could, my gaze would probe beneath their surfaces[,] still now, tracing the angle of the veins' incline, conjuring the forms, the fractures that lie hidden, wrapped in years of mystery like a child unborn lying in the mother's womb, its fingers scratching faintly at the ice" (83). Drawing on a conceptual approach similar to Adorno's critique of a "paradoxical dynamic at a standstill," Gopal tries to understand the essential transformational quality of a stone that may have crystallized thousands of years ago. (His deliberations seem odd, given that outside of geologists and perhaps nature writers, few of us ever really pause to consider a stone's history.)[64] The stone appears to be perfectly solid and unchangeable to the naked eye, but it was not always in such a state. It was at one time fluid in the form of molten lava. In its solidity, it possesses a geological history that could go back centuries if not millennia. In effect, Gopal's ponderings on the history embedded in rigidified stone parallel the novel's obsessive meditation on the history inherently ingrained in reified narratives or in art forms generally. Gopal takes the comparison a step further, effectively commenting on the reification of consciousness via a close examination of the concreteness of stones. Reflecting on his "darkness," he realizes:

> Some gray dawn—not just the stone—overtook me in mist, exiled me to a world of black or gray, condemned me to pry apart the porousness of a stone gone dark, forgetful of the fire that gave it life, that spilled it from the stony womb of earth and sent it coiling down dark hillsides, trailing sparks in the night with each sweep of its serpent robes, stone tongues licking, devouring the rice, setting fire to whole villages, entombing the living with the dead, feeding, ravening till sated, it curled up at last and went to sleep. . . . Even

> now, touching it, prodding it with my chisel . . . does the stone remember? Does the chisel remind it of the fire? (37–38)

Aside from the poetic power in the narrator's contemplative musings, what stands out in this passage is the profundity of Gopal's thoughts regarding the reified character of stones. What has been reified, however, is not only the stone, but the consciousness of the person examining the stone as such. When Gopal asks if the stone remembers, he is really wondering about his own astonishing capacity to forget—in particular, to forget the history that gives life to his stone carvings. Whereas the history he has forgotten can be understood in terms of reification, his efforts to remember might be understood as dereification. Martin Jay writes that "the concept of dereification implied [for Lukács] a certain type of remembering, for what had to be recaptured were the human origins of a social world that had been mystified under capitalism as a kind of 'second nature.'"[65] Similarly, when Gopal asks if the chisel can instigate memory, he is exploring the possibility that artworks can potentially draw out the "human origins of a social world" implied in their own making. Gopal's awareness of his forgetfulness provides a small opening through which he catches a glimpse of the historicity in his stonework, scratching from inside—like the unborn child in the mother's womb—for a chance to get out. If we can reach this conclusion about Gopal's narrative, carved literally in stone, then surely we must also reach the same conclusion about *Frieze* itself, which repeatedly reveals traces of the author's efforts to capture a "paradoxically dynamic" history "at a standstill" in her writing.

This desire might be best exemplified in the advice that Maya—Gopal's first wife and "the one of his heart"—gives to him.[66] (Maya displays an artist's sensibility even though she practices no craft.) As a young man in his early twenties and a newlywed, Gopal has already developed an advanced skill in stone carving. The images he carves are technically precise, but they are also flat and lifeless. He experiences difficulty in understanding how to make his carvings convey more than what is represented on their hard surfaces. Something is lacking in his art that he cannot fully grasp. Sensing his frustration, Maya tells him to follow her to a window, where she shows him a bowl of water filled to the brim. She taps the bowl so that the sunlight shimmers with the movement on the surface of the water: "now a pearl, now a mirror, now catching, now repelling the sunlight of the courtyard." She tells him to "trap it," to capture the movement of the water in his art. "Tell this in stone!" she says (22). The advice haunts

Gopal not only at the moment of its utterance, but for the rest of his life, as he struggles to comprehend its meaning and, more significantly, to put it into practice. Essentially Maya advises him to create movement within an otherwise static object, to make the inorganic organic, to give life to solid stone, to make the speechless speak, to remember what has been forgotten, to dereify the reified—or, recalling the three levels of the Borobudur temple, to surpass the spheres of desire and form and enter the sphere of "formlessness," where formlessness might be defined as a resolution to the conflict between narrative and narration.[67] Maya's stunning advice displays, within the logic of the argument I have been developing, a profound comprehension of the life movements implied in static art forms. Her advice can also be read as a revelation of what the author herself has attempted to accomplish in *Frieze:* to tell a story in stone.

Face and *Frieze:* "Upsetting Comfortable Mythologies"

Like the other novels I have analyzed, Pineda's *Face* and *Frieze* engage in dereifying the discourses they represent. But unlike the novels of Ruiz de Burton, Acosta, and Santiago, which aspire toward a broad comprehension of the social totality via the representation of specific racial experiences, Pineda's novels, in one sense, invert the logic of the comparison between standpoint epistemology and the standpoint of the proletariat. Rather than "digging for" class consciousness in representations of group experience, Pineda's novels track back in the opposite direction, attempting to dig up the specificity of Chicano experience in allegories of reified identity and class struggle. In so doing, Pineda's fiction can be said to dereify the boundaries established around predetermined conceptions of the Chicano novel not by representing the immediacy of experience, but by "occupying itself in breaking barriers" and "upsetting comfortable mythologies, whether of content or form."[68] Like Santiago, who demonstrates in his writing of *Famous All Over Town* that an author does not need to be Chicano to write a compelling novel about Chicano experience, Pineda shows in *Face* and *Frieze* that an author does not need to write specifically or exclusively about Chicano characters to produce a novel that contributes to a comprehension of the Chicano-ness of Chicano novels.

I started this long discussion of Pineda's novels by asserting that *Face* and *Frieze* can be read as two aspects of a singular novelistic project that gestures symbolically toward a creative dialectical interplay between individuals and history. The two novels complement one another: each novel shedding light, symbolically, on separate aspects of the same contradiction. *Face* explores the manner in which individuals must take decisive action to change their situations and to rupture the rigidity of their dehistoricized identities; *Frieze* serves as the logical counterpart to Pineda's first novel, contemplating the stone-hard limits that history places on individuals in their efforts to change themselves and their social environments. Together they wage a fierce battle to break free from beneath the rigid surfaces of their own narratives; in so doing, they carve out an aesthetic space that lies beyond reification.

EPILOGUE

CHICANO NOVELS

Necessarily Embracing What They Must Also Abolish

> Marx pointed out that capital is a social relation, though mediated by the instrumentality of things. Literary theorists should take a cue from Marx and recognize that the fictional text is likewise a social relation, mediated through the instrumentality of objectifiable textual features.
>
> —Barbara Foley, *Telling the Truth*

> I stared at the [farm worker] as he returned to the endless rows of cotton. That had been me as a girl, I thought. Not a girl, but a robot, expected to have no feelings, no brain. . . . Getting legal status was easier said than done, naturally. We had to get our papers in order. That's all every immigrant in the world wants, to get her papers in order. To officially become a person.
>
> —Ana Castillo, *The Guardians*

IN THE PRECEDING FOUR CHAPTERS, I analyzed the forms and themes in several Chicano novels, drawing on the theory of reification as outlined in chapter 1. All of these novels display the anxieties associated with assuming social identities in the face of class conflict and the global expansion of capital. In *Who Would Have Thought It?* and *The Squatter and the Don*, María Amparo Ruiz de Burton creates an aesthetic response to the objective conditions of her historical moment, which was marked by the onset of primitive accumulation and the proletarianization of Mexican Americans in the decades following the U.S.-Mexico War of 1846–48. The process of capitalist accumulation necessitated the naturalizing (or reifying) of Mexicans as laborers well suited for assuming the lowest-paid and most physically demanding jobs, resulting in the formation of Mexican Americans as a social group racialized in class terms. The experiences associated with the political and economic developments in the Southwest during the last half of the nineteenth century, as represented in Ruiz de Burton's novels and as alluded to in the epigraph by Castillo, have left their mark on the content and forms of Chicano cultural production for over 150 years, as cultural critics and historians have documented.

The other novels I have written about respond to various effects of capitalist accumulation from the perspective of later historical moments. The narrator in Oscar Zeta Acosta's *The Autobiography of a Brown Buffalo* endeavors desperately to escape the psychological damage caused by growing up in a racialized California barrio in the 1940s and 1950s, and *The Revolt of the Cockroach People* documents a Chicano social rebellion against class exploitation, racism, and state repression in Los Angeles during the late 1960s. *Revolt* also dramatizes the political weaknesses of the Chicano Movement and the failures of cultural nationalism, the loosely unified and highly contradictory ideological positions that fueled and gave direction to the movement. Set in the early 1960s but written and published after the Chicano Movement, Danny Santiago's *Famous All Over Town* responds to the ideological contradictions of cultural authenticity and identity politics during the 1970s and early 1980s. Santiago's novel exposes the manner in which racism, nationalism, and sexism become internalized as destructive ideologies within a working-class Chicano family. Cecile Pineda's *Face* and *Frieze* allegorize the losses suffered by the U.S. working class generally—and racialized workers in particular—with the end of Fordism and the rise of a period (sometimes referred to as postmodernity) marked by the flexible accumulation of capital and the policies of neoliberalism. Written during the final years of the Cold War, Pineda's novels criticize the convergence of class power and the state in late capitalism, constructing fictional worlds that highlight the formal similarities between commodity fetishism, the reification of identity, and literary form. The characters in all these novels experience severe alienation, but they do not achieve a level of class consciousness that would enable them to understand the causes of their alienation. Some of the characters develop a sense of individual or collective identity in response to the conflicts they experience, but they nonetheless fail "to think totality"—that is, they fail to comprehend the social forces at work that necessitated the formation of racial identity in the first place. Despite the limited viewpoints they embody, these novels nonetheless aspire to convey a sense of society as a whole, which is to say, they reveal via their contradictory ideological positions the class contradictions implicit in the politics they critique and the losses they lament.

Moreover, all of these novels challenge normative conceptions of the Chicano novel, in part because they not only represent racial identities but also allude to their transformation or negation. Thus they lend themselves to an interpretive approach outlined by Terry Eagleton in an essay on nationalism and literature. Eagleton warns that literary representations of social identities, such as those based on nationalism and gender, "ontologically empty though they may be, continue to exert an implacable political force. It would be the worst form of premature utopianism," he adds, to circumvent identities based on nationality or gender in favor of some abstract notion of universal humanism. It would be equally idealist to "celebrat[e] only the particular and polymorphous."[1] He suggests, alternatively, that nationalist identities—and by implication, identities based on gender, race, and ethnicity—are much like social class affiliations in that they must embrace what inevitably they need to abolish if they are to avoid the slippery relativism of irreducible difference, on the one hand, and the arrogant idealism of abstract universalism, on the other. In an essay first published in 1938, Richard Wright made an argument similar to that of Eagleton. Wright argued for a kind of literature that represents the culture of African Americans as fragmented. The purpose of such a literature, he asserted, was to nurture an awareness of social totality: "of the *whole*, nourishing culture from which they were torn in Africa, and of the long, complex (and for the most part, unconscious) struggle to regain in some form and under alien conditions of life a *whole* culture again."[2] As implied in Wright's essay, debates over the relation among the categories of nation, race, and class have been part and parcel of left politics for the better part of the last century.

In the present context, what we stand to learn from Chicano novels—and what the novels of Ruiz de Burton, Acosta, Santiago, and Pineda imply—is that racialized subjects must become conscious of themselves as members of a historically situated politicized group, primarily for the purpose of abolishing all divisions based on racial, ethnic, and national difference, including those differences resulting from self-fashioned or self-conceptualized identities. As Eagleton puts it, "[A]ny emancipatory politics must begin with the specific . . . but must in the same gesture leave it behind." Or, employing a more pointed language, he suggests that alienated subjects must "try somehow to go right through those estranging definitions [of identity] to emerge somewhere on the other side."[3] The novels of Ruiz de Burton, Acosta, Santiago, and Pineda engage with racial and ethnic identity in this way, beginning with the specificity of Chicano identity—either thematically or, as in the case of Pineda's novels, philosophically and allegorically—but simultaneously challenging and eventually attempting to surpass the reification of identity. Consequently, they have been misinterpreted, criticized, ignored, or censored for attempting to "go right through" the "ontologically empty" category of racial identity in an effort to "emerge somewhere on the other side," which is to say, beyond reification. With this said, what remains to be done in the final pages of this book is to draw some conclusions about the links among the key theoretical concepts I have been employing in my study of Chicano novels, insofar as I have been arguing that these concepts—which include contradiction, commodity fetishism, reification, cultural identity, and literary form—can best be understood in their dialectical relations to one another.

Some critics have attempted to explain the meaning of dialectics as a closed system with the triadic formula of thesis, antithesis, and synthesis. For others, the dialectic is a formulaic method that, through sleight of hand, enables the dialectician to explain anything and everything—or, in the case of those who would rather explain nothing at all, it enables the critic to "oscillate wildly,"[4] as one writer puts it, between stagnant categories so as to remain forever trapped in the interstices between the colonizing poles of antinomic subject positions. Further, dialectics is often erroneously equated with Marxism, but, to paraphrase David Harvey, not all Marxists are dialecticians and not all dialecticians are Marxists.[5] I would add to Harvey's assertion, however, that the most critically astute Marxists are indeed dialecticians and vice versa.[6]

Nevertheless, as José Saldívar points out, "[M]any scholars and critics trained to read texts within the Anglocentric tradition have yet to learn to think dialectically."[7] His observation comes at a time that bears witness to a widespread discrediting of the basic principles of Marxist dialectics, including the concept of "contradiction." As an alternative to nondialectical thinking, Saldívar raises the following provocative question: "Might not Adorno's aesthetic philosophy of nonidentity and negative dialectics be more appropriate than a 1960s Sartrean philosophy of engagement?"[8] In the present context we might frame the same question as follows: What would happen if we placed a dialectical Marxist critique of cultural identity at the center of Chicano literary studies? Taking my cue from Saldívar's question, I suggest that Adorno's negative dialectic can indeed offer

Chicano critics an appropriate way of thinking about both identity and literary form. To be clear, I am not proposing that Adorno is the answer to all the problems associated with the interpretation of Chicano literature. One cannot overlook Adorno's political weaknesses, which have been well documented. Yet as a theorist of culture and literature—and moreover, as a dialectician and a historical materialist—Adorno has much to offer Chicano literary criticism. If we were to rely only on the theoretical works of political purists, we would have very few critics indeed to stack up in support of our arguments. In general, Chicano literary criticism—and perhaps ethnic literary studies generally—has not made sufficient use of Adorno and other theorists of the dialectical tradition. My point is similar to Keya Ganguly's claim regarding postcolonial studies; Ganguly writes that "Frankfurt School social philosophy . . . has yet to find its way into postcolonial analysis."[9] With the exception of a few critics, the same could be said for Chicano literary criticism or ethnic studies generally. I shall now explain briefly my purpose for analyzing Adorno's negative dialectic and its relation to the critique of Chicano novels. But first, I need to distinguish Adorno's negative dialectic from traditional Marxism's dialectical materialism.

To be sure, Adorno's dialectic differs from that of Marx. For Marx, the historical dialectic progresses forward through the increasing antagonism of social class contradictions. As long as class societies exist, class contradictions are never fully resolved. Historical transformations occur when the struggles between social classes result in the rise to power by one social class over another. Roughly speaking, this leads to the replacement of an old qualitative state by a new one, as in the transition (incomplete and uneven as these transitions always are) from one mode of production to another. The process is not linear, predictable, or inevitable, despite the misinformed critics who routinely condemn the Marxist dialectic for being teleological. But the critique of teleology—the view that history develops toward an inevitable end by natural design rather than as the result of human agency and social conflict—often has more to do with condemning Marxist politics than with criticizing the idea of an absolute telos.[10]

Adorno's dialectic evolves out of the Hegelian and Marxist philosophical traditions, but it does not necessarily move forward from one historical stage to another. Nor is there a reconciliation of opposites. Adorno describes his dialectic as "negative" because it never produces a "positive" state, as in Hegel's Absolute Spirit. The movement of Adorno's dialectic never ceases to pursue negation, even to the point of abnegation. Thus at the end of *Negative Dialectics,* Adorno argues that the dialectical critic must "extinguish" the claim of an absolute dialectical knowledge through a "negation of the negation that will not become a positing."[11] He asserts, "To this end, dialectics is obliged to make a final move: being at once the impression and the critique of the universal delusive context, it must now turn even against itself."[12] Jameson responds to this moment of absolute negativity by explaining that Adorno's "negative dialectic" is a "counteraffirmation . . . in which the classical dialectic seeks, by biting its own tail, to deconstruct itself."[13] As Jameson correctly points out, Adorno's self-deconstructing dialectic is problematic for political projects aimed at instigating historical transformation. But what I find useful in Adorno's negative dialectic is the refusal to negate one entity for the purpose of positing another. On the contrary, he argues vehemently against any kind of positivism—even a dialectical kind.

Let me emphasize that although Adorno rejects the notions of reconciliation and synthesis, he does not abandon the principle of contradiction. His dialectic remains rigorously "persistent," criticizing above all the idea of a "dialectical positivism": the act of affirmation by way of negation. In the preface to *Negative Dialectics,* Adorno states his criticism clearly in describing the purpose of his book: "As early as Plato, dialectics meant to achieve something positive by means of negation; the thought figure of a 'negation of negation' later became the succinct term. This book seeks to free dialectics from such affirmative traits without reducing its determinacy."[14] Later in the book he reasons, "In criticizing ontology we do not aim at another ontology, not even at one of being nonontological."[15] Following from these observations, we could argue that to read a Chicano novel—indeed, any novel—in a manner consistent with Adorno's negative dialectic would require a rigorous critique of its reified themes and forms. Granted, the representations of racism, sexism, and class conflicts in Chicano novels remain exceedingly important, but acknowledging their importance does not mean that we need to close one eye to open the other. That is, the representations of identity or personal experience in Chicano novels may not always be as transparent as they seem. Adorno's dialectic helps us come to terms with that which is not readily apparent in Chicano novels—the unseen, the unstated, the repressed, and the abstract.

If Adorno's negative dialectic successfully provides a critical tool for rethinking literary representations of identity formation, it is because of its basis in the Marxist theory of the commodity exchange abstraction. We must acknowledge that the connotation of "identity" as used in Adorno's "critique of identity" differs from that of "cultural identity" as employed by most contemporary cultural critics. Adorno's critique of identity takes issue with philosophies that claim the possibility of an identity between subject and object, between signifier and signified—or more simply, between consciousness and social reality. Cultural identity refers generally to personal consciousness and an individual's awareness of his or her group affiliation. Adorno himself clarifies, however, that these different connotations of identity are not entirely unrelated, recognizing that in "modern philosophy, the word 'identity' has had several meanings," including that of a "personal consciousness."[16] For Adorno, identity as "personal consciousness" differs from the epistemological assertion that "subject and object coincide," but he admonishes, "Not even Kant keeps [these] two layers of meaning strictly apart."[17] This is so because both refer to a process of cognition, to an attempt to know the world (including one's place in the world) by naming it. Adorno postulates that, in a society based on commodity exchange, it is impossible for "subject and object to coincide," even when both subject and object take the form of a "personal consciousness." Interestingly, however, the nonidentity of subject and object is not necessarily an eternal or absolute condition. On the contrary, identity thinking emerges historically from a capitalist system based on commodity exchange, as explained in the following crucial passage from *Negative Dialectics:*

> If mankind is to get rid of the coercion to which the form of identification really subjects it, it must attain identity with its concept at the same time. . . . The barter principle, *the reduction of human labor to the abstract universal concept of average working hours*, is fundamentally akin to the principle of identification. Barter is the social model of the principle, and without the principle there would be no barter; it is through barter that non-identical individuals and performances become commensurable and identical.[18]

In this passage Adorno argues that the principle of identity originates in the process of commodity exchange. Even though the term *barter* usually refers to a system of trade that precedes commodity exchange, Adorno's qualification of the term—"the reduction of human labor to the abstract universal of average working hours"—desribes a process that occurs only with the development of commodity exchange.[19] I am not alone in reading Adorno's critique of identity in this way. In arguing to debunk "post-Marxist" interpretations of Adorno's critique of identity, Jameson comments:

"Of identity we have seen that it is in fact Adorno's word for the Marxian concept of exchange relationship (a term he also frequently uses)."[20] Jameson adds that in discussing Adorno's critique of "identity, the abstraction itself—very much including its most sophisticated philosophical equivalent in logic and in the form of universals—is revealed at another level to be at one with the logic of equivalence and exchange; that is to say, with the logic of capital."[21] From this basic materialist view, Adorno does not rule out the possibility of a historical moment when the "coercion" of identity no longer exists, which implicitly makes the identity of subject and object—thought and reality—historically conceivable. Since identity "is fundamentally akin" to commodity exchange, eradicating the "coercion" of identity would require a social transformation to a system of relations other than capitalism: "From olden times, the main characteristic of the exchange of equivalents has been that unequal things would be exchanged in its name, that the surplus value of labor would be appropriated. If comparability as a category of measure were simply annulled, the rationality which is inherent in the barter principle—as ideology of course, but also as a promise—would give way to direct appropriation, to force, and nowadays to the naked privilege of monopolies and cliques."[22]

Adorno explains that in the process of commodity exchange, unequal things get exchanged as if they were equal, hence the accumulation of surplus value. To make exchange appear equal when it is really not, a deception must take place in the form of ideology: where the nonequality of "equivalents" in commodity exchange translates directly into the nonidentity of subject and object in abstract thinking. These abstractions—of commodity exchange and cognition—serve also as the social synthesis, or the glue, that keeps the system functional.[23] Without the deception that takes place as a result of these abstractions—that is, if the hidden secret in commodity exchange were made transparent—ideology would self-destruct, and "monopolies" and "cliques" would be forced to use brute force to keep the system running. Again, Adorno states:

> When we criticize the barter principle as the identifying principle of thought, we want to realize the ideal of free and just barter. To date, this ideal is only a pretext. Its realization alone would transcend barter. Once critical theory has shown it up for what it is—an exchange of things that are equal and yet unequal—our critique of the inequality within equality aims at equality too, for all our skepticism of the rancor involved in the bourgeois egalitarian ideal that tolerates no qualitative difference. *If no man had part of*

> *his labor withheld from him any more, rational identity would be a fact*, and society would have transcended the identifying mode of thinking.[24]

One need not stretch the imagination to realize that here Adorno alludes to a Communist society. Call it something else, if you must, but essentially he describes an egalitarian society without commodity exchange, without the exploitation of labor, without surplus value, and without ideology.[25] Additionally, these passages call into question the postmodernist conception of Adorno's negative dialectic as the absence of historical development or a static constellation. To achieve the kind of society Adorno describes here would require the abolition of social classes. More importantly, for the purposes of this book, he argues that the mystification that takes place in commodity exchange, the obfuscation of unequal social relations embedded in the very structure of the commodity—a process oftentimes referred to as reification—reproduces itself identically in the abstract thinking of human subjects. As I have been arguing throughout these chapters, this obfuscation also reproduces itself identically in the formal features of novels, such as those of Ruiz de Burton, Acosta, Santiago, and Pineda. With this point in mind, we might be motivated to explore in greater depth the manner in which both cultural identities and literary works of other (non-Chicano) social groups are intricately linked to the abstraction of commodity exchange, wherein nonequivalence gets mistaken for equivalence—where what you see is not exactly what you get, even in terms of "personal consciousness." Whereas the abstraction that takes place in the exchange of commodities obfuscates the accumulation of surplus value, the abstraction at work in cultural identity results in the formation of a reified consciousness unable to conceptualize its own complicity in reproducing certain hegemonic relations of production. In Chicano novels, narrators and characters develop a critical awareness of themselves as members of a historically situated racialized group, but this awareness, useful as it is for surviving in a world of variable oppressions, runs the risk of becoming reified if the ultimate goal, to recall Eagleton, falls short of "going right through" the "ontologically empty" category of racial identity in an effort to "emerge somewhere on the other side," or beyond reification.

The novels of Ruiz de Burton, Acosta, Santiago, and Pineda can be interpreted—as I have attempted to do—as representing the contradictions of social situations and literary forms, along with those of identity and consciousness itself. In this regard, they depict the partially successful efforts of their protagonists in determining their own identities and social spaces, but only from within the limits imposed by the political, cultural, and economic structures of their fictional worlds. We might think of each of these novels as allegorical equivalents of Marx's enormously influential declaration in *The Eighteenth Brumaire of Louis Bonaparte:* "Men [and women] make their own history, but they do not make it just as they please; they do not make it under circumstances chosen by themselves, but under circumstances directly found, given and transmitted from the past."[26] Not satisfied with simplistic notions of human agency and history, Marx demonstrated great insight in recognizing the dialectical relation between exploited classes engaged in efforts to change the world, and ruling classes that resist those efforts at every step, often with the use of brute force. Even today, the women, men, and youth involved in movements to create a new world are not unaffected by "the tradition of all the dead generations [weighing] like a nightmare on the brain of the living."[27] The genius of Marx was to critique the contradictions of capitalism not only in politics and economics, but in all forms of social practice, including literature and art, and then to conceptualize the possibility of a resolution to those contradictions, which inescapably would involve the transformation of a social world that on its surface appears utterly unchangeable. The novels of Ruiz de Burton, Acosta, Santiago, and Pineda do not come close in scope and depth to the *The Eighteenth Brumaire* in terms of political and historical insight. Nevertheless, what these novels do, they do well—gesturing symbolically toward an epistemologically realist representation of the dialectical tension between the reified worlds of their narrators and characters, on the one hand, and the possibilities of a world beyond racial and class distinctions, on the other.

NOTES

INTRODUCTION

1. María Amparo Ruiz de Burton, *The Squatter and the Don* (Houston: Arte Público Press, 1992), originally published in 1885, and *Who Would Have Thought It?* (Houston: Arte Público Press, 1995), originally published in 1872; Daniel Venegas, *Las aventuras de Don Chipote o cuando los pericos mamen* (Mexico City: Secretaría de Educación Pública, Centro de Estudios Fronterizos del Norte de México, 1984), originally published in 1928; Josephina Niggli, *Mexican Village* (Albuquerque: University of New Mexico Press, 1994), originally published in 1945, and *Step Down, Elder Brother* (New York: Rinehart, 1947).

2. Jovita González-Mireles and Eve Raleigh, *Caballero: A Historical Novel* (College Station: Texas A&M University Press, 1996); Jovita González-Mireles, *Dew on the Thorn* (Houston: Arte Público Press, 1997); Américo Paredes, *George Washington Gómez* (Houston: Arte Público Press, 1990). These novels were written in the 1930s.

3. Raymond Barrio, *The Plum Plum Pickers* (1969); Josephina Niggli, *Miracle for Mexico* (1964); John Rechy, *City of Night* (1963), *Numbers* (1967), and *This Day's Death* (1969); Floyd Salas, *Tattoo the Wicked Cross* (1967) and *What Now My Love* (1969); and José Antonio Villareal, *Pocho* (1959).

4. For general studies of the Chicano novel, see Sister Helena Monohan, "The Chicano Novel: Toward a Definition and Literary Criticism," Ph.D. diss., Saint Louis University, 1972; Ramón Saldívar, "A Dialectic of Difference: Towards a Theory of the Chicano Novel," *MELUS* 6:3 (1979): 73–92; Faye Nell Vowell, "The Chicano Novel: A Study in Self-Definition," Ph.D. diss., University of Cincinnati, 1979; Marvin A. Lewis, "Introduction to the Chicano Novel," University of Wisconsin–Milwaukee, Spanish Speaking Outreach Institute Paper Series (1982): 1–74; Charles M. Tatum, "Contemporary Chicano Novel," in *Chicano Literature* (Boston: Twayne, 1982), 102–37; Juan Bruce-Novoa, "History as Content, History as Act: The Chicano Novel," *Aztlán* 18:1 (Spring 1987): 29–44; Ramón Saldívar,

Chicano Narrative: The Dialectics of Difference (Madison: University of Wisconsin Press, 1990); Mario T. García, "History, Literature, and the Chicano Working-Class Novel: A Critical Review of Alejandro Morales' *The Brick People*," *Critica* 2:2 (Fall 1990): 189–201; Héctor Calderón, "The Novel and the Community of Readers: Rereading Tomás Rivera's *Ý no se lo tragó la tierra*," in *Criticism in the Borderlands: Studies in Chicano Literature, Culture, and Ideology*, ed. Calderón and José David Saldívar (Durham, N.C.: Duke University Press, 1991), 97–113; Erlinda Gonzales-Berry, "Unveiling Athena: Women in the Chicano Novel," in *Chicana Critical Issues: Mujeres Activas en Letras y Cambio Social (MALCS)*, ed. Norma Alarcón et al. (Berkeley, Calif.: Third Woman Press, 1993), 33–44; María C. González, *Contemporary Mexican-American Women Novelists: Toward a Feminist Identity* (New York: Peter Lang, 1996); Annie Eysturoy, *Daughters of Self-Creation: The Contemporary Chicana Novel* (Albuquerque: University of New Mexico Press, 1996); Sheila Ortiz Taylor, "*Coachella:* The Novel as Community," *Tema y Variaciones de Literatura* 14:1 (2000): 87–103; and Ralph E. Rodríguez, *Brown Gumshoes: Detective Fiction and the Search for Chicana/o Identity* (Austin: University of Texas Press, 2005).

5. Cherríe Moraga, *Loving in the War Years: Lo que nunca pasó por sus labios* (Cambridge, Mass.: South End Press, 1983) and Gloria Anzaldúa, *Borderlands/la frontera: The New Mestiza* (San Francisco: Aunt Lute Books, 1987).

6. Ray González, ed., *Mirrors beneath the Earth: Short Fiction by Chicano Writers* (Willimantic, Conn.: Curbstone, 1992), 9.

7. Moyra Haslett writes that "Adorno's own theories of 'totality' are responses to and continuations of *History and Class Consciousness.*" See Haslett, *Marxist Literary and Cultural Theories* (New York: St. Martin's Press, 2000), 102. Even more emphatically, Neil Lazarus states that "if we read the Hungarian Marxist pre-eminently as the theorist of reification, Adorno was more thoroughly Lukácsian than Lukács himself." See Lazarus, "Modernism and Modernity: T. W. Adorno and Contemporary White South African Literature," *Cultural Critique* 5 (Winter 1986–87): 137.

8. I could have included any of several other novels in my study of Chicano novels and reification, among them Ronald Ruiz's *Happy Birthday Jesús;* Ana Castillo's *Sapogonia;* Helena Viramontes's *Under the Feet of Jesus;* Dagoberto Gilb's *The Last Known Residence of Mickey Acuña;* Américo Paredes's *George Washington Gómez;* and John Rechy's *The Miraculous Day of Amalia Gómez.*

9. Lukács derives his ideas on Balzac's realism from comments made by Frederick Engels in his famous letter to novelist Margaret Harkness in April 1888. Lukács subsequently elaborated upon Engels's views of realism at length in *The Historical Novel* and other works.

10. Mario Barrera, *Race and Class in the Southwest: A Theory of Racial Inequality* (Notre Dame, Ind.: University of Notre Dame Press, 1979), 39.

11. Oscar Zeta Acosta, *The Autobiography of a Brown Buffalo* (New York: Vintage, 1989), 86.

12. José Limón, *Mexican Ballads, Chicano Poems: History and Influence in Mexican-American Social Poetry* (Berkeley and Los Angeles: University of California Press, 1992), 164.

13. R. Saldívar, *Chicano Narrative*, 213–14.

CHAPTER 1

1. Ruiz de Burton, *Squatter and Don*, 364.

2. Rosemary Hennessy, *Profit and Pleasure: Sexual Identities in Late Capitalism* (New York: Routledge, 2000), 103.

3. Hennessy, *Profit and Pleasure*, 95.

4. Moishe Postone, "The Holocaust and the Trajectory of the Twentieth Century," in *Catastrophe and Meaning: The Holocaust and the Twentieth Century*, ed. Postone and Eric Santner (Chicago: University of Chicago Press, 2003), 90; emphasis added.

5. Susan Oyama, *Evolution's Eye: A Systems View of the Biology-Culture Divide* (Durham, N.C.: Duke University Press, 2000), 138.

6. See Georg Lukács, *History and Class Consciousness: Studies in Marxist Dialectics*, trans. Rodney Livingstone (Cambridge: MIT Press, 1971); Theodor W. Adorno, various works, including *Negative Dialectics*, trans. E. B. Ashton (New York: Continuum, 1994), 189–92, originally published in German in 1966; Fredric Jameson, *Signatures of the Visible* (London: Routledge, 1992), especially the essay entitled "Reification and Utopia in Mass Culture," 9–34, originally published in *Social Text* 1:1 (Fall 1979): 130–48; Jameson, *The Political Unconscious: Narrative as a Socially Symbolic Act* (Ithaca, N.Y.: Cornell University Press, 1981); and Hennessy, *Profit and Pleasure*, especially 74–110.

7. Timothy Bewes, *Reification, or the Anxiety of Late Capitalism* (London: Verso, 2002), 12.

8. Jameson, *Signatures of the Visible*, 24.

9. Edward Said, *The World, the Text, and the Critic* (Cambridge: Harvard University Press, 1983), 231. Said writes that "there is . . . one form of experience that concretely represents the essence of reification as well as its limitation: crisis" (231). He acknowledges that at one level capitalism appears to be total in its ability to quantify, commodify, and rationalize everything—human and nonhuman. "But there are moments," he argues, "when . . . 'irrational' things such as sentiment, passion, chance . . . suddenly become the decisive factor. . . . At such a moment, then, mind or 'subject' has its one opportunity to escape reification: by thinking through what it is that causes reality to appear to be only a collection of objects and economic *données*. . . . Crisis, in short, is converted into criticism of the status quo" (232). Said criticizes Lukács's theory of reification on several counts, but his description of crisis as the moment of dereification is useful for literary criticism. Similarly, Hennessy points out that while Lukács may overstate the pervasiveness and reach of reification in advanced capitalist societies, "he does not finally see this process as all determining. The chapter on reification [in *History and Class Consciousness*] ends with his well-known consideration of the ways the worker, because of his historical position, can and does interrupt reification because wherever he imagines himself to be the subject of his own life he finds this to be an illusion" (Hennessy, *Profit and Pleasure*, 96). Though there are significant differences between experientially based identities and social class, there are also similarities, especially in the case of identities that have been conceptualized and formed in class terms, such as in the racialization of Chicanos. In this case, the racialized subject

"can and does interrupt reification" upon discovering normalized subjectivity to be an illusion.

10. Eric Schocket, *Vanishing Moments: Class and American Literature* (Ann Arbor: University of Michigan Press, 2006), 25.

11. Bewes, *Reification*, 4. For additional excellent critical commentaries on the theory of reification, see J. M. Bernstein, *The Philosophy of the Novel: Lukács, Marxism, and the Dialectics of Form* (Minneapolis: University of Minnesota Press, 1984), 1–43; Said, *World, Text, and Critic*, 230–40; Gillian Rose, *The Melancholy Science* (New York: Columbia University Press, 1978), especially chapter 3, "The Lament over Reification," 27–51; Carolyn Porter, *Seeing and Being: The Plight of the Participant Observer in Emerson, James, Adams, and Faulkner* (Middletown, Conn.: Wesleyan University Press, 1981), especially chapter 2, "Reification and American Literature," 23–53; and Kevin Floyd, "Rethinking Reification: Marcuse, Psychoanalysis, and Gay Liberation," *Social Text* 66, 19:1 (Spring 2001): 103–28. For a somewhat dated but interesting study of reification from a socio-psychoanalytical perspective, see Joseph Gabel, *False Consciousness: An Essay on Reification*, trans. Margaret A. Thompson with the assistance of Kenneth A. Thompson (New York: Harper and Row, 1975), originally published as *La fausse conscience* (Paris: Editions de Minuit, 1962).

12. Kirsten Silva Gruesz, "Utopía Latina: *The Ordinary Seaman* in Extraordinary Times," *Modern Fiction Studies* 49:1 (Spring 2003): 57.

13. In addition to the benefits for literary studies afforded by close reading, other positive aspects of the New Criticism, even those that perhaps were unintended, should be recognized. Richard Ohmann, for example, writes that "although new critical close reading carried with it a lot of ahistorical and apolitical baggage, it also came into literary studies as a democratization of reading: anyone could be a skilled reader by learning new critical procedures, it seemed, in the late 1940s, not just those who had come into high culture by birth. In fact, [I. A.] Richards' *Practical Criticism* seemed to show that the young inheritors of high culture at Cambridge were rotten readers of poetry" (Richard Ohmann, posted on an email list sponsored by the Radical Caucus of the Modern Language Association, February 2, 2006).

14. José Limón, *Mexican Ballads, Chicano Poems: History and Influence in Mexican-American Social Poetry* (Berkeley and Los Angeles: University of California Press, 1992), 3–4.

15. Neil Lazarus, *Nationalism and Cultural Practice in the Postcolonial World* (Cambridge: Cambridge University Press, 1999), 15.

16. Joseph Sommers, "From the Critical Premise to the Product: Critical Modes and Their Applications to a Chicano Literary Text," *New Scholar* 5:2 (1977): 51–80. This essay was originally presented at the MLA in 1975. A short version of the essay was published as "Critical Approaches to Chicano Literature" in *De Colores* 3:4 (1977): 15–21. A slightly revised version of this shorter essay was also reprinted in *The Identification and Analysis of Chicano Literature*, ed. Francisco Jiménez (New York: Bilingual Press/Editorial Bilingüe, 1979), 143–52. The *New Scholar* version also appears in *New Directions in Chicano Scholarship*, ed. Ricardo Romo and Raymund Paredes (La Jolla: Chicano Studies Program, University of

California, San Diego, 1978), 51–80. All citations in this chapter are from the 1977 *New Scholar* article.

17. Sommers marks 1968 as the start of a movement to establish Chicano studies as a legitimate discipline in U.S. universities. Rolando Hinojosa points out that the Modern Language Association included for the first time "a workshop on Chicano literature at its convention in 1970." He adds that the "Midwest MLA followed this by accepting a [*single*] paper on Chicano literature for its 1971 session." See Hinojosa, "Mexican-American Literature: Toward an Identification," *Books Abroad* 49:3 (Summer 1975): 422.

18. Sommers, "Critical Premise to Product," 63.

19. Sommers, "Critical Premise to Product," 57.

20. Sommers, "Critical Premise to Product," 68.

21. Sommers, "Critical Premise to Product," 59; emphasis added .

22. The cases of John Rechy and Sheila Ortiz Taylor, as pointed out by Juan Bruce-Novoa, are interesting in this regard. Rechy and Taylor are Mexican American writers, but their works do not represent Chicano experiences exclusively. For years, their works were excluded from the "Chicano canon," but their exclusion has been contested by scholars critical of reductive notions of cultural authenticity. See Bruce-Novoa, *Retrospace: Collected Essays on Chicano Literature* (Houston: Arte Público Press, 1990), especially the essay "Canonical and Non-canonical Literature" (132–45). See also Karen Christian, "Will the 'Real Chicano' Please Stand Up? The Challenge of John Rechy and Sheila Ortiz Taylor to Chicano Essentialism," *The Americas Review* 20:2 (1992): 89–104. In chapters 4 and 5, I make a similar case for including the novels of Cecile Pineda and Danny Santiago (Daniel James) in Chicano literature courses and research projects.

23. Sommers, "Critical Premise to Product," 59.

24. Gilbert G. González and Raul Fernández, *A Century of Chicano History: Empire, Nations, and Migration* (New York: Routledge, 2003), 1–2. For a similar argument, see Juan Gómez-Quiñones, "Toward a Concept of Culture," *Revista Chicano-Riqueña* 5:2 (Spring 1977): 29–47.

25. Edén E. Torres, *Chicana without Apology, Chicana sin vergüenza: The New Chicana Cultural Studies* (New York: Routledge, 2003). See chapter 2: "Rich in Culture, Low on Capital: Cultural Studies and the Global Economy," 47–71.

26. Arif Dirlik, "Chinese History and the Question of Orientalism," *History and Theory* 35:4 (1996): 117.

27. Sommers, "Critical Premise to Product," 61; emphasis added.

28. Sommers, "Critical Premise to Product," 60.

29. Sommers, "Critical Premise to Product," 60.

30. Bruce-Novoa, *Retrospace*, 169, 170. Bruce-Novoa's rebuke was instigated by Sommers, who wrote that the former "retain[s] the formalist insistence on separating the text from historical reality or social context" ("Critical Premise to Product," 55). But Sommers's assessment was not accurate. Bruce-Novoa certainly pays close attention to the formal aspects of literary texts, but he also expresses concern for the dynamic relation between literature and history. Moreover, he has taken positions not altogether different from those of Sommers, assuming a staunch stance against "those ideologues" in the 1960s and 1970s

"who arrogated to themselves the right to define Chicano authenticity" (Bruce-Novoa, *Retrospace*, 63).

31. R. Saldívar, "A Dialectic of Difference," 73. Saldívar's essay was one of the first serious efforts to theorize the Chicano novel. Saldívar later incorporated a revised version of this essay in *Chicano Narrative: The Dialectics of Difference* (Madison: University of Wisconsin Press, 1990), after dropping references to Sommers's essay—and after changing the focus of his study from the Chicano *novel* to the broader category of Chicano *narrative*.

32. Bruce-Novoa, *Retrospace*, 170.

33. R. Salvidar, "A Dialectic of Difference," 88.

34. R. Saldívar, *Chicano Narrative*, 5.

35. From a more celebratory perspective, Angie Chabram describes Sommers's essay as "ground-breaking" and "a benchmark" in Chicano literary studies. In Chabram's opinion, the essay should be considered "undoubtedly the most comprehensive study" of Chicano literary criticism published between 1977 and 1988. Chabram credits Sommers with inspiring "a string of writers to take cognizance of the developments in Chicano criticism" and "other forms of metacritical activity," even as she recognizes the need to "update" Sommers's assessment and proposed method (Angie Chabram, "Conceptualizing Chicano Critical Discourse," in Calderón and Saldívar, *Criticism in the Borderlands*, 128). Similarly, Chicano poet Alurista (Alberto Urista) acknowledges the importance of Sommers's scholarship and mentorship by paying tribute to him posthumously in a poem entitled "compañero," which appears as the epigraph to Alurista's 1983 dissertation. The poem, written entirely in lowercase with the exception of two letters, ends with the following lines: "i, for one / will remember u / with a capital S / Sommers" (Alberto Heredia Urista, "Oscar Z. Acosta: In Context," Ph. D. diss., University of California, San Diego, 1983, vi).

36. Limón, *Mexican Ballads, Chicano Poems*, 165, 167.

37. For examples of work by the "new Chicano critics," see Chabram, "Conceptualizing Chicano Critical Discourse"; Héctor Calderón, "To Read Chicano Narratives: Commentary and Metacommentary," *Mester* 11 (1983): 3–14; Calderón and Saldívar, *Criticism in the Borderlands;* Teresa McKenna, *Migrant Song: Politics and Process in Contemporary Chicano Literature* (Austin: University of Texas Press, 1997); José David Saldívar, "The Limits of Cultural Studies," *American Literary History* 2:2 (Summer 1990): 251–66; José David Saldívar, *The Dialectics of Our America: Genealogy, Cultural Critique, and Literary History* (Durham, N.C.: Duke University Press, 1991); José David Saldívar, *Border Matters: Remapping American Cultural Studies* (Berkeley and Los Angeles: University of California Press, 1997); Ramón Saldívar, *Figural Language in the Novel: The Flowers of Speech from Cervantes to Joyce* (Princeton, N.J.: Princeton University Press, 1984); R. Saldívar, *Chicano Narrative;* and Rosaura Sánchez, *Chicano Discourse: Socio-historic Perspectives* (Rowley, Mass.: Newbury House, 1983).

38. Limón, *Mexican Ballads, Chicano Poems*, 167

39. Limón, *Mexican Ballads, Chicano Poems*, 167.

40. There are of course exceptions to this claim: John Rechy's *City of Night* and Cecile Pineda's *Face* and *Frieze* may be considered Chicano novels even though

they do not represent Chicano characters centrally, but I would argue that the Chicano-ness of these novels resides as much in their forms as in their themes. I address this issue more fully in my chapter on Pineda and—from a somewhat different perspective—in my chapter on Danny Santiago.

41. Ruiz de Burton, *The Squatter and the Don* (1885, 1992) and *Who Would Have Thought It?* (1872, 1995); González-Mireles and Raleigh, *Caballero;* González-Mireles, *Dew on the Thorn;* Paredes, *George Washington Gómez.* The González-Mireles and Paredes novels were written in the 1930s.

42. See the six volumes of *Recovering the U.S. Hispanic Literary Heritage* (Houston: Arte Público Press), vol. 1, ed. Ramón Gutiérrez and Genaro Padilla (1993); vol. 2, ed. Erlinda Gonzales-Berry and Chuck Tatum (1996); vol. 3, ed. María Herrera-Sobek and Virginia Sánchez Korrol (2000); vol. 4, ed. José F. Aranda Jr. and Silvio Torres-Saillant (2002); vol. 5, ed. Kenya Dworkin-Mendez and Anges Lugo-Ortiz (2006); and vol. 6, ed. Antonia I. Castañeda and A. Gabriel Meléndez (2007). Other works have also contributed in significant ways to establishing a pre-1959 Chicano or U.S. Latino literary tradition: Genaro Padilla, *My History, Not Yours: The Formation of Mexican American Autobiography* (Madison: University of Wisconsin Press, 1993); Rosaura Sánchez, *Telling Identities: The Californio Testimonios* (Minneapolis: University of Minnesota Press, 1995); Tey Diana Rebolledo, *Women Singing in the Snow: A Cultural Analysis of Chicana Literature* (Tucson: University of Arizona Press, 1995); Leticia M. Garza-Falcón, *Gente Decente: A Borderlands Response to the Rhetoric of Dominance* (Austin: University of Texas Press, 1998); Kirsten Silva Gruesz, *Ambassadors of Culture: The Transamerican Origins of Latino Writing* (Princeton, N.J.: Princeton University Press, 2002); José F. Aranda Jr., *When We Arrive: A New Literary History of Mexican America* (Tucson: University of Arizona Press, 2003); and Amelia María de la Luz Montes and Anne Elizabeth Goldman, eds., *María Amparo Ruiz de Burton: Critical and Pedagogical Perspectives* (Lincoln: University of Nebraska Press, 2004).

43. Bruce-Novoa, *Retrospace,* 167.

44. Alma M. García, *Chicana Feminist Thought: The Basic Historical Writings* (London: Routledge, 1997).

45. *De Colores* 3:3 (1977). A special issue: "La Cosecha: Literatura y la Mujer Chicana," issue editors: Linda Morales Armas, Sue Molina, and Teresa Marquez.

46. Lupe Anguiano, "World Women's Challenge—a New Society Based on Justice and Peace," *De Colores* 2:3 (1975): 32.

47. Theodor W. Adorno, *Aesthetic Theory,* trans. Robert Hullot-Kentor (Minneapolis: University of Minnesota, 1997), 142.

48. Adorno, *Aesthetic Theory,* 144; emphasis added. Timothy Bewes offers an insightful analysis of Adorno's dialectical concept of mediation as it relates to the interpretation of artworks. He points out that "[m]ediation is simultaneously mediation and immediacy, just as contemplation, for Adorno, is simultaneously action and contemplation. The attempt to maintain them in opposition—to privilege action over contemplation, for example—is the truly contemplative procedure, the product of a reified consciousness which attributes reality, precisely, to the conceptual world as given. Likewise, what is immediate, in-itself . . . is accessible only in

the process of its mediation; only in its mediation, in fact, does the mediated achieve immediacy" (*Reification*, 164).

49. José Limón, *Dancing with the Devil: Society and Cultural Poetics in Mexican-American South Texas* (Madison: University of Wisconsin Press, 1994), 181.

50. Limón, *Dancing with the Devil*, 181.

51. Jameson, *The Political Unconscious*, 141. I draw on the work of various Marxist theorists (Lukács, Adorno, Sartre, Althusser, Jameson, and Eagleton, among others) who do not agree on every issue related to the study of literature. In fact, they seem to express irreconcilable differences when it comes to such key interpretive categories as modernism, realism, reification, mediation, form, and the dialectic itself. See, for example, Adorno et. al., *Aesthetics and Politics*, translation ed. Ronald Taylor (London: Verso, 1977).

52. Richard Chase, *The American Novel and Its Tradition* (Baltimore: Johns Hopkins University Press, 1957), 1–12 and 243–46.

53. Wallace Martin, *Recent Theories of Narrative* (Ithaca, N.Y.: Cornell University Press, 1986), 21.

54. Fredric Jameson, "Reflections in Conclusion," in Adorno et al., *Aesthetics and Politics*, 204. This essay was later published as "Reflections on the Brecht-Lukács Debate" in Jameson's *The Ideologies of Theory: Essays 1971–1986*, vol. 2, *Syntax of History* (Minneapolis: University of Minnesota Press, 1988), 133–47.

55. Jameson has made similar comments about Lukács's career elsewhere. See Jameson's *Marxism and Form: Twentieth-Century Dialectical Theories of Literature* (Princeton, N.J.: Princeton University Press, 1971), 160–205; and the introduction to Lukács's *The Historical Novel*, trans. Hannah Mitchell and Stanley Mitchell (Lincoln: University of Nebraska Press, 1983), 1–8.

56. Fredric Jameson, "*History and Class Consciousness* as an 'Unfinished Project,'" *Rethinking Marxism* 1:1 (Spring 1988): 52.

57. Jameson, "Unfinished Project," 66.

58. Lukács, *History and Class Consciousness*, 17.

59. Lukács, *History and Class Consciousness*, 203.

60. Jameson, "Unfinished Project," 52–53.

61. For a comprehensive study of the concept of totality, see Martin Jay, *Marxism and Totality: The Adventures of a Concept from Lukács to Habermas* (Berkeley and Los Angeles: University of California Press, 1984). See also Andrew Feenberg, *Lukács, Marx, and the Sources of Critical Theory* (Oxford: Oxford University Press, 1986.)

62. Jameson, "Unfinished Project," 53.

63. Jameson, "Unfinished Project," 54.

64. Writing from a Marxist-Feminist perspective, Teresa Ebert also recognizes the continuing importance of Lukács's concept of totality. Critical of the "antitotality" arguments of postmodernist theorists, she writes, "I think a more productive way to deal with totality is to go back to Lukács—a Lukács whose Hegelian idealism one should be very careful about. Lukács argues in *History and Class Consciousness*, that bourgeois thought is by its very constitution detotalized and detotalizing: it is a fragmentary mode of knowing," or what Lukács refers to as reified consciousness. Ebert's interest, however, lies not only in reified consciousness, but also

in what Lukács "proposes as the *other* of bourgeois thought: 'concrete analysis,' which means 'the relation to society as a whole.' Totality is far from being an abstraction that forgets about specific differences (which is after all the charge postmodernism levels at totality)—it is a concrete recognition of the diverse relations that produce the social." See Ebert, "Rematerializing Feminism," *Science and Society* 69:1 (January 2005): 54.

65. Jameson, "Unfinished Project," 52.

66. Jameson writes, for example, that literary "modernism and reification are parts of the same immense process which expresses the contradictory inner logic and dynamics of late capitalism. [But] modernism—far from being a mere reflection of . . . reification. . . —is also a revolt against that reification and a symbolic act which involves a whole Utopian compensation for increasing dehumanization on the level of daily life" (*The Political Unconscious*, 42). Further: "Lukács is not wrong to associate the emergence of . . . modernism with the reification which is its precondition; but he oversimplifies and deproblematizes a complicated and interesting situation by ignoring the Utopian vocation of the newly reified sense" (63).

67. Jameson, *The Political Unconscious*, 236.

68. Fredric Jameson, "Marxism and the Historicity of Theory: An Interview with Fredric Jameson," interview by Xudong Zhang, *New Literary History* 29:3 (1998): 361.

69. Jameson employs Lukács's theory of reification to explain postmodernism's attack on the concept of "totality" and the repudiation of Marxism generally. As Jameson proposes, "[A]t least a few of the most strident of the anti-totality positions are based on that silliest of all puns, the confusion of 'totality' with 'totalitarianism,'" adding that "what is here staged as a principled fear of Stalinism is probably often little more than a fear of socialism itself" ("Unfinished Project," 60).

70. In *Postmodern Theory: Critical Interrogations* (New York: Guilford Press, 1997), Steven Best and Douglas Kellner argue that identity politics bears the influence of postmodernist theory. Their definition of identity politics merits quoting at length: "The concept of 'identity politics' refers to a politics in which individuals construct their cultural and political identities through engaging in struggles that advance the interests of the groups in which they identify. Identity politics emerges from the splintering of the social movements of the 1960s and 1970s, in which, for example, some black groups pursued a solely black nationalist and separatist program, and some women pursued a strictly feminist agenda. Many other groups also pursued their own agendas, eschewing the movement and alliance politics that had emerged during the mid-1960s to bring people together to oppose the Vietnam War and to transform United States society. By the 1980s and 1990s, the now often warring and highly fragmented political groups were pursuing a politics of identity marked by cultural politics, single-issue group focus on the concerns of one's chosen social group, and rejection of alliance politics. Such versions of identity politics advocate the interests of specific groups over alliances and coalitions, following upon earlier forms of cultural nationalism and separatism" (33 n. 6).

71. Jameson, *The Seeds of Time* (New York: Columbia University Press, 1994), 50.

72. For a critique of postmodernism as it relates to Chicano literature, see

Marcial González, "Postmodernism, Historical Materialism, and Chicana/o Cultural Studies," *Science and Society* 68:2 (Summer 2004): 161–86.

73. Limón, *Mexican Ballads, Chicano Poems,* 159. Limón focuses mainly on poetry, not fiction, but the implications of his argument for "critical modernism" are applicable to Chicano literature generally.

74. Limón, *Mexican Ballads, Chicano Poems,* 165.

75. Limón, *Mexican Ballads, Chicano Poems,* 164.

76. Jameson, "Unfinished Project," 64 n 19.

77. Jameson, "Unfinished Project," 69.

78. Jameson, "Unfinished Project," 70.

79. Jameson, "Unfinished Project," 64; emphasis added.

80. Karl Marx, "Theses on Feuerbach," in *The Marx-Engels Reader,* 2nd ed. (New York: Norton, 1978), 143–45.

81. Lukács, *History and Class Consciousness,* 21.

82. Lukács, *History and Class Consciousness,* 21.

83. Jameson, "Reification and Utopia in Mass Culture," *Signatures of the Visible,* 22.

84. Jameson, "Reification and Utopia in Mass Culture," 5.

85. Rey Chow, *The Protestant Ethnic and the Spirit of Capitalism* (New York: Columbia University Press, 2002), 40.

86. The notion of epistemic access implicit in Jameson's revision of the "standpoint of the proletariat" approximates (and can also be compared to) the concept of "epistemic privilege" as theorized by the postpositivist realists. The difference, however, is that the latter are interested in knowledge derived from experience, while Jameson is interested in gaining access to class consciousness by way of cultural representations. For works of postpositivist realism, see the collection by Paula Moya and Michael R. Hames-García, eds., *Reclaiming Identity: Realist Theory and the Predicament of Postmodernism* (Berkeley and Los Angeles: University of California Press, 2000). See also Satya P. Mohanty, *Literary Theory and the Claims of History: Postmodernism, Objectivity, Multicultural Politics* (Ithaca, N.Y.: Cornell University Press, 1997).

87. Hennessy, *Profit and Pleasure,* 96.

88. Hennessy, *Profit and Pleasure,* 97.

89. Bewes, *Reification,* xi.

CHAPTER 2

1. María Amparo Ruiz de Burton, *The Squatter and the Don* (Houston: Arte Público Press, 1992) and *Who Would Have Thought It?* (Houston: Arte Público Press, 1995). My references to Ruiz de Burton's novels come from these two editions. Arte Público printed a second edition of *The Squatter and the Don* in 1997 with altered pagination; my citations do not correspond to the later edition. As noted on the cover of *The Squatter,* this was "the first literary text to be issued by a national project to reconstruct the literary history of Hispanics of the United States: *Recovering the U. S. Hispanic Literary Heritage.*"

2. Montes and Goldman, *María Amparo Ruiz de Burton.*

3. Sánchez and Pita wrote an equally impressive introduction to the 1995 edition of Ruiz de Burton's *Who Would Have Thought It?*

4. Ruiz de Burton, *Squatter and Don*, 5.

5. Ruiz de Burton, *The Squatter and the Don* (New York: Random House, 2004), xvi. See Ana Castillo's introduction (xiii–xviii).

6. Anne E. Goldman, "'Who Ever Heard of a Blue-Eyed Mexican?': Satire and Sentimentality in María Amparo Ruiz de Burton's *Who Would Have Thought It?*" in *Recovering Hispanic Literary Heritage*, vol. 2, ed. Gonzales-Berry and Tatum, 75.

7. Roberto Schwarz, "A Brazilian Breakthrough," *New Left Review* 36 (November–December 2005): 91–107. In this study of Joaquim Maria Machado de Assis's *The Posthumous Memoirs of Brás Cubas*—a novel published in Brazil five years before *The Squatter* and bearing a formal similarity to Ruiz de Burton's novel—Schwarz describes Machado's novel as "an aesthetic solution to objective problems" (91) lodged in the contradictions of Brazilian culture and postcolonial societies generally.

8. Lukács, *The Historical Novel*, 176.

9. Schwarz, "A Brazilian Breakthrough," 92.

10. Ruiz de Burton, *Squatter and Don*, xviii.

11. Rodolfo Acuña, *Occupied America: A History of Chicanos*, 3rd ed. (New York: Harper Collins, 1988), 125. Tiburcio Vásquez was executed in 1875.

12. John Chavez, *The Lost Land: The Chicano Image of the Southwest* (Albuquerque: University of New Mexico Press, 1984), 87.

13. Jesse Alemán, "'Thank God, Lolita Is Away from Those Horrid Savages': The Politics of Whiteness in *Who Would Have Thought It?*" in Montes and Goldman, *María Amparo Ruiz de Burton*, 99.

14. R. Saldívar, *Chicano Narrative*, 14.

15. Quoted from chapter 39 of Charles Dickens's *Bleak House*.

16. Acuña, *Occupied America*, 124–25.

17. Chavez, *The Lost Land*, 49.

18. Martha Menchaca, *Recovering History, Constructing Race: The Indian, Black, and White Roots of Mexican Americans* (Austin: University of Texas Press, 2001), 215.

19. In arguing for a political and moral "rectitude," Don Mariano articulates what might be considered a nineteenth-century version of late-twentieth-century "political correctness."

20. Sánchez and Pita, introduction to *Who Would Have Thought It?* 6.

21. Sánchez and Pita, introduction to *Who Would Have Thought It?* 30–31.

22. Sánchez and Pita, introduction to *Who Would Have Thought It?* 8; emphasis added.

23. Schwarz, "A Brazilian Breakthrough," 105.

24. R. Saldívar, *Chicano Narrative*, 213.

25. María Amparo Ruiz de Burton, *Conflicts of Interest: The Letters of María Amparo Ruiz de Burton*, edited with commentary by Rosaura Sánchez and Beatrice Pita (Houston: Arte Público Press, 2001), xvii. The quoted passage comes from the introduction, written by Sánchez and Pita.

26. Sánchez, *Telling Identities*, 34.

27. Alemán, "Thank God, Lolita," 97.

28. John M. González, "Romancing Hegemony: Constructing Racialized Citizenship in María Amparo Ruiz de Burton's *The Squatter and the Don*," in *Recovering Hispanic Literary Heritage*, vol. 2, ed. Gonzales-Berry and Tatum, 26.

29. González, "Romancing Hegemony," 30.

30. González cautions against an easy dismissal of nationalism as an oppositional discourse, arguing that Chicano nationalism, "despite its shortcomings, nonetheless continues as a powerful articulation of communal memory and resistance." Notwithstanding the critiques of sexism and other forms of separatism within Chicano nationalist projects, González adds, somewhat controversially, that nationalism "remains a necessary but not sufficient condition for a critical practice" ("Romancing Hegemony," 27).

31. Manuel M. Martín Rodríguez, "Textual and Land Reclamation: The Critical Reception of Early Chicana/o Literature," in *Recovering Hispanic Literary Heritage*, vol. 2, ed. Gonzales-Berry and Tatum, 47.

32. Rodríguez, "Textual and Land Reclamation," 46.

33. José Aranda, "Contradictory Impulses: Maria Amparo Ruiz de Burton, Resistance Theory, and the Politics of Chicano/a Studies," *American Literature* 70:3 (September 1998): 554.

34. Aranda, "Contradictory Impulses," 554; emphasis added.

35. Aranda, "Contradictory Impulses," 561.

36. Aranda, "Contradictory Impulses," 573. In a later essay, Aranda mollifies his criticism of Saldívar, stating that "Saldívar's idea of Ruiz de Burton as a mediator has been, I must admit, tantalizing, but if she was not a subaltern mediator, then what kind of mediator was she, and why?" See "Returning California to the People: Vigilantism in *The Squatter and the Don*," in Montes and Goldman, *María Amparo Ruiz de Burton*, 13.

37. J. Saldívar, *Border Matters*, 170.

38. J. Saldívar, *Border Matters*, 180.

39. J. Saldívar, *Border Matters*, 170.

40. J. Saldívar, *Border Matters*, 182.

41. Aranda, "Contradictory Impulses," 573.

42. Aranda, "Returning California," 13.

43. Sánchez, *Telling Identities*, 34.

44. *The Bostonians* first appeared serially in the *Century Magazine* from February 1885 to February 1886. The first complete edition was published in 1886.

45. Anne Goldman, *Continental Divides: Revisioning American Literature* (New York: Palgrave, 2000), 21–37.

46. Julie Ruiz, "Captive Identities: The Gendered Conquest of Mexico in *Who Would Have Thought It?*" in Montes and Goldman, *María Amparo Ruiz de Burton*, 121.

47. Carrie Tirado Bramen, *The Uses of Variety: Modern Americanism and the Quest for National Distinctiveness* (Cambridge: Harvard University Press, 2000), 130–42.

48. Garza-Falcón, *Gente Decente*, 9, 10.

49. Roberto Schwarz, *A Master on the Periphery of Capitalism: Machado de Assis*, trans. John Gledson (Durham, N.C.: Duke University Press, 2001), 119. Schwarz

adds: "[W]e can say that the question of honesty in narrative changes in quality and takes on its present-day aspect from 1848 on, when the tide of popular revolutions forced the European bourgeoisies to recognize the particular nature of their own interests" (119).

50. V. N. Volosinov, *Marxism and the Philosophy of Language*, trans. L. Matejka and I. R. Tutunik (New York: Seminar, 1973) (originally published in 1930), 23.

51. Sánchez, *Telling Identities*, 54, 64.

52. Karl Marx, *Capital: A Critique of Political Economy*, vol. 1, Translated by Ben Fowkes, introduction by Ernest Mandel (London: Penguin, 1990), 929.

53. See Albert Camarillo, *Chicanos in a Changing Society: From Mexican Pueblos to American Barrios in Santa Barbara and Southern California, 1848–1930* (Cambridge: Harvard University Press, 1979), 126-41; David Montejano, *Anglos and Mexicans in the Making of Texas, 1836–1986* (Austin: University of Texas Press, 1987), 106–219.

54. John Borrego, "Capitalist Accumulation and Revolutionary Accumulation: The Context for Chicano Struggle," Ph.D. diss., University of California, Berkeley, 1978, 35.

55. Marx, *Capital*. In the opening lines of part 8 of *Capital*, vol. 1, Marx writes, "[T]he accumulation of capital presupposes surplus-value; surplus-value presupposes capitalist production; capitalist production presupposes the availability of considerable masses of capital and labour-power in the hands of commodity producers. The whole movement, therefore, seems to turn around in a never-ending circle, which we can only get out of by assuming a primitive accumulation (the 'previous accumulation' of Adam Smith) which precedes capitalist accumulation; an accumulation which is not the result of the capitalist mode of production but its point of departure" (873).

56. For an excellent analysis of the effects of primitive accumulation in the late twentieth century, see Michael Perelman, *The Invention of Capitalism: Classical Political Economy and the Secret History of Primitive Accumulation* (Durham, N.C.: Duke University Press, 2000). Perelman argues that the concept of primitive accumulation should not be understood restrictively as a transitory moment between precapitalist social relations and the early stages of industrial capitalism, but rather, primitive accumulation is an ongoing process that continues alongside the general process of capital accumulation proper. For Chicano history, primitive accumulation, then, does not refer merely to the experiences of land loss and proletarianization that took place in the decades following 1848 and the U.S. annexation of the Southwest; it refers also to practices that continue to take place in the present. For instance, how different were the enclosures of eighteenth-century England, which forced peasants off their land and into the cities to meet the labor needs of an expanding industrialism, from NAFTA and other neoliberal policies and practices of the United States, which have forced huge numbers of workers, farmers, and professionals to abandon their homes in Latin America and migrate to the United States to find work? See also Silvia Federici, *Caliban and the Witch: Women, the Body, and Primitive Accumulation* (Brooklyn, N.Y.: Autonomedia, 2004). Federici constructs a history of patriarchy that coincides with the emergence of capitalism and primitive accumulation. She refers to the latter as "the historical context in which the history of women and reproduction in the transition from feudalism to capital-

ism must be placed; for the changes which the advent of capitalism introduced in the social position of women—especially at the proletarian level—were primarily dictated by the search for new sources of labor as well as new forms of regimentation and division of the work-force" (66).

57. For two sources on the relation of "free labor" and capitalist accumulation, see Tomas Almaguer, *Racial Faultlines: The Historical Origins of White Supremacy in California* (Berkeley and Los Angeles: University of California Press, 1994), 32–37; and Jairus Banaji, "The Fictions of Free Labour: Contract, Coercion and So-Called Unfree Labour," *Historical Materialism* 11:3 (2003): 69–95.

58. Mario Barrera, *Race and Class in the Southwest: A Theory of Racial Inequality* (Notre Dame, Ind.: University of Notre Dame Press, 1979), 34–57.

59. For an early essay that argues for the usefulness of the internal colony model, see Carlos Muñoz, Mario Barrera, and Charles Ornelas, "The Barrio as an Internal Colony," in *La Causa Política: A Chicano Politics Reader*, ed. F. Chris Garcia (Notre Dame, Ind.: University of Notre Dame Press, 1974), 281–301. This article was first published in *Urban Affairs Annual Review* 6 (1972): 465–98.

60. Barrera, *Race and Class*, 7. Gilbert G. González and Raul A. Fernández point out that the Californios and other sectors of the landowning Mexicans in the Southwest did not make up a significant portion of the emergent colonial labor force. They formed a relatively small social grouping compared to the amount of labor that would be required to drive certain industries in California and the Southwest. Most of that labor force would be comprised of Mexicans immigrating to the United States after 1900. The Californios are nonetheless important historically for understanding the social developments that led to the class-based racialization of Mexicans beginning in the nineteenth century. See González and Fernández, *A Century of Chicano History: Empire, Nations, and Migration* (London: Routledge, 2003), 1–28.

61. Barrera, *Race and Class*, 39–53.

62. I use the term *organic intellectual* here in the Gramscian sense. Quintin Hoare and Geoffrey Nowell Smith define organic intellectuals as "the thinking and organizing element of a particular fundamental social class." Their function is to direct "the ideas and aspirations of the class to which they belong" (3). See Antonio Gramsci, *Selections from the Prison Notebooks of Antonio Gramsci*, ed. and trans. Q. Hoare and G. N. Smith (New York: International Publishers, 1971).

63. Frederick Jackson Turner, *The Frontier in American History* (Tuscon: University of Arizona Press, 1992), 219. The essays in this volume were published from 1893 to 1920.

64. Gilbert González, "American Writers and the Ideology of Empire: The U.S. and Mexico, 1880–1930," Working Paper Series in Cultural Studies, Ethnicity and Race Relations, Department of Comparative American Cultures, Washington State University (1999), 2. For a stark exposé of racist attitudes toward Mexicans in the nineteenth century, see Arnoldo De León, *They Called Them Greasers: Anglo Attitudes toward Mexicans in Texas, 1821–1900* (Austin: University of Texas Press, 1983).

65. To cite just one example, consider the case of Frederick Remington, a personal friend of Theodore Roosevelt. Remington describes Mexicans as occupying "the tiniest mental world, hardly larger than the *patio*" (47), and as having no windows in their dwellings (48), metaphorical for having no eyes in their heads—no ca-

pacity for envisioning the future. Remington describes Mexicans as dirty, lazy, listless, ugly, subservient, animal-like, childlike, slothful, wild, disorderly, and docile. Mexicans are not fully human, and "while the dogs and pigs lie about . . . little brown vaqueros are ripening in the sun." The image here is one of cultivation, the raising of a new crop, a new generation of obedient dark people and laborers: the reproduction of the relations of production. The Mexican vaquero is a "fatalist, with less wants than the pony he rides"; thus he will gladly accept low wages. Inhabiting a "land where *poco tiempo* means forever" (61), the Mexican lacks a conception of historical time, a characteristic sometimes referred to as the *mañana* syndrome. See Remington, *Pony Tracks* (Norman: University of Oklahoma Press, 1989); originally published in 1893.

66. Mark Seltzer, *Bodies and Machines* (London: Routledge, 1992), 25.

67. Seltzer, *Bodies and Machines,* 43.

68. Lukács, *The Historical Novel,* 176.

69. Lukács, *The Historical Novel,* 178.

70. This passage comes from an essay entitled "Schiller" in Thomas Carlyle, *Critical and Miscellaneous Essays* (Boston: Phillips, Sampson, 1855), 226.

71. As Tirado Bramen points out, drawing on Spencer's own declarations, Spencer "believed that interracial unions among widely divergent 'varieties' were 'physically injurious' to the offspring, producing a 'worthless type of mind—a mind fitted neither for the kind of life led by the higher of the two races, nor for that led by the lower—a mind out of adjustment to all conditions of life" (*The Uses of Variety,* 202).

72. Herbert Spencer, "Representative Government—What Is It Good For?" from *Essays: Scientific, Political, and Speculative,* vol. 3 (New York and London: D. Appleton, 1892), 283–325. For passage quoted, see page 323. This essay was first published in *Westminster Review,* October 1857, 454–86.

73. The passage quoted by Mechlin comes from Spencer, "Representative Government," 315. Stanford is a character in the novel based on the actual Leland Stanford.

74. Lukács, *The Historical Novel,* 173.

75. Barbara Foley, *Telling the Truth: The Theory and Practice of Documentary Fiction* (Ithaca, N.Y.: Cornell University Press, 1986), 65. Similarly, Fredric Jameson writes that literature produces "analogous subjects and forms of historical consciousness," and that "the work of art . . . certainly reflects something, but what it reflects is not so much the class in itself as some autonomous cultural configuration, as rather the situation of that class, or, in short, class conflict" (*Marxism and Form,* 381–82).

76. Schwarz, "A Brazilian Breakthrough," 105.

77. Raymond Williams, *Marxism and Literature* (Oxford: Oxford University Press, 1977), 121–27.

78. Foley, *Telling the Truth,* 146.

79. My use of the terms *consent* and *coercion* comes from Gramsci, *Prison Notebooks.* He describes these terms as dialectical opposites within the process of hegemony. See especially chapter 2, "State and Civil Society," 206–76.

80. Vincent Pérez, "Remembering the Hacienda: Land and Community in Californio Narratives," in Montes and Goldman, *María Amparo Ruiz de Burton,* 29.

81. Aranda, "Returning California," 21.

82. Terry Eagleton, "Nationalism: Irony and Commitment," in Eagleton, Fredric Jameson, and Edward Said, *Nationalism, Colonialism, and Literature* (Minneapolis: University of Minnesota Press, 1990), 35.

CHAPTER 3

1. Leonard Pitt, *Decline of the Californios* (Berkeley and Los Angeles: University of California Press, 1966), 160.

2. Ernesto Chávez, *"¡Mi Raza Primero!" (My People First): Nationalism, Identity, and Insurgency in the Chicano Movement in Los Angeles, 1966–1978* (Berkeley and Los Angeles: University of California Press, 2002), 70. In addition to Salazar, two other persons were killed at the demonstration: Angel Gilberto Díaz died in an auto accident while trying to leave the area, and "Lynn Ward, a fifteen-year-old Brown Beret, received fatal wounds from an explosion that hurled him through a plate-glass window" (Chávez 70). Approximately four hundred persons were arrested.

3. Oscar Zeta Acosta. *The Revolt of the Cockroach People* (New York: Vintage, 1989); originally published by Straight Arrow Books in 1973 and reprinted by Bantam in 1974. All page references in this chapter are from the 1989 edition.

4. Fredric Jameson, *Sartre: The Origins of a Style* (New York: Columbia University Press, 1984), vii. Originally published in 1961 by Yale University Press.

5. Oscar Zeta Acosta, *Autobiography of a Brown Buffalo* (New York: Vintage, 1989). Originally published by Straight Arrow Books, 1972. All page references are from the 1989 edition. Henceforward I shall refer to the novel as *Autobiography*. For the sake of clarity, I treat the narrators in Acosta's two novels as separate characters: Oscar in *Autobiography* and Zeta Brown in *Revolt*.

6. Raymund A. Paredes, "Los Angeles from the Barrio: Oscar Zeta Acosta's *The Revolt of the Cockroach People*," in *Los Angeles Fiction: A Collection of Original Essays*, edited by David Fine (Albuquerque: University of New Mexico Press, 1984), 213. Paredes's description of Acosta's writing style as a "literary equivalent of a Molotov cocktail" borrows from Juan Bruce-Novoa's characterization of Hunter Thompson's "Gonzo journalism" as an "alternative to armed revolution, a literary Molotov cocktail" in "Fear and Loathing on the Buffalo Trail," *MELUS* 6:4 (Winter 1979): 40.

7. Paredes, "Los Angeles from the Barrio," 213.

8. For other interpretations of Acosta's Gonzo style, see Bruce-Novoa, "Fear and Loathing," and Yvette C. Doss, "The Lost Legend of the Real Dr. Gonzo," *Los Angeles Times*, June 5, 1998, 2. Doss explains that "new journalism" was the stylistic precursor of "Gonzo journalism." Two practitioners of "new journalism" were Tom Wolfe and Norman Mailer. Genaro Padilla compares Acosta's writing style in *Revolt* to that of Norman Mailer's *Armies of the Night*. Padilla writes, "Not content to remain merely an external observer of the crazy house of history, the writer forces his way into the house of mirrors, narrates his own vigorous movements and perceptions, and, consequently, becomes the protagonist of his own story." See "The Progression from Individual to Social Consciousness in Two Chicano Novel-

ists: José Antonio Villarreal and Oscar Zeta Acosta," Ph.D. diss., University of Washington, 1981, 213.

9. For drafts of the novels, see Acosta's "The Autobiography of the Brown Buffalo," *Con Safos* 2:7 (Winter 1971): 34–46; and "The Revolt of the Cockroach People," *La Gente*, November–December 1973, 4–5, 12. "Autobiography" was reprinted in *Growing Up Latino: Memoirs and Stories*, ed. Harold Augenbraum and Ilan Stavans (Boston: Houghton Mifflin, 1993), 193–207; and both drafts were reprinted in Acosta's *Uncollected Works*, ed. Stavans (Houston: Arte Público Press, 1996), 149–73 and 177–90.

10. Norman D. Smith refers to *Revolt* as a "literary compilation documentary" in "Buffaloes and Cockroaches: Acosta's Siege at Aztlán," *Latin American Literary Review* 5:10 (Spring–Summer 1977): 94. This article was reprinted in *Contemporary Chicano Fiction: A Critical Survey*, ed. Vernon E. Lattin (Binghamton, N.Y.: Bilingual Press/Editorial Bilingüe, 1986), 82–93.

11. The film Zeta Brown describes in *Revolt* was made by the police, not one of the protesters. In the novel, the district attorney, Torrez, tells Sheriff Peaches, "[W]e have seen the film your department prepared" (202). This fact does not diminish the symbolic importance of the film and the light it sheds on Acosta's writing style. The film is important to Zeta Brown because it can be read as being produced by a participant-observer. For an example of the kind of film Zeta Brown describes, see David Garcia's *Requiem 29* (Los Angeles: NLCC Educational Media, 1997), a documentary film produced with footage from the August 1970 Chicano Moratorium demonstration in Los Angeles, California. The film documents the confrontation between police and Chicanos during and after the demonstration, and it includes scenes from the subsequent inquest hearing into the death of Rubén Salazar.

12. Smith, "Buffaloes and Cockroaches," 91.

13. Bruce-Novoa, "Fear and Loathing," 45.

14. Erich Auerbach, *Mimesis: The Representation of Reality in Western Literature*, trans. Willard R. Trask (Princeton, N.J.: Princeton University Press, 1953), 115. Auerbach analyzes paratactic constructions in Homeric poetry, not modern novels. Nonetheless, his conception of parataxis is highly instructive for untangling some of the formal complexities in modern novels such as *Revolt*. See also Rose, *The Melancholy Science*. In describing the symbolic significance of Theodor Adorno's writing style, Rose explains, "'Parataxis' means placing propositions one after the other without indicating relations of co-ordination or subordination between them" (13). For another excellent description and analysis of Adorno's paratactic style, see Robert Hullot-Kentor's "Translator's Introduction," in Adorno's *Aesthetic Theory*, xi–xxi. Hullot-Kentor describes *Aesthetic Theory* as a "paratactical text" in which "every sentence undertake[s] to be the topic sentence . . . each of which stems under the obligation to present the book as a whole" (xiv).

15. I refer to Acosta's novels as hybrid because they employ both hypotactic and paratactic narrative strategies. Other critics have described his novels as "hybrid" because they mix genres. Bruce-Novoa explains that "Acosta's books are . . . hybrids of fiction, journalism, and autobiography" ("Fear and Loathing," 44).

Horst Tonn describes *Revolt* as "clearly a 'hybrid' form—a combination of the elements of journalistic reporting, autobiography and the novel." See Tonn's "Fiction and Politics in Acosta's *The Revolt of the Cockroach People*," in *Missions in Conflict: Essays on U.S.-Mexican Relations and Chicano Culture*, ed. Renate von Bardeleben, Dietrich Briesemeister, and Juan Bruce-Novoa (Tübingen, Germany: Gunter Narr Verlag, 1986), 195.

16. Robert Weisberg, *Poethics and Other Strategies of Law and Literature* (New York: Columbia University Press, 1992), 104–16. Weisberg employs the term *inside narrative* in his formal analysis of Herman Melville's *Billy Budd, Sailor*. He argues that Melville's novella is structured with a "covert" inside narrative that has been overlooked by critics and casual readers alike. He takes the term *inside narrative* from the subtitle of *Billy Budd*, which is "(An inside narrative)."

17. Richard Lanham, *Analyzing Prose*, 2nd ed. (London: Continuum Company, 2003), 47.

18. Smith, "Buffaloes and Cockroaches," 95.

19. Lanham, *Analyzing Prose*, 47.

20. Hullot-Kentor, "Translator's Introduction," xvi.

21. Auerbach, *Mimesis*, 71.

22. Jeanne Thwaites, "The Use of Irony in Oscar Zeta Acosta's *Autobiography of a Brown Buffalo*," *The Americas Review* 20:1 (Spring 1992): 74.

23. Arthur Ramírez, "Reseñas: Book Review of *The Autobiography of a Brown Buffalo* and *The Revolt of the Cockroach People*," *Revista Chicano-Riqueña* 3:3 (Summer 1975): 50.

24. Ramírez, "Reseñas," 51.

25. N. Katherine Hayles, "Postmodern Parataxis: Embodied Texts, Weightless Information," *American Literary History* 2:3 (Fall 1990): 400.

26. Hayles, "Postmodern Parataxis," 396.

27. Alan Munton, "Quoting the Culture: The New British Sentence and the Politics of Parataxis in the Avant-garde, 1914–2001," *Critical Survey* 14:2 (September 2002): 22.

28. Quoted in Rose, *The Melancholy Science*, 13.

29. Lanham, *Analyzing Prose*, 29.

30. Alan C. Hunsaker, "Book Review: *The Autobiography of a Brown Buffalo* and *The Revolt of the Cockroach People*," *Hispanic Journal of Behavioral Sciences* 12:3 (August 1990): 332.

31. Hunsaker, "Book Review," 333.

32. Dorothy Healey is a minor fictional character in the novel based on the real person with the same name.

33. Smith maintains that the "[j]uxtaposing portraits of vatos, spiritual and militant leaders, and martyrs gives Acosta's work a sense of immediacy" (94), and Lionel Rolfe writes that Acosta's "intermingling of cultural paradigms . . . gives his books . . . their real significance." See "Why I Still Love Oscar Zeta Acosta," in *Literary L.A.* (Los Angeles: California Classics, 2002), 57.

34. In *Autobiography*, the narrator identifies himself as "a brown-eyed child of the sun" and "[j]ust a peach-picker's boy from the West Side" (54).

35. According to James Smethurst, the representation of the *vato loco* in *Revolt* is consistent with the 1960s politics of the New Left, which tended to view the

lumpenproletariat as revolutionary because as a social group it was the "most alienated from society and therefore the most radical." See Smethurst, "The Figure of the Vato Loco and the Representation of Ethnicity in the Narratives of Oscar Z. Acosta," *MELUS* 20:2 (Summer 1995): 127. The view that the *lumpenproletariat* constitutes a strategic revolutionary class is not limited to the New Left of the 1960s. Historian Marcus Rediker formulated a similar argument in a talk he gave at the Working Class Studies Conference, Youngstown State University on May 18, 2001. The untitled talk was part of a panel called "Workers, Prisoners, and Resistance from Olden Days to Mumia Abu-Jamal."

36. Some critics argue that *Revolt* privileges one or another of these strategies; others question whether the novel, ultimately, privileges any particular strategy at all. Tonn argues that the "juxtaposition of adversary and sometimes contradictory outlooks" is the "central narrative paradigm" in *Revolt* ("Fiction and Politics," 198), but he concludes that Acosta's novel does not make the case for any single "ideology" and that *Revolt* will "frustrate any reader's attempt to align the text with a given political stance" (201).

37. For a critique of Acosta's sexism and homophobia in relation to cultural nationalism, see Carl Gutiérrez-Jones, *Rethinking the Borderlands: Between Chicano Culture and Legal Discourse* (Berkeley and Los Angeles: University of California Press, 1995), 123–39.

38. R. Saldívar, *Chicano Narrative*, 96.

39. Michael A. Olivas, "'Breaking the Law' on Principle," in *The Latino/a Condition: A Critical Reader*, ed. Richard Delgado and Jean Stefancic (New York: New York University Press, 1998), 320–31.

40. Michael Hames-Garcia, "Dr. Gonzo's Carnival: The Testimonial Satires of Oscar Zeta Acosta," *American Literature* 72:3 (September 2000): 483.

41. Ian F. Haney López, *Racism on Trial: The Chicano Fight for Justice* (Cambridge: Harvard University Press, 2003).

42. In a personal essay, Acosta himself writes, "Lawyers are basically peddlers of flesh. They live off other people's misery. . . . I have no respect for the courts and I make it clear to them from the minute I walk in that I have no respect for the system. That I'm against it and would destroy it in one second if I had the physical power to do it" (*Uncollected Works*, 14).

43. Bruce-Novoa, "Fear and Loathing," 46.

44. According to Sam Blazer, *Revolt* exposes "the hypocrisy and the falseness of the judicial process for anyone—juror, reporter or victim—who can afford the luxury of understanding." See Blazer, "Review: *The Revolt of the Cockroach People*," *The Nation*, April 13, 1974, 469.

45. In *Revolt*, Zeta Brown receives more than half a million votes in the election for sheriff. In actuality, Acosta received just over 100,000 votes, substantially less than the incumbent, Peter Pitchess (portrayed by Sheriff Peaches in the novel) but still quite impressive. Pitchess received 1.3 million votes. The day after the election, Rubén Salazar wrote, "Acosta, easily recognized in court by his loud ties and flowered attaché case with a Chicano Power sticker, didn't come close to [winning] but he did beat Everett Holladay, Monterey Park chief of police" for second place. Salazar adds, "[I]n the Chicano community Acosta's impressive loss was an enigmatic ray of sunshine." See Rubén Salazar, *Border Correspondent: Selected Writings*,

1955–1970, ed. Mario T. García (Berkeley and Los Angeles: University of California Press, 1995), 259.

46. Bruce-Novoa, *Retrospace*, 137. His essay "Canonical and Non-canonical Texts" in this collection was originally published in *The Americas Review* 14:3–4 (Fall–Winter 1986): 119–35.

47. Bruce-Novoa, *Retrospace*, 138.

48. Louis Mendoza, "On Buffaloes, Body Snatching, and Bandidismo: Ilan Stavans's Appropriation of Oscar Acosta and the Chicano Experience," *Bilingual Review/La Revista Bilingüe* 26:1 (January–April 2001–2): 83.

49. Most critics have interpreted Acosta's novels as a "search for identity" from one angle or another. Some have read the novels as being successful in this search; others conclude that Acosta ultimately fails to find his identity. A few have read Acosta's quest in a positive light, while others have interpreted the journey as inevitably futile. Some have focused on the narrator's individual identity; others have argued that *Revolt* posits a collective identity based on ethnicity, culture, or nationalist politics. What almost all the criticism has in common, however, is the claim that Acosta's novels essentially trace the author's attempt to find his identity. Carlotta Cárdenas de Dwyer describes *Autobiography* as "an unholy pilgrimage to self and identity" in her dissertation, "Chicano Literature 1965–1975: The Flowering of the Southwest," SUNY Stony Brook, 1976, 184. Raymund Paredes maintains that "[a]t the root of [Acosta's] troubles is a lack of self-identity" in "Contemporary Mexican-American Literature, 1960–Present," *A Literary History of the American West* (Fort Worth: Texas Christian University Press, 1987), 1111. Francisco R. Alvarez identifies the epiphany of *Autobiography* as "el momento de identificación con el grupo o comunidad," in "*The Autobiography of a Brown Buffalo* de Oscar Zeta Acosta: Escritura, ser e ideología en la autobiografía chicana de los 70," *Monographic Review/Revista Monografica* 9 (1993): 169. Padilla argues that Acosta's "sojourn has led to an expansive communal identity through which he projects his own role in the destiny of his people" ("Progression," 55). According to María del Carmen Trouvé, "Acosta describe su viaje . . . espiritual hacia la comprensión y aceptación de su identidad chicana." See Trouvé's "La Mujer en la Negociación de la Identidad Chicana: *The Autobiography of a Brown Buffalo* de Oscar Zeta Acosta," in *XXVIII Jornadas de la Asociación Argentina de Estudios Americanos*, ed. Picazo, Boiero, and Celi (Rio Cuarto, Argentina: Universidad Nacional de Rio Cuarto, 1997), 377. Smith also characterizes Acosta as undertaking "a spiritual quest searching for both personal identity and a place within two countries" ("Buffaloes and Cockroaches," 87). For Ramírez, *Autobiography* represents a "budding desire to . . . affirm his Chicano identity" and a "desperate search for personal and collective identity . . . and a kind of salvation" ("Reseñas," 48, 51). Likewise, as Charles Tatum observes, Acosta becomes "aware that he is culturally rootless" and undertakes a quest for the "attainment of his true identity as a Chicano" (*Chicano Literature*, 112–13). According to Manuel Luis Martínez, Acosta and Mexican Americans of his period abnegated "their 'American' cultural persona, and in effect [became] stateless subjects . . . opting for a mythical Aztlán." See Martínez's *Countering the Counterculture: Reading Postwar American Dissent from Jack Kerouac to Tomás Rivera* (Madison: University of Wisconsin Press, 2003), 172. In a series of articles that

span a decade, Joe D. Rodríguez asserts the centrality of identity in Acosta's novels: in "God's Silence and the Shrill of Ethnicity in the Chicano Novel," *Explorations in Ethnic Studies* 4:2 (July 1981), he writes that *Autobiography* "is a boisterous account of a lawyer without a sure sense of identity . . . who casts himself adrift on a voyage of self-discovery" (16); in "The Chicano Novel and the North American Narrative of Survival," *Denver Quarterly* 16 (Fall 1981), Rodríguez argues that in *Revolt* the narrator "has forgotten his culture . . . and wonders if he is a turncoat or vendido" (66); in "Oscar Zeta Acosta," *Chicano Literature: A Reference Guide*, ed. Francisco Lomelí and Julio A. Martínez (Westport, Conn.: Greenwood Press, 1985), he maintains that Acosta's novels "recklessly and doggedly pursue . . . ethnic identity" (4); and in "Oscar Zeta Acosta," *Dictionary of Literary Biography*, vol. 82, *Chicano Writers, First Series*, ed. Francisco Lomelí and Carl R. Shirley (Detroit: Gale Research, 1989), Rodríguez holds that "[e]thnicity was Acosta's literary mission" (9). Paul Guajardo writes the most troublesome interpretation of Acosta's novels. In *Chicano Controversy: Oscar Acosta and Richard Rodriguez* (New York: Peter Lang, 2002), Guajardo complains that Acosta fails to convince "that he has put together all the pieces of his identity puzzle" (38), and he claims Acosta "is never completely at home with his Chicano heritage" (55). Then he lambastes Acosta for being "an opportunist who spent much of his life rejecting his culture (dis-assimilating) and then frantically trying to reclaim it . . . unsuccessfully" (1). He adds, "There is little progression of Acosta as an individual; he is a static character in terms of development and change" (61). Guajardo's biggest mistake (and he is not alone in doing this) is to conflate the author with the narrator in Acosta's novels. Guajardo treats Acosta's narrators as real persons rather than as socially symbolic figures.

50. On this point, I agree with Carlos Gallego, who argues that "identity, although an important concept to be considered in philosophical and political debates, as well as [in] literary studies, cannot be prioritized as a category for social change due to its primary psychic-ideological function." See "Chicano Literature and the Problem of Identity," an unpublished manuscript presented at the Sixteenth Annual Arizona Quarterly Symposium on American Literature and Culture, University of Arizona, March 25, 2004.

51. The 1968 walkouts are dramatized in a film entitled *Walkout*, produced by Moctesuma Esparza and directed by Edward James Olmos (HBO Films, 2006).

52. Haney López, *Racism on Trial*, 3.

53. Juan Bruce-Novoa, "Homosexuality and the Chicano Novel," *Confluencia: Revista Hispanica de Cultura y Literatura* 2:1 (Fall 1986): 73.

54. The word *alacrán* in Spanish means "scorpion" in English.

55. Frederick Luis Aldama writes that Acosta "actively invents or changes details such as his name and age" in *Autobiography* and *Revolt*. In so doing, he argues, Acosta "invents himself as character and frees himself to promote his ideological agenda." See Aldama's *Postethnic Narrative Criticism: Magicorealism in Oscar "Zeta" Acosta, Ana Castillo, Julie Dash, Hanif Kureishi, and Salman Rushdie* (Austin: University of Texas Press, 2003), 66.

56. Critics have tended to interpret Acosta's distortions of facts either as a weakness of the text or as an attempt to avoid legal action against him. Rodríguez argues that Acosta's motive for changing facts "appears to have been [to avoid]

prosecution and civil liability" ("Oscar Zeta Acosta," 8). By contrast, Alurista writes that Acosta's novels are "founded on verifiable documents such as court cases, [but] the narrative, far from maintaining an objective posture, suffers from a deliberately unrestrained subjectivity." See Alurista's essay, "Acosta's *The Revolt of the Cockroach People:* The Case, The Novel, and History," in Lattin, *Contemporary Chicano Fiction*, 94; originally published in Spanish as "El caso, la novella y la historia de la obra de Acosta: *Revolt of the Cockroach People*," *Maize* 2:3 (Spring 1979): 6–13.

57. Guajardo, *Chicano Controversy*, 45. Guajardo argues that Acosta's novels do not hold up to expectations of "authenticity" and "veracity" normally associated with autobiographies, proclaiming that "it is unsafe to use the words 'Acosta' and 'truth' in the same sentence" (36). Guajardo displays the problems with attempting to interpret autobiographical novels literally rather than figuratively. He complains that Acosta omits any mention of his two marriages and his son, Marco, in *Autobiography* and *Revolt*, especially in light of the author's "philandering." Guajardo announces that readers would feel less sympathy for Acosta "were we to know that his escapades occurred while he was a husband and father" (37). Setting aside the moralistic assumptions of his statement, Guajardo places the weight of his interpretive method on a literal reading of Acosta's novel. He makes no effort to separate Acosta from Zeta Brown. Thus he ends up attacking the author for the actions and thoughts of a fictive character.

58. Hunsaker, "Book Review," 330.

59. Kimberly A. Kowalczyk, "Oscar Zeta Acosta: The Brown Buffalo and His Search for Identity," *The Americas Review* 16:3–4 (Fall–Winter 1988): 203.

60. Kowalczyk, "Oscar Zeta Acosta," 203. Kowalczyk refers to a single narrator in *Autobiography* and *Revolt.* As stated earlier, I treat the narrators of Acosta's novels as two distinct characters.

61. In a manner similar to my own interpretation of *Revolt*, Aldama develops a highly useful analysis that distinguishes between Acosta as writer, as narrator, and as character (*Postethnic Narrative Criticism*, 63–75).

62. Alvarez contends it does not matter if Acosta changed facts as they relate to persons, places, and events. Nor does it matter if he changed some facts but not others since autobiography relates experiences, not actual events. "Dicha traición o falsificación, si existe, resulta irrelevante a fin de cuentas ya que el problema central de la autobiografía es que el autor relata experiencias y no hechos" (164).

63. See Richard Weisberg, "Law in and as Literature: Self-Generated Meaning in the 'Procedural Novel,'" in *The Comparative Perspective on Literature: Approaches to Theory and Practice*, ed. Clayton Koelb and Susan Noakes (Ithaca, N.Y.: Cornell University Press, 1988), 226.

64. Saldívar, *Chicano Narrative*, 74–98.

65. Thwaites, "Use of Irony," 75.

66. Acosta, *Uncollected Works*, 36.

67. Alurista writes that "Zeta Brown falsely claims he is in Acapulco" on August 29, 1970, and adds, "This claim is false, at least on the date mentioned" ("Acosta's *Revolt*," 102, 104 n. 6). Alurista does not specifically state that Acosta was in Los Angeles on the day of the march, but he emphatically asserts that he was not

in Acapulco. Bruce-Novoa also states that "Acosta was involved in the Chicano Moratorium of 1970" as a witness and a participant in this "key occurrence" ("Fear and Loathing," 45). Chávez more assuredly places Acosta in Los Angeles on August 29, 1970, announcing that at the rally in Laguna Park on that day, "[t]hirteen speakers from a variety of organizations, among them Rodolfo 'Corky' Gonzales of Denver's Crusade for Justice, attorney Oscar Acosta, and Rosalío Muñoz, addressed the crowd" (*Mi Raza Primero,* 69).

68. Bruce-Novoa, "Fear and Loathing," 45.

69. A. Robert Lee, "Chicanismo's Beat Outrider? The Texts and Contexts of Oscar Zeta Acosta," in *The Beat Generation: Critical Essays,* ed. Kostas Myrsiades (New York: Peter Lang, 2002), 270. Originally published in *College Literature* 27:1 (Winter 2000): 158–76.

70. Guajardo, *Chicano Controversy,* 48.

71. Mary Helen Ponce, *Boyle Heights: An Autobiography* (Albuquerque: University of New Mexico Press, 1993), ix.

72. Acosta did not have a twin, nor did he have a brother named Jesús. In *Autobiography,* the narrator describes a brother named Bob who is two years older and noticeably different in physical appearance and personality. In actuality, Acosta had two brothers, Robert and Al.

73. Padilla, "Progression," 234.

74. As *Revolt* ends, Zeta Brown states that he is leaving Los Angeles in the "Spring of '72," but the last event in the novel, the verdict of the Tooner Flats Seven and the bombing of the Los Angeles Hall of Justice, takes place in April 1971. Zeta Brown's last year in Los Angeles remains untold in *Revolt.*

75. These statistics represent both combat and noncombat deaths. The number of Vietnamese deaths includes figures for soldiers of the North and South Vietnamese armies, nongovernment rebels of the National Liberation Front, and civilians from both North and South Vietnam.

76. For novels about Chicanos in Vietnam, see David Cano, *Shifting Loyalties* (Houston: Arte Público Press, 1995); and Alfredo Vea, *Gods Go Begging* (New York: Plume, 2000).

77. Alurista, "Acosta's *Revolt,*" 104.

78. Carl Oglesby, "The Revolted," in *Containment and Change: Two Dissenting Views of American Foreign Policy,* ed. Oglesby and Richard Shaull (New York: Collier-Macmillan), 141.

79. For an excellent analysis of "social death," see Abdul JanMohamed, *The Death-Bound-Subject: Richard Wright's Archaeology of Death* (Durham, N.C.: Duke University Press, 2005). JanMohamed wrote on this topic in a much earlier work as well: "Negating the Negation as a Form of Affirmation in Minority Discourse: The Construction of Richard Wright as Subject," *Cultural Critique* 7 (Fall 1987): 245–66.

80. Paredes, "Los Angeles from the Barrio," 217.

81. Oglesby, "The Revolted," 149.

82. Schwarz, "A Brazilian Breakthrough," 92.

83. Mendoza, "Buffaloes, Body Snatching," 83.

CHAPTER 4

1. Danny Santiago, *Famous All Over Town* (New York: Plume, 1983). Page references to this work will be found in the text.

2. Ricardo Sánchez, *Hechizospells*, Creative Series No. 4 (Los Angeles: UCLA Chicano Studies Center Publications, 1976), xi. Sánchez also states, "What makes Chicano literature *Chicano* is the fact that it is created by Chicanos and expresses the way Chicanos see not only their lives, but the lives of other people" (xi).

3. For the Pilger scene, see pages 65–68.

4. John Gregory Dunne, *Crooning: A Collection* (New York: Simon and Schuster, 1990), 47. Dunne's exposé, entitled "The Secret of Danny Santiago," originally appeared in the *The New York Review of Books*, August 16, 1984, 17–18, 20, 22, 24–27. Dunne later added a postscript to the article, included it in his book *Crooning*, and retitled the piece "An American Education" (21–56). My page references correspond to this later version.

5. Dunne, *Crooning*, 23.

6. For the sake of clarity, I shall refer to the author of *Famous All Over Town* as Daniel James but will occasionally refer to him as Danny Santiago, where appropriate. Tellingly, the novel's original title from the uncorrected proofs of the manuscript was *My Name Will Follow You Home*, an indication that James was cognizant of the problems that could eventually arise from his use of a Latino *nom de plume*.

7. Jonah Raskin, "Danny Santiago (Daniel James)," *Dictionary of Literary Biography*, vol. 122, *Chicano Writers, Second Series*, ed. Carl R. Shirley (Detroit: Gale Research, 1992), 248.

8. Raskin, "Danny Santiago," 251.

9. Jameson, *The Political Unconscious*, 39–40.

10. Jameson, *The Political Unconscious*, 226.

11. Jameson, *The Political Unconscious*, 179.

12. Jameson, *The Political Unconscious*, 180; my emphasis.

13. Jameson, *The Political Unconscious*, 43.

14. Aside from running his own business, James's father was an amateur painter and playwright; he was sympathetic to left politics and enjoyed bringing writers and artists to their home in Carmel Highlands on the central coast of California. At Carmel during the 1930s, James met various figures who influenced his views on literature and politics, including Sinclair Lewis, John Steinbeck, Ella Winter, Langston Hughes, Lincoln Steffens, and Charlie Chaplin.

15. One *New York Times* reviewer wrote that *Winter Soldiers* is "a perfect portrait of that other column which also carries on the war for freedom" (Dunne, *Crooning*, 34). And in *New Masses*, Alvah Bessie wrote, "*Winter Soldiers* possesses values apparent in no other play on the boards today." See Bessie, "Winter Soldiers," *New Masses*, December 15, 1942, 31. The play was produced by Erwin Piscator and premiered in the fall of 1942 at the New School of Social Research in New York City, where it played twenty-five performances. That same year, *Winter Soldiers* was awarded the Sidney Howard Memorial Award and a fifteen-hundred-dollar prize from the Playwrights Company.

16. Raskin, "Danny Santiago," 249.

17. Raskin, "Danny Santiago," 249.

18. Edwin McDowell, "A Noted 'Hispanic' Novelist Proves to Be Someone Else," *New York Times*, July 22, 1984, 44.

19. Two professional librettists, Sid Herzig and Fred Saidy, added music and dance to the play, producing the libretto. According to Dunne, Herzig and Saidy's work on the manuscript "made more room for song and dance by planing away the dialectic" (Dunne, *Crooning*, 35). A *New Masses* reviewer described the play as "a unique freedom-loving musicale" in which "we witness the early efforts of women to achieve both suffrage and dignity." See Harry Taylor, "On Broadway," *New Masses*, October 24, 1944, 29. Several years later, NBC-TV bought the rights to produce *Bloomer Girl* for *Producer's Showcase*, a television program. When NBC producers became aware of the Jameses' history, they insisted on removing the Jameses' names from the program's credits; otherwise the show would be canceled. *Bloomer Girl* aired on May 28, 1956.

20. James describes *The Hockadays* as a "novel of manners." He explains that he sought "to explore my own background with the tools of Marxism so I set about and wrote a very bad novel about a young girl in upper petit-bourgeois Kansas City circles." See Jonah Raskin, "The Man Who Would Be Danny Santiago," *San Francisco Bay Guardian*, November 28, 1984, 18.

21. Dunne, *Crooning*, 31.

22. James recalled that he carried a copy of Voltaire's *Candide* in his pocket during his testimony. "I had planned to say Voltaire published that work under the pseudonym M. le Docteur Ralph, and that if the Committee was successful, American writers would have to follow in his footsteps and disguise their identities with pen names." He made no mention of Voltaire in his testimony (Raskin, "Danny Santiago," 250).

23. Dunne, *Crooning*, 37.

24. Raskin, "Danny Santiago," 252. At the ceremony, John Kenneth Galbraith announced, "*Famous All Over Town* adds luster to the enlarging literary genre of immigrant experience, of social, cultural and psychological threshold-crossing. . . . The durable young narrator spins across a multi-cultured scene of crime, racial violence and extremes of dislocation, seeking and perhaps finding his own space" (Dunne, *Crooning*, 22).

25. Dunne, *Crooning*, 41–42; Alberto Huerta, "Daniel James (1911–1988): Socrates and Santiago in California," *The Californians* 6 (December 1988): 50.

26. Dunne, *Crooning*, 41–43; Huerta, "Daniel James," 49–50.

27. Raskin, "Danny Santiago," 249.

28. Raskin, "Danny Santiago," 250.

29. Clover Street and the Eastside Clover Gang were the inspiration for the novel's Shamrock Street and Chato's street gang, the Jesters. See Huerta, "Daniel James," 53.

30. Huerta, "Daniel James," 53.

31. Dunne, *Crooning*, 47.

32. Jonah Raskin, email to Marcial González, April 15, 2004, 2.

33. Jonah Raskin, email to Marcial González, June 2, 2003.

34. Raskin, "Danny Santiago," 249.

35. Raskin, "Danny Santiago," 251.
36. Huerta, "Daniel James," 49.
37. Huerta, "Daniel James," 49.
38. Raskin, "Man Who Would Be," 14.
39. Raskin, "Man Who Would Be," 14.
40. Dunne, *Crooning*, 36. Henry Wallace, vice president during Franklin Roosevelt's third term, ran for president in 1948 on the Progressive Party ticket. He received approximately a million votes and was officially endorsed by the Communist Party USA.
41. Albert Maltz, a Party member and one of the Hollywood Ten, wrote in 1946, "I have come to believe that the accepted understanding of art as a weapon is not a useful guide but a straightjacket. . . . I have felt this in my own work and in the work of others. In order to write at all, it has become necessary for me to repudiate it and abandon it" (19). Maltz acknowledges that art can indeed function as an instrument to raise political consciousness, but he also asserts that "where art is a weapon, it is only so when it is art" (22)." See Maltz, "What Shall We Ask of Writers?" *New Masses*, February 12, 1946.
42. Raskin, "Man Who Would Be," 14.
43. In response to James's 1984 interview with Raskin, Alan Wald writes, "I think [James] is quite clear that he left the CP in 1948 because he felt that support of the Wallace campaign was 'left sectarian.' This tells me that he was to the 'right' of the [William Z.] Foster leadership" (email, Alan Wald to Marcial González, March 24, 2004).
44. Dunne, *Crooning*, 30.
45. Dunne, *Crooning*, 31.
46. Raskin, "Danny Santiago," 251.
47. Raskin, "Danny Santiago," 249.
48. Dunne, *Crooning*, 36.
49. I address the Party's 1940 debates on politically committed literature in "Before Dan James Became Danny Santiago: the Duclos Letter and the Maltz Affair," an unpublished paper presented at the American Studies Annual Colloquium, University of California, Berkeley, May 11, 2007.
50. Joyce Carol Oates writes, "Though *Famous All Over Town* alone should have been the issue, and not its author's identity, the awards committee confessed that they might have had second thoughts about giving the novel their prize, had they known its author was 'Anglo' and not 'Chicano.'" See *(Woman) Writer: Occasions and Opportunities* (New York: Dutton, 1988), 385. The essay entitled "Pseudonymous Selves" in *(Woman) Writer* originally appeared as "Success and the Pseudonymous Writer: Turning over a New Self," *New York Times Book Review*, December 6, 1987, 12, 14.
51. Edwin McDowell, "Publishing: Endowment Gives Four Writers $25,000," *New York Times*, August 10, 1984, C23.
52. McDowell, "Noted 'Hispanic,'" 44. Lewis admits that had the committee known that Santiago was not Chicano "it would have given us pause. . . . [I]t does raise all kinds of interesting questions" (44).
53. Gerald Haslam, "A Question of Authenticity, or, Who Can Write What?" *Western American Literature* 20:3 (Fall 1985): 247.

54. Haslam, "A Question of Authenticity," 247.

55. Haslam, "A Question of Authenticity," 247.

56. McDowell, "Noted 'Hispanic,'" 44.

57. Dunne, *Crooning*, 53.

58. Felipe de Ortego y Gasca, "Danny Santiago and the Ethics of Deception," *Nuestro* 8 (November 1984): 51.

59. The passages from Burciaga, Arias, and Islas are quoted in Ortego y Gasca, "Ethics of Deception," 50. Similarly, Felix Garcia remarks, "You don't have to be a Latino to write on the Latino experience," but, he adds, "Dan James should write as Dan James, because a piece should stand on the merit of the writing, not the author's name." See Raskin, "Danny Santiago," 252.

60. Stavans and Augenbraum, *Growing Up Latino*, xxvii.

61. Francisco A. Lomelí and Donaldo W. Urioste coined the phrase "literatura chicanesca" or "chicanesque literature" to designate literature written about Chicana/os by non-Chicana/o writers, in *Chicano Perspectives in Literature: A Critical and Annotated Bibiography* (Albuquerque: Pajarito, 1976).

62. Juan Bruce-Novoa, "Canonical and Non-canonical Texts," *Retrospace*, 141.

63. Bruce-Novoa, "Canonical and Non-canonical Texts," 140.

64. Haslam, "A Question of Authenticity," 248.

65. Haslam, "A Question of Authenticity," 247.

66. Anne C. Roark, "When Is a Pseudonym a Lie?" *San Francisco Chronicle*, "This World" section, August 12, 1984, 17.

67. Huerta, "Daniel James," 51.

68. Carolyn See, who wrote a generous review of the novel when it first came out, exclaims, "[A]nyone who makes a fuss over the use of a pseudonym doesn't know diddly about the book world" (Roark, "When Is a Pseudonym a Lie?" 17); Thomas Sanchez, author of *Zoot Suit Murders*, reasons, "I know this whole thing is being politicized, but I think it shouldn't be. . . . Should we say that Shakespeare shouldn't have written a certain play located in Verona because he didn't 'culturally identify' with an Italian girl named Juliet?" (Roark "When Is a Pseudonym a Lie?" 17).

69. Roark, "When Is a Pseudonym a Lie?" 17.

70. Raskin, "Danny Santiago," 252.

71. Garry Abrams, "The Three Lives of Dan James," *Los Angeles Times*, June 19, 1988, IV, 1.

72. Huerta, "Daniel James," 48.

73. Huerta, "Daniel James," 53.

74. Alexander Cockburn, "Naming as Ritual," *The Nation*, August 4–11, 1984, 71.

75. Haslam, "A Question of Authenticity," 249.

76. Henry Louis Gates Jr., "'Authenticity' or the Lesson of Little Tree," *New York Times Book Review*, November 24, 1991, 1. Leonard Feather published his blindfold test with Roy Eldridge (nicknamed Little Jazz) in "Little Jazz Goes Color Blind," *Down Beat*, July 13, 1951, 12. The results of the test were reprinted in Feather's *The Book of Jazz, from Then till Now; a Guide to the Entire Field*, rev. ed. (New York: Horizon, 1965), 47.

77. Gates, "Authenticity," 1.

78. Gates, "Authenticity," 29.

79. Dunne, *Crooning*, 47.

80. Huerta, "Daniel James," 50.

81. David Quammen, "Three Novels," *New York Times Book Review*, April 24, 1983, 12. Quammen describes Santiago as "a writer with the delicate, precious trick of keeping a reader off balance yet engaged, with not just a keen eye but a keen ear, a keen wit and a feel for those narrative contours that make a good novel quite different from a padded short story or a veiled diary" (12).

82. Flores 147.

83. Raskin, "Danny Santiago," 251.

84. Huerta, "Daniel James," 50.

85. Lauro Flores, untitled book review, *Minnesota Review* 22 (Spring 1984): 147.

86. Rodolfo Acuña, "Troubled Angels," in *Anything but Mexican: Chicanos in Contemporary Los Angeles* (New York: Verso, 1996), 275. Acuña cites two articles: Amy Wallace, "Riots Changed Few Attitudes, Poll Finds," *Los Angeles Times*, September 3, 1992, and "Money and Power," *Los Angeles Times*, November 18, 1992.

87. In 1968, the year Chato would have been a senior in high school, ten thousand Chicano students walked out of five high schools in East Los Angeles in defiance against racism and the generally depressed conditions in schools. For more on this topic, see chapter 3 above.

88. Laura Browder, *Slippery Characters: Ethnic Impersonators and American Identities* (Chapel Hill: University of North Carolina Press, 2000), 237, 243.

89. Louis Althusser, *Lenin and Philosophy and Other Essays*, trans. Ben Brewster (New York: Monthly Review Press, 1971), 162.

90. Jameson differentiates Althusser's definition of ideology from that of Lukács. For Althusser, it is not—as it is for Lukács—that the *representation* is reified, but rather that the *relation* represented is other than real. Althusser writes, "What is represented in ideology is therefore not the system of real relations which govern the existence of individuals, but the *imaginary* relation of those individuals to the real relations in which they live" (Althusser, *Lenin*, 165). Recognizing this difference, Jameson attempts to find a common ground where the two conceptions of ideology come together, arguing that "we may now refine [Althusser's] 'definition' and its narrative conditions of possibility: the former [Althusser's definition] is precisely the wish-fulfilling daydream or fantasy text . . . which can be indefinitely enlarged to include [the author's] vision of himself." Lukács's definition takes the shape of "narrative presuppositions which one must 'believe,' those empirical preconditions which must have been secured, in order for the subject successfully to tell itself this particular daydream" (Jameson, *The Political Unconscious*, 182). Thus, the difference is not a fundamental one; it is rather a different emphasis on the various conceptual moments of ideology.

91. Theodor W. Adorno, "The Position of the Narrator in the Contemporary Novel," in *Notes to Literature*, vol. 1 (New York: Columbia University Press, 1991), 30.

92. Adorno, "Position of the Narrator," 32.

93. Adorno, "Position of the Narrator," 33.

94. For the sake of analytical clarity, I have separated the categories of form and content in this discussion of *Famous*. In actuality, these categories do not operate separately but are aspects of the novel's integrated totality.

95. Raskin, "Danny Santiago," 251.

96. Flores, untitled book review, 147.

97. Adorno, "Position of the Narrator," 32.

98. Adorno, "Position of the Narrator," 32.

99. For literary criticism the concept of reification should not be understood strictly in negative terms. Reification should not be "overhastily" categorized purely in terms of "loss and constraint." Rather, "[T]he effects of reification—the sealing off of the psyche, the division of labor of the mental faculties, the fragmentation of the bodily and perceptual sensorium—also determine the opening up of whole new zones of experience and the production of new types of linguistic content" (Jameson, *The Political Unconscious*, 160).

100. *San Francisco Chronicle*, "Young Latin Author Is Neither," (July 23, 1984), 16.

101. Gates, "Authenticity," 30.

102. In *The Cultural Front: The Laboring of American Culture in the Twentieth Century* (New York: Verso, 1997), Michael Denning argues for the historical importance of proletarian literature, but he also draws a genealogical link between proletarian literature and ethnic American literature: "If we fail to understand the proletarian literature movement, its contradictory successes and failures, its conscious aesthetic goals and its often ironic results, then we fail to understand much of American fiction from John Dos Passos, Richard Wright, and Tillie Olsen to Toni Morrison and E. L. Doctorow. For the proletarian literature movement has had far greater influence on the subsequent half century of American fiction than the experimental modernism of Stein and Hemingway. . . . [T]he renaissance ignited by the proletarian avant-garde was responsible for two key developments in American literary history: the emergence of a generation of plebeian ethnic writers who represented—in several senses of the word—the new working-class cultures of America and who were to transform American letters in the decades to follow; and the creation of a genre—the ghetto or tenement pastoral—that is still at the heart of the American novel" (201). Literary scholars have covered much ground in historicizing and theorizing the connections between proletarian literature and the African American literary tradition, but much less work has been done to show this connection for other U.S. ethnic literary traditions, including Chicano literature.

103. Danny Santiago (Daniel James), "Danny Santiago Makes a Call on Daniel James," *Los Angeles Times*, August 15, 1984, II, 5.

CHAPTER 5

1. Cecile Pineda, *Face* (New York: Viking, 1985); *Frieze* (New York: Viking, 1986). All page references in the text correspond to these editions unless otherwise indicated. A revised edition of *Face* was reissued by Wings Press, San Antonio, 2003.

2. *The Love Queen of the Amazon: A Novel* (Boston: Little Brown, 1992); *Bardo99* (Lincoln, Nebr.: Writers Club Press, 2000); *Redoubt* (Lincoln, Nebr.: Writers Club Press, 2000); *Fishlight: A Dream of Childhood* (San Antonio: Wings Press, 2001). *Face* won the Sue Kaufman Prize awarded by the American Academy and Institute of Art and Letters, and the Gold Medal from the Commonwealth

Club of California, and was nominated for the American Book Award for First Work. *Fishlight* is described by its publisher as "autobiographical fiction." Pineda refers to *Bardo99* and *Redoubt* as "mononovels," which she defines as "writing that occurs in the singular mind of one protagonist: visions, conversations, happenings, sensations, events—all within one imagining mind." See Jeff Biggers, "Pineda Unbound: An Interview with Cecile Pineda," *Bloomsbury Review* 24:5 (September–October 2004): 3.

3. Bruce-Novoa began calling attention to Pineda's work soon after *Face* appeared in print. In 1986 he wrote, "The two women I consider the best of the published fiction writers, Shiela Ortiz Taylor and Cecile Pineda, have not figured in any of the Chicana collections, nor to my knowledge have they been written about, discussed, or even mentioned in the Chicano context until now." See *Retrospace*, 145. He also refers to her as "a leading Chicana novelist" in "Deconstructing the Dominant Patriarchal Text: Cecile Pineda's Narratives," in *Breaking Boundaries: Latina Writing and Critical Readings*, ed. Asunción Horno-Delgado et al. (Amherst: University of Massachusetts Press, 1989), 72. For another early review of Pineda's work, see Erlinda Gonzales-Berry's "Review of *Face*" in *The Americas Review* 15:2 (Summer 1987): 107–9.

4. Bruce-Novoa, "Deconstructing Dominant Patriarchal Text," 72.

5. See Bruce-Novoa, "Canonical and Non-canonical Texts" and "Deconstructing Dominant Patriarchal Text"; Gonzales-Berry, "Review of *Face*"; Biggers, "Pineda Unbound"; Francisco Lomelí, "Cecile Pineda's *Face* and Ralph Ellison's *Invisible Man:* Poetics of Synthesizing an Identity," in *El Poder Hispano: Actas del V Congreso de Culturas Chicanas de los Estados Unidos*, ed. Alberto Moncala Lorenzo et al. (Madrid: Universidad de Alcalá, 1994): 465–72; and "Cecile Pineda" in *Dictionary of Literary Biography*, vol. 209, *Chicano Writers, Third Series*, ed. Francisco Lomelí and Carl R. Shirley (Detroit: Gale Group, 1999), 202–11; Frank N. Magill, "Book Review of *Face*," in *Masterpieces of Latino Literature* (New York: HarperCollins, 1994), 157–60; Karen Christian, *Show and Tell: Identity as Performance* (Albuquerque: University of New Mexico Press, 1997); John S. Christie, *Latino Fiction and the Modernist Imagination: Literature of the Borderlands* (New York: Garland, 1998); Barbara Rodríguez, *Autobiographical Inscriptions* (Oxford: Oxford University Press, 1999), 177–204; and Anne Connor, "Desenmascarando a Ysrael: The Disfigured Face as Symbol of Identity in Three Latino Texts," *Cincinnati Romance Review* 21 (2002): 148–62.

6. Rodríguez, *Autobiographical Inscriptions*, 177.

7. Rodríguez, *Autobiographical Inscriptions*, 189.

8. Lomelí, "Cecile Pineda," 203.

9. Lomelí, "Cecile Pineda," 203.

10. Bruce-Novoa, "Deconstructing Dominant Patriarchal Text," 80.

11. Rafael Pérez-Torres, *Movements in Chicano Poetry: Against Myths, against Margins* (Cambridge: Cambridge University Press, 1995), 27.

12. Michael Bérubé, *Marginal Forces/Cultural Centers: Tolson, Pynchon, and the Politics of the Canon* (Ithaca, N.Y.: Cornell University Press, 1992), 2–3.

13. Bérubé, *Marginal Forces*, 5.

14. Bérubé, *Marginal Forces*, 134.

15. Bérubé, *Marginal Forces*, 135.

16. Pineda, "Deracinated," 65.

17. Sophia A. McClennen, *The Dialectics of Exile: Nation, Time, Language, and Space in Hispanic Literature* (West Lafayette, Ind.: Purdue University Press, 2004), 2, 44.

18. Biggers, "Pineda Unbound," 23.

19. Biggers, "Pineda Unbound," 23.

20. Public Forum, Santa Rosa Junior College, Petaluma, California, April 19, 2000.

21. Bruce-Novoa identifies several similarities in *Face* and *Frieze:* of the two protagonists, one is blind, and the other is facially disfigured; one cannot see, while people do not want to look at the other. Both novels have male protagonists; "[n]either achieves wealth, fame, or the social position he had envisioned, and both lose the woman they most desire" ("Deconstructing Dominant Patriarchal Text," 75). Additionally, the protagonists are forced to leave their homes midway through their narratives to a distant land: a radical translocation in *Face*, from the urban "Capital," Rio de Janeiro, to the rural "Hinterland," Rio das Pedras; and an equally jolting geographical displacement in *Frieze*, from ninth-century India, "then considered a First World zone," according to Bruce-Novoa, to "'a boarded-up backwater' in Java" (74).

22. Biggers, "Pineda Unbound," 24.

23. Jean-Paul Sartre, *Search for a Method*, trans. Hazel E. Barnes (New York: Vintage, 1968), 104 n. 6.

24. David E. Johnson criticizes Pineda for not foregrounding her ethnicity in the novel and describes the novel as a "fiction of assimilation" (79) in the tradition of Oscar Hijuelos and Richard Rodriguez. In his view, her "book is written in a homogenous and homogenizing English." He concludes that the novel displays the desire to be white and thus promotes universalism. Johnson argues in favor of diversity in American literature and points out that the "whiteness of the academy and the reading public for years sustained exclusionary policies that resulted in the denationalization, the un-Americanness, of certain literatures: women's writing, Black literature, Chicano literature, [and] Japanese and Chinese American literatures" (75). But in his zeal to defend U.S. ethnic literatures (a worthy cause in and of itself) Johnson underestimates *Face*, not taking into account the possibility that Chicano literature need not focus on Chicano themes and characters (in some absolute sense) to engage with conditions and developments that have affected the lives of Chicanos historically. See Johnson, "Face Value (An Essay on Cecile Pineda's *Face*)," *The Americas Review* 19:2 (Summer 1991): 73–93.

25. "Postpositivist realist" critics emphasize the importance of this point in their work. See the collection by Paula M. L. Moya, *Learning from Experience: Minority Identities, Multicultural Struggles.* See also the collection by Moya and Hames-García, *Reclaiming Identity.*

26. Johnson writes, "There is no economic register that records and values the face's utility. The face is cosmetic at best; unless one is a model, the face as such goes unused. Unlike the hands . . . the face appears beyond the limits of economic

appropriation and determination. . . . The face's utility, then, must belong . . . to an order as yet uncircumscribed by economics, by the market" ("Face Value," 85).

27. In an early handwritten draft of *Face*, the term "police squads" was originally "extermination squads." See Lomelí, "Cecile Pineda," 204.

28. Schwarz, "A Brazilian Breakthrough," 92.

29. Christie, *Latino Fiction*, 5. The passage, "heap of broken images," quoted by Christie, comes from line 22 of T. S. Eliot's "The Waste Land."

30. Christie, *Latino Fiction*, 12, 14.

31. In addition to Lomelí and Bruce-Novoa, who read *Face*, along with *Frieze*, as an allegory, Frank Magill reads *Face* as "psychological realism" (Magill, "Book Review of *Face*," 157), and Barbara Rodríguez writes that *Face* can be categorized as a self-conscious commentary on "fictional autobiography" (Rodríguez, *Autobiographical Inscriptions*, 182). Magill analyzes *Face* from a sympathetic point of view, characterizing the novel as a "masterpiece." But like Christie, who privileges fragmentation at the expense of social reference, Magill emphasizes the intrinsic qualities of Pineda's novel while minimizing its extrinsic thrust. He asserts that the novel "scrupulously" depicts the social conditions in Rio de Janeiro and Rio das Pedras, but "such realistic features are not the essence of the book." He holds rather that "[w]hat is central to the novel is the examination of psychological issues of identity that Helio's experience provokes" (159). Magill's psychological reading of *Face* downplays the novel's representation of social conflicts, even as Helio himself finds difficulty in doing so. "Not content to play the role of victim that European philosophies would assign him," Magill explains, "Helio reacts to his situation with a committed spirit of Third World resistance. This political and ethical undertone is all the more powerful because of the novel's meticulous avoidance of obvious political themes" (159). Magill recognizes the political issues addressed in the novel but reads them as the psychological effects of the protagonist, while implying the aesthetic distastefulness of "obvious political themes." Rodríguez asserts that "although Pineda does not identify the narrative as autobiography, she nevertheless constructs an image that thematizes and comments on the theory of autobiography." Drawing on Barbara Johnson's reading of Mary Shelley's *Frankenstein* as "female autobiography," Rodríguez argues that *Face* can be read "as female autobiography *through* the re-facement of a male" (*Autobiographical Inscriptions*, 186). She also takes issue with David Johnson's reading of *Face* as a "fiction of assimilation," criticizing him for ignoring "the difference of gender when he argues that Pineda's novel is logically aligned with [Richard] Rodriguez's autobiography [*Hunger of Memory*]" (194).

32. Lomelí, "Cecile Pineda," 205.

33. See Lomelí's comparison of Elllison's *Invisible Man* and *Face* ("Cecile Pineda").

34. Christie, *Latino Fiction*, 13.

35. Limón, *Mexican Ballads, Chicano Poems*, 164.

36. Robert Schwarz, *Misplaced Ideas: Essays on Brazilian Culture* (New York: Verso, 1992), 140.

37. Volosinov, *Marxism and Philosophy of Language*, 23.

38. Eugene Lunn, *Marxism and Modernism: An Historical Study of Lukács,*

Brecht, Benjamin and Adorno (Berkeley and Los Angeles: University of California Press, 1982), 21.

39. Jameson, *The Political Unconscious*, 266.

40. Jameson, *The Political Unconscious*, 266.

41. Adorno, *Aesthetic Theory*, 31.

42. Adorno, *Aesthetic Theory*, 322.

43. Bruce-Novoa, "Deconstructing Dominant Patriarchal Text," 75. Bruce-Novoa defines asceticism as "the doctrine that through the renunciation of the desires of the flesh and of pleasure in worldly things and through self-mortification or self-denial one can subdue her or his appetites and discipline oneself so as to reach a high spiritual or intellectual state" (1989, 81 n.4). The practice of asceticism, as Wim Swaan confirms, is normally associated with the desire to arrive at oneness with the innermost self, the absolute or universal being. Swaan clarifies that "[t]his path of progressive detachment leads ultimately to an extinction of the Self . . . and *nirvana*, a blissful state of Non-Existence or reabsorption into the Absolute." See Swaan, *The Lost Cities of Asia: Ceylon, Burma, Cambodia* (London: Elek Books, 1966), 14. The ascetic seeks to transcend space and time to enter a state of pure knowledge or universal truth—a truth beyond the material-earthly qualities of the social world. Thus "aesthetic asceticism" represents the ultimate form of idealism, wherein the social subject itself has been totally eradicated. "In both novels," argues Bruce-Novoa, "Pineda's deep structure is essentially that of the ascetic journey of self-discovery through suffering, degradation, renunciation, and disciplined work. . . . Pineda's is an ancient message meant for our time; the *true meaning of life* is found only through sacrifice, self-encounter, and rebirth" ("Deconstructing Dominant Patriarchal Text," 76; emphasis added). Bruce-Novoa's conceptualization of asceticism differs from that of Michel Foucault, for whom asceticism stands as a kind of genealogical-critical approach that allows one to go against nature—to denaturalize the self. See Michel Foucault, "Friendship as a Way of Life," in *Foucault Live*, ed. Sylvère Lotringer, trans. John Johnston (New York: Semiotext(e), 1989), 206.

44. Bruce-Novoa, "Deconstructing Dominant Patriarchal Text," 80.

45. Bruce-Novoa, "Deconstructing Dominant Patriarchal Text," 80. Bruce-Novoa uses the term "differed difference" rather than the customary Derridean term of "deferred difference" to connote the concept of *différance*.

46. Keya Ganguly, "Adorno, Authenticity, Critique," in *Marxism, Modernity and Postcolonial Studies*, ed. Crystal Bartolovich and Neil Lazarus (Cambridge: Cambridge University Press, 2002), 243.

47. Bruce-Novoa, *Retrospace*, 138.

48. The prologue is fictional, delivered by the imaginary Godoy. But the novel is based on a real incident, incredible as the story sounds. Pineda read a newspaper article entitled, "A Man Reconstructs His Own Face," *San Francisco Chronicle*, May 21, 1977, 1, 12. The story stuck with her, and three years later, she began writing the novel.

49. Names assume symbolic significance in Pineda's novels: Cardoso is a barber who teaches Helio basic surgical techniques during the latter's apprenticeship as a young man, thus enabling Helio to "change" himself upon his return to Rio das Pe-

dras years later. *Cardoso* is derived from the Latin root *cardo,* which was the name of the Roman goddess of *thresholds* and *change.* Bertha is a motherly nurse who sneaks into Helio's hospital room at night to comfort him; she is in fact the only one to offer him any kind of compassion or tenderness. *Bertha* comes from the German word, *beraht,* meaning "bright," but which is also the name of a legendary character who sneaks into nurseries and rocks children to sleep. Durga, Gopal's second wife, bears his children and tirelessly maintains his household; she even cares for his first wife, Maya, after Maya loses her touch with reality. *Durga* means "unattainable" in Sanskrit, but in Hindu mythology it is also the name of the twelve-armed wife of Shiva. The etymologies of other names in *Face* and *Frieze* can be traced in similar fashion to reveal their symbolic content; this holds true for minor as well as for major characters. Given Pineda's obvious attention to the symbolism of names, we could reasonably suspect the name *Godoy* to be a cross between Beckett's Godot and Malloy.

50. Adorno, *Aesthetic Theory,* 81.

51. Adorno refers to Beckett's plays as "novels" because, as he points out, Beckett himself "sardonically" called them novels (*Aesthetic Theory,* 30).

52. See Walter Benjamin, *The Arcades Project,* trans. Howard Eiland and Kevin McLaughlin (Cambridge: Belknap Press of Harvard University Press, 1999). In a study of the historicity of the image, Benjamin writes, "Every present day is determined by the images that are synchronic with it: each 'now' is the now of a particular recognizability. In it, truth is charged to the bursting point with time. . . . It is not that what is past casts its light on what is present, or what is present its light on what is past; rather, image is that wherein what has been comes together in a flash with the now to form a constellation. In other words: image is *dialectics at a standstill.* For while the relation of the present to the past is purely temporal, the relation of what-has-been to the now is dialectical: not temporal in nature but figural" (462–63; emphasis added).

53. Adorno, *Aesthetic Theory,* 153.

54. Adorno, *Aesthetic Theory,* 364. Beckett's works were so important to Adorno that, according to Gretel Adorno and Rolf Tiedemann, Adorno would have dedicated *Aesthetic Theory* to Beckett had he not died before finishing it (Adorno, *Aesthetic Theory,* 366).

55. Jean-Paul Sartre, *No Exit and Three Other Plays* (New York: Vintage, 1949), 47.

56. These questions come from "The Birth, Life, and Rebirth of *Face* as Witnessed by the Author," which appears as a preface in the revised edition of *Face* (San Antonio: Wings Press, 2003), xiii–xvi.

57. Adorno, *Negative Dialectics,* 320.

58. Pineda, *Face,* 192.

59. Bernstein, *Philosophy of the Novel,* xviii; emphasis added. According to Bernstein, the philosophical positions set forth by Lukács in *The Theory of the Novel* can be traced back to the "Kantian distinction between the transcendental subject and empirical subject, between . . . the subject which gives form to experience and the subject so formed. . . . This division within the self as manifested in the novel tells the story of how the self has become unnarratable, unable to tell its story" (xxi–xxii). This division also roughly characterizes the conflict between narrative and narration.

60. Pineda, *Frieze,* viii.

61. For an essay on the Chicano working-class novel, see García, "Chicano Working-Class Novel."

62. J. Hillis Miller, *Fiction and Repetition: Seven English Novels* (Cambridge: Harvard University Press, 1982), 9.

63. For an intriguing comparison of commodity fetishism and novelistic form, see Andrew Feenberg, "Fetishism and Form: Erotic and Economic Disorder in Literature," in *Violence and Truth: On the Work of René Girard*, ed. Paul Dumouchel (Stanford, Calif.: Stanford University Press, 1988), 134–51. Feenberg draws on but also takes issue with Lucien Goldmann's argument for a homology of the commodity form and the form of the novel. For the latter, see Goldmann, "Introduction to the Problems of a Sociology of the Novel," in *Marxist Literary Theory: A Reader*, ed. Terry Eagleton and Drew Milne (Oxford: Blackwell, 1996), 204–20.

64. A similar fascination with the history of stones can be found in Helena María Viramontes's *Under the Feet of Jesus* (New York: Penguin, 1995). In this novel, a young Chicano farmworker dreams of escaping his hard life in the fields by going to college. He has a passion for geology and compares the formation of his identity to the formation of stones. "He loved stones and the history of stones because he believed himself to be a solid mass of boulder thrust out of the earth and not some particle lost in infinite and cosmic space. With a simple touch of the hand and a hungry wonder of his connection to it all, he not only became a part of the earth's history, but would exist as the boulders did, for eternity" (52). Like Pineda's novels, *Under the Feet of Jesus* can be read as an attempt to comprehend and critique the reification of identity and the class-based racialization of Chicana and Chicano subjects.

65. Jay, *Marxism and Totality*, 228.

66. The name *Maya* is significant. In Sanskrit, *maya* means "illusion." In Hebrew, *mayim* means "water." In the Buddhist tradition, as in the novel, Maya is the name of the mother of Siddhartha Gautama, the Buddha. The name also evokes the great Mayan civilization.

67. Critical artworks may achieve a quality that gives the appearance of formlessness, but in actuality formlessness is unattainable. It is an ideal. It is the *aspiration* toward formlessness rather than its *achievement* that constitutes the novel's critical aesthetic.

68. Biggers, "Pineda Unbound," 24.

EPILOGUE

1. Eagleton, "Nationalism," 24.

2. See "Blueprint for Negro Writing," in *The Portable Harlem Renaissance Reader*, ed. David Lewis (New York: Penguin, 1995), 203. Thanks to Barbara Foley for bringing Wright's essay to my attention.

3. Eagleton, "Nationalism," 30, 24.

4. See Peter Hitchcock, *Oscillate Wildly: Space, Body, and Spirit of Millennial Materialism* (Minneapolis: University of Minnesota Press, 1999).

5. See David Harvey, *Justice, Nature, and the Geography of Difference* (Malden, Mass.: Blackwell, 1996), 47.

6. The best example of a kind of Marxism that opposes dialectics may be found in the works of the rational choice Marxists (RCM). For an excellent collection of essays on RCM, see Terrell Carver and Paul Thomas, eds., *Rational Choice Marxism* (University Park: Pennsylvania State University Press, 1995). In particular, see the article entitled "Rational Choice Marxism: Is the Game Worth the Candle?" by Ellen Meiksins Wood (79–135).

7. J. Saldívar, *Dialectics of Our America*, 26.

8. J. Saldívar, *Border Matters*, 102.

9. See Ganguly, "Adorno, Authenticity, Critique," 242.

10. Jameson argues that the "poststructuralist attack on 'historicism,' which emerges from a no less problematic affirmation of the priority of 'synchronic' thought," can be understood as a repudiation of teleological forms of narrative, which amounts to a "repudiation of the idea of 'progress'" (*The Ideologies of Theory*, 153). He adds that "[a]s desirable as it may be to rid Marxism of any vestiges of a properly bourgeois notion of 'progress,' it would seem a good deal less desirable nervously to abandon any Marxian vision of the future altogether (an operation in which Marxism itself is generally abandoned in the process)" (154).

11. Adorno, *Negative Dialectics*, 406.

12. Adorno, *Negative Dialectics*, 406.

13. Jameson, *The Political Unconscious*, 54. For an excellent analysis of Adorno's deconstructing dialectic, see Neil Larsen, "Negation of the Abnegation: Dialectical Criticism in the 1990s," *Rethinking Marxism* 5:2 (1992): 109–17.

14. Adorno, *Negative Dialectics*, xix.

15. Adorno, *Negative Dialectics*, 136.

16. Adorno, *Negative Dialectics*, 142.

17. Adorno, *Negative Dialectics*, 142.

18. Adorno, *Negative Dialectics*, 146; emphasis added.

19. Jameson, *Late Marxism: Adorno, or, The Persistence of the Dialectic* (London: Verso, 1990). Jameson complains about the poor translations of Adorno's books, including 1994 edition of *Negative Dialectics*, translated by E. B. Ashton. Jameson points out that readers "should make a note of the most urgent howlers," among them, "*Tauschverhaltnis* [which] is in particular not 'barter' but simply 'exchange system' (very much as in 'exchange value')" (x).

20. Jameson, *Late Marxism*, 26.

21. Jameson, *Late Marxism*, 28.

22. Adorno, *Negative Dialectics*, 146–47.

23. Adorno's critique of the commodity exchange abstraction in *Negative Dialectics* draws on Alfred Sohn-Rethel's analysis of the exchange abstraction and the conversion of the real abstraction into the conceptual abstraction. In a letter to Walter Benjamin dated November 28, 1936, Adorno writes, "The most significant événement of the last week was a visit from Alfred Sohn-Rethel, who first wrote me an extremely stimulating letter about his own project and then came and discussed the project itself with me in some detail. From a quite different angle, he has arrived at certain conclusions which are remarkably similar to those of my own current efforts. I regard this mutual discussion between us as very important for the issues in question." See Theodor W. Adorno and Walter Benjamin, *The Complete*

Correspondence: 1928–1940, ed. Henri Lonitz, trans. Nicholas Walker (Cambridge: Harvard University Press, 1999), 162. See also Alfred Sohn-Rethel, *Intellectual and Manual Labor: A Critique of Epistemology* (Atlantic Highlands, N.J.: Humanities Press, 1978).

24. Adorno, *Negative Dialectics*, 147; emphasis added.

25. I realize that in my reading of Adorno I run the risk of being accused of choosing selective passages to make a specific argument in a way that misrepresents a broader understanding of Adorno's work in general and of negative dialectics in particular. But in reading these passages from the perspective I have chosen, I make no claim that they represent the totality of Adorno's critical theory. I have already stated that Adorno is a problematical theorist, not easily pigeon-holed into an identifiable theoretical project. His critique of identity implies that he would himself resist a categorization of any kind that would posit his work ontologically.

26. Karl Marx, *The Marx-Engels Reader*, 2nd ed., ed. R. C. Tucker (New York: Norton, 1978), 595.

27. Marx, *The Marx-Engels Reader*, 595.

BIBLIOGRAPHY

Abrams, Garry. "The Three Lives of Dan James." *Los Angeles Times*, June 19, 1988, IV, 1, 12.

Acosta, Oscar Zeta. "Autobiography." In *Growing Up Latino: Memoirs and Stories*, ed. Harold Augenbraum and Ilan Stavans, 193–207. Boston: Houghton Mifflin, 1993.

Acosta, Oscar Zeta. *The Autobiography of a Brown Buffalo.* New York: Vintage, 1989. Originally published by Straight Arrow Books in 1972.

Acosta, Oscar Zeta. "The Autobiography of the Brown Buffalo." *Con Safos* 2:7 (Winter 1971): 34–46.

Acosta, Oscar Zeta. "The Revolt of the Cockroach People." *La Gente*, November–December 1973, 4–5, 12.

Acosta, Oscar Zeta. *The Revolt of the Cockroach People.* New York: Vintage, 1989. Originally published by Straight Arrow Books in 1973 and reprinted by Bantam in 1974.

Acosta, Oscar Zeta. *The Uncollected Works.* Ed. Ilan Stavans. Houston: Arte Público Press, 1996.

Acuña, Rodolfo. *Anything but Mexican: Chicanos in Contemporary Los Angeles.* New York: Verso, 1996.

Acuña, Rodolfo. *Occupied America: A History of Chicanos.* 3rd ed. New York: HarperCollins, 1988.

Adorno, Theodor W. *Aesthetic Theory.* Ed. Gretel Adorno and Rolf Tiedemann. Trans. Robert Hullot-Kentor. Minneapolis: University of Minnesota Press, 1997.

Adorno, Theodor W. *Negative Dialectics.* Trans. E. B. Ashton. New York: Continuum, 1994. Originally published in German in 1966.

Adorno, Theodor W. *Notes to Literature.* Vol. 1. Ed. Rolf Tiedemann. Trans. Shierry Weber Nicholsen. New York: Columbia University Press, 1991.

Adorno, Theodor W. "Reconciliation under Duress." In *Aesthetics and Politics*, ed. Ronald Taylor, 151–76. London: New Left Books, 1977.

Adorno, Theodor W., and Walter Benjamin. *The Complete Correspondence: 1928–1940.* Ed. Henri Lonitz. Trans. Nicholas Walker. Cambridge: Harvard University Press, 1999.

Adorno, Theodor W., Walter Benjamin, Ernst Bloch, Bertolt Brecht, and Georg Lukács. *Aesthetics and Politics.* Afterword by Fredric Jameson. Translation ed. Ronald Taylor. London: New Left Books, 1977.

Aldama, Frederick Luis. *Postethnic Narrative Criticism: Magicorealism in Oscar "Zeta" Acosta, Ana Castillo, Julie Dash, Hanif Kureishi, and Salman Rushdie.* Austin: University of Texas Press, 2003.

Alemán, Jesse. "'Thank God, Lolita Is Away from Those Horrid Savages': The Politics of Whiteness in *Who Would Have Thought It?*" In *María Amparo Ruiz de Burton: Critical and Pedagogical Perspectives* Montes, ed. Amelia María de la Luz and Anne Elizabeth Goldman, 95–111. Lincoln: University of Nebraska Press, 2004.

Almaguer, Tomas. *Racial Faultlines: The Historical Origins of White Supremacy in California.* Berkeley and Los Angeles: University of California Press, 1994.

Alvarez, Francisco R. "*The Autobiography of a Brown Buffalo* de Oscar Zeta Acosta: Escritura, ser e ideología en la autobiografía chicana de los 70." *Monographic Review/Revista Monografica* 9 (1993): 162–75.

Althusser, Louis. *Lenin and Philosophy and Other Essays.* Trans. Ben Brewster. New York: Monthly Review Press, 1971.

Alurista. See Alberto H. Urista.

Anguiano, Lupe. "World Women's Challenge—a New Society Based on Justice and Peace." *De Colores* 2:3 (1975): 32–40.

Anzaldúa, Gloria. *Borderlands/la frontera: The New Mestiza.* San Francisco: Aunt Lute Books, 1987.

Aranda, José. "Contradictory Impulses: Maria Amparo Ruiz de Burton, Resistance Theory, and the Politics of Chicano/a Studies." *American Literature* 70:3 (September 1998): 551–79.

Aranda, José. "Returning California to the People: Vigilantism in *The Squatter and the Don.*" In *María Amparo Ruiz de Burton: Critical and Pedagogical Perspectives,* ed. Amelia María de la Luz Montes and Anne Elizabeth Goldman, 11–26 Lincoln: University of Nebraska Press, 2004.

Aranda, José. *When We Arrive: A New Literary History of Mexican America.* Tucson: University of Arizona Press, 2003.

Armas, Linda Morales, Teresa Marquez, and Sue Molina, eds. "La Cosecha: Literatura y La Mujer Chicana." Special issue of *De Colores* 3:3 (1977).

Auerbach, Erich. *Mimesis: The Representation of Reality in Western Literature.* Trans. Willard R. Trask. Princeton, N.J.: Princeton University Press, 1953.

Augenbraum, Harold and Ilan Stavans, eds. *Growing Up Latino: Memoirs and Stories.* Boston: Houghton Mifflin, 1993.

Banaji, Jairus. "The Fictions of Free Labour: Contract, Coercion and So-Called Unfree Labour." *Historical Materialism* 11:3 (2003): 69–95.

Barrera, Mario. *Race and Class in the Southwest: A Theory of Racial Inequality.* Notre Dame, Ind.: University of Notre Dame Press, 1979.

Barrera, Mario, Carlos Muñoz, and Charles Ornelas. "The Barrio as an Internal

Colony." In *La Causa Política: A Chicano Politics Reader*, ed. F. Chris Garcia, 281–301. Notre Dame, Ind.: University of Notre Dame Press, 1974. First published in Harlan Hahn, ed., *Urban Affairs Annual Review* 6 (1972): 465–98.

Barrio, Raymond. *The Plum Plum Pickers*. Guerneville, Calif.: Ventura Press, 1969.

Benjamin, Walter. *The Arcades Project*. Trans. Howard Eiland and Kevin McLaughlin. Cambridge: Belknap Press of Harvard University Press, 1999.

Bernstein, J. M. *The Philosophy of the Novel: Lukács, Marxism, and the Dialectics of Form*. Minneapolis: University of Minnesota Press, 1984.

Bérubé, Michael. *Marginal Forces/Cultural Centers: Tolson, Pynchon, and the Politics of the Canon*. Ithaca, N.Y.: Cornell University Press, 1992.

Bessie, Alvah. "Winter Soldiers." *New Masses*, December 15, 1942, 30–31.

Best, Steven, and Douglas Kellner. *Postmodern Theory: Critical Interrogations*. New York: Guilford Press, 1997.

Bewes, Timothy. "What Is a Literary Landscape? Immanence and the Ethics of Form." *Differences* 16:1 (2005): 63–102.

Bewes, Timothy. *Reification, or the Anxiety of Late Capitalism*. London: Verso, 2002.

Biggers, Jeff. "Pineda Unbound: An Interview with Cecile Pineda." *Bloomsbury Review* 24:5 (September–October 2004): 3, 24.

Blazer, Sam. "Review: *The Revolt of the Cockroach People*." *The Nation*, April 13, 1974, 469–71.

Borrego, John. "Capitalist Accumulation and Revolutionary Accumulation: The Context for Chicano Struggle." Ph.D. diss., University of California, Berkeley, 1978.

Bramen, Carrie Tirado. *The Uses of Variety: Modern Americanism and the Quest for National Distinctiveness*. Cambridge: Harvard University Press, 2000.

Browder, Laura. *Slippery Characters: Ethnic Impersonators and American Identities*. Chapel Hill: University of North Carolina Press, 2000.

Bruce-Novoa, Juan. "Canonical and Non-canonical Texts." *The Americas Review* 14:3–4 (Fall—-Winter 1986): 119–35.

Bruce-Novoa, Juan. "Deconstructing the Dominant Patriarchal Text: Cecile Pineda's Narratives." In *Breaking Boundaries: Latina Writing and Critical Readings*, ed. Asunción Horno-Delgado et al., 72–81. Amherst: University of Massachusetts Press, 1989.

Bruce-Novoa, Juan. "Fear and Loathing on the Buffalo Trail." *MELUS* 6:4 (Winter 1979): 39–50.

Bruce-Novoa, Juan. "History as Content, History as Act: The Chicano Novel." *Aztlán* 18:1 (Spring 1987): 29–44.

Bruce-Novoa, Juan. "Homosexuality and the Chicano Novel." *Confluencia: Revista Hispánica de Cultura y Literatura* 2:1 (Fall 1986): 69–77.

Bruce-Novoa, Juan. *Retrospace: Collected Essays on Chicano Literature*. Houston: Arte Público Press, 1990.

Calderón, Héctor. "The Novel and the Community of Readers: Rereading Tomás Rivera's *Ý no se lo tragó la tierra*." In *Criticism in the Borderlands: Studies in Chicano Literature, Culture, and Ideology*, ed. Héctor Calderón and José David Saldívar, 97–113. Durham, N.C.: Duke University Press, 1991.

Calderón, Héctor. "To Read Chicano Narratives: Commentary and Metacommentary." *Mester* 11 (1983): 3–14.

Calderón, Héctor, and José David Saldívar, eds. *Criticism in the Borderlands: Studies in Chicano Literature, Culture, and Ideology*. Durham, N.C.: Duke University Press, 1991.

Camarillo, Albert. *Chicanos in a Changing Society: From Mexican Pueblos to American Barrios in Santa Barbara and Southern California, 1848–1930*. Cambridge: Harvard University Press, 1979.

Cano, David. *Shifting Loyalties*. Houston: Arte Público Press, 1995.

Cárdenas de Dwyer, Carlotta. "Chicano Literature 1965–1975: The Flowering of the Southwest." Ph.D. diss., SUNY Stony Brook, 1976.

Carlyle, Thomas. *Critical and Miscellaneous Essays*. Boston: Phillips, Sampson, 1855.

Carver, Terrell, and Paul Thomas, eds. *Rational Choice Marxism*. University Park: Pennsylvania State University Press, 1995.

Castillo, Ana. *The Guardians: A Novel*. New York: Random House, 2007.

Castillo, Ana. *Sapogonia: An Anti-Romance in 3/8 Meter*. New York: Anchor Books, 1994.

Cervantes, Lorna Dee. "Poema Para Los Californios Muertos." In *Emplumada*, 42–43. Pittsburgh: University of Pittsburgh Press, 1981.

Chabram, Angie. "Conceptualizing Chicano Critical Discourse." In *Criticism in the Borderlands: Studies in Chicano Literature, Culture, and Ideology*, ed. Héctor Calderón and José David Saldívar, 127–48. Durham, N.C.: Duke University Press, 1991. Originally published as "Conceptualizing Chicano Critical Discourse: An Emerging Practice," *Aztlán* 18 (1987): 45–90.

Chase, Richard. *The American Novel and Its Tradition*. Baltimore: Johns Hopkins University Press, 1957.

Chávez, Ernesto. "*¡Mi Raza Primero!" (My People First): Nationalism, Identity, and Insurgency in the Chicano Movement in Los Angeles, 1966–1978*. Berkeley and Los Angeles: University of California Press, 2002.

Chávez, John. *The Lost Land: The Chicano Image of the Southwest*. Albuquerque: University of New Mexico Press, 1984.

Christian, Karen. *Show and Tell: Identity as Performance*. Albuquerque: University of New Mexico Press, 1997.

Christian, Karen. "Will the 'Real Chicano' Please Stand Up? The Challenge of John Rechy and Sheila Ortiz Taylor to Chicano Essentialism." *The Americas Review* 20:2 (1992): 89–104.

Chow, Rey. *The Protestant Ethnic and the Spirit of Capitalism*. New York: Columbia University Press, 2002.

Christie, John S. *Latino Fiction and the Modernist Imagination: Literature of the Borderlands*. New York: Garland, 1998.

Cockburn, Alexander. "Naming as Ritual." *The Nation*, August 4–11, 1984, 71.

Connor, Anne. "Desenmascarando a Ysrael: The Disfigured Face as Symbol of Identity in Three Latino Texts." *Cincinnati Romance Review* 21 (2002): 148–62.

De León, Arnoldo. *They Called Them Greasers: Anglo Attitudes toward Mexicans in Texas, 1821–1900*. Austin: University of Texas Press, 1983.

Denning, Michael. *The Cultural Front: The Laboring of American Culture in the Twentieth Century*. New York: Verso, 1997.

Derwin, Susan. *The Ambivalence of Form: Lukács, Freud, and the Novel.* Baltimore: Johns Hopkins University Press, 1992.

Dickens, Charles. *Bleak House*. New York: Norton, 1977.

Dirlik, Arif. "Chinese History and the Question of Orientalism." *History and Theory* 35:4 (1996): 96–118.

Doss, Yvette C. "The Lost Legend of the Real Dr. Gonzo." *Los Angeles Times*, June 5, 1998, F, 2–3.

Dunne, John Gregory. *Crooning: A Collection*. New York: Simon and Schuster, 1990.

Dunne, John Gregory. "The Secret of Danny Santiago." *New York Review of Books*, August 16, 1984, 17–18, 20, 22, 24–27.

Eagleton, Terry. "Nationalism: Irony and Commitment." In Eagleton, Fredric Jameson, and Edward Said, *Nationalism, Colonialism and Literature*, 23–39. Minneapolis: University of Minnesota Press, 1990.

Ebert, Teresa. "Rematerializing Feminism." *Science and Society* 69:1 (January 2005): 33–55.

Escobar, Edward J. "The Dialectics of Repression: The Los Angeles Police Department and the Chicano Movement, 1968–1971." *Journal of American History* 79:4 (March 1993): 1483–1514.

Eysturoy, Annie. *Daughters of Self-Creation: The Contemporary Chicana Novel.* Albuquerque: University of New Mexico Press, 1996.

Feather, Leonard. "Little Jazz Goes Color Blind." *Down Beat*, July 13, 1951, 12. Reprinted in Leonard Feather, *The Book of Jazz, from Then till Now; a Guide to the Entire Field*, rev. ed. (New York: Horizon, 1965), 47.

Federici, Silvia. *Caliban and the Witch: Women, the Body, and Primitive Accumulation.* Brooklyn: Autonomedia, 2004.

Feenberg, Andrew. "Fetishism and Form: Erotic and Economic Disorder in Literature." In *Violence and Truth: On the Work of René Girard.* ed. Paul Dumouchel, 134–51. Stanford, Calif.: Stanford University Press, 1988.

Feenberg, Andrew. *Lukács, Marx, and the Sources of Critical Theory.* Oxford: Oxford University Press, 1986.

Flores, Lauro. Untitled book review. *Minnesota Review* 22 (Spring 1984): 145–48.

Floyd, Kevin. "Rethinking Reification: Marcuse, Psychoanalysis, and Gay Liberation." *Social Text* 66, 19:1 (Spring 2001): 103–28.

Foley, Barbara. *Radical Representations: Politics and Form in U.S. Proletarian Fiction, 1929–1941*. Durham, N.C.: Duke University Press, 1993.

Foley, Barbara. *Telling the Truth: The Theory and Practice of Documentary Fiction.* Ithaca, N.Y.: Cornell University Press, 1986.

Folkart, Burt A. "Daniel James Who Masqueraded as a Latino." *Los Angeles Times*, May 21, 1988, 22.

Foucault, Michel. "Friendship as a Way of Life." In *Foucault Live: Collected Interviews, 1961–1984*, ed. Sylvère Lotringer, trans. Lysa Hochroth and John Johnston, 308–12. New York: Semiotext(e), 1989.

Gabel, Joseph. *False Consciousness: An Essay on Reification.* New York: Harper and Row, 1975. Trans. Margaret A. Thompson with the assistance of Kenneth A.

Thompson. Originally published as *La fausse conscience* (Paris: Editions de Minuit, 1962).

Gallego, Carlos. "Chicano Literature and the Problem of Identity." Presented at the Sixteenth Annual Arizona Quarterly Symposium on American Literature and Culture, University of Arizona, March 25, 2004.

Ganguly, Keya. "Adorno, Authenticity, Critique." In *Marxism, Modernity, and Postcolonial Studies*, ed. Crystal Bartolovich and Neil Lazarus, 240–56. Cambridge: Cambridge University Press, 2002.

García, Alma M. *Chicana Feminist Thought: The Basic Historical Writings.* London: Routledge, 1997.

García, David. *Requiem 29.* Los Angeles: NLCC Educational Media, 1997. Videocassette, 31 minutes.

García, Mario T. "History, Literature, and the Chicano Working-Class Novel: A Critical Review of Alejandro Morales' *The Brick People.*" *Critica* 2:2 (Fall 1990): 189–201.

Garza-Falcón, Leticia M. *Gente Decente: A Borderlands Response to the Rhetoric of Dominance.* Austin: University of Texas Press, 1998.

Gates, Henry Louis, Jr. "'Authenticity' or the Lesson of Little Tree." *New York Times Book Review*, November 24, 1991, 1, 26–30.

Gilb, Dagoberto. *The Last Known Residence of Mickey Acuña.* New York: Grove Press, 1994.

Goldman, Anne E. "'Who Ever Heard of a Blue-Eyed Mexican?': Satire and Sentimentality in María Amparo Ruiz de Burton's *Who Would Have Thought It?*" In *Recovering the U.S. Hispanic Literary Heritage*, vol. 2, ed. Erlinda Gonzales-Berry and Chuck Tatum, 59–78. Houston: Arte Público Press, 1996.

Goldman, Anne E. *Continental Divides: Revisioning American Literature.* New York: Palgrave, 2000.

Goldmann, Lucien. "Introduction to the Problems of a Sociology of the Novel." In *Marxist Literary Theory: A Reader*, ed. Terry Eagleton and Drew Milne, 204–20. Oxford: Blackwell, 1996.

Gómez-Quiñones, Juan. "Toward a Concept of Culture." *Revista Chicano-Riqueña* 5:2 (Spring 1977): 29–47.

González, Gilbert G. "American Writers and the Ideology of Empire: The U.S. and Mexico, 1880–1930." Working Paper Series in Cultural Studies, Ethnicity and Race Relations, Department of Comparative American Cultures, Washington State University. 1999.

González, Gilbert G., and Raul A. Fernández, *A Century of Chicano History: Empire, Nations, and Migration.* New York: Routledge, 2003.

González, John M. "Romancing Hegemony: Constructing Racialized Citizenship in María Amparo Ruiz de Burton's *The Squatter and the Don.*" In *Recovering the U.S. Hispanic Literary Heritage*, vol. 2, ed. Erlinda Gonzales-Berry and Chuck Tatum, 23–39. Houston: Arte Público Press, 1996.

González, Marcial. "Before Dan James Became Danny Santiago: The Duclos Letter and the Maltz Affair," an unpublished paper presented at the American Studies Annual Colloquium, University of California, Berkeley, May 11, 2007.

González, Marcial. "Jameson's 'Arrested Dialectic': From Structuralism to Postmodernism." *Cultural Logic: Marxist Theory and Practice* 2:2 (Spring 1999). http://clogic.eserver.org/2–2/2-2index.html.

González, Marcial. "A Marxist Critique of Borderlands Postmodernism: Adorno's *Negative Dialectics* and Chicano Cultural Criticism." In *Left of the Color Line: Race, Radicalism, and Twentieth-Century Literature of the United States*, ed. Bill Mullen and James Smethurst, 279–97. Chapel Hill: University of North Carolina Press, 2003.

González, Marcial. "Postmodernism, Historical Materialism, and Chicana/o Cultural Studies." *Science and Society* 68:2 (Summer 2004): 161–86.

González, María C. *Contemporary Mexican-American Women Novelists: Toward a Feminist Identity*. New York: Peter Lang, 1996.

González, Ray, ed. *Mirrors beneath the Earth: Short Fiction by Chicano Writers*. Willimantic, Conn.: Curbstone, 1992.

Gonzales-Berry, Erlinda. "Review of *Face*." *The Americas Review* 15:2 (Summer 1987): 107–9.

Gonzales-Berry, Erlinda. "Unveiling Athena: Women in the Chicano Novel." In *Chicana Critical Issues: Mujeres Activas en Letras y Cambio Social (MALCS)*, ed. Norma Alarcón et al., 33–44. Berkeley, Calif.: Third Woman Press, 1993.

Gonzales-Berry, Erlinda, and Chuck Tatum, eds. *Recovering the U.S. Hispanic Literary Heritage*. Vol. 2. Houston: Arte Público Press, 1996.

González-Mireles, Jovita. *Dew on the Thorn*. Houston: Arte Público Press, 1997.

González-Mireles, Jovita, and Eve Raleigh. *Caballero: A Historical Novel*. College Station: Texas A&M University Press, 1996.

Gramsci, Antonio. *Selections from the Prison Notebooks of Antonio Gramsci*. Ed. and trans. Quintin Hoare and Geoffrey Nowell Smith. New York: International Publishers, 1971.

Gruesz, Kirsten Silva. *Ambassadors of Culture: The Transamerican Origins of Latino Writing*. Princeton, N.J.: Princeton University Press, 2002.

Gruesz, Kirsten Silva. "Utopía Latina: *The Ordinary Seaman* in Extraordinary Times." *Modern Fiction Studies* 49:1 (Spring 2003): 54–83.

Guajardo, Paul. *Chicano Controversy: Oscar Acosta and Richard Rodriguez*. New York: Peter Lang, 2002.

Gutiérrez-Jones, Carl. *Rethinking the Borderlands: Between Chicano Culture and Legal Discourse*. Berkeley and Los Angeles: University of California Press, 1995.

Hames-Garcia, Michael. "Dr. Gonzo's Carnival: The Testimonial Satires of Oscar Zeta Acosta." *American Literature* 72:3 (September 2000): 463–93.

Haney López, Ian F. *Racism on Trial: The Chicano Fight for Justice*. Cambridge: Harvard University Press, 2003.

Harvey, David. *Justice, Nature, and the Geography of Difference*. Malden, Mass.: Blackwell, 1996.

Haslam, Gerald. "A Question of Authenticity, or, Who Can Write What?" *Western American Literature* 20:3 (Fall 1985): 246–50.

Haslett, Moyra. *Marxist Literary and Cultural Theories*. New York: St. Martin's Press, 2000.

Hayles, N. Katherine. "Postmodern Parataxis: Embodied Texts, Weightless Information." *American Literary History* 2:3 (Fall 1990): 394–421.

Hennessy, Rosemary. *Profit and Pleasure: Sexual Identities in Late Capitalism.* London: Routledge, 2000.

Hinojosa, Rolando. "Mexican-American Literature: Toward an Identification." *Books Abroad (World Literature Today)* 49:3 (Summer 1975): 422–30.

Hitchcock, Peter. *Oscillate Wildly: Space, Body, and Spirit of Millennial Materialism.* Minneapolis: University of Minnesota Press, 1999.

Huerta, Alberto. "Daniel James (1911–1988): Socrates and Santiago in California." *The Californians* 6 (December 1988): 48–53.

Hullot-Kentor, Robert. "Translator's Introduction." In Theodor Adorno, *Aesthetic Theory*, xi–xxi. Minneapolis: University of Minnesota Press, 1997.

Hunsaker, Alan C. "Book Review: *The Autobiography of a Brown Buffalo* and *The Revolt of the Cockroach People.*" *Hispanic Journal of Behavioral Sciences* 12:3 (August 1990): 328–34.

James, Daniel. See Danny Santiago.

Jameson, Fredric. "*History and Class Consciousness* as an 'Unfinished Project.'" *Rethinking Marxism* 1:1 (Spring 1988): 49–72.

Jameson, Fredric. *The Ideologies of Theory: Essays 1971–1986.* Vol. 2, *Syntax of History.* Minneapolis: University of Minnesota Press, 1988.

Jameson, Fredric. *Late Marxism: Adorno, or, The Persistence of the Dialectic.* London: Verso, 1990.

Jameson, Fredric. *Marxism and Form: Twentieth-Century Dialectical Theories of Literature.* Princeton, N.J.: Princeton University Press, 1971.

Jameson, Fredric. "Marxism and the Historicity of Theory: An Interview with Fredric Jameson." Interview by Xudong Zhang. *New Literary History* 29:3 (1998): 353–83.

Jameson, Fredric. *The Political Unconscious: Narrative as a Socially Symbolic Act.* Ithaca, N.Y.: Cornell University Press, 1981.

Jameson, Fredric. "Reflections in Conclusion." In Theodor Adorno et al., *Aesthetics and Politics*, 196–213. London: New Left Books, 1997. Subsequently published as "Reflections on the Brecht-Lukács Debate," in *The Ideologies of Theory: Essays 1971–1986*, vol. 2, *Syntax of History* (Minneapolis: University of Minnesota Press, 1988), 133–47.

Jameson, Fredric. "Reification and Utopia in Mass Culture." *Social Text* 1:1 (Fall 1979): 130–48.

Jameson, Fredric. *Sartre: The Origins of a Style.* New York: Columbia University Press, 1984. Originally published in 1961 by Yale University Press.

Jameson, Fredric. *The Seeds of Time.* New York: Columbia University Press, 1994.

Jameson, Fredric. *Signatures of the Visible.* London: Routledge, 1992.

JanMohamed, Abdul. *The Death-Bound-Subject: Richard Wright's Archaeology of Death.* Durham, N.C.: Duke University Press, 2005.

JanMohamed, Abdul. "Negating the Negation as a Form of Affirmation in Minority Discourse: The Construction of Richard Wright as Subject." *Cultural Critique* 7 (Fall 1987): 245–66.

Jay, Martin. *Marxism and Totality: The Adventures of a Concept from Lukács to Habermas.* Berkeley and Los Angeles: University of California Press, 1984.

Johnson, David E. "Face Value: An Essay on Cecile Pineda's *Face*." *The Americas Review* 19:2 (Summer 1991): 73–93.

Kowalczyk, Kimberly A. "Oscar Zeta Acosta: The Brown Buffalo and His Search for Identity." *The Americas Review* 16:3–4 (Fall–Winter 1988): 198–209.

Lanham, Richard. *Analyzing Prose.* 2nd ed. London: Continuum, 2003.

Larsen, Neil. *Determinations: Essays on Theory, Narrative, and Nation in the Americas.* New York: Verso, 2001.

Larsen, Neil. "Negation of the Abnegation: Dialectical Criticism in the 1990s." *Rethinking Marxism* 5:2 (1992): 109–17.

Lazarus, Neil. "Modernism and Modernity: T. W. Adorno and Contemporary White South African Literature." *Cultural Critique* 5 (Winter 1986–87): 131–55.

Lazarus, Neil. *Nationalism and Cultural Practice in the Postcolonial World.* Cambridge: Cambridge University Press, 1999.

Lee, A. Robert. "Chicanismo's Beat Outrider? The Texts and Contexts of Oscar Zeta Acosta." In *The Beat Generation: Critical Essays*, ed. Kostas Myrsiades, 259–80. New York: Peter Lang, 2002. Originally published in *College Literature* 27:1 (Winter 2000): 158–76.

Lewis, Marvin A. "Introduction to the Chicano Novel." University of Wisconsin–Milwaukee, Spanish Speaking Outreach Institute Paper Series. 1982.

Limón, José. *Dancing with the Devil: Society and Cultural Poetics in Mexican-American South Texas.* Madison: University of Wisconsin Press, 1994.

Limón, José. *Mexican Ballads, Chicano Poems: History and Influence in Mexican-American Social Poetry.* Berkeley and Los Angeles: University of California Press, 1992.

Lomelí, Francisco. "Cecile Pineda." In *Dictionary of Literary Biography*, vol. 209, *Chicano Writers, Third Series*, ed. Lomelí and Carl R. Shirley, 202–11. Detroit: Gale Group, 1999.

Lomelí, Francisco. "Cecile Pineda's *Face* and Ralph Ellison's *Invisible Man:* Poetics of Synthesizing an Identity." In *El Poder Hispano: Actas del V Congreso de Culturas Chicanas de los Estados Unidos*, ed. Alberto Moncala Lorenzo et al., 465–72. Madrid: Universidad de Alcalá, 1994.

Lomelí, Francisco A., and Donaldo W. Urioste. *Chicano Perspectives in Literature: A Critical and Annotated Bibiography.* Albuquerque: Pajarito, 1976.

Lukács, Georg. *The Historical Novel.* Trans. Hannah Mitchell and Stanley Mitchell. Lincoln: University of Nebraska Press, 1983.

Lukács, Georg. *History and Class Consciousness: Studies in Marxist Dialectics.* Trans. Rodney Livingstone. Cambridge: MIT Press, 1971.

Lunn, Eugene. *Marxism and Modernism: An Historical Study of Lukács, Brecht, Benjamin, and Adorno.* Berkeley and Los Angeles: University of California Press, 1982.

Magill, Frank N. "Book Review of *Face*." In *Masterpieces of Latino Literature*, 157–60. New York: HarperCollins, 1994.

Maltz, Albert. "What Shall We Ask of Writers?" *New Masses*, February 12, 1946, 19–22.

"A Man Reconstructs His Own Face." *San Francisco Chronicle*, May 21, 1977, 1, 12.

Martin, Wallace. *Recent Theories of Narrative.* Ithaca, N.Y.: Cornell University Press, 1986.

Martínez, Manuel Luis. *Countering the Counterculture: Reading Postwar American Dissent from Jack Kerouac to Tomás Rivera.* Madison: University of Wisconsin Press, 2003.

Marx, Karl. *Capital: A Critique of Political Economy.* Vol. 1. Trans. Ben Fowkes. Intro. Ernest Mandel. London: Penguin, 1990.

Marx, Karl. *The Marx-Engels Reader.* 2nd ed. Ed. Robert C. Tucker. New York: Norton, 1978.

McClennen, Sophia A. *The Dialectics of Exile: Nation, Time, Language, and Space in Hispanic Literature.* West Lafayette, Ind.: Purdue University Press, 2004.

McCracken, Ellen. *New Latina Narrative: The Feminine Space of Postmodern Ethnicity.* Tucson: University of Arizona Press, 1999.

McDowell, Edwin. "A Noted 'Hispanic' Novelist Proves to be Someone Else." *New York Times,* July 22, 1984, 1, 44.

McDowell, Edwin. "Publishing: Endowment Gives Four Writers $25,000." *New York Times,* August 10, 1984, C23.

McKenna, Teresa. *Migrant Song: Politics and Process in Contemporary Chicano Literature.* Austin: University of Texas Press, 1997.

Menchaca, Martha. *Recovering History, Constructing Race: The Indian, Black, and White Roots of Mexican Americans.* Austin: University of Texas Press, 2001.

Mendoza, Louis Gerard. *Historia: The Literary Making of Chicana and Chicano History.* College Station: Texas A&M University Press, 2001.

Mendoza, Louis Gerard. "On Buffaloes, Body Snatching, and Bandidismo: Ilan Stavans's Appropriation of Oscar Acosta and the Chicano Experience." *Bilingual Review/La Revista Bilingüe* 26:1 (January–April 2001–2): 79–86.

Miller, J. Hillis. *Fiction and Repetition: Seven English Novels.* Cambridge: Harvard University Press, 1982.

Mohanty, Satya P. *Literary Theory and the Claims of History: Postmodernism, Objectivity, Multicultural Politics.* Ithaca, N.Y.: Cornell University Press, 1997.

Monohan, Sister Helena. "The Chicano Novel: Toward a Definition and Literary Criticism." Ph.D. diss., Saint Louis University, 1972.

Montejano, David. *Anglos and Mexicans in the Making of Texas, 1836–1986.* Austin: University of Texas Press, 1987.

Montes, Amelia María de la Luz , and Anne Elizabeth Goldman, eds. *María Amparo Ruiz de Burton: Critical and Pedagogical Perspectives.* Lincoln: University of Nebraska Press, 2004.

Moraga, Cherríe. *Loving in the War Years: Lo que nunca pasó por sus labios.* Cambridge, Mass.: South End Press, 1983.

Moya, Paula M. L. *Learning from Experience: Minority Identities, Multicultural Struggles.* Berkeley and Los Angeles: University of California Press, 2002.

Moya, Paula M. L., and Michael R. Hames-García, eds. *Reclaiming Identity: Realist Theory and the Predicament of Postmodernism.* Berkeley and Los Angeles: University of California Press, 2000.

Mullen, Bill V. *Afro-Orientalism.* Minneapolis: University of Minnesota Press, 2004.

Munton, Alan. "Quoting the Culture: The New British Sentence and the Politics of Parataxis in the Avant-garde, 1914–2001." *Critical Survey* 14:2 (September 2002): 22–36.

Niggli, Josephina. *Mexican Village*. Albuquerque: University of New Mexico Press, 1994. Originally published in 1945.

Niggli, Josephina. *A Miracle for Mexico*. Greenwich, Conn: New York Graphic Society, 1964.

Niggli, Josephina. *Step Down, Elder Brother*. New York: Rinehart, 1947.

Oates, Joyce Carol. "Success and the Pseudonymous Writer: Turning Over a New Self." *New York Times Book Review*, December 6, 1987, 12, 14.

Oates, Joyce Carol. *(Woman) Writer: Occasions and Opportunities*. New York: Dutton, 1988.

Oglesby, Carl. "The Revolted." In *Containment and Change: Two Dissenting Views of American Foreign Policy*, ed. Oglesby and Richard Shaull, 140–56. New York: Macmillan, 1967.

Olivas, Michael A. "'Breaking the Law' on Principle." In *The Latino/a Condition: A Critical Reader*, ed. Richard Delgado and Jean Stefancic, 320–31. New York: New York University Press, 1998.

Ortego y Gasca, Felipe de. "Danny Santiago and the Ethics of Deception." *Nuestro* 8 (November 1984): 50–51.

Oyama, Susan . *Evolution's Eye: A Systems View of the Biology-Culture Divide*. Durham, N.C.: Duke University Press, 2000.

Padilla, Genaro. *My History, Not Yours: The Formation of Mexican American Autobiography*. Madison: University of Wisconsin Press, 1993.

Padilla, Genaro. "The Progression from Individual to Social Consciousness in Two Chicano Novelists: José Antonio Villarreal and Oscar Zeta Acosta." Ph.D. diss. University of Washington, 1981.

Paredes, Américo. *George Washington Gómez*. Houston: Arte Público Press, 1990.

Paredes, Raymund A. "Contemporary Mexican-American Literature, 1960–Present." In *A Literary History of the American West*, 1101–18. Fort Worth: Texas Christian University Press, 1987.

Paredes, Raymund A. "Los Angeles from the Barrio: Oscar Zeta Acosta's *The Revolt of the Cockroach People*." In *Los Angeles Fiction: A Collection of Original Essays*, ed. David Fine, 209–22. Albuquerque: University of New Mexico Press, 1984.

Perelman, Michael. *The Invention of Capitalism: Classical Political Economy and the Secret History of Primitive Accumulation*. Durham, N.C.: Duke University Press, 2000.

Pérez, Vincent. "Remembering the Hacienda: Land and Community in Californio Narratives." In *María Amparo Ruiz de Burton: Critical and Pedagogical Perspectives*, ed. Amelia María de la Luz Montes and Anne Elizabeth Goldman, 27–55. Lincoln: University of Nebraska Press, 2004.

Pérez-Torres, Rafael. *Movements in Chicano Poetry: Against Myths, against Margins*. Cambridge: Cambridge University Press, 1995.

Pineda, Cecile. *Bardo99*. Lincoln, Nebr.: Writers Club Press, 2000.

Pineda, Cecile. "Deracinated: The Writer Re-invents Her Sources." In *Máscaras*, ed. Lucha Corpi, 57–70. Berkeley, Calif.: Third Woman Press, 1997.

Pineda, Cecile. *Face.* New York: Viking, 1985.
Pineda, Cecile. *Face.* San Antonio: Wings Press, 2003.
Pineda, Cecile. *Fishlight: A Dream of Childhood.* San Antonio: Wings Press, 2001.
Pineda, Cecile. *Frieze.* New York: Viking, 1986.
Pineda, Cecile. *The Love Queen of the Amazon: A Novel.* Boston: Little Brown, 1992.
Pineda, Cecile. *Redoubt.* Lincoln, Nebr.: Writers Club Press, 2000.
Pitt, Leonard. *Decline of the Californios.* Berkeley and Los Angeles: University of California Press, 1966.
Ponce, Mary Helen. *Boyle Heights: An Autobiography.* Albuquerque: University of New Mexico Press, 1993.
Porter, Carolyn. *Seeing and Being: The Plight of the Participant Observer in Emerson, James, Adams, and Faulkner.* Middletown, CT: Wesleyan University Press, 1981.
Postone, Moishe. "The Holocaust and the Trajectory of the Twentieth Century." In *Catastrophe and Meaning: The Holocaust and the Twentieth Century*, ed. Postone and Eric Santner, 81–116. Chicago: University of Chicago Press, 2003.
Quammen, David. "Three Novels." *New York Times Book Review*, April 24, 1983, 12, 33.
Ramírez, Arthur. "Reseñas: Book Review of *The Autobiography of a Brown Buffalo* and *The Revolt of the Cockroach People.*" *Revista Chicano-Riqueña* 3:3 (Summer 1975): 46–53.
Raskin, Jonah. "Danny Santiago (Daniel James)." In *Dictionary of Literary Biography*, vol. 122, *Chicano Writers, Second Series*, ed. Carl R. Shirley, 247–54. Detroit: Gale Research, 1992.
Raskin, Jonah. "The Man Who Would Be Danny Santiago." Interview. *San Francisco Bay Guardian*, November 28, 1984, 13–14, 19.
Rebolledo, Tey Diana. *Women Singing in the Snow: A Cultural Analysis of Chicana Literature.* Tucson: University of Arizona Press, 1995.
Rechy, John. *City of Night.* New York: Grove Press, 1963.
Rechy, John. *The Miraculous Day of Amalia Gómez.* New York: Arcade, 1991.
Rechy, John. *Numbers.* New York: Grove Press, 1967.
Rechy, John. *This Day's Death.* New York: Grove Press, 1969.
Remington, Frederick. *Pony Tracks.* Norman: University of Oklahoma Press, 1989. Originally published in 1893.
Rivera, Tomás. *. . . y no se lo tragó la tierra / . . . and The Earth Did Not Part.* Trans. Herminio Rios. Berkeley, Calif.: Editorial Justa, 1977.
Roark, Anne C. "When Is a Pseudonym a Lie?" *San Francisco Chronicle*, "This World" section, August 12, 1984, 17.
Rodríguez, Barbara. *Autobiographical Inscriptions.* Oxford: Oxford University Press, 1999.
Rodríguez, Joe D. "The Chicano Novel and the North American Narrative of Survival." *Denver Quarterly* 16 (Fall 1981): 64–70.
Rodríguez, Joe D. "God's Silence and the Shrill of Ethnicity in the Chicano Novel." *Explorations in Ethnic Studies* 4:2 (July 1981): 14–21.
Rodríguez, Joe D. "Oscar Zeta Acosta." In *Chicano Literature: A Reference Guide*, ed. Francisco Lomelí and Julio A. Martínez, 3–16. Westport, Conn.: Greenwood Press, 1985.

Rodríguez, Joe D. "Oscar Zeta Acosta." In *Dictionary of Literary Biography*, vol. 82, *Chicano Writers, First Series*, ed. Francisco Lomelí and Carl R. Shirley, 3–10. Detroit: Gale Research, 1989.

Rodríguez, Manuel M. Martín. "Textual and Land Reclamation: The Critical Reception of Early Chicana/o Literature." In *Recovering the U.S. Hispanic Literary Heritage*, vol. 2, ed. Erlinda Gonzales-Berry and Chuck Tatum, 40–58. Houston: Arte Público Press, 1996.

Rodríguez, Ralph E. *Brown Gumshoes: Detective Fiction and the Search for Chicana/o Identity*. Austin: University of Texas Press, 2005.

Rolfe, Lionel. *Literary L.A.*. Los Angeles: California Classics, 2002.

Rose, Gillian. *The Melancholy Science*. New York: Columbia University Press, 1978.

Ruiz, Julie. "Captive Identities: The Gendered Conquest of Mexico in *Who Would Have Thought It?*" In *María Amparo Ruiz de Burton: Critical and Pedagogical Perspectives*, ed. Amelia María de la Luz Montes and Anne Elizabeth Goldman, 112–32. Lincoln: University of Nebraska Press, 2004.

Ruiz, Ronald L. *Happy Birthday Jesús*. Houston: Arte Público Press, 1994.

Ruiz de Burton, María Amparo. *Conflicts of Interest: The Letters of María Amparo Ruiz de Burton*. Ed. with commentary by Rosaura Sánchez and Beatrice Pita. Houston: Arte Público Press, 2001.

Ruiz de Burton, María Amparo. *The Squatter and the Don*. Introduction by Rosaura Sánchez and Beatrice Pita. Houston: Arte Público Press, 1992. Originally published in 1885.

Ruiz de Burton, María Amparo. *The Squatter and the Don*. Introduction by Ana Castillo. New York: Random House, 2004.

Ruiz de Burton, María Amparo. *Who Would Have Thought It?* Introduction by Rosaura Sánchez and Beatrice Pita. Houston: Arte Público Press, 1995. Originally published in 1872.

Said, Edward. *The World, the Text, and the Critic*. Cambridge: Harvard University Press, 1983.

Salas, Floyd. *What Now My Love*. New York: Grove Press, 1969.

Salas, Floyd. *Tattoo the Wicked Cross*. New York: Grove Press, 1967.

Salazar, Rubén. *Border Correspondent: Selected Writings, 1955–1970*. Ed. Mario T. García. Berkeley and Los Angeles: University of California Press, 1995.

Saldívar, José David. *Border Matters: Remapping American Cultural Studies*. Berkeley and Los Angeles: University of California Press, 1997.

Saldívar, José David. *The Dialectics of Our America: Genealogy, Cultural Critique, and Literary History*. Durham, N.C.: Duke University Press, 1991.

Saldívar, José David. "The Limits of Cultural Studies." *American Literary History* 2:2 (Summer 1990): 251–66.

Saldívar, Ramón. *Chicano Narrative: The Dialectics of Difference*. Madison: University of Wisconsin Press, 1990.

Saldívar, Ramón. "A Dialectic of Difference: Towards a Theory of the Chicano Novel." *MELUS* 6:3 (1979): 73–92.

Saldívar, Ramón. *Figural Language in the Novel: The Flowers of Speech from Cervantes to Joyce*. Princeton, N.J.: Princeton University Press, 1984.

Sánchez, Ricardo. *Hechizospells*, Creative Series No. 4. Los Angeles: UCLA Chicano Studies Center Publications, 1976.

Sánchez, Rosaura. *Chicano Discourse: Socio-historic Perspectives.* Rowley, Mass.: Newbury House, 1983.

Sánchez, Rosaura. *Telling Identities: The Californio Testimonios.* Minneapolis: University of Minnesota Press, 1995.

Santiago, Danny (Daniel James). "Danny Santiago Makes a Call on Daniel James." *Los Angeles Times,* August 15, 1984, II, 5.

Santiago, Danny (Daniel James). *Famous All Over Town.* New York: Plume, 1983.

Sartre, Jean-Paul. *No Exit and Three Other Plays.* New York: Vintage, 1949.

Sartre, Jean-Paul. *Search for a Method.* New York: Vintage, 1968.

Schocket, Eric. *Vanishing Moments: Class and American Literature.* Ann Arbor: University of Michigan Press, 2006.

Schwarz, Robert. "A Brazilian Breakthrough." *New Left Review* 36 (November–December 2005): 91–107.

Schwarz, Robert. *A Master on the Periphery of Capitalism: Machado de Assis.* Trans. John Gledson. Durham, N.C.: Duke University Press, 2001.

Schwarz, Robert. *Misplaced Ideas: Essays on Brazilian Culture.* New York: Verso, 1992.

Seltzer, Mark. *Bodies and Machines.* London: Routledge, 1992.

Smethurst, James. "The Figure of the Vato Loco and the Representation of Ethnicity in the Narratives of Oscar Z. Acosta." *MELUS* 20:2 (Summer 1995): 119–32.

Smith, Norman D. "Buffaloes and Cockroaches: Acosta's Siege at Aztlán." *Latin American Literary Review* 5:10 (Spring–Summer 1977): 86–97. Reprinted in *Contemporary Chicano Fiction: A Critical Survey,* ed. Vernon E. Lattin (Binghamton, N.Y.: Bilingual Press/Editorial Bilingüe, 1986), 82–93.

Sohn-Rethel, Alfred. *Intellectual and Manual Labor: A Critique of Epistemology.* Trans. Martin Sohn-Rethel. Atlantic Highlands, N.J.: Humanities Press, 1978.

Sommers, Joseph. "From the Critical Premise to the Product: Critical Modes and Their Applications to a Chicano Literary Text." *New Scholar* 5:2 (1977): 51–80.

Spencer, Herbert. "Representative Government—What Is It Good For?" In *Essays: Scientific, Political, and Speculative,* vol. 3, 283–325. New York: D. Appleton, 1892. First published in *Westminster Review* (October 1857): 454–86.

Swaan, Wim. *The Lost Cities of Asia: Ceylon, Burma, Cambodia.* London: Elek Books, 1966.

Tatum, Charles M. "Contemporary Chicano Novel." In *Chicano Literature,* 102–37. Boston: Twayne, 1982.

Taylor, Harry. "On Broadway." *New Masses,* October 24, 1944, 29–31.

Taylor, Sheila Ortiz. "*Coachella:* The Novel as Community." *Tema y Variaciones de Literatura* 14:1 (2000): 87–103.

Thwaites, Jeanne. "The Use of Irony in Oscar Zeta Acosta's *Autobiography of a Brown Buffalo.*" *The Americas Review* 20:1 (Spring 1992): 73–82.

Tonn, Horst. "Fiction and Politics in Acosta's *The Revolt of the Cockroach People.*" In *Missions in Conflict: Essays on U.S.-Mexican Relations and Chicano Culture,* ed. Renate von Bardeleben, Dietrich Briesemeister, and Juan Bruce-Novoa, 195–202. Tübingen, Germany: Gunter Narr Verlag, 1986.

Torres, Edén E. *Chicana without Apology, Chicana sin vergüenza: The New Chicana Cultural Studies.* New York: Routledge, 2003.

Torres, Hector A. "The Ethnographic Component in Chicano/a Literary Discourse." *Aztlán* 25:1 (Spring 2000): 149–66.

Trouvé, María del Carmen. "La Mujer en la Negociación de la Identidad Chicana: *The Autobiography of a Brown Buffalo* de Oscar Zeta Acosta." In *XXVIII Jornadas de la Asociación Argentina de Estudios Americanos,* ed. Picazo, Boiero, and Celi, 377–86. Rio Cuarto, Argentina: Universidad Nacional de Rio Cuarto, 1997.

Turner, Frederick Jackson. *The Frontier in American History.* Tuscon: University of Arizona Press, 1992.

Urista (Alurista), Alberto Heredia. "Acosta's *The Revolt of the Cockroach People:* The Case, The Novel, and History." In *Contemporary Chicano Fiction: A Critical Survey,* ed. Vernon E. Lattin, 94–104. Binghamton, N.Y.: Bilingual Press/Editorial Bilingüe, 1986. Originally published in Spanish as "El caso, la novella y la historia de la obra de Acosta: *Revolt of the Cockroach People,*" *Maize* 2:3 (Spring 1979): 6–13.

Urista (Alurista), Alberto Heredia. "Oscar Z. Acosta: In Context." Ph.D. diss., University of California, San Diego, 1983.

Vea, Alfredo. *Gods Go Begging.* New York: Plume, 2000.

Venegas, Daniel. *Las aventuras de Don Chipote o cuando los pericos mamen.* Mexico City: Secretaría de Educación Pública, Centro de Estudios Fronterizos del Norte de México, 1984. Originally published in 1928.

Vigil, Ernesto B. *The Crusade for Justice: Chicano Militancy and the Government's War on Dissent.* Madison: University of Wisconsin Press, 1999.

Villareal, José Antonio. *Pocho.* Garden City, N.Y.: Doubleday, 1959.

Viramontes, Helena María. *Under the Feet of Jesus.* New York: Penguin, 1995.

Volosinov, V. N. *Marxism and the Philosophy of Language.* Trans. L. Matejka and I. R. Tutunik. New York: Seminar, 1973. Originally published in 1930.

Vowell, Faye Nell. "The Chicano Novel: A Study in Self-definition." Ph.D. diss., University of Cincinnati, 1979.

Walkout. Director, Moctesuma Esparza. Producer, Edward James Olmos. HBO Films, 2006.

Weisberg, Richard. "Law in and as Literature: Self-Generated Meaning in the 'Procedural Novel.'" In *The Comparative Perspective on Literature: Approaches to Theory and Practice,* ed. Clayton Koelb and Susan Noakes, 224–32. Ithaca, N.Y.: Cornell University Press, 1988.

Weisberg, Richard. *Poethics and Other Strategies of Law and Literature.* New York: Columbia University Press, 1992.

Williams, Raymond. *Marxism and Literature.* Oxford: Oxford University Press, 1977.

Wright, Richard. "Blueprint for Negro Writing." In *The Portable Harlem Renaissance Reader,* ed. David L. Lewis, 194–205. New York: Penguin, 1995. Originally published in *New Challenge* 2 (Fall 1937).

"Young Latin Author Is Neither." *San Francisco Chronicle,* July 23, 1984, 1, 16.

INDEX